AQA GCSE German

Higher

Andy Holland, Helen Kent, Sabine Leitner, Wanda Marshall, Ben Merritt, Lisa Probert

Published by Pearson Education Limited, 80 Strand, London, WC2R ORL.

www.pearsonschoolsandfecolleges.co.uk

Copies of official specifications for all Pearson qualifications may be found on the website: qualifications.pearson.com

Text © Pearson Education Limited 2024
Edited by Pearson and Newgen
Designed and typeset by Kamae Design
Original illustrations © Pearson Education Limited 2024
Illustrated by Beehive Illustrations (Afua Bediako, Tamara Joubert, Andy Keylock, Daniel Limón, Mauro Marchesi, Andrew Pagram) and Newgen KnowledgeWorks
Cover design by Kamae Design
Cover photo © Shutterstock/Hybrid Gfx
Audio recorded at Chatterbox Studios, London, with thanks to Rowan Laxton

Written by Andy Holland, Helen Kent, Sabine Leitner, Wanda Marshall, Ben Merritt and Lisa Probert.

The rights of Andy Holland, Helen Kent, Sabine Leitner, Wanda Marshall, Ben Merritt and Lisa Probert to be identified as authors of this work have been asserted by them in accordance with the Copyright, Designs and Patents Act 1988.

This publication is protected by copyright, and permission should be obtained from the publisher prior to any prohibited reproduction, storage in a retrieval system, or transmission in any form or by any means, electronic, mechanical, photocopying, recording, or otherwise.

For information regarding permissions, request forms and the appropriate contacts, please visit https://www.pearson.com/us/contact-us/permissions.html Pearson Education Limited Rights and Permissions Department.

Pearson Education Limited is an exclusive trademark owned by Pearson Education Limited and/or Pearson or its affiliates in the United Kingdom and/ or other countries.

Unless otherwise indicated herein, any third party trademarks that may appear in this work are the property of their respective owners and any references to third party trademarks, logos or other trade dress are for demonstrative or descriptive purposes only. Such references are not intended to imply any sponsorship, endorsement, authorisation, or promotion of Pearson Education Limited products by the owners of such marks, or any relationship between the owner and Pearson Education Limited or its affiliates, authors, licensees or distributors.

First published 2024

28 27 26 25 24

10 9 8 7 6 5 4 3 2 1

British Library Cataloguing in Publication Data

A catalogue record for this book is available from the British Library

ISBN 978 1 292 736839

Copyright notice

All rights reserved. No part of this publication may be reproduced in any form or by any means (including photocopying or storing it in any medium by electronic means and whether or not transiently or incidentally to some other use of this publication) without the written permission of the copyright owner, except in accordance with the provisions of the Copyright, Designs and Patents Act 1988 or under the terms of a licence issued by the Copyright Licensing Agency, 5th Floor, Shackleton House, 4 Battle Bridge Lane, London, SE1 2HX (www.cla.co.uk). Applications for the copyright owner's written permission should be addressed to the publisher.

Printed in the UK by Bell & Bain Ltd, Glasgow

Acknowledgements

We would like to thank Vicki Baxter, Sarah Bench, Kate Bonail, Gillian Eades, Gabriela Hallas, Andy Holland, Helen Kent, Monika Lee, Sabine Leitner, Stephen Lyons, Wanda Marshall, Antoinette Meehan, Ben Merritt, Lisa Probert, Frances Reynolds, Judith Rifeser, Mario Rogic, Elizabeth Weatherup, Melissa Weir, the teams at Newgen and Kamae, and everyone else involved, for their invaluable work in the development of this course. We would also like to thank Rowan Laxton and the team at Chatterbox Studios: Daniel Alexander, Phoebe Shepherd Gartner, Britta Gartner, Emilia Kreutzmann Gravioto, Lara Marie Straka, Finn Humphrey, Leo Peithmann and Damien Saini. Andy Holland would like to thank his husband, Michael, his mother, Nicole, and his fellow authors, Sabine and Ben. Sabine Leitner would like to thank her fellow author, Wanda. Wanda Marshall would like to thank her husband, Joe. Ben Merritt would like to thank his wife, Abi, and his daughters, Molly and Matilda. Lisa Probert would like to thank her husband, Roy.

The authors and publisher would like to thank the following individuals and organisations for permission to reproduce photographs:

123RF: stillfx 6, grebeshkovmaxim 6, Olga Popova 7, seventyfour74 8, Cathy Yeulet 25, yurkina 27, ssilver 34, imagesource 42, euregiocontent 44, wavebreakmediamicro 47, yurkina 51, yurkina 77, Koonsiri Boonnak 84, dotshock 84, Ken Easter 87, kobackpacko 87, chassenet 93, Cathy Yeulet 99, yurkina 101, Ratchanida Thippayos 111, iriana88w 115, Roman Babakin 123, yurkina 125, Zoltan Tukacs 132, iriana88w 136, alphaspirit 164, Anastasiia Guseva 165, Kubko 166, stanciuc 170, yurkina 177, Katarzyna Białasiewicz 180, Cathy Yeulet 180, kubko 182, Kasper Ravlo 182, Natalia Klenova 185, Ian Allenden 199, yurkina 201, jakobradlgruber 210, sborisov 214, Imagesource 221, Moodboard Stock Photography 225; **Alamy Images:** MBI 10, Galinast 13, Canetti 14, Jürgen Fälchle 14, MBI 14, dpa picture alliance 30, Science History Images 30, Björn Deutschmann 30, Adam Stoltman, 36, United Archives GmbH 38, WENN Rights Ltd 38, Panther Media GmbH 38, Associated Press 56, dpa picture alliance archive 56, imageBROKER.com GmbH & Co. KG 56, Associated Press 57, blickwinkel 57, Maren Winter 72, Classic Collection, Shotshop GmbH 80, Associated Press 91, idp french collection 109, Retro AdArchives 118, Intense Images 132, dpa picture alliance 161, Panther Media GmbH 186, Travelscape Images 192, Sean Pavone 218; **Getty Images:** Westend61 6, Stuart Fox 10, Jan Wlodarczyk 10, Oliver Rossi 13, ozgurdonmaz 13, Hill Street Studios 14, Kali9 14, Kammata 19, JohnnyGreig 23, MBI 25, Andreas Rentz 31, Stefan Matzke - sampics 36, Westend61 40, Mehmet Hilmi Barcin 40, John Eder 45, william87 57, adamkaz 60, Marc Piasecki 63, Paula Bronstein 63, Deepak Sethi 67, Counter 68, FlamingoImages 70, SolStock 75, Klaus Vedfelt 76, simonkr 80, Westend61 80, Lumi Images/ Pupeter-Secen 80, Jasmin Merdan 80, SDI Productions 80, Jenner Images 84, MarsYu 86, Yasser Chalidz 87, Erik Isakson 90, Alexander Spatari 104, Joe Daniel Price 104, Feng Wei Photography 105, SerrNovik 107, Anderson Rodrigues da Silva 107, Christopher Lee/Stringer 112, Natalija Juric 115, ewg3D 115, Yellow Dog Productions 115, Maremagnum 117, RgStudio 123, Evgenij84 124, Nikada 132, © Marco Bottigelli 132, Westend61 142, Nicolas Micolani 151, iStock 152, NurPhoto/Contributor 156, SolStock 158, skynesher 158, Deepak Sethi 159, Moorefam 160, Rachel Carbonell 160, luoman 160, shaifulzamri 160, Maja Hitij/Staff 161, SolStock 163, NurPhoto 164, Ddoble-d 175, AleksandarGeorgiev 180, Joos Mind 180, mgstudyo 180, Westend61 180, Willie B. Thomas 180, Getty Images 183, SDI Productions 186, FOTOGRAFIA INC. 186, vitaliymateha 188, sturti 188, Edwin Tan 189, sturti 189, Courtney Hale 190, Tony Anderson 190, shironosov 197, Sturti 199, Nevena1987 200, Zeljkosantrac 212, mladenbalinovac 213, ljubaphoto, 217, SolStock 217, Westend61 223, Kali9 225; **Pearson Education Ltd:** Jon Barlow 34, Handan Erek 62, Miguel Dominguez Muñoz 62, Jules Selmes 80, Gareth Boden 82, Justin Hoffmann 88, Jon Barlow 140, Lord and Leverett 186; **Shutterstock:** Mistervlad (background graphic in header), Hybrid Gfx 6, KALABUKHAVA IRYNA 6, FamVeld/Shutterstock 6, MBI 7, Shutterstock 7, Karkas 7, Billion Photos 7, Africa Studio 7, NYS 7, Darren Baker 9, CarlosBarquero 10, Sky Designs 11, tele52 11, ShutterStockStudio 14, CatwalkPhotos 14, Rafael Ramirez Lee 15, fizkes 16, Prostock-studio 17, Motortion films 17, Shutterstock 17, Vectomart 18, Ermolaev Alexander 20, Dan Rentea 21, Geartooth Productions 26, archideaphoto 30, insta_photos 34, Zoia Kostina 34, Olimpik 35, Ground Picture 37, Praszkiewicz 38, WB Television/Netflix/Kobal 38, WB Television/Netflix/Kobal 38, Moviestore 38, Africa Studio 40, Jojje 41, Eastimages 42, PeopleImages.com - Yuri A 46, Atstock Productions 49, sirtravelalot 49, David Davis 50, David Irlweg 56, FooTToo 56, Isopix 56, Stokkete 57, Frank Uffmann 57, justaa 59, agil73 60, Darren Baker 62, Andrew Rybalko 64, Kobby Dagan 64, Heide Pinkall 65, Toa55 65, Gorodenkoff 66, Wavebreakmedia 67, lithian 69, AJR_Photo 71, astarot 75, WAYHOME studio 82, sianc 82, Estudio Grafico Ve 83, Kekyalyaynen 84, Pixel-Shot 85, denio109 87, Syda Productions 88, STILLFX 88, SeDmi 88, oneinchpunch 97, Boiarkina Marina 99, Alexander Raths 100, S-F 104, Visions-AD 104, Alexey Fedorenko 104, R.M. Nunes 104, trabantos 104, Parilov 105, Nate Hovee 107, Peter Stein 108, RossHelen 110, Altug Galip 113, Stephen Bridger 118, Zurijeta 121, BorisB 132, VOJTa Herout 133, Christian Kaehler 134, kootzz 134, SARYMSAKOV ANDREY 136, Sukpaiboonwat 136, Alpay Erdem 136, Grand Warszawski 136, Atlaspix 136, PointImages 137, Blend Images 137, Sky Designs 138, Altrendo Images 138, Carboxylase 140, PETROV ARTEM 142, Arts Illustrated Studios 143, saiko3p 147, Zurijeta 149, Cultura Motion 151, LeStudio 156, Stefano Garau 156, Shahrul Azman 158, Vladimir Toropov 160, LifetimeStock 160, Valmedia 163, Stella Sophie 164, Julinzy 165, Pro-Stock Studio 167, Martin D. Vonka 167, Motortion Films 168, Piyaset 170, elwynn 170, Rich Carey 171, Daisy Daisy 172, AnnGaysorn 173, Phovoir 175, Sepp photography 176, Bumble Dee 180, Shutterstock 180, Viktoriia Hnatiuk 180, shurkin_son 186, Shutterstock 186, Daisy Daisy 188, angiolina 190, Joshua Resnick 190, Science Photo 191, Stella Sophie 191; **International Committee of the Red Cross:** Thierry Gassmann/ICRC. © International Committee of the Red Cross 164; **SafeSpace:** Printed with permission of Nour Idelbi 185; **Save the Children:** www.savethechildren.org 164; **United Nations [2024].** Reprinted with the permission of the United Nations 165; **World Health Organization:** ©World Health Organization/Pierre Albouy/© WHO 2024 164

Text extracts reproduced with permission from:

Young Green Switzerland: Fanny Zürn Generalsekretärin | Secrétaire générale Junge Grüne Schweiz 163

Notes from the publisher

Pearson has robust editorial processes, including answer and fact checks, to ensure the accuracy of the content in this publication, and every effort is made to ensure this publication is free of errors. We are, however, only human, and occasionally errors do occur. Pearson is not liable for any misunderstandings that arise as a result of errors in this publication, but it is our priority to ensure that the content is accurate. If you spot an error, please do contact us resourcescorrections@pearson.com so we can make sure it is corrected.

Inhalt

Kapitel 1 Zurück zur Schule! — Theme 1: People and lifestyle

Kulturzone Meine Schule, deine Schule — 6
- Understanding the school system in Great Britain and in the German-speaking world
- Using articles and plural nouns

Einheit 1 Welche Fächer hast du dieses Jahr? — 8
- Talking about your school subjects
- Using the present tense
- Using *weil* to give and justify opinions

Einheit 2 Was trägst du in der Schule? — 10
- Talking about school uniforms
- Using adjectives with nouns
- Describing a photo

Einheit 3 Sind Schulregeln wirklich nötig? — 12
- Talking about school rules
- Using modal verbs: *müssen, dürfen, sollen*
- Using opinion phrases with *dass*

Einheit 4 Schultage: die beste Zeit deines Lebens? — 14
- Talking about special events at school
- Using the perfect and imperfect tenses
- Practising the *w* sound in German

Einheit 5 Austausch geht auch online! — 16
- Describing school life
- Speaking and writing in the past and present
- Practising the 90-word exam question

Grammatik 1 — 18
Grammatik 2 — 20
Lese- und Hörtest — 22
Mündlicher Test — 24
Schreibtest — 26
Wörter — 28

Kapitel 2 Endlich mal Freizeit! — Theme 2: Popular culture; Theme 3: Communication and the world around us

Kulturzone Kennst du diese Musiker? — 30
- Learning about German-speaking musicians
- Giving opinions

Einheit 1 Was machst du gern in deiner Freizeit? — 32
- Talking about your free time
- Expressing preferences
- Using frequency phrases with correct word order

Einheit 2 Was machst du online? — 34
- Discussing how you spend time online
- Using separable verbs in the present tense
- Expressing advantages and disadvantages of life online

Einheit 3 Das Leben als Star — 36
- Discussing the pros and cons of celebrity culture
- Asking questions
- Practising the role-play section of the exam

Einheit 4 Wie war der Film? — 38
- Expressing preferences about films and TV shows
- Using the imperfect and perfect tenses together
- Practising the *eu* sound in German

Einheit 5 Hast du Pläne? — 40
- Using the future tense to describe plans for the weekend
- Understanding the 'time – manner – place' rule
- Using sequencers

Grammatik 1 — 42
Grammatik 2 — 44
Lese- und Hörtest — 46
Mündlicher Test — 48
Schreibtest — 50
Wörter — 52
Grammatik: Wiederholung Kapitel 1–2 — 54

Kapitel 3 Meine Welt, deine Welt — Theme 1: People and lifestyle; Theme 2: Popular culture

Kulturzone Feste in der deutschsprachigen Welt — 56
- Describing festivals and cultural events
- Giving opinions and justifications

Einheit 1 Wie ist deine Familie? — 58
- Describing family members
- Using possessive adjectives
- Using relative pronouns

Einheit 2 Deine Beziehungen — 60
- Saying how you get on with people and why
- Using pronouns and possessive adjectives in the dative
- Writing about a friend using three time frames

Einheit 3 Wer ist dir wichtig? — 62
- Discussing role models
- Using two time frames together: past and present
- Using qualifiers and intensifiers

Einheit 4 Wir haben gefeiert! — 64
- Describing a family celebration in the past
- Practising word order
- Using time phrases

Einheit 5 Partyzeit! — 66
- Discussing a party
- Using two time frames together: past and future
- Using *in* + accusative or dative

Grammatik 1 — 68
Grammatik 2 — 70
Lese- und Hörtest — 72
Mündlicher Test — 74
Schreibtest — 76
Wörter — 78

drei 3

Inhalt

Kapitel 4 Bleib gesund!
**Theme 1: People and lifestyle;
Theme 2: Popular culture**

Kulturzone Ich liebe Sport **80**
- Learning about favourite sports in the German-speaking world
- Using comparative and superlative adjectives and adverbs

Einheit 1 Willst du fit und gesund sein? **82**
- Talking about healthy lifestyles
- Using *um ... zu*
- Practising an extended conversation

Einheit 2 Es geht mir nicht gut **84**
- Talking about accidents and illnesses
- Using modal verbs in the imperfect tense
- Using *seit*

Einheit 3 Was möchte ich verbessern? **86**
- Talking about good and bad habits
- Revising present, past and future tenses
- Using infinitive constructions with *zu*

Einheit 4 Gute Tage, schlechte Tage **88**
- Talking about wellbeing
- Using *wenn*
- Using set phrases with *zu*

Einheit 5 Das finde ich wichtig! **90**
- Talking about what is important to you
- Asking questions in different tenses
- Writing about lifestyle and wellbeing

Grammatik 1 **92**
Grammatik 2 **94**
Lese- und Hörtest **96**
Mündlicher Test **98**
Schreibtest **100**
Wörter **102**

Kapitel 5 Meine Gegend
Theme 3: Communication and the world around us

Kulturzone Wo spricht man Deutsch? **104**
- Learning key facts about German-speaking countries
- Revising the superlative

Einheit 1 Wo wohnst du? **106**
- Describing where you live
- Using prepositions followed by the dative
- Using a variety of adjectives with intensifiers and qualifiers

Einheit 2 Wie fährst du? **108**
- Discussing transport in your local area
- Using prepositions with the accusative
- Using correct word order with modal verbs and *weil*

Einheit 3 Wo gehst du gern einkaufen? **110**
- Discussing shopping habits
- Using dual-case prepositions followed by the dative
- Using plurals of nouns

Einheit 4 Mein idealer Wohnort **112**
- Describing an ideal place to live
- Using the imperfect tense
- Revising the conditional

Einheit 5 Bei mir zu Hause **114**
- Describing your home
- Using dual-case prepositions with the accusative
- Working out the meaning of compound nouns

Grammatik 1 **116**
Grammatik 2 **118**
Lese- und Hörtest **120**
Mündlicher Test **122**
Schreibtest **124**
Wörter **126**
Grammatik: Wiederholung Kapitel 1–5 **128**

Kapitel 6 Schöne Ferien!
Theme 3: Communication and the world around us

Kulturzone Im Urlaub und unterwegs **132**
- Learning about German-speaking travel destinations
- Forming the imperative

Einheit 1 Wo fahren wir hin? **134**
- Describing different holiday destinations
- Forming questions
- Discussing advantages and disadvantages

Einheit 2 Wo werden wir wohnen? **136**
- Describing types of holiday accommodation
- Using *wer, wen* and *wem*
- Recognising negatives

Einheit 3 Mein schrecklicher Urlaub **138**
- Describing problems on holiday
- Revising possessive adjectives
- Practising a holiday role-play

Einheit 4 Wie waren die Schulferien? **140**
- Describing a past holiday
- Using prepositions with the genitive
- Talking about the weather in the past

Einheit 5 Ich möchte um die Welt reisen! **142**
- Describing future and ideal holidays
- Using interrogative and demonstrative adjectives
- Practising the *w* and *v* sounds in German

Grammatik 1 **144**
Grammatik 2 **146**
Lese- und Hörtest **148**
Mündlicher Test **150**
Schreibtest **152**
Wörter **154**

Kapitel 7 Unsere Welt

Theme 1: People and lifestyle;
Theme 3: Communication and the world around us

Kulturzone *Wir verbessern die Welt!*   156
- Learning more about activism in German-speaking countries
- Using more prepositions with the genitive

Einheit 1 *Was ist dir wichtig?*   158
- Discussing issues facing young people today
- Using verbs followed by prepositions
- Asking questions which include prepositions

Einheit 2 *Unser armer Planet*   160
- Discussing how environmental issues are being addressed
- Revising compound nouns
- Using phrases of argument and disagreement

Einheit 3 *Jeder kann was tun!*   162
- Discussing personal responsibilities and actions
- Using *wollen* (to want to)
- Using three different time frames in speaking

Einheit 4 *Wir wollen eine bessere Welt!*   164
- Discussing international responsibilities and actions
- Using the conditional of *sollen*
- Using *man* to avoid the passive

Einheit 5 *Dialog ist wichtig!*   166
- Expressing and justifying complex opinions and points of view
- Using phrases of debating in speaking
- Pronouncing *r* sounds correctly

Grammatik 1   168
Grammatik 2   170
Lese- und Hörtest   172
Mündlicher Test   174
Schreibtest   176
Wörter   178

Kapitel 8 Wie sieht die Zukunft aus?

Theme 1: People and lifestyle

Kulturzone *Ich will helfen*   180
- Learning about military and civilian service
- Revising verbs and constructions with *zu*

Einheit 1 *Was wirst du nach deinen Prüfungen machen?*   182
- Discussing plans for after exams
- Using reflexive verbs
- Revising ways to refer to the future

Einheit 2 *Was ist dein Traumberuf?*   184
- Discussing what jobs you would like to do in the future
- Revising the conditional and imperfect subjunctive
- Using *werden* in different tenses

Einheit 3 *Was kannst du gut?*   186
- Discussing characteristics and skills
- Revising subordinating conjunctions
- Extending your written work

Einheit 4 *Ein Zwischenjahr? Warum nicht?*   188
- Discussing gap years
- Using adjectives as nouns
- Formulating an argument

Einheit 5 *Meine Träume für die Zukunft*   190
- Discussing hopes for the future
- Dealing with unfamiliar vocabulary
- Consolidating key language and grammar points

Grammatik 1   192
Grammatik 2   194
Lese- und Hörtest   196
Mündlicher Test   198
Schreibtest   200
Wörter   202
Grammatik: Wiederholung Kapitel 1–8   204

Wiederholung

Kapitel 1	Zurück zur Schule!	210	**Kapitel 5** Meine Gegend	218
Kapitel 2	Endlich mal Freizeit!	212	**Kapitel 6** Schöne Ferien!	220
Kapitel 3	Meine Welt, deine Welt	214	**Kapitel 7** Unsere Welt	222
Kapitel 4	Bleib gesund!	216	**Kapitel 8** Wie sieht die Zukunft aus?	224

Speaking support

Speaking test revision: Conversation questions	226
Speaking test revision: German phonics	228
Speaking test revision: Role-play skills	230
Speaking test revision: Photo card task	232
Verb tables	234
Derivational morphology	240

Kapitel 1: Zurück zur Schule!

Meine Schule, deine Schule
- Understanding the school system in Great Britain and in the German-speaking world
- Using articles and plural nouns

a) Deutschland
- Typischer Schultag: 7:30–13:00 Uhr
- Ferien: 10–13 Wochen
- Hausaufgaben: 2–3 Stunden
- Noten: 1–6
- Mit dem Rad zur Schule: 11%

b) die Schweiz
- Typischer Schultag: 8:00–16:00 Uhr
- Ferien: 12–14 Wochen
- Hausaufgaben: 2–3 Stunden
- Noten: 1–6
- Mit dem Rad zur Schule: 18%

c) Großbritannien
- Typischer Schultag: 8:30–15:30 Uhr
- Ferien: 13–15 Wochen
- Hausaufgaben: 1–2 Stunden
- Noten: 9–1 (*GCSEs*), A–D (*Nationals*, Schottland)
- Mit dem Rad zur Schule: 2%

d) Österreich
- Typischer Schultag: 7:30–13:00 Uhr
- Ferien: 14–16 Wochen
- Hausaufgaben: 2–3 Stunden
- Noten: 1–5
- Mit dem Rad zur Schule: 20%

e) Austausch in Großbritannien: Schule einmal anders!

Maximillian von Reichelt

In Deutschland gehen wir mit sechs Jahren in die Grundschule, aber in Großbritannien gehen die Kinder schon mit vier oder fünf Jahren in die Schule – ja, so früh! Und ohne Schultüte!

Die Schultypen sind auch anders. Die meisten Schulen sind Gesamtschulen und es gibt auch Privatschulen. Bei uns gibt es mehr als vier Schultypen! Ich besuche ein Gymnasium.

Mit 15 oder 16 Jahren schreiben sie in Großbritannien wichtige Prüfungen: *GCSEs* oder *Nationals*. Das kann man mit unserer Mittlere-Reife-Prüfung vergleichen und das Abitur heißt *A-levels* oder *Highers*. Aber sie müssen nie sitzenbleiben, auch wenn sie viele schlechte Noten haben.

Bei den Lehrern gibt es auch Unterschiede – in Deutschland unterrichten die Lehrer normalerweise jede Stunde in einem anderen Klassenzimmer, aber in England haben die Lehrer meistens ihr eigenes Klassenzimmer.

Und, *last but not least* (ein bisschen Englisch für euch): in Großbritannien tragen fast alle eine Schuluniform – das finde ich ein bisschen komisch!

die Schultüte	a cone of treats children get on their first day at primary school
die Gesamtschule	comprehensive school
die Mittlere-Reife-Prüfung	GCSE exam equivalent

Kulturzone   Kapitel 1

Lesen 1 Read the statistics (a–d) about typical schools in Germany, Switzerland, Great Britain and Austria. Copy and complete the sentences below in English.

1 The school day in Germany begins at …
2 Students in Switzerland have … hours of homework.
3 Students in Great Britain have … weeks' holiday.
4 …% of students cycle to school in Great Britain compared to …% in Austria.
5 School ends at 1:00 p.m. in … and …, but at … in Switzerland.
6 Most of the countries have different systems for …

Lesen 2 Read the article (e) about Maximillian's exchange trip to Great Britain. Write down <u>five</u> key differences between schools in Great Britain and in Germany.

Lesen 3 Look at the flyer. Write the letter of the correct item of clothing (a–f) for each German word.

1 das T-Shirt
2 die Schuhe
3 die Hose
4 das Hemd
5 der Rock
6 die Jacke

Hören 4 Listen to the conversation. Look at the pictures in exercise 3. Write down a–f. Tick (✓) the items they buy and cross (✗) the ones they don't.

Schreiben 5 Copy and complete the sentences with the singular and plural items of clothing from exercise 3.

Ich brauche ein T-Shirt, …
Ich habe T-Shirts, …

> The word *Umlaut* means 'sound changer'.
> Listen and repeat the words.
> Then practise reading them out.
> R**o**ck (skirt)   R**ö**cke (skirts)
> Sch**u**le (school)   Sch**ü**ler (pupils)

G In German, there are several ways of forming **plural nouns**: you can't just add an **-s** as in English.

When you learn a new noun, learn its plural as well as its gender. In a dictionary, plurals are usually shown in brackets after the noun.

	singular	plural
m	der Rock (¨-e) der Schuh (-e)	die Röck**e** die Schuh**e**
f	die Jacke (-n) die Hose (-n)	die Jacke**n** die Hose**n**
nt	das Hemd (-en) das T-Shirt (-s)	die Hemd**en** die T-Shirt**s**

Sprechen 6 Memory game: In pairs, take turns to say what you are buying, adding an extra item each time.

● *Ich gehe einkaufen und ich kaufe einen Rock.*
■ *Ich gehe einkaufen und ich kaufe einen Rock und Schuhe …*

G

	definite article 'the'		indefinite article 'a'	
	nominative	accusative	nominative	accusative
m	der	den	ein	einen
f	die	die	eine	eine
nt	das	das	ein	ein
pl	die	die	–	–

Nom (subject): **Ein** Rock kostet 25 Euro. **Der** Rock ist teuer!
Acc (direct object): Ich brauche **einen** Rock. Ich kaufe **den** Rock.

Page 18

sieben 7

1 Welche Fächer hast du dieses Jahr?

- Talking about your school subjects
- Using the present tense
- Using *weil* to give and justify opinions

 Hören 1 Listen to the students talking about their school subjects. Decide if each person is talking about the timetable below (✓) or not (✗). (1–8)

	Montag	Dienstag	Mittwoch	Donnerstag	Freitag
1. Stunde	Mathe	Chemie	Englisch	Deutsch	Physik
2. Stunde	Biologie	Englisch	Mathe	Englisch	Chemie
Pause					
3. Stunde	Deutsch	Französisch	Geschichte	Kunst	Theater
4. Stunde	Englisch	Kunst	Deutsch	Spanisch	Mathe
5. Stunde	Erdkunde	Informatik	Religion	Musik	Biologie
Mittagspause					
6. Stunde	Musik	Sport	Physik	Sport	Französisch

Informatik Computing

 Hören 2 Listen again. Write down <u>eight</u> opinion adjectives you hear and translate them into English.

Be careful with cognates! Words can look similar to English but sound different in German.

Listen and repeat the words. Then practise reading them out.

- g **B**i**o**l**og**ie
- sp **Sp**ort
- ch **Ch**emie
- th Ma**th**e, **Th**eater
- e **E**nglisch
- y Ph**y**sik

 Use the **present tense** to talk about what you **do** or **are doing** now.

*Ich **lerne** Deutsch.* I **learn** German. / I **am learning** German.

	regular verbs: *lernen*	verbs with a stem ending in -d or -t: *finden*	*haben*	*sein*
ich (*I*)	lern**e**	find**e**	hab**e**	bin
du (*you*)	lern**st**	find**est**	hast	bist
er/sie/es/man (*he/she/it/one*)	lern**t**	find**et**	hat	ist
wir (*we*)	lern**en**	find**en**	hab**en**	sind
ihr (*you plural*)	lern**t**	find**et**	hab**t**	seid
Sie (*you formal, sg and pl*)	lern**en**	find**en**	hab**en**	sind
sie (*they*)	lern**en**	find**en**	hab**en**	sind

Page 19

 Sprechen 3 In pairs, take turns to ask and answer questions about your school subjects. Be careful with cognates.

- Was hast du dieses Jahr am <u>Montag</u> in der <u>ersten</u> Stunde?
- Am <u>Montag</u> in der <u>ersten</u> Stunde habe ich <u>Englisch</u>.
- Wie findest du <u>Englisch</u>?
- Ich finde es <u>schwierig</u>. Was hast du am <u>Freitag</u> nach der Pause?
- Am <u>Freitag</u> nach der Pause habe ich …

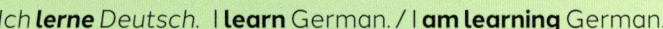

Was hast du (am Montag) in der (ersten/zweiten/dritten) Stunde?
Am (Montag) in der (ersten) Stunde habe ich …
Wie oft hast du (Mathe)?
Ich habe (Mathe) (einmal/zweimal/dreimal) pro Woche / pro Tag.
Wie viele Stunden hast du (am Nachmittag / nach der Pause)?
Wie findest du (Englisch)?
Ich finde es einfach/anstrengend/nützlich/schwierig.
Was ist dein Lieblingsfach?
Mein Lieblingsfach ist (Deutsch).

4 Listen to and read the interview with Sarah. Translate the words in blue into English. Then translate the phrases in **bold** into English.

? *Hallo Sarah! Welche Fächer lernst du dieses Jahr?*
Dieses Jahr lerne ich Mathe, Englisch, Deutsch, Religion, Sport, Geschichte, Informatik, Kunst, Theater und Musik.

? *Was ist dein Lieblingsfach?*
Mein Lieblingsfach ist Englisch, **weil es interessant ist**.

? *Warum?*
Weil ich es total nützlich finde. Ich höre sehr gern Musik mit englischen Texten.

? *Wann hast du Englisch?*
Ich habe am Dienstag, am Mittwoch und am Freitag Englisch. Ich finde das toll, **weil ich Sprachen liebe**.

? *Welches Fach magst du nicht und warum?*
Ich mag Mathe nicht. Ich finde Mathe kompliziert und schwer, **weil ich schwach in Mathe bin**.

? *Wie findest du Sport?*
Ich finde Sport praktisch und wichtig, aber manchmal ist es auch ein bisschen anstrengend.

? *Was machst du in der Pause?*
In der Pause trinke ich viel Wasser und ich esse Obst, **weil ich oft Hunger habe**.

? *Was machst du in der Mittagspause?*
Normalerweise esse ich in der Kantine und ich spreche mit meinen Freundinnen. Ich mache auch oft meine Hausaufgaben und jeden Mittwoch spiele ich Fußball in der Mittagspause. Das finde ich toll, **weil ich sportlich bin**.

5 In pairs, take turns to ask and answer the questions in the interview in exercise 4.

	es	interessant wichtig nützlich einfach/leicht praktisch schwer/schwierig anstrengend kompliziert	ist.
Ich mag (Englisch), Ich liebe (Deutsch), Ich mag (Mathe) (nicht),	weil ich es		finde.
	ich (nicht)	gut in (Mathe) schwach in (Musik)	bin.
In der Pause	esse ich … / trinke ich … / spiele ich … spreche ich mit meinen Freunden.		

G *weil* sends the verb to the **end** of the clause:

Ich mag Englisch. Ich finde es nützlich.
I like English. I find it useful.

Ich mag Englisch, weil ich es nützlich finde.
I like English **because** I find it useful.

Page 19

6 Translate the sentences into German.

'I am learning' and 'I learn' are the same in German.

What is different about the verb endings of *finden*?

1 My favourite subject is art.
2 Languages are very interesting.
3 I am learning German, music and history.
4 Anna finds maths great because it's easy.
5 After the lunch break we have PE.
6 On Tuesday in the third lesson, Thomas has English.

Remember, *weil* sends the verb to the end.

2 Was trägst du in der Schule?

- Talking about school uniforms
- Using adjectives with nouns
- Describing a photo

Read the speech bubbles. Write the letter of the correct photo (a–d) for each speech bubble.

1. Die Mädchen tragen ein grünes Kleid. Die Jungen tragen braune Shorts und ein braunes Hemd. Sie tragen alle braune Schuhe und braune oder weiße Socken.

2. Die Schüler und Schülerinnen tragen meistens Jeans, ein T-Shirt, eine Jacke und Sportschuhe. Sie haben keine Schuluniform.

3. Sie tragen alle eine dunkelblaue Jacke, ein weißes Hemd und eine rot-weiße Krawatte. Die Mädchen tragen einen grauen Rock und die Jungen tragen eine graue Hose.

4. Die Jugendlichen tragen alle ein weißes Hemd. Sie tragen entweder eine schwarze Hose oder einen schwarzen Rock und schwarze Schuhe.

die Krawatte	tie
die Sportschuhe	trainers

Deutschland

Großbritannien

Südafrika

Japan

Listen to some students describing what they wear to school. For each person, write down the items they wear, the colour and any extra information. (1–5)

rot, orange, gelb, grün, blau, hellblau, dunkelblau, schwarz, grau, weiß, braun

Two adjectives can be combined in German to form a new adjective:
hell (light) + blau (blue) → hellblau (light blue)
dunkel (dark) + blau (blue) → dunkelblau (dark blue)

Adjectives used before nouns must **agree** with the noun.

Ich trage	einen keinen	blauen	Pullover. Rock.
	eine keine	blaue	Hose. Jacke.
	ein kein	blaues	Hemd. Kleid.
	–	blaue	Schuhe.
	keine	blauen	Sportschuhe.

kein (not, not a) has the same endings as the indefinite article:
Sie tragen **keine** rot**e** Hose.

Page 18

zehn

3 Translate the sentences into German.

> Trousers are singular in German.

> Remember that irregular verbs take an umlaut in some forms.

> Remember that *kein* must agree with the noun.

1 I wear black trousers, a grey shirt and a blue jumper.
2 I wear a grey skirt and a green T-shirt at school.
3 She wears a blue dress and black shoes.
4 The girls wear a yellow dress and a dark blue jacket.
5 The boys wear a red T-shirt and black trainers.
6 We wear black trousers but no jumper.

Some **irregular verbs** change their **vowel sounds** in the *du* and *er/sie/es/man* forms of the present tense.

	tragen (*to wear*)	fahren (*to drive, go*)
ich	trage	fahre
du	tr**ä**gst	f**ä**hrst
er/sie/es/man	tr**ä**gt	f**ä**hrt

Page 19

4 Listen to and read the forum and decide which statements about school uniforms are positive (**P**), negative (**N**) or both (**P+N**). Then translate the phrases in **bold** into English. Write down two opinions you agree with.

Wie findest du Schuluniformen?

1 Ganz-froh: Ich finde Schuluniformen **sehr praktisch**.

2 Elfmeter: Aber **eine Schuluniform ist sehr teuer**!

3 Modefan: Kleider machen Leute! **Meine Kleidung zeigt meinen Charakter**!

4 Einmaleins: Ja, und **Schuluniformen verhindern Mobbing**, aber auf der anderen Seite sind sie langweilig und unbequem.

5 Mitzi: Ja, das finde ich auch. **Ich bin total gegen Schuluniformen, weil man seine Individualität verliert**.

6 Bergfex: Das finde ich nicht. Die Schuluniform ist ein gutes Image für die Schule und **es gibt keinen Unterschied zwischen den Schülern**.

7 Lorelei: Das kann sein, aber **normale Kleidung kostet oft mehr als eine Uniform**.

8 Fata Morgana: Ich bin mehr als meine Kleidung! **Meine Kleidung ist nicht meine Identität! Eine Schuluniform hat sowohl Vorteile als auch Nachteile**!

die Kleider	clothes
unbequem	uncomfortable

5 Listen to the description and decide which photo in exercise 1 is being described. Then write down the answers the person gives to the two questions below.

1 Was trägst du in der Schule?
2 Wie findest du Schuluniformen?

Auf dem Foto sieht man (drei) Jugendliche: (zwei) Jungen und (ein) Mädchen.
Sie sind ungefähr (15) Jahre alt.
Der Junge vorne trägt …
Das Mädchen im Hintergrund trägt …
Die Jungen/Mädchen tragen …
Sie sind (in der Schule / in einem Park / draußen).
Sie (sprechen miteinander / lachen).

6 In pairs, take turns to describe a photo from exercise 1 and answer the two questions in exercise 5 for yourself.

3 Sind Schulregeln wirklich nötig?

- Talking about school rules
- Using modal verbs: *müssen, dürfen, sollen*
- Using opinion phrases with *dass*

Lesen 1
Read the school rules. Write the letter of the correct picture (a–f) for each one.

1 Man muss Respekt zeigen.
2 Man muss seine Hausaufgaben machen.
3 Man soll für den Mathetest lernen.
4 Man soll im Gang leise sein.
5 Man darf im Unterricht nicht frech sein.
6 Man darf im Klassenzimmer nicht essen.

a

b

c

d

e

f

Lesen 2
Find the German in exercise 1 for the English phrases below.
1 You must / have to …
2 You should / ought to …
3 You are not allowed to …

Hören 3
Listen. Copy and complete the table in English. (1–5)

	rules	opinions
1	not allowed to eat in the classroom	OK
	not allowed to …	…

| Man | muss darf soll | im Klassenzimmer im Computerraum im Gang im Unterricht in der Turnhalle in der Kantine in der Schule draußen | ruhig sein. leise sein. (nicht) frech sein. (nicht) laufen. Fußball spielen. langsam gehen. (nicht) essen. (nicht) trinken. eine Uniform tragen. Respekt zeigen. seine Hausaufgaben machen. |

Modal verbs are irregular and must be used with another verb in the infinitive at the end of the sentence.
müssen: Man **muss** seine Hausaufgaben machen.
dürfen: Man **darf** Fußball spielen.
sollen: Man **soll** im Gang leise sein.

Use **man** with modal verbs to mean 'you' generally.

	müssen (must, have to)	dürfen (be allowed to)	sollen (should, ought to)
ich	muss	darf	soll
du	musst	darfst	sollst
er/sie/es/man	muss	darf	soll
wir	müssen	dürfen	sollen
ihr	müsst	dürft	sollt
Sie	müssen	dürfen	sollen
sie	müssen	dürfen	sollen

The *ich* and *er/sie/es/man* forms of modal verbs are the same.

Page 20

4 Write <u>six</u> sentences about your school rules using *man*.

Example: 1 *Man muss eine Schuluniform tragen.*

man **muss**	you **have to**
man **muss** … **nicht**	you **don't** have to (**not** you must **not**)
man **darf** … **nicht**	you **are not** allowed to / you **must not**

5 Listen and read. Translate the phrases in **bold** into English.

Lukas

Wir haben einen neuen Direktor und jetzt muss man aufstehen, wenn der Lehrer kommt. **Ich finde, dass es blöd ist**.

Wir müssen auch im Gang langsam gehen und dürfen nicht laufen. **Ich finde, dass es notwendig ist**, weil es gefährlich sein kann.

Ayaan

Wir dürfen nur in der Kantine essen. **Ich glaube, dass diese Regel falsch ist**. Unsere Kantine ist viel zu klein und es gibt nicht genug Platz für alle.

Wir dürfen auch Handys nicht in der Schule benutzen. **Ich finde, dass es unfair ist**, weil es in der Pause niemanden stört.

Malik

Wir müssen im Unterricht total leise sein und dürfen überhaupt nie sprechen. Es ist streng, aber **ich denke, dass es richtig ist**.

Jedoch bekommen wir jeden Tag so viele Hausaufgaben. **Ich bin der Meinung, dass es nicht richtig ist**, weil ich nicht genug Freizeit habe.

stören	to disturb, to bother

6 Read the texts again and answer with the correct name.

Who thinks …?
1. standing up when a teacher enters is stupid
2. not being allowed to talk in lessons is reasonable
3. there is not enough space in the school canteen
4. mobile phones don't disturb anyone during break
5. they don't have enough free time
6. running in the corridor can be dangerous

G *dass* also sends the verb to the end, like **weil**.
Page 19

7 In pairs, take turns to agree or disagree with the school rules in exercise 1 and give your opinion.

- *Man darf im Klassenzimmer nicht essen. Was denkst du?*
- *Ich glaube, dass es unfair ist.*
- *Warum?*
- *Weil es in der Kantine nicht genug Platz gibt.*

Ich finde, Ich denke, Ich glaube, Ich bin der Meinung,	dass	es diese Regel	sehr ziemlich nicht	(un)fair wichtig notwendig richtig falsch nötig	ist.
Warum?	Weil	es unbequem es (nicht) praktisch/notwendig/nötig es (un)fair/(un)gerecht			ist.
		ich nicht genug Freizeit			habe.
		es in der Kantine nicht genug Platz			gibt.

4 Schultage: die beste Zeit deines Lebens?

- Talking about special events at school
- Using the perfect and imperfect tenses
- Practising the *w* sound in German

  Look at the photos. Write the letter of the correct event (a–h) for each photo.

a Konzert **b** Sporttag **c** Modenschau **d** Skiwoche
e Wandertag **f** Theaterstück **g** Schulausflug **h** Kreativwoche

  Listen to and read the sentences. Write the letter of the correct event (a–h) from exercise 1 for each sentence.

1 Ich habe den ganzen Tag Sport gemacht.
2 Ich bin mit der Schule für eine Woche Skifahren gegangen.
3 Ich habe ein Musical gemacht und ich habe die Hauptrolle gespielt.
4 Ich habe im Chor gesungen und das Orchester hat gespielt.
5 Ich habe die ganze Woche in jedem Fach kreative Sachen gemacht.
6 Ich bin an einem Tag 16km zu Fuß gegangen.
7 Ich habe tolle Kleidung gezeigt.
8 Ich bin mit der Schule zu einem Freizeitpark gefahren.

| der Chor | choir |
| der Freizeitpark | theme park |

  Find the German for the phrases below in exercise 2. In what way are the phrases in 2 and 5 different from the others?

1 I did …
2 I went …
3 I played …
4 I sang …
5 I walked …
6 I showed …

In the German-speaking world, 'hiking days' (*Wandertage*) are part of the school curriculum. In Austria and Switzerland, these can also be whole-school ski days and in some areas, schools organise a week of skiing to give every child the opportunity to learn this national sport.

  Listen to the students talking about special events at school. (1–4) Which <u>four</u> events from exercise 1 do they mention? Write the letters.

5 Read the text and write down the missing words. Then listen and check.

Letztes Jahr **1** wir einen Schulausflug nach Phantasialand gemacht. Wir **2** mit dem Bus gefahren und ich **3** im Bus Musik gehört. Das Wetter war super. Am Morgen **4** wir vier Fahrten gemacht. Zu Mittag gab es Hotdogs – lecker! Am Nachmittag **5** ich mit der Achterbahn gefahren. Mein Freund **6** viele Fotos gemacht und ich **7** ein Geschenk für meinen Bruder gekauft. Um fünf Uhr **8** wir wieder mit dem Bus zurück zur Schule gefahren und wir **9** alle im Bus geschlafen. Wir waren sehr müde, aber der Tag **10** super und wir hatten Spaß!

| die Fahrt (-en) | ride |
| die Achterbahn | roller coaster |

6 Find <u>three</u> sentences containing *war*, *gab* or *hatten* in exercise 5 and translate them into English.

7 In pairs, use the words to make <u>six</u> sentences in the perfect tense. Add an opinion using the imperfect tense. Pay attention to the **w** sounds.

| ich | du | wir | sie | er |

| hat | hast | haben | bin | bist | habe |

| Fußball | Pommes frites | Postkarten |
| im Meer | nach Österreich | ins Café |

| gefahren | gekauft | geschwommen |
| gespielt | gegangen | gegessen |

| super | schlecht | wunderbar | es | war |

The **perfect tense** is used to describe actions in the past. In German, the perfect tense consists of **two** parts: an <u>auxiliary verb</u> (part of *haben* or *sein*) and the **past participle**.

*Ich <u>habe</u> Musik **gehört**.*   I **listened** to music.
*Ich <u>bin</u> 16km zu Fuß **gegangen**.*   I **walked** 16km.

The past participle usually starts with **ge-** and can end in **-t** (regular verbs) or **-en** (irregular verbs). Most verbs take **haben** in the perfect tense, but a few take **sein**. These are mostly verbs of movement and changes of state.

Learn these six common verbs that take *sein*:

Ich **bin gegangen**.	I went (on foot).
Ich **bin gefahren**.	I went (by means of transport).
Ich **bin geflogen**.	I flew.
Ich **bin gekommen**.	I came.
Ich **bin geschwommen**.	I swam.
Ich **bin geblieben**.	I stayed.

Page 20

These **imperfect tense** phrases are often used to describe how things were in the past.

*Ich **war** / Wir **waren** froh.*   *Das Wetter **war** super.*
I **was** / We **were** happy.   The weather **was** great.

*Ich **hatte** / Sie **hatte** / Wir **hatten** Spaß.*
I **had** / She **had** / We **had** fun.

*Es **gab** eine Achterbahn. Es **gab** viele Fahrten.*
There was a rollercoaster. **There were** many rides.

Page 21

w in German is always pronounced like the English 'v' sound.

Listen and repeat the sentence. Then practise saying it. How quickly can you say it?

*Der **W**andertag **w**ar **w**underbar, **w**eil **w**ir auch sch**w**immen **w**aren und das **W**asser **w**arm **w**ar.*

8 In pairs, ask and answer questions about an interesting school event.

- *Hast du letztes Jahr etwas Interessantes in der Schule gemacht?*
- *Ja, es gab eine Kreativwoche.*
- *Was hast du gemacht?*
- *Ich habe …*
- *Wie war es?*
- *Es war …*

fünfzehn 15

5 Austausch geht auch online!

- Describing school life
- Speaking and writing in the past and present
- Practising the 90-word exam question

Hören 1
Listen to and read the video chat between Nala and Alina. Then find the German for the phrases below.

Nala in Leeds

Hallo Alina! Ich heiße Nala und ich bin deine online Austauschpartnerin. Hier in Leeds ist es zwölf Uhr und wir haben gerade Deutsch. Was hast du gerade?

Ja, ich besuche eine ziemlich große Gesamtschule. Wir haben jeden Tag fünf Stunden und eine Stunde dauert 60 Minuten. Und bei dir?

In der kleinen Pause verbringe ich Zeit mit meinen Freunden und in der Mittagspause esse ich in der Kantine. Manchmal mache ich auch Sport, oder ich gehe in einen Club. Und du?

Gestern bin ich um vier Uhr nach Hause gekommen und ich hatte eine kurze Pause, weil ich so müde war. Danach habe ich meine Hausaufgaben gemacht. Und du?

Ich lerne auch ein Instrument: Ich lerne Gitarre, aber ich lerne es in der Schule.

Tschüss. Bis zum nächsten Mal!

Alina in Köln

Hallo Nala, schön dich kennenzulernen. Hier in Köln ist es ein Uhr und wir haben gerade Englisch. Kannst du deine Schule beschreiben?

Eine Stunde dauert bei uns 50 Minuten und wir haben fünf oder sechs Stunden pro Tag. Was machst du in der Pause?

Ja, ich esse meinen Imbiss und spreche mit meinen Freunden. Ich habe keine Mittagspause, weil die Schule am Mittag endet, also esse ich zu Hause. Was hast du gestern nach der Schule gemacht?

Nach dem Mittagessen hatte ich gestern eine Cellostunde. Ich lerne Cello in der Musikschule. Und du?

Nala, meine Stunde ist aus. Ich muss jetzt nach Hause gehen. Tschüss!

die Gitarre	guitar
Tschüss	bye

1 exchange partner
2 What do you have right now?
3 nice to meet you
4 to describe
5 comprehensive school
6 A lesson lasts 60 minutes.
7 I spend time with my friends.
8 I also do sports.
9 snack
10 My lesson is over.

Lesen 2
Read the video chat again. Copy and complete the sentences in English.

1 Nala goes to a ... school.
2 A lesson at Alina's school lasts ...
3 At lunch, Nala sometimes ... or ...
4 At midday, Alina's school ...
5 Yesterday, Nala went home at ...
6 Nala learns the ... at ...

Sprechen 3 — In pairs, take turns to ask and answer the questions.

- *Was machst du normalerweise in der Mittagspause?*
- *In der Mittagspause ... ich normalerweise ...*
- *Was hast du gestern in der Mittagspause gemacht?*
- *Gestern in der Mittagspause ... ich ...*
- *Was hast du gestern nach der Schule gemacht?*
- *Gestern nach der Schule ... ich ...*

> The **verb** is always the second idea in a German sentence. If you start with a <u>time phrase</u>, the verb and the subject change place.
> <u>Gestern</u> **habe** ich Sport gemacht.

In der Pause/ Mittagspause	esse	ich (normalerweise)	meinen Imbiss. in der Kantine.
	spreche		mit meinen Freunden.
	verbringe		Zeit mit Freunden.
	mache		Sport. meine Hausaufgaben.
	gehe		in einen Club. in die Kantine.
Gestern in der Pause/ Mittagspause	habe	ich	in der Kantine gegessen. mit meinen Freunden gesprochen. Zeit mit Freunden verbracht. Sport gemacht.
Gestern nach der Schule	bin		in die Stadt gegangen.

Hören 4 — Listen to Oliver and Finn discussing school uniforms, rules and memorable school days. Select the <u>three</u> correct statements.

a Oliver likes not having to think about clothes in the morning.
b Oliver has a non-uniform day this week.
c Finn always wears comfortable clothes.
d Oliver thinks that there are too many exams.
e Finn did a 14km hike with his class.
f The water was too cold for swimming.

Schreiben 5 — Write approximately 90 words about your school. Include the following points:

- your school day
- your opinion about school rules
- a special event at school last year.

The 90-word question

For this question on the writing exam paper, you need to cover the three bullet points given and write in German. The word count is a guide only, but try to stick to it.

For the highest marks, you should:
- cover all three bullet points
- develop your ideas with opinions and reasons
- write as accurately as you can
- write in all the time frames required by the bullet points.

Wir haben jeden Tag ... Stunden und ... Pausen.
In der Schule lerne ich ...
Mein Lieblingsfach ist ..., weil ... Aber ich mag ... nicht, weil ...
In der Pause/Mittagspause ... ich normalerweise ...
In der Schule muss ich ... tragen. Ich finde ...
In meiner Schule müssen wir ...
Im Klassenzimmer dürfen wir (nicht) ...
Ich finde, dass es ... ist.
Letztes Jahr hatten wir ...
Es war ..., weil ...
Es gab ...
Wir haben ... gemacht.

siebzehn

Grammatik 1

Definite articles and plural nouns (Culture, page 7)

 1 Listen and write down the definite articles (the) you hear. Then write down the gender of the nouns (m, f, nt).

Example: 1 die Jacke (f)

1 ▢ Jacke ist zu teuer.
2 ▢ Hose ist zu klein.
3 ▢ Hemd kostet €18,50.
4 Wo ist ▢ Lehrerin?
5 ▢ Klassenzimmer ist groß.
6 Wann beginnt ▢ Schultag?

German also uses these gender-neutral forms:

gender-neutral form	instead of
Lehrer*innen	Lehrer und Lehrerinnen
Schüler*innen	Schüler und Schülerinnen

 2 Write down the plural forms of the nouns from exercise 1.

Example: 1 die Jacke → die Jacken

Nominative and accusative cases (Culture, page 7; Unit 2, page 10)

 3 Copy and complete the sentences with the correct definite (the) or indefinite articles (a, no) in the accusative case.

1 Ich habe *eine* Pause. (f, a)
2 Ich mag ▢ Mittagspause. (f, the)
3 Wir müssen ▢ Uniform tragen. (f, a)
4 In Deutschland tragen die Schüler ▢ Schuluniform. (f, no)
5 Meine Freundin hat ▢ T-Shirt. (nt, a)
6 Aber sie hat ▢ Rock. (m, no)

 A 'case' represents the relationship between the subject and the object of a sentence.

In the following sentence, Oliver is the **subject** (who is doing the action of buying) and the jumper is the <u>object</u> (the thing that is being bought).

Oliver kauft <u>einen Pullover</u>.   **Oliver** buys <u>a jumper</u>.

The **nominative case** is always used for the **subject**.
The **accusative case** is always used for the **direct object**.

 4 Translate the sentences into German. Think carefully about which case to use.

Example: 1 Sie hat einen Rock und ein T-Shirt.

1 She has a skirt (*m*) and a T-shirt (*nt*).
2 The skirt (*m*) costs €18.
3 We need shoes (*pl*).
4 He has a jacket (*f*) and the trousers (*f*).
5 The T-shirt (*nt*) is expensive!
6 She needs a shirt (*nt*) and she has no jacket (*f*).

Using adjectives before nouns (Unit 2, page 10)

 5 Copy and complete the sentences with the correct form of the adjectives in brackets.

1 Ich trage ein ▢ Hemd. (*weiß*)
2 Trägst du eine ▢ Schuluniform? (*bequem*)
3 Wir tragen alle ▢ Schuhe. (*schwarz*)
4 Sofie trägt einen ▢ Pullover. (*grün*)

18 achtzehn

The present tense (Unit 1, page 8; Unit 2, page 11)

Copy and complete the sentences with the correct form of the verb in brackets.

1 Ich **lerne** gern Deutsch. (*lernen*)
2 Was ___ du in der Pause? (*machen*)
3 Mein Bruder ___ Geschichte. (*lieben*)
4 Wir ___ Mathe toll. (*finden*)
5 Sie ___ ihre Hausaufgaben. (*machen*)
6 ___ du ein Instrument? (*spielen*)

Select the correct verb form to complete each sentence.
Example: 1 *fahre*

1 Ich **fahre / fahrt / fährst** mit dem Rad zur Schule.
2 Wir **habt / haben / habe** am Montag Deutsch und Englisch.
3 Meine Freundin **ist / bist / bin** sehr gut in Mathe.
4 **Trage / Trägst / Trägt** du gern eine Schuluniform?
5 Was **habe / hat / hast** du in der dritten Stunde?
6 Ich **ist / bin / bist** total gegen Schuluniformen.

Go back to pages 8 and 11 and look at the verb tables to refresh your memory of verb endings in the present tense. Then test a partner.

Translate the sentences into German.
Example: 1 *Joel lernt Englisch und Französisch.*

1 Joel learns English and French.
2 We don't wear a school uniform.
3 Arya has English three times a week.
4 How do you find biology?
5 My favourite subject is German.
6 He is playing football.

weil and dass (Unit 1, page 9; Unit 3, page 13)

In pairs, take turns to link the sentences using *weil*.
Example: 1 *Ich liebe Kunst, weil es einfach ist.*

1 Ich liebe Kunst. Es ist einfach.
2 Ich mag Chemie nicht. Es ist schwierig.
3 Wir finden Englisch schwer. Wir sind schwach in Englisch.
4 Ich mag Mathe. Ich finde es nützlich.
5 Sascha findet Fußball toll. Er ist sportlich.
6 Du isst Obst in der Pause. Du hast oft Hunger.

Put the words in the correct order to make sentences starting with the words in bold. Then translate the sentences into English.
Example: 1 *Wir glauben, dass ... / We believe that ...*

1 nicht fair **Wir glauben,** dass ist es
2 der Meinung, diese Regel notwendig **Ich bin** ist dass
3 du, Uniformen sind dass **Findest** bequem
4 dass denke, Schulausflug **Ich** war der toll

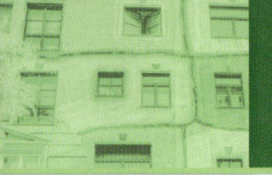

Grammatik 2

Modal verbs (Unit 3, page 12)

1 Rewrite the sentences using the correct form of the modal verb in brackets.

Example: 1 *Ich soll für den Mathetest lernen.*

1 Ich lerne für den Mathetest. (*sollen*)
2 Wir tragen eine Schuluniform. (*müssen*)
3 Ich benutze das Handy nicht in der Schule. (*dürfen*)
4 Wir essen nicht im Klassenzimmer. (*dürfen*)
5 Ich zeige Respekt. (*müssen*)
6 Wir sind leise im Gang. (*sollen*)

2 Translate the sentences into English.

Example: 1 *I don't have to leave my mobile phone at home.*

1 Ich muss mein Handy nicht zu Hause lassen.
2 Ich darf mein Handy nicht in der Schule benutzen.
3 Ich muss nicht zu Mittag in der Schule essen.
4 Ich darf im Klassenzimmer nicht essen.
5 Ich muss heute keine Hausaufgaben machen.
6 Ich darf meine Hausaufgaben nicht vergessen.

Go back to page 12 to refresh your memory on modal verbs. Then test a partner.

Remember *ich muss nicht* means 'I don't have to', not 'I mustn't'.

The perfect tense (Unit 4, page 15)

3 Copy and complete the table.

infinitive	past participle
machen	gemach**t**
spielen	1
kaufen	2
gehen	gegang**en**
essen	3
trinken	4
treffen	5
fahren	6
schlafen	7
schwimmen	8
besuchen	**be**sucht

Remember:
- past participles of regular verbs end in **-t**
- past participles of irregular verbs end in **-en**
- past participles of verbs starting with **be-**, **ent-**, **er-**, **ge-**, **über-** and **ver-** don't add **ge-**.

4 Identify the <u>three</u> verbs from exercise 3 that take *sein* as the auxiliary verb.

5 In pairs, take turns to create sentences using the past participles from exercise 3.

Example: 1 *Ich bin in die Stadt gegangen.*

1 ich – in die Stadt (*went*)
2 er – ein Eis (*bought*)
3 wir – zu Fuß (*went*)
4 sie (sg) – Kuchen (*ate*)
5 du – Cola (*drank*)
6 ich – meine Oma (*visited*)
7 wir – Fußball (*played*)
8 sie (pl) – Freunde (*met*)

The imperfect tense (Unit 4, page 15)

 Rewrite these sentences using the imperfect tense.

Example: 1 *Es war langweilig.*

1. Es ist langweilig.
2. Wir sind müde.
3. Ich habe eine Schuluniform.
4. Wir haben dreimal pro Woche Deutsch.
5. Es gibt eine Turnhalle.
6. Im Klassenzimmer gibt es viele Bücher.
7. Wir haben einen Sporttag und es gibt viele Spiele.
8. Ich bin in einem Freizeitpark und es gibt eine Achterbahn.
9. Sie haben eine Kreativwoche und es gibt viel zu tun.
10. Ich habe jeden Tag Biologie und es ist schwierig.

 haben and *sein* are often used in the imperfect tense.

	haben	sein
ich	hatte	war
du	hattest	warst
er/sie/es/man	hatte	war
wir	hatten	waren
ihr	hattet	wart
Sie	hatten	waren
sie	hatten	waren

Es gab (there was) is also common in the imperfect tense.

Using the perfect and imperfect tenses (Unit 5, page 17)

 Listen and write down the missing perfect and imperfect tense verbs that you hear.

Gestern **1** *hatte* ich sechs Stunden in der Schule. Der Vormittag **2** langweilig, weil ich Mathe und Geschichte **3** . Aber in Chemie **4** wir ein Experiment **5** und das **6** ziemlich interessant. Nach der Schule **7** ich mich mit meinen Freunden im Park **8** und wir **9** Fußball **10** . Das Wetter **11** gut und danach **12** wir in ein Café **13** und **14** Kuchen **15** und Cola **16** . Wir **17** **18** und es **19** Spaß **20** .

der Vormittag morning

Los geht's!

 Translate the sentences into German.

1. I love music because it is interesting.
2. I think that maths is very difficult.
3. Yesterday I had maths, English, history, German and drama.
4. I have to revise (*lernen*) for maths because I have a test on Monday.
5. I went into town and I bought a T-shirt, a jumper and a skirt.
6. We played football outside.
7. We are not allowed to run in the corridor.
8. I think that school uniforms are very unfair.
9. I have art once a week and it is useful.
10. Yesterday after school I went into town.

 Pay particular attention to word order when translating. Remember the following:
- The verb is always the second idea.
- *weil/dass* sends the verb to the end of the clause.
- Modal verbs are used with another verb in the infinitive, which goes at the end of the clause.

Kapitel 1 Lese- und Hörtest

Reading

Lesen 1

School life. You read this email from your German friend, Matteo. Write the correct letter, **A**, **B** or **C**, to complete each sentence.

> Hallo!
> Ich gehe ziemlich gern ins Gymnasium. Ich habe zehn Fächer und ich finde sie alle interessant. Geschichte ist nützlich, Sport finde ich leicht, aber Mathe ist kompliziert.
>
> Wir müssen eine Schuluniform tragen und das finde ich schlecht. Meine Eltern finden die Kleidung praktisch, aber ich denke, dass sie zu unbequem ist.
>
> Letzte Woche hat meine Klasse einen Film gesehen. Ich war der Meinung, dass er langweilig war, aber meine Freunde haben ihn spannend gefunden.
>
> Dein Matteo

Always read the title and the instructions for each question so you know the context of the reading passage and who the people are.

What do you think you should do first? Read the text or the questions? Discuss with your partner and decide which works best for you and why.

1 Matteo likes …
   A school.   B going to the gym.   C his school uniform.
2 Matteo finds … easy.
   A history   B PE   C maths
3 Matteo's parents think his school uniform is …
   A expensive.   B practical.   C uncomfortable.
4 Matteo thought the film was …
   A relaxing.   B exciting.   C boring.

In this task, you have to choose the correct answer from three possible options each time. Often, the incorrect options will also be mentioned in the text, so read carefully and look out for negatives and other small words which might change the meaning of a sentence.

Lesen 2

Opinions about school. Read Mia's blog and answer the questions.

> Ich mag die Schule, weil meine Freunde und ich gute Noten bekommen. Viele Schüler finden den Unterricht schwierig, aber für mich ist er nützlich und interessant.
>
> Die Schule beginnt um neun Uhr und wir haben sechs Stunden pro Tag. Jede Stunde dauert fünfzig Minuten. Wir bekommen viele Hausaufgaben und wir müssen auch Prüfungen schreiben. Das finde ich notwendig, aber meinen Rock und meine **Bluse** finde ich total unbequem. Ich trage lieber Jeans und ein T-Shirt.
>
> Es gibt viele Regeln in der Schule: man darf im Gang nicht laufen und das Handy ist total verboten, und das finde ich total unfair. Wir dürfen auch im Unterricht nicht sprechen. Das finde ich aber gerecht, weil wir lernen müssen.

In this task, you have to work out the meaning of a word that you might not have come across before. Read the sentences around it carefully, as there are likely to be clues there to help you. Use the context to help you too: for example, here, both meinen Rock and meine Bluse are described as unbequem.

1 What does Mia think of her lessons? Give **two** details.
2 Which **two** aspects of school does Mia find necessary?
3 Which **two** school rules does Mia **not** agree with?
4 Read the second paragraph again. What would you do with a **Bluse**? Write the correct letter, **A**, **B** or **C**.
   A study it   B eat it   C wear it

22 *zweiundzwanzig*

Lesen 3

Translate these sentences into English.

1. In der Pause habe ich mit meinen Freunden gesprochen.
2. Nächsten Sommer machen wir einen Ausflug nach München.
3. Der Lehrer sagt, dass Mobbing immer schlecht ist.
4. Ich finde, dass der Unterricht viel zu früh beginnt.
5. In der Mittagspause dürfen die Schüler im Klassenzimmer nicht essen.

 Kapitel 1

- Which preposition could you use instead of 'with' to translate *mit*?
- *machen* usually means 'to do' or 'to make', but how would you translate it in this context?
- Remember that some German place names have an English equivalent.
- Make sure you account for every word in your translation.
- Think carefully about how to translate *dürfen* when it is used with *nicht*.

Don't be afraid to alter the word order or your choice of words if it sounds more natural in English. Read your sentences through when you've finished, to be sure they make sense.

Listening

Hören 4

Opinions about school. Some German pupils are talking about different aspects of school life. What opinions do they have? Write **P** for a **positive** opinion, **N** for a **negative** opinion, **P+N** for a **positive and negative** opinion.

1. Sophie
2. Noah
3. Ella
4. Leon

Listen carefully for words that mean 'I like' or 'I don't like', but remember that you will also hear opinions expressed in other ways. The speaker might use an adjective with the word *zu* (too) before it, giving it a positive or negative meaning. If you hear words like *aber* (but), it may suggest that the person is expressing both a positive and a negative viewpoint.

Hören 5

Listen to Luisa giving her opinion about school rules. Answer the questions in English.

1. Which rule does she mention?
2. Why does she disagree with this rule?

Dictation

Hören 6

You will hear five short sentences. Write down exactly what you hear in German.

When writing down what you hear, think about how these sounds are pronounced. Remember that with cognates, the German and English words are often pronounced differently.
u, ü,
-ig, w

dreiundzwanzig

Kapitel 1 — Mündlicher Test

Role-play

1 Look at the role-play and prepare what you are going to say.

> Describe any aspect of your school. It could be the size, school buildings, school type, the number of teachers and/or students.

> You are talking to your Austrian friend.
> 1 **Describe** your school. (Give **two** details.)
> 2 Say what you usually do at lunchtime. (Give **one** detail.)
> 3 Say what you think of school uniform and why. (Give **one** opinion and **one** reason.)
> 4 Say what you did yesterday after school. (Give **two** details.)
> 5 ? Ask your friend a question about a school subject.

> Make sure you include the correct number of details. Remember that you must include at least one verb in response to each task.

> You need to include both an opinion and a reason here.

> At least one point will require you to use a past or future tense. Here you need to use the past tense.

> For example, you could ask what their favourite subject is or say *Wie findest du …?* with any subject.

2 Practise what you have prepared. Then, using your notes, listen and respond to the teacher.

> Make notes to prepare your answers. They can be full sentences and you can read from them when you respond to the questions.

3 Listen to Ethan's answers. Make a note of:
   a how he answers the questions for points 1–4
   b what question he asks for point 5.

Reading aloud

4 Look at this task. With a partner, read the sentences aloud, paying attention to the underlined letters.

> In England geht man normalerweise mit fünf Jahren in die Schule.
>
> Die Schultypen sind anders als in Österreich.
>
> Normalerweise tragen die Schüler eine Schuluniform.
>
> Meine Schwester trägt ein weißes Hemd, einen grünen Rock und schwarze Schuhe.
>
> Man lernt Fächer wie Englisch, Chemie, Physik und Biologie, und nach der Schule kann man Theater oder Sport machen.

> Be careful with cognates as they are not pronounced exactly the same way in German. Think carefully about how to pronounce the cognates and these sounds:
> o, ö, u, ü
> w

5 Listen and check your pronunciation.

6 Listen to the teacher asking four follow-up questions. Translate each question into English and prepare your own answer for each one. Then listen again and respond to the teacher.

vierundzwanzig

Photo card

 Look at the photos and listen to Ethan describing them. Write down the German for these words and phrases.

1 In the first photo there is …
2 On the table there are …
3 The teacher is sitting …
4 In the second photo I see …
5 I think it is …
6 They are sitting …
7 In the background there are …

You will be asked to talk about the content of these photos. You must say at least one thing about each photo.

After you have spoken about the content of the photos, you will be asked questions related to any of the topics within the theme of **People and lifestyle**.

Your responses should be as **full and detailed** as possible.

 Prepare your own description of the photos. Then, with a partner, take turns asking and answering the following question:

> Sag mir etwas über die Fotos.

 Listen to the teacher's first follow-up question, *Wie findest du deine Schule?*, and Ethan's response. Write the letters (a–e) in the order in which Ethan mentions these points.

a sport   b not too big   c homework   d modern   e teachers

 The teacher then asks Ethan, *Was hast du gestern in der Schule gemacht?* Listen and write down the missing word for each gap.

Gestern hatte ich **1** und Deutsch vor der **2**. Dann hatten wir **3**. Am Nachmittag haben wir **4** gemacht. Das habe ich toll gefunden, weil das mein **5** ist und weil ich den **6** mag. Wir sind in die **7** gegangen und haben Basketball gespielt. Die letzte Stunde war **8**.

- Listen carefully to the question words used by the teacher. **Wie viele** Stunden …? is asking you **how many**, rather than **which**, lessons you have.
- If you don't understand the whole question, the question word can help you make a sensible guess. For example, if the question word is **wer** (who), then you know you need to include a person or people in your response.

 Listen to two more follow-up questions and prepare your answers. Then respond to the recording. Make your answers as full as possible, including opinions and reasons.

Aim to use a variety of different structures, vocabulary and tenses you have learned in this module. Try using:
- modal verbs + infinitive: *Ich **muss/soll/darf** Deutsch **lernen**.*
- adjectives: *Meine Jacke **ist grau** und ich trage **einen blauen** Rock.*
- additional details such as qualifiers: *Mathe finde ich **ein bisschen** kompliziert. Ich mache **viel** Sport.*
- regular and irregular past participles in the perfect tense: *Gestern **bin** ich in die Turnhalle **gegangen** und ich **habe** Basketball **gespielt**.*
- more complex opinions: *Ich **mag** die Schule, weil die Stunden **interessant** sind, und ich **finde**, dass die Uniform sehr **bequem** ist.*

 Prepare your own answers to as many of the Module 1 questions on page 226 as you can. Then practise with your partner.

fünfundzwanzig

Kapitel 1 Schreibtest

Translation

Read the English sentences and correct the mistakes in Julie's translation of them.

1 She wears trousers and a blue jacket.
2 I am not allowed to eat in the classroom.
3 We find the teachers very strict.
4 Yesterday he didn't do his homework.
5 I like the school uniform because it is practical.

1 Er trägt eine Hose und ein blaues Hemd.
2 Ich muss im Gang nicht essen.
3 Wir finden die Schüler streng.
4 Morgen macht er seine Hausaufgaben nicht.
5 Ich trage die Schuluniform, weil sie nützlich ist.

Translate these sentences into German.
1 I wear a black jacket and a red skirt.
2 You are not allowed to talk with friends.
3 The pupils find the subjects difficult.
4 Yesterday she didn't do English.
5 He likes the school because it is modern.

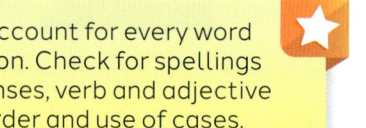
Make sure you account for every word in your translation. Check for spellings and umlauts, tenses, verb and adjective endings, word order and use of cases.

90-word writing task

You are writing to your German friend about your school life.

Write approximately **90** words in **German**.

You must write something about each bullet point.

Describe:
- the subjects you study
- a school activity you took part in last week
- a school trip which is planned for the future.

Look at this writing exam task and then, for each bullet point:
1 think about the vocabulary and structures you have learned, which you could use in your answers. For example:
   - **nouns** and **verbs** to write about school subjects
   - language for **narrating a story** about what you did/where you went
   - how to explain what you are **planning to do** in the future.
2 write down three or four ideas you could write about
3 write down which tense(s) you will need to use in your answer.

To refer to the future in German, you can use the present tense with a **future time phrase**.

Heute nach der Schule gehe ich in den Park.
I am going to the park **after school today**.

Kapitel 1

 Lesen 4 Read Julie's answer to the exam task on page 26. Answer the questions in the coloured boxes (1–5).

1 These are examples of **complex language**. What do they mean? Find <u>three</u> more examples of complex language in the text.

2 Julie uses a **variety of adjectives**. What do these words mean? Find <u>two</u> more examples.

3 Which **tense** is this? What other examples can you find? Does Julie use any other time frames?

In der Schule lerne ich zehn Fächer. Natürlich muss ich Mathe und Englisch lernen, aber ich lerne auch Geschichte und Deutsch, weil ich sie interessant finde. Mein Lieblingsfach ist Musik. Ich finde, dass Chemie sowohl nutzlos als auch schwer ist, aber meine Freundin findet Chemie leicht.

Letzte Woche haben wir einen Wandertag gemacht und wir sind 15 Kilometer gelaufen! Ich möchte das nicht wieder machen. Ich habe es sehr anstrengend gefunden.

Nächsten Monat fährt meine Klasse nach London. Ich darf mitfahren. Das finde ich toll, weil Ausflüge viel Spaß machen. Wir müssen leider Schuluniform tragen.

4 How could Julie **avoid repetition** by using a synonym here?

5 Which <u>two</u> connectives could you use here to form an **extended sentence**? What other connectives does Julie use?

 Lesen 5 Read Julie's answer again. Copy and complete the sentences.

1 Julie studies ▓ subjects at school.
2 She finds ▓ and ▓ interesting.
3 She disagrees with her friend about ▓.
4 She took part in a ▓ last week.
5 She found that very ▓.
6 She is planning to go on a trip to London with her ▓.

 Schreiben 6 Prepare your own answer to the task.

- Think about how you can develop each bullet point.
- Look back at your notes from exercises 3 and 4.
- Look at the 'Challenge checklist' and consider how you can show off your German!
- Write a **brief** plan and organise your answer into paragraphs.
- Write your answer and then check carefully for accuracy.

Challenge checklist

🥨	✓ Past, present and future time frames ✓ Connectives and time phrases ✓ Some extended sentences ✓ An opinion verb and simple adjectives
🥨🥨	✓ A wider range of tenses and different verbs ✓ Different persons of the verb ✓ More varied opinion verbs and adjectives ✓ Intensifiers and qualifiers (*sehr, zu, total, überhaupt*) ✓ A wider range of interesting vocabulary
🥨🥨🥨	✓ Phrases with more than one tense ✓ Modal verb with an infinitive ✓ Complex language (subordinating conjunctions, subject–verb inversion, modal verbs + infinitive) ✓ Use of different cases ✓ Adjectival agreement ✓ More varied conjunctions (*weil, dass*)

siebenundzwanzig

Kapitel 1 Wörter

Key:
bold = this word will appear in higher exams only
* = this word is not on the vocabulary list but you may use it in your own sentences

Meine Schule, deine Schule (pages 6–7):

Das Schulleben	School life
der **Austausch**	exchange
die *Gesamtschule	comprehensive school
die **Grundschule**	primary school
die Note	mark, grade
die Prüfung	exam, test
das **Abitur**	A-level equivalent
das **Gymnasium**	grammar school
die Hausaufgaben	homework
sitzenbleiben	to repeat a school year

Welche Fächer hast du dieses Jahr? (pages 8–9):

Schulfächer	School subjects
Was hast du (am Montag) in der (ersten/zweiten/dritten) Stunde?	What do you have on Monday in the (first/second/third) lesson?
Am (Montag) in der (ersten) Stunde habe ich …	On (Monday) my (first) lesson is …
Biologie	biology
Chemie	chemistry
Deutsch	German
Englisch	English
Erdkunde	geography
Französisch	French
Geschichte	history
*Informatik	computing
Kunst	art
Mathe	maths
Musik	music
Physik	physics
Religion	religious education
Spanisch	Spanish
Sport	sport
Sprachen	languages
Theater	theatre/drama
Wissenschaften	sciences

Tage	Days
Montag	Monday
Dienstag	Tuesday
Mittwoch	Wednesday
Donnerstag	Thursday
Freitag	Friday

Wie oft hast du (Mathe)? — How often do you have (maths)?
Ich habe (Mathe) (einmal/zweimal/dreimal) pro Woche / pro Tag. — I have (maths) (once / twice / three times) a week / a day.
Wie viele Stunden hast du (am Nachmittag / nach der Pause)? — How many lessons do you have (in the afternoon / after break)?
Was ist dein Lieblingsfach? — What is your favourite subject?
Mein Lieblingsfach ist (Deutsch). — My favourite subject is (German).
Wann hast du (am Dienstag) (Englisch)? — When do you have (English) (on Tuesday)?

Fragen	Questions
Wann …?	When …?
Was …?	What …?
Wie …?	How …?
Wie viel(e) …?	How much / How many …?
Wie oft …?	How often …?
Warum …?	Why …?
Welcher/Welche/Welches …?	Which …?

Welches Fach magst du (nicht) und warum? — Which subject do you (not) like and why?
Wie findest du …? — What do you think about …?
Ich mag … (nicht), weil es …ist. — I (don't) like … because it is …
Ich liebe …, weil ich es … finde. — I love … because I find it …

anstrengend	demanding
einfach	easy
interessant	interesting
kompliziert	complicated
langweilig	boring
leicht	easy
nützlich	useful
praktisch	practical
schwer	difficult/hard/tough
schwierig	difficult/hard/tough
wichtig	important

… weil ich gut in (Mathe) bin. — because I'm good at (maths).
… weil ich schwach in (Musik) bin. — because I'm weak at (music).
… weil ich sportlich bin. — because I'm sporty.
… weil ich Sprachen liebe. — because I love languages.

In der Pause … — At break …
　spreche ich mit meinen Freunden/Freundinnen. — I talk to my friends.
　esse ich … — I eat …
　trinke ich … — I drink …
　spiele ich … — I play …

Was trägst du in der Schule? (pages 10–11):

Schuluniform	School uniform
Was trägst du in der Schule?	What do you wear to school?
Ich trage …	I wear …
einen *Pullover	a sweater
einen Rock	a skirt
eine Hose	trousers
eine Jacke	a jacket
(eine) *Jeans	(a pair of) jeans
eine *Krawatte	a tie
eine Schuluniform	school uniform
ein Hemd	a shirt
ein Kleid	a dress
ein T-Shirt	a T-shirt
*Sportschuhe	trainers

Farben	Colours
blau	blue
braun	brown
gelb	yellow
grau	grey
grün	green
*orange	orange
rot	red
schwarz	black
weiß	white

Wie findest du Schuluniformen? — What do think of school uniforms?
Ich finde (Schuluniformen) … (sehr) praktisch — I find (school uniforms) … (very) practical

Auf der anderen Seite sind sie …	On the other hand they are …
langweilig	boring
teuer	expensive
unbequem	uncomfortable
Was sieht man auf dem Foto?	What can you see on the photo?
Auf dem Foto sieht man (drei) Jugendliche: (zwei) Jungen und (ein) Mädchen.	On the photo you can see (three) young people: (two) boys and (one) girl.
Sie sind ungefähr (15) Jahre alt.	They are about (15) years old.
Es sind Schüler und Schülerinnen, weil sie eine Schuluniform tragen.	They are students/pupils because they are wearing school uniforms.
Der Junge trägt …	The boy is wearing …
Die Jungen tragen …	The boys are wearing …
Das Mädchen trägt …	The girl is wearing …
Die Mädchen tragen …	The girls are wearing …
Sie sind (in einem Park) (draußen) und sie (sprechen miteinander).	They are (in a park) (outside) and they (are talking to each other).
vorne	at the front
im Hintergrund	in the background
Der Vorteil/Nachteil ist …	The advantage/disadvantage is …

Sind Schulregeln wirklich nötig? (pages 12–13):

Schulregeln und Meinungen	School rules and opinions
Man muss …	You have to / must …
Man soll …	You should / ought to …
Man darf …	You are allowed to …
Man darf nicht …	You must not / are not allowed to …
im Klassenzimmer	in the classroom
im Computerraum	in the computer room
im Gang	in the corridor
im Unterricht	during lessons
in der *Bibliothek	in the library
in der Kantine	in the canteen
in der Schule	in school
in der **Turnhalle**	in the gym/sports hall
draußen	outside
(nicht) **frech** sein	(not) be cheeky
ruhig sein	be quiet
leise sein	be quiet
(nicht) laufen	(not) run
langsam gehen	walk slowly
eine Uniform tragen	wear a uniform
*Respekt zeigen	show respect
seine Hausaufgaben machen	do your homework
Ich denke, dass …	I think (that) …
Ich glaube, dass …	I believe (that) …
Ich bin der Meinung, dass diese Regel (ist) …	I am of the opinion that this rule (is) …
blöd	stupid
(un)fair	(un)fair
(un)gerecht	(un)fair
falsch	wrong
notwendig/nötig	necessary
(nicht) praktisch	(not) practical
richtig	right
wichtig	important
weil ich nicht genug Freizeit habe.	because I don't have enough free time.
weil es in der Kantine nicht genug Platz gibt.	because there isn't enough room in the canteen.

Schultage: die beste Zeit deines Lebens? (pages 14–15):

Verben	Verbs
Ich habe / Wir haben …	I/We …
gegessen	ate
gespielt	played
gemacht	did
gezeigt	showed
gehört	heard/listened
gekauft	bought
geschlafen	slept
Ich bin / Wir sind …	I/We …
gegangen	went
gefahren	drove/travelled
geflogen	flew
gekommen	came
geschwommen	swam
geblieben	stayed
Ich war / Wir waren	I was / We were
Ich hatte / Wir hatten	I had / We had
Es gab	There was/were

Austausch geht auch online! (pages 16–17):

Der Schultag	The school day
Was machst du normalerweise in der (Mittags)pause?	What do you normally do in your (lunch) break?
In der (Mittags)pause …	In my (lunch) break, I (normally) …
esse ich (normalerweise) meinen Imbiss / in der Kantine.	eat my snack / in the canteen.
spreche ich mit meinen Freunden.	talk with my friends.
verbringe ich Zeit mit Freunden.	spend time with friends.
mache ich Sport / meine Hausaufgaben.	do sports / my homework.
gehe ich in einen Club / in die Kantine.	go to a club / to the canteen.
Ich habe keine (Mittags)pause.	I don't have a (lunch) break.
Was hast du gestern in der Mittagspause gemacht?	What did you do in your lunch break yesterday?
Gestern in der Mittagspause habe ich …	Yesterday in my lunch break I …
Was hast du gestern nach der Schule gemacht?	What did you do after school yesterday?
Gestern nach der Schule habe ich …	Yesterday after school I …
mit meinen Freunden gesprochen.	talked with friends.
Zeit mit Freunden verbracht.	spent time with friends.
Sport gemacht.	did sports.
Ich bin in die Stadt gegangen.	I went into town.
Wir haben jeden Tag … Stunden und … Pausen.	Every day we have … lessons and … breaks.
In der Schule lerne ich …	At school I'm learning …
Letztes Jahr hatten wir …	Last year we had …
Es war …, weil …	It was … because …

Kapitel 2 — Endlich mal Freizeit!

Kennst du diese Musiker?
- Learning about German-speaking musicians
- Giving opinions

Ein musikalisches Abenteuer mit deutschsprachigen Stars!

Bist du eher Die Prinzen oder Wise Guys Fan? Hörst du lieber elektronische Musik oder Rap?

Herbert Grönemeyer
- Stil: Popmusik
- Beliebtes Lied: „Der Weg"
- Schöne Lyrik: *Es war ein Stück vom Himmel, Dass es dich gibt.*
- Geburtsdatum: 12. April 1956
- Geburtsort: Göttingen, Deutschland
- Aktive Jahre: 1978–heute

Herbert Grönemeyer ist ein deutscher Sänger und Schauspieler. Er produziert auch Musik und spielt viele Instrumente. Er ist extrem erfolgreich in Deutschland und singt über Familie, Liebe und sein Leben als Kind in Deutschland. Seine Lieder sind also oft leise und traurig, aber sie sind manchmal auch schön.

Wolfgang Amadeus Mozart
- Stil: klassische Musik
- Beliebtes Lied: „Eine kleine Nachtmusik"
- Geburtsdatum: 27. Januar 1756
- Geburtsort: Salzburg, Österreich
- Aktive Jahre: 1761–1791

Mozart war ein berühmter Musiker und ist für seine wunderbare klassische Musik weltweit bekannt. Er hat über 600 Musikstücke geschrieben und er hat sein erstes Stück im Alter von fünf Jahren geschrieben! Seine Musik ist normalerweise schnell und laut, aber einige Lieder sind wirklich ruhig und sehr angenehm.

Namika
- Stil: Rap
- Beliebtes Lied: „Lieblingsmensch"
- Schöne Lyrik: *Hallo, Lieblingsmensch! Ein Riesenkompliment dafür, dass du mich so gut kennst!*
- Geburtsdatum: 23. August 1991
- Geburtsort: Frankfurt, Deutschland
- Aktive Jahre: 2013–heute

Sängerin und Rapperin Namika ist sehr beliebt und ihr Nummer-eins-Hit „Lieblingsmensch" war zehn Monate in den Charts! Ihre Rap-Musik ist weder schnell noch langsam, aber immer modern. Namikas Familie ist in den 70er Jahren von Marokko nach Deutschland gekommen und das hört man an ihrer Musik.

Die Ärzte
- Stil: Punkrock und Pop
- Musiker: Farin Urlaub, Bela B und Rodrigo González
- Beliebtes Lied: „Hurra"
- Schöne Lyrik: *Hipp, hipp, hurra! Alles ist super, alles ist wunderbar!*
- Gegründet: Berlin, Deutschland
- Aktive Jahre: 1982–heute

Die Ärzte sind eine sehr berühmte deutsche Band. Sie haben viele Fans in Deutschland, aber die Band ist auch international erfolgreich. Ihre Musik ist oft spannend und kann auch ziemlich verrückt klingen!

der Musiker (-)	musician
deutschsprachig	German-speaking
weder ... noch	neither ... nor

Kulturzone — Kapitel 2

1 Hören Listen to and read the article. Copy and complete the sentences. Use words from the box. There are more words than gaps.

1. Herbert Grönemeyer is one of Germany's most … musicians.
2. His songs are often … and sad.
3. Mozart's music is normally … and loud.
4. Namika's rap songs are always …
5. Die Ärzte are a very … German rock band.
6. Their music is often … and can be a bit …

exciting	strange
pleasant	modern
crazy	quiet
relaxing	famous
fast	successful

2 Lesen Translate the text into English.

Meine Lieblingssängerin ist Helene Fischer. Sie ist auch Tänzerin und stammt aus Russland. Sie wurde 1984 geboren. Sie singt Popmusik auf Deutsch und auf Englisch und sie ist besonders erfolgreich. Ihre beliebte Musik ist manchmal schnell und laut, aber immer spannend und nie langweilig.

wurde … geboren was born

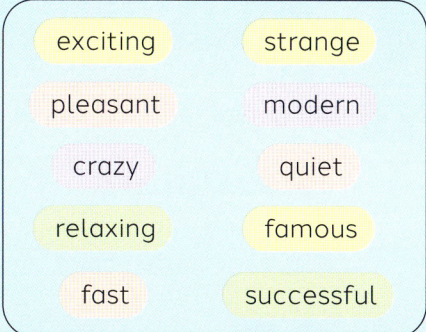

3 Sprechen Read out the text in exercise 2. Pay attention to the *ie*, *ei* and *i* sounds.

ie is pronounced like the English letter 'e':
bel**ie**bt L**ie**der L**ie**be v**ie**le

ei is pronounced like the English letter 'i':
erfolgr**ei**ch l**ei**se **ei**ne weltw**ei**t

i on its own is a long 'ee' sound before a single consonant:
Mus**i**k Nam**i**ka

i is a short 'i' sound before two or more consonants, like in the English word 'bit':
n**i**cht K**i**nd

Listen and repeat the words.

4 Hören Listen to two friends discussing their music preferences. Write down <u>two</u> descriptions given for each type of music below.

1. classical music
2. Wise Guys' music
3. rap music
4. Cro's music

To say 'I **don't** like…', use *ich mag (Metal) **nicht***. *Nicht* comes after the type of music.

Wie findest du (Rockmusik)?
Magst du die Musik von (Helene Fischer)?
Was ist deine Lieblingsmusik?

Ich	liebe mag hasse	Metal, Rap, Rock,		er	zu extrem besonders sehr wirklich ganz ziemlich nicht	aufregend. interessant. komisch. langweilig. laut. leise. modern. schnell. spannend.
Meine Lieblingsmusik ist		die Musik von (Mozart), elektronische Musik, klassische Musik, Popmusik, Tanzmusik,	denn	ist sie		

5 Sprechen In pairs, take turns to ask and answer the questions below.

- Wie findest du <u>klassische Musik</u>?
- Ich <u>liebe</u> <u>klassische Musik</u>, denn sie ist <u>wirklich</u> <u>spannend</u>.
- Magst du die Musik von <u>Namika</u>?
- Ich <u>mag</u> die Musik von <u>Namika</u>, denn sie ist <u>besonders</u> <u>modern</u>.
- Was ist deine Lieblingsmusik?
- Meine Lieblingsmusik ist <u>Popmusik</u>, denn sie ist <u>ganz</u> <u>laut</u>.

Remember to add **intensifiers and qualifiers** (*sehr*, *ganz*) to your opinions to make them more varied. You can use *denn* (because) to add reasons to your opinions. Unlike *weil*, *denn* does not send the <u>verb</u> to the end of the phrase.

Ich hasse Popmusik, **denn** sie <u>ist</u> **sehr** langweilig.

einunddreißig 31

1 Was machst du gern in deiner Freizeit?

- Talking about your free time
- Expressing preferences
- Using frequency phrases with correct word order

Hören 1 Listen and read. Write the letter of the correct set of pictures (a–d) for each forum post.

Freizeitfieber!

Was machen diese deutschen Jugendlichen gern in ihrer Freizeit? Ist ihre Freizeit eine tolle Zeit oder Zeitverschwendung?

1 Lea Ich bin jeden Tag ziemlich aktiv – ich bin fast nie zu Hause! Ich spiele sehr gern Basketball, aber ich gehe lieber schwimmen. Ich schwimme sehr oft am Wochenende, weil es Spaß macht! Ich gehe manchmal mit Freunden in die Stadt und wir gehen am liebsten ins Kino.

2 Matteo Ab und zu machen wir in der Schule Sport, aber ich spiele nicht gern Basketball oder Fußball. Meine Eltern gehen gern wandern, aber ich gehe selten mit. Ich male gern und ich interessiere mich sehr für Kunst – ich finde es super. Ich zeichne also täglich Bilder für meine Familie und Freunde.

3 Clara Am liebsten höre ich Musik, aber ich lese auch gern Bücher – ich lese jeden Tag Romane von Thomas Brezina – er ist ein österreichischer Autor. Meine beste Freundin liest nicht gern, denn sie macht lieber Fotos. Sie geht am liebsten mit ihrer Kamera in die Stadt.

4 Leon Meine Freunde und ich singen sehr gern und wir kochen auch jeden Donnerstag in einem Schulclub – das macht so viel Spaß! Ich spiele oft am Computer und manchmal sehe ich auch gern Filme in meinem Zimmer.

die Zeitverschwendung — waste of time

Lesen 2 Translate Lea's text into English.

Lesen 3 Find the frequency expressions in the forum posts in exercise 1 and translate them into English.

Example: jeden Tag — every day

G To say how much we like doing something, we add (*nicht*) *gern*, *lieber* or *am liebsten* after the verb.

- ✗ Meine Eltern spielen **nicht gern** Fußball.
- ♥ Meine beste Freundin geht **(sehr) gern** ins Kino.
- ♥♥ Wir spielen **lieber** am Computer.
- ♥♥♥ Ich gehe **am liebsten** wandern.

Page 43

G Remember we use the **present tense** to talk about what we do or like to do regularly. Always check that the **verb** matches the subject of the sentence and that the **conjugated verb** is in the second position.

first idea	second idea (verb)	rest of sentence
Ich	**bin**	**jeden Tag** ziemlich aktiv.
Meine Freundin	**spielt**	**am liebsten** Fußball.
Meine Eltern	**gehen**	**ab und zu** wandern.

If a sentence starts with a **frequency expression** or **am liebsten**, then the **conjugated verb** remains in the second position and is followed by the subject of the sentence.

first idea	second idea (verb)	rest of sentence
Jeden Tag	**bin**	ich ziemlich aktiv.
Am liebsten	**spielt**	meine Freundin Fußball.
Ab und zu	**gehen**	meine Eltern wandern.

Page 42

Kapitel 2

4 Copy and complete the translations. Then <u>underline</u> the verb(s) in each sentence.

1 I read books and novels very often.
Ich <u>lese</u> sehr oft …

2 I like to go swimming best of all.
Am liebsten …

3 I watch TV now and again, but I prefer listening to music.
Ich <u>sehe</u> …

4 My parents play tennis at the weekend, but I don't like to play.
Meine Eltern …

5 Listen. Copy and complete the table in English. (1–3)

	activities they like	activities they don't like
1	art, painting	visiting art exhibitions

> The **a** sound in German is a long 'aah' sound when it is followed by a single consonant (e.g. **A**b**e**nd). It is usually a short 'ah' sound when it is followed by two or more consonants (e.g. **Wa**ndern) or when it is a one-syllable word.
>
> Listen and repeat this tongue-twister.
>
> M**a**ler m**a**chen M**a**lerei **a**m N**a**chmitt**a**g, m**a**nchm**a**l Fußb**a**ll, m**a**nchm**a**l B**a**sketb**a**ll. **A**b und zu w**a**ndern sie in die St**a**dt für **A**thletik und Rom**a**ne **a**m **A**bend!

6 Listen again and write down any additional details.

7 In pairs, take turns to ask and answer the questions about free time using the pictures for ideas. Remember to use frequency expressions and pay attention to the **a** sounds.

- *Was machst du gern in deiner Freizeit?*
- *Ich interessiere mich sehr für Einkaufen und ich mache oft Fotos. Meine Freunde und ich gehen manchmal ins Kino.*
- *Was machst du nicht gern?*
- *Ich höre nicht gern Musik – ich finde das ganz langweilig.*

Was machst du gern in deiner Freizeit?		
Mein Lieblingshobby ist Meine Lieblingsfreizeitaktivität ist		Sport. Fernsehen. Einkaufen. Lesen. Fahrradfahren. Gaming.
Ich	interessiere mich (sehr/nicht) für	
	spiele	am Computer.
	gehe	wandern. in die Stadt. einkaufen. schwimmen. ins Kino.
	besuche	nicht gern (sehr) gern lieber am liebsten	Freunde. Ausstellungen.
	mache		Fotos.
	höre	(fast) nie selten ab und zu manchmal am Wochenende oft jeden Tag täglich	Musik.
	sehe		fern. Filme.
	lese		Bücher. Romane.
	male/zeichne		Bilder.
	treffe mich		mit meinen Freunden.
	bleibe		zu Hause.
	koche		
	tanze		in einem Schulclub.
	singe		

8 Write your own forum post about your free time. Use exercise 1 as a model.

dreiunddreißig

2 Was machst du online?

- Discussing how you spend time online
- Using separable verbs in the present tense
- Expressing advantages and disadvantages of life online

1 Listen and read. Answer the questions below in English.

Hallo! In meinem Zimmer habe ich einen Computer und ich habe auch ein Smartphone. Was mache ich online? Ich **lade** oft Musik **herunter** und ich bin auch in sozialen Medien sehr aktiv. Ich **lade** jeden Tag viele Fotos **hoch** und chatte immer mit Freunden. Ich **sehe** nie **fern**, aber ich **rufe** ganz oft meine Freunde **an** und wir streamen auch sehr gern Filme.

Leonie

Ich bin nie auf sozialen Medien, weil ich sie gefährlich finde. Neue Technologie und Geräte gefallen mir nicht! Ich habe also kein Smartphone und keine Spielkonsole. Ich habe einen Laptop, aber ich benutze ihn selten – nur für meine Hausaufgaben. Musik spielen ist mein Ding, und ich **nehme** im Moment ein neues Album und ein neues Musikvideo **auf**!

die Spielkonsole — games console

Bruno

Ich verbringe viel Zeit online und benutze verschiedene Geräte, wie mein Smartphone, meinen Laptop, mein Tablet und meine Spielkonsole. Mein Handy **bietet** viele Daten **an** und ich **bringe** es überall **mit**! Ich lese täglich Nachrichten, und ich schicke oft E-Mails. Ich **sehe** mir jeden Tag YouTube-Videos **an** und ich folge vielen YouTube-Stars. Ich **gebe** jeden Monat ungefähr €50 für Technologie **aus**!

Aaliyah

1 Whose phone offers lots of data?
2 Who is very active on social media?
3 Who only uses a laptop for school work?
4 Who phones their friends a lot?
5 Who is recording music at the moment?
6 Who takes their phone everywhere with them?

> **G** Separable verbs contain a **separable prefix**. In the present tense, this prefix 'snaps off' and goes to the end of the sentence.
> **herunterladen** (to download)   Ich **lade** oft Musik **herunter**.
> **anrufen** (to call, to phone)   Mein Bruder **ruft** jeden Abend Freunde **an**.
> **fernsehen** (to watch TV)   Meine Eltern und ich **sehen** im Wohnzimmer **fern**.
> Page 43

Lesen 2 Read the texts again. Find the German for the phrases below.
Find <u>three</u> more sentences containing separable verbs.

1 I never watch TV.
2 I watch YouTube videos every day.
3 I call my friends quite often.
4 I spend approximately €50 every month on technology.
5 I upload many photos every day.
6 I often download music.

Hören 3 Listen to a journalist interviewing people. Copy and complete the table in English. (1–3)

	devices at home	activities they do	how often?
1	mobile phone ...	uses social media ...	every day ...

34 *vierunddreißig*

4 Hören
Listen again to the journalist's introduction. Write down the words you hear to complete the text.

> Hallo zusammen! Ich 1 einen 2 über Technologie im täglichen 3 und 4 mit einer 5 von 6 und 7 aus Hamburg. Also, ein herzliches Willkommen an 8 !

German words with **sch**, **sp** or **st** at the start usually sound like 'sh', 'shp' and 'sht'. Some words borrowed from English don't follow this pattern, but some do.
Listen and repeat the words.

schreiben   **Sp**ielkonsole   **St**udent
Stars   **st**reamen

5 Sprechen
In pairs, take turns to ask and answer the questions below. Pay attention to the **sch**, **sp** and **st** sounds.

- Welche Geräte benutzt du zu Hause?
- Ich benutze …
- Was machst du online? Und wie oft?
- Ich streame jeden Tag Musik und …
  Und du? Welche Geräte benutzt du?
- Ich habe …
- Was machst du online? Und wie oft?
- Ich lade häufig Apps herunter und …

Welche Geräte benutzt du?

Ich habe / Wir haben	einen Computer/Laptop. eine Spielkonsole.
Ich benutze / Wir benutzen	ein Handy/Smartphone/Tablet.

Was machst du online? Und wie oft?

Ich sehe mir		Filme/Videos an.
Ich lade		Musik hoch / Apps herunter.
Ich nehme	normalerweise	Videos auf.
Ich rufe	häufig	meine Freunde an.
Ich benutze	jeden Nachmittag	soziale Medien.
Ich spreche	jeden Abend	mit Freunden.
Ich schreibe/ lese/schicke	jede Woche	Nachrichten. E-Mails.
Ich folge	immer	Stars / berühmten Persönlichkeiten.
Ich streame		Filme/Musik/Serien.

6 Hören
Listen to and read the statements. Decide which you feel are positive (**P**) and which are negative (**N**).

Was sind die Vorteile von Technologie?
Und was sind die Nachteile?

1 Man kann mit Freunden in Kontakt bleiben.
2 Man kann Computer-Viren bekommen.
3 Man kann Filme und Musik herunterladen.
4 Man kann Informationen schnell finden.
5 Man kann falsche Informationen oder Nachrichten lesen.
6 Man kann Probleme mit Mobbing bekommen.

der Virus (Viren pl**)**   virus

> **G** Just like other **modal verbs** (dürfen, müssen, sollen), **können** is used with another verb in its infinitive at the end of the sentence.
> Man **kann** Filme streamen.
> You **can** stream films.
> Page 43

7 Schreiben
Write answers in German to the interview questions below about your life online.

1 Welche Geräte benutzt du?
  Guten Tag! Ich habe einen Laptop …

2 Was machst du online? Und wie oft?
  Ich chatte täglich mit Freunden und …

3 Was sind die Vorteile von Technologie?
  Man kann Informationen schnell finden und …

4 Und was sind die Nachteile?
  Man kann Computer-Viren bekommen und …

3 Das Leben als Star

- Discussing the pros and cons of celebrity culture
- Asking questions
- Practising the role-play section of the exam

 Lesen 1 Read the information cards. Copy and complete the table in English.

1

Name: Jamal Musiala
Beruf: Fußballprofi
Leistung / Erfolg: Er war der jüngste Torschütze für Bayern München (mit 17 Jahren).
Vorteile: Er kann sein Hobby als Beruf machen. Es ist aufregend und macht Spaß.
Nachteile: Er hat kein Privatleben. Es gibt Mobbing von Fans, wenn man schlecht spielt.

| der Profi | professional |
| der Torschütze | goal scorer |

2

Name: Angelique Kerber
Beruf: Tennisspielerin
Leistung / Erfolg: Sie hat viele internationale Spiele gewonnen.
Vorteile: Sie kann um die Welt reisen und neue Leute kennenlernen.
Nachteile: Sie muss immer fit sein und stundenlang trainieren.

| stundenlang | for hours |

	profession	successes/ achievements	advantages	disadvantages
1				

 Sprechen 2 Prepare your answers to the role-play below, then practise the dialogue with a partner.

You are talking to your Austrian friend.
Your teacher will play the part of your friend and will speak first.

- *Wer ist deine Lieblingspersönlichkeit?*
1 **Say which celebrity you like and why. (Give one opinion and one reason.)**
- *Was ist er/sie von Beruf?*
2 **Say what job this person does.**
- *Was hat er/sie gemacht?*
3 **Say what this person has done in their life.**
- *Sag mir einen Vorteil und einen Nachteil von seinem/ihrem Leben.*
4 **Give one advantage and one disadvantage of their life.**
- *Interessant!*
5 **Ask your friend a question about celebrities.**

Er Sie	ist	Fußballprofi. Tennisspieler(in). Musiker(in). Sänger(in).	
	kann	sehr gut extrem gut	Fußball spielen. singen.
	ist	sehr talentiert. ein Vorbild.	
	hat	viele Spiele gewonnen. viel Musik gemacht.	
Ein Vorteil von seinem/ ihrem Leben ist,		er/sie ist ein Vorbild. er/sie kann um die Welt reisen.	
Ein Nachteil ist,		er/sie muss immer fit sein. er/sie muss immer gut aussehen. er/sie hat kein Privatleben.	

3 Listen to and read the interview. Answer the questions in English.

Mein Leben als Influencerin!

Was macht diese berühmte deutsche Influencerin den ganzen Tag? Wir finden es heraus!

Hallo Annika! Wie geht's?
Gut, danke!

Möchtest du uns etwas über deinen Alltag sagen?
Ja, klar! Ich stehe um sieben Uhr auf und gucke sofort nach meinem Handy. Super! Ich habe über Nacht zweitausend neue Followers bekommen! Das ist extrem wichtig für mich, denn ohne Followers habe ich keinen Job. Dann mache ich ein Video und zeige meinen Followern mein Frühstück! Ich esse immer super gesund und es sieht wie immer sehr lecker aus.

Was machst du nach dem Frühstück?
Danach mache ich mich bereit und gehe in die Stadt. Ich gehe in viele Geschäfte, wo ich die neuen Moden sehe und ein Video mit meinen Meinungen dazu mache. Meine Followers lieben meine Videos und ich chatte auch gern mit meinen Fans – sie hören mir immer zu und sind wie Freunde für mich!

Was musst du auch oft machen?
Ich muss immer meinen Followern neue Kleidung zeigen und sagen, was ich darüber denke. Ich reise auch viel, fast jede Woche, aber diese Woche bin ich zu Hause und ich möchte mich entspannen.

Willst du immer Influencerin sein? Auch wenn du älter bist?
Also man weiß nie, was das Leben bringt, aber im Moment gefällt mir mein Job sehr. Ich treffe immer neue Leute, habe viel moderne Kleidung und kann oft reisen – mein Leben ist das Beste!

1. What is the first thing Annika does when she wakes up?
2. Why are her followers so important for her?
3. What is her first video of the day about?
4. Why does she go to so many shops?
5. What does she have to do with new clothes? (Give **two** details.)
6. Why is this week more relaxing than usual?
7. What does she say about the future?
8. Why does she feel her life is so good? (Give **three** details.)

4 Translate the interview questions in **bold** into English.

5 In pairs, read the interview aloud.

6 Listen to the conversation between Erik and Yusuf. Select the correct option to complete each statement.
1. Erik is **tired** / **sorry**.
2. Erik went to **Berlin** / **Wacken** for three days.
3. He finds **going shopping** / **fashion** boring.
4. He **was ill** / **took selfies** at the music festival.
5. He **likes** / **dislikes** his job at the moment.
6. He gets **money** / **no money** by creating videos and photos.

> **G**
> To form a yes/no question, start with the **verb**. You can use the modals **Möchtest du …?** (Would you like …?) or **Willst du …?** (Do you want …?).
>
> Remember to put the infinitive at the end of the question when using modal verbs:
> **Möchtest du** berühmt sein?   Would you like to be famous?
> **Willst du** einkaufen gehen?   Do you want to go shopping?
>
> To ask other types of questions, you can use a question word (e.g. wann, wo, wie, warum) and swap the verb and subject round:
> **Was** machst du nach dem Frühstück?   **What** do you do after breakfast?
>
> Page 43

> Be careful with **o** and **ö** – they are different sounds in German.
> Listen and repeat the words.
> M**o**de   M**o**ment
> W**o**che   **o**ft
> k**ö**nnen   m**ö**chte

7 Choose a celebrity or an influencer. Write a paragraph about what they do, what they have done in their life and the advantages and disadvantages of their celebrity life.

4 Wie war der Film?

- Expressing preferences about films and TV shows
- Using the imperfect and perfect tenses together
- Practising the *eu* sound in German

Lesen 1 Read the descriptions of some TV shows. Write the letter of the best show (a–f) for each person in the sentences below.

< Gestern   Heute   Morgen >
< 14:00   15:00   16:00 >

a Emil und die Detektive
Emil und seine Freunde sind auf einer spannenden Mission durch Berlin. Ein klassischer Actionfilm für die ganze Familie!

b Die Tagesschau
Die neuesten Nachrichten, Sport und Wetter aus Deutschland, Europa und der Welt. Die Tagesschau: Deutschlands älteste und meistgesehene Nachrichtensendung.

c Türkisch für Anfänger
Lachen Sie mit dieser beliebten, kulturellen und lustigen Serie über eine deutsch-türkische Familie. Genießen Sie die witzigen Momente voller Humor.

d Dark
Eine überzeugende und spannende Fantasy-Serie über Zeitreisen. Perfekt für alle, die komische Geschichten und Serien wie *Doctor Who* lieben.

e Nosferatu: Phantom der Nacht
Erleben Sie einen klassischen, deutschen Horrorfilm. Im Film geht es um einen verrückten Vampir und der Film hat eine spannende Stimmung.

f Conchita: Unstoppable
Ein wirklich interessanter Film über die weltberühmte Sängerin Conchita und ihr Leben, mit Interviews mit ihrer Familie.

> **überzeugend** convincing

1. Ich liebe Komödien.
2. Aktion gefällt mir sehr und ich sehe gern mit meinen Eltern Filme.
3. Am liebsten sehe ich mit Freunden Horror.
4. Ich mag Realityshows nicht, aber ich erfahre gern interessante Informationen.
5. Ich interessiere mich sehr für Science-Fiction-Filme, wie *Avatar 3*.
6. Ich bin Fußball-Fan – ich sehe also lieber Sendungen, die über Sport berichten.

Lesen 2 Sort the words on the right into two categories: 'qualifiers/intensifiers' or 'adjectives'. Then translate them into English.

sehr | total | witzig | interessant
super | ganz | langweilig | toll
ziemlich | wunderbar | zu | kompliziert

Hören 3 Listen. (1–3) Write the letters of the three correct statements.

a Oskar likes comedies.
b He thinks they are very boring.
c Charlotte's favourite film is a documentary.
d She finds action films particularly interesting.
e Bente likes to watch game shows.
f He finds them too complicated.

Sprechen 4 In pairs, take turns to ask and answer questions about your favourite types of film and TV show. Remember to include qualifiers.

- *Wie findest du Sportsendungen?*
- *Ich finde Sportsendungen ein bisschen langweilig. Ich mag Sport nicht. Und du?*
- *Ich finde Sportsendungen ganz interessant. Ich bin Fußball-Fan.*

Kapitel 2

5 Listen to and read the film review. Copy and complete the sentences below with words from the box. There are more words than gaps.

Aktion-Katzen
Eine echte KATastrophe!
★☆☆☆☆

Kritik: Heute Abend bin ich mit meinem Freund ins Kino gegangen und ich habe den neuen Actionfilm für Kinder *Aktion-Katzen* gesehen. Es war eine echte Zeitverschwendung. Im Film ging es um drei Katzen und die Geschichte fand in Berlin statt – toll, oder? Nein! Es gab zu viele langweilige Szenen und der Film hatte keine Spannung. Es war traurig, dass der Film so lang und kompliziert war. Die Schauspieler und Schauspielerinnen haben mich nicht überzeugt. Es gab auch keine Gewalt – das war gut für die jungen Zuschauer, aber meiner Meinung nach war der Film sehr schwach. Ich empfehle den Film gar nicht!

| a school | weak | complicated |
| plot | actors | a city |

1 The story took place in …
2 The … did not convince the reviewer.
3 Overall, the reviewer found the film very …

G The **perfect tense** is used in spoken German and more informal writing.
The **imperfect tense** is used more in written narrative accounts, stories and reviews:

Es ging um … It was about …
Es fand in Berlin statt. It took place in Berlin.

Some verbs are used more commonly in the imperfect than the perfect tense:

ich war I was   *ich hatte* I had
es gab there was/were

Page 44

6 Translate the six underlined sentences in the review in exercise 5 into English.

7 Read out the review in exercise 5. Pay attention to the *eu* sounds. Then listen again and check.

The **eu** sound in German is pronounced 'oy' as in 'b**oy**'.

Listen and repeat these words.
n**eu**lich   Fr**eu**ndin   überz**eu**gen   D**eu**tschland

8 Write approximately 90 words about films and TV shows. Include the following points:
- your opinions on different TV shows
- a description of a film you have seen recently
- what you are watching this evening.

| Das ist | ein Film/Krimi. |
| | eine Serie/Seifenoper/Komödie. |

Im Film ging es um eine Familie / zwei Schüler(innen).
Es ging um eine Reise.
Die Sendung fand in Berlin statt.

Es gab	keine	Gewalt.
(Der Film) hatte	(zu) viel	Spannung.
	wenig	Stimmung.

Der Film war …
Die Schauspieler(innen) waren …
Ich habe (den Film) … gefunden.
Heute Abend sehe ich vielleicht …

Try to vary the **adjectives** you use in your description:
kompliziert   schwach
lang   spannend
langweilig   traurig
lustig

Adding qualifiers and intensifiers will also make your writing more interesting:
besonders   sehr
ein bisschen   völlig
extrem   wirklich
nicht   zu

Der Film war zu lang.

5 Hast du Pläne?

- Using the future tense to describe plans for the weekend
- Understanding the 'time – manner – place' rule
- Using sequencers

 1 Listen and read. Write the letters of the correct weekend plans (a–h) for each person.

Was wirst du am Wochenende machen?

Alex

1 Nächstes Wochenende wird wunderbar sein! Ich werde zuerst am Samstag Fußball mit meinen Freunden im Park spielen. Danach werden wir einkaufen gehen und ich werde Karten für eine Vorstellung kaufen. Ich gehe nicht gern allein in die Stadt, denn das ist ganz langweilig.

2 Ich interessiere mich sehr für Sport und am Sonntag werde ich viel Sport machen. Meine Mutter und ich werden zuerst in der Stadt Tennis spielen. Danach werden wir mit meinem Onkel, meiner Tante und meinen Cousins am Strand Volleyball spielen! Schließlich werde ich um 19:00 Uhr nach Hause gehen und viel schlafen!

Noah

Elif

3 Dieses Wochenende werde ich keine Hausaufgaben machen! Ich liebe soziale Medien, denn man kann mit Freunden in Kontakt bleiben. Ich werde also am Samstagmorgen mein Handy benutzen und ich werde Videos hochladen und viele Nachrichten schicken. Mein Vater sagt immer, „Wirst du das ganze Wochenende online sein?!", aber am Sonntag werde ich keine Zeit haben, online zu sein. Ich werde mit meiner Stiefmutter ins Sportzentrum gehen – ich werde schwimmen und sie wird ins Fitness-Studio gehen.

 a  b
 c  d
 e  f
 g  h

 2 Find all the time phrases and sequencers in exercise 1. Make two lists.

Example: Time phrases: *nächstes Wochenende*
Sequencers: *zuerst*

> **Sequencers** help to indicate the order in which events take place.
> Here are some useful sequencing words:
> zuerst — firstly / first of all
> danach — afterwards
> dann — then
> nachdem — after
> schließlich — finally

 3 Translate Alex's text into English.

 4 Fill in the gaps with the correct form of *werden*.

1 Es … toll sein.
2 Ihr … online sein.
3 Ich … Basketball spielen.
4 Jan und Mia … heute Nacht gut schlafen.
5 Du … allein wandern gehen.
6 Wir … das Museum besuchen.
7 … Sie im Sportzentrum schwimmen gehen, Herr Schmidt?

> **G** To form the **future tense** in German, use the correct form of **werden** and put the infinitive at the end of the clause.
>
> | ich werde | wir werden |
> | du wirst | ihr werdet |
> | er/sie/es/man wird | Sie/sie werden |
>
> *Dieses Wochenende* **werde** *ich keine Hausaufgaben* machen.
> This weekend, I **will** not do any homework.
> *Nächstes Wochenende* **wird** *wunderbar* sein!
> Next weekend **will** be wonderful!
>
> You can also talk about the future by using the **present tense** with a future time expression.
> *Morgen* **spiele** *ich Tennis*.
> Tomorrow I **am playing** tennis.

 Page 45

5 Listen to Kian talking about his plans for this weekend. Copy and complete the table in English. (1–5)

	when?	with whom?	where?	activity
1				

 6 In pairs, take turns to talk about your future plans using the notes below. Then create your own conversations about your plans for the weekend. Pay attention to the **ä** sounds.

- Was wirst du um 16:00 Uhr machen?
- Ich werde um 16:00 Uhr mit Freunden in der Stadt einen Film sehen.

1
- um 16:00 Uhr
- mit Freunden
- in der Stadt
- einen Film sehen

2
- nächsten Samstag
- allein
- zu Hause
- Bücher lesen

3
- später
- mit meiner Familie
- zu Hause
- fernsehen

> The **ä** sound in German can be a short sound like the English 'e' in 'g**et**' or a longer sound like the 'ay' in 's**ay**'. Listen and repeat these words and decide if they have the short or long **ä** sound.
> n**ä**chstes   Aktivit**ä**t
> gef**ä**llt mir   sp**ä**ter

 7 Translate the sentences into German.
1. This weekend I will play basketball with my friend in the park.
2. That will be particularly great, because it is my favourite activity.
3. Afterwards, we will go into town and see a film.
4. I saw a horror film last weekend, but I prefer seeing action films.
5. I am really interested in the cinema!
6. Finally, I will visit an exhibition with my family in Leipzig.

> **G** The correct **word order** for elements in a German sentence is:
> **time** (when) – **manner** (how) – **place** (where).
>
> *Mein Halbbruder und ich werden* **nächsten Sonntag** **mit Freunden** **im Park** *Fußball spielen.*
>
> Remember that you can start your sentences with the time phrase – just make sure the **verb** is in the second position:
>
> **Nächsten Sonntag** *werden mein Halbbruder und ich* **mit Freunden** **im Park** *Fußball spielen.*
>
> Page 45

 8 Write a paragraph about your own plans for this weekend. Use exercise 1 as a model and use the pictures for ideas if needed.

Was wirst du am Wochenende machen?				
Ich werde Er/Sie wird Wir werden	später heute Nachmittag heute Abend heute Nacht morgen (früh) nächsten (Samstag) am Wochenende	allein mit meinem Freund mit meiner Freundin mit meiner Familie mit meinen Freunden mit meinen Freundinnen	am Strand im Park in der Stadt(mitte) im Kino in Stuttgart zu Hause	(Rockmusik) hören. (Fußball) spielen. (einkaufen) gehen. (Bücher) lesen. (soziale Medien) benutzen. (Videos) hochladen. (einen Film) sehen.
Ich werde das Das wird	besonders total sehr/wirklich ganz/ziemlich ein bisschen nicht	toll lustig spannend anstrengend langweilig schlecht	finden, weil sein, weil	ich es liebe. es meine Lieblingsaktivität ist. ich es nicht mag.

Grammatik 1

Regular verbs in the present tense (Unit 1, page 32)

1 Copy and complete the table with the correct form of the regular verbs.

	spielen	gehen	machen
ich	spiel**e**	5	10
du	**1** spiel**st**	geh**st**	11
er/sie/es/man	2	6	mach**t**
wir	spiel**en**	7	12
ihr	3	geh**t**	13
Sie	4	8	mach**en**
sie	spiel**en**	9	14

Irregular verbs in the present tense (Unit 1, page 32)

2 Listen. Copy and complete the table with the correct form of the irregular verbs.

	sehen	lesen	fahren	essen
ich	**1** s**e**h**e**	4	fahr**e**	ess**e**
du	s**ie**h**st**	l**ie**s**t**	7	**i**ss**t**
er/sie/es/man	2	5	f**ä**hr**t**	10
wir	3	les**en**	fahr**en**	ess**en**
ihr	seh**t**	les**t**	8	11
Sie	seh**en**	les**en**	fahr**en**	12
sie	seh**en**	6	9	ess**en**

Some verbs, such as **sehen** (to see), **lesen** (to read), **fahren** (to go, to travel) and **essen** (to eat) are **irregular**.

The endings are the same as for regular verbs, but there are changes to the stem in the **du** and the **er/sie/es/man** forms.

Word order: verb as second idea (Unit 1, page 32)

Remember that the conjugated verb is always the second idea in a German sentence.

3 Rewrite the sentences starting with the **bold** words.

Example: 1 **Später** werde ich am Strand Volleyball spielen.

1 Ich werde **später** am Strand Volleyball spielen.
2 Wir werden **heute Nachmittag** im Park Rockmusik hören.
3 Mein Stiefvater besucht **am liebsten** Ausstellungen in der Stadt.
4 Die Nachrichten waren **letzte Woche** ganz schlecht.
5 Meine Freunde und ich gehen **ab und zu** wandern.
6 Ich möchte **jeden Tag** soziale Medien benutzen.

4 Read out the sentences from exercise 3.

Using gern, lieber and am liebsten (Unit 1, page 32)

5 Write sentences using *(nicht) gern, lieber* and *am liebsten*.
Example: 1 Ich fahre am liebsten Fahrrad.

1 ♥♥♥
2 ✗
3 ♥
4 ♥♥♥
5 ♥♥

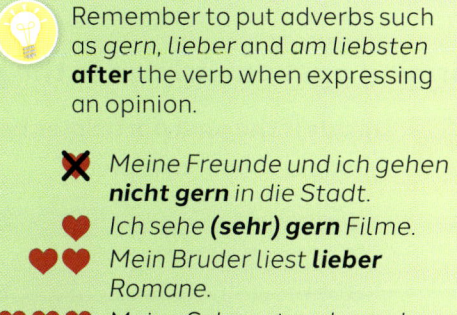

Remember to put adverbs such as *gern, lieber* and *am liebsten* **after** the verb when expressing an opinion.

✗ *Meine Freunde und ich gehen **nicht gern** in die Stadt.*
♥ *Ich sehe **(sehr) gern** Filme.*
♥♥ *Mein Bruder liest **lieber** Romane.*
♥♥♥ *Meine Schwestern besuchen **am liebsten** Ausstellungen.*

Separable verbs in the present tense (Unit 2, page 34)

6 Copy and complete the sentences with the correct form of the separable verb in brackets. Then translate them into English.

1 Ich *rufe* meine Freunde jeden Tag *an*. (anrufen)
2 Wir ___ oft Videos ___. (aufnehmen)
3 Er ___ normalerweise jeden Abend ___. (fernsehen)
4 Ich ___ mir häufig Actionfilme ___. (ansehen)
5 Meine Familie und ich ___ Fotos ___. (hochladen)
6 Mein Bruder ___ ein Handy ___. (mitnehmen)

Man kann … (Unit 2, page 35)

7 Put the words in the correct order to make sentences starting with *Man kann …*

1 Man   in   kann   bleiben   Kontakt
2 herunterladen   Musik   kann   Man
3 kann   Man   Computer-Viren   bekommen
4 finden   Informationen   schnell   Man   kann
5 streamen   Filme   kann   Man
6 Man   Informationen   lesen   kann   falsche

Asking questions with möchten and wollen (Unit 3, page 37)

8 Put the words in the correct order to make questions.

1 morgen in die Stadt Möchtest gehen du?
2 die Ausstellung Sie Möchten sehen?
3 ihr spielen Möchtet Fußball?
4 sein Willst berühmt du?
5 im Restaurant essen Sie Wollen?
6 Wollt sehen ihr einen Film?

möchten	wollen
ich möchte	ich will
du möchtest	du willst
er/sie/es/man möchte	er/sie/es/man will
wir möchten	wir wollen
ihr möchtet	ihr wollt
Sie möchten	Sie wollen
sie möchten	sie wollen

dreiundvierzig

Grammatik 2

Forming past participles in the perfect tense (Unit 4, page 39)

 1 Decide if the past participles below use *haben* or *sein*. Write two lists.

Example: haben: gespielt, …

1 gespielt
2 gegangen
3 gehört
4 besucht
5 gesehen
6 gefahren
7 gelesen
8 gefunden
9 ferngesehen
10 geschwommen

 Remember that most verbs take **haben** in the perfect tense. Those that take **sein** usually involve movement or a change of state, e.g. *gehen* (to go), *aufstehen* (to get up).

 2 Copy and complete the sentences with the correct form of *haben* or *sein* and the past participle of the verb in brackets. Then listen and check your answers.

 Remember that the past participle usually starts with **ge-** and can end in **-t** (regular verbs) or **-en** (irregular verbs). Don't add **ge-** if the verb starts with **be-**, **ent-**, **er-**, **ge-**, **über-** or **ver-**.

1 Meine Freundinnen und ich sind gestern in die Stadt gefahren . (*fahren*)
2 Ich ___ Freunde in Köln ___ . (*besuchen*)
3 Mein Bruder ___ letztes Wochenende ins Kino ___ . (*gehen*)
4 Meine Eltern ___ schwimmen ___ . (*gehen*)
5 Lola ___ den ganzen Tag elektronische Musik ___ . (*hören*)
6 Wir ___ danach einen guten Film ___ . (*sehen*)

Köln

The imperfect tense (Unit 4, page 39)

 3 Translate these sentences into English.

1 Ich hatte ein Hobby.
2 Wir waren sehr erfolgreich.
3 Der Film fand in Graz statt.
4 Es ging um eine Reise.

 4 Translate these sentences into German.

1 It was about a big family.
2 Mozart was particularly popular.
3 She had a laptop.
4 There was no violence.

 The **imperfect tense** is mainly used in written texts and stories. However, some verbs are used more commonly in the imperfect than the perfect tense.

	Common irregular verbs		Other common irregular phrases
	haben	sein	es gab *there was/were* es fand … statt *it took place* es ging um *it was about*
ich	hatte	war	
er/sie/es/man	hatte	war	
wir	hatten	waren	

The future tense (Unit 5, page 40)

 Put the words in the correct order to make sentences starting with the words in bold.

1. werden   Musik   **Wir**   hören
2. Freund   **Mein**   einkaufen   gehen   wird
3. kaufen   die   nächsten   **Ich**   Samstag   Karten   werde
4. ich   werden   Schwester   herunterladen   und   **Meine**   Apps

> Remember: to form the **future tense** in German, use the correct form of **werden** and put the infinitive at the end of the clause.

Word order: time – manner – place (Unit 5, page 41)

 Decide if the phrases in the box are 'time', 'manner' or 'place' phrases. Copy and complete the table.

time	manner	place
heute Abend		

mit meiner Familie   am Strand
mit meinen Freundinnen   in Österreich
später   morgen
heute Abend   nächstes Wochenende
mit meinem Bruder   zu Hause
allein   ins Kino

Translate the sentences into German. Use the table from exercise 6 to help you.

1. I will listen to music at home with my brother this evening.
2. I will go shopping next weekend in Austria with my friends.
3. I will go to the cinema with my family later.
4. Tomorrow I will read books alone on the beach.

Los geht's!

 Read the text and find as many examples as you can of each of the six grammar features.

1. Separable verbs (e.g. **fern**sehen)
2. Opinions using *gern, lieber* and *am liebsten*
3. Verb as second idea following frequency phrase (e.g. *Jeden Tag* **spiele ich** …)
4. Perfect tense (e.g. *Ich* **habe** *Basketball* **gespielt**.)
5. Imperfect tense (e.g. *Wir* **waren** *ganz erfolgreich*.)
6. Future tense (e.g. *Er* **wird** *in die Stadt* **gehen**.)

Letzte Woche hatte ich Geburtstag und ich habe ein neues Handy bekommen. Es ist perfekt, weil es sehr modern ist. Ich liebe neue Technologie: Ich lade sehr gern Musik herunter. Am liebsten chatte ich mit Freunden und ich rufe jetzt jeden Tag meine Freunde an! Von meiner Tante habe ich ein neues Buch bekommen, aber ich interessiere mich nicht für Lesen und ich sehe lieber Filme. Ich werde also am Samstag mit Freunden ins Kino gehen. Letztes Wochenende haben wir einen schlechten Film gesehen. Es war ein Actionfilm und es ging um eine Reise durch Japan!

 Prepare a presentation about your free time. Use exercise 8 to help you, and try to include at least one example of all six grammar features. Then read it out to your partner.

fünfundvierzig

Kapitel 2 Lese- und Hörtest

Reading

Free-time activities. Read Mila's blog. What does it say about her hobbies?

Ich bin sehr aktiv und habe viele Interessen. Früher habe ich gern Basketball gespielt, aber jetzt gehe ich lieber schwimmen. Das mache ich jeden Morgen vor der Schule. Manchmal gehen meine Freunde in die Stadt einkaufen, und morgen gehen sie zusammen in die Geschäfte, aber ich war gestern mit meinen Eltern dort, also werde ich zu Hause Musik hören. Meine Schwester und ich sehen am liebsten Actionfilme und wir werden am Sonntag ins Kino gehen. Es wird ein toller Abend sein.

Write **P** for something that she did in the past, **N** for something that she does now and **F** for something that she will do in the future.

A	Basketball
B	Swimming
C	Shopping with parents
D	Listening to music
E	Cinema

Look out for time phrases.

The word *Morgen* (upper case M) means morning and *morgen* (lower case m) means tomorrow.

Read these sentences carefully to see if there is a past, present or future meaning.

Hobbies. Translate these sentences into English.

1 Im Krimi gab es zu viel Gewalt.
2 Morgen werden wir zu Hause fernsehen.
3 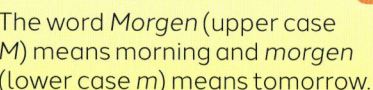 Ich will Schauspieler werden, weil ich gern ins Theater gehe.
4 Gestern Abend bin ich mit meiner Familie ins Kino gegangen.
5 Meine Freundin interessiert sich für Kunst und besucht eine Ausstellung in der Stadt.

Before you start, make a note of which tense (past, present, future) is required for each sentence.

Does this mean the same in English or is it a false friend?

You may not have come across this word before, but can you work out its meaning from the context? The clues are *Kunst* and *Stadt*.

46 sechsundvierzig

Listening

Technology. You hear Sofie and Tim talking about the advantages and disadvantages of using technology. Which **two** aspects does each person mention? Write the **two** correct letters for each person.

A	Shopping is easy
B	Find information quickly
C	Bullying
D	Stay in touch with friends
E	Read false news
F	Buy too many things

Be prepared to listen out for pros and cons. Look at the answer options before you listen and note which are advantages and which are disadvantages.

There will be one mark for each aspect. If you only understand one half of what someone says, think about the context and have a guess at what the other aspect might be. Never leave it blank.

Before you listen, think of language you might hear relating to each of the answer options. Then listen out for key words when you hear the recording.

My weekend. Katrin is talking about her weekend activities. Listen to the recording and write **A**, **B** or **C** to complete each sentence.

1 Katrin often goes …
   A to a friend's house.
   B swimming.
   C shopping.

2 Katrin …
   A likes going to the cinema.
   B doesn't like watching films.
   C thinks the cinema is expensive.

3 Katrin uses her mobile phone …
   A all the time.
   B at home.
   C sometimes.

Read the questions before you start listening and try to anticipate the words and phrases you might expect to hear for each answer option.

Aspects of all the answer options are mentioned at some point in the recording, so listen carefully. Don't choose an answer based on the first word you hear that matches an answer option. Listen to the end of the sentence for negatives and the context in which the words are mentioned. Listen again the second time round to make sure your choice is correct.

Dictation

You will hear five short sentences. Write down exactly what you hear in German.

Think carefully about how these sounds are pronounced when writing down what you hear:
a, ä
o, ö
ie, ei, i
eu

au
ch
sp, st, sch

siebenundvierzig 47

Kapitel 2 Mündlicher Test

Role-play

 1 Look at the role-play card and prepare what you are going to say.

 Your response to each point (1–5) must have a verb in it.

Include both elements. Keep it simple and use words you know. (It does not have to be true.)

You are talking to your German friend.
1 Say how often and where you listen to music.
2 Say what sort of music you like and why. (Give **one** detail and **one** reason.)
3 Say what you watched recently on TV. (Give **two** details.)
4 Say whether you prefer watching films on TV or in the cinema. (Give **one** detail.)
5 ? Ask your friend a question about what they do at the weekend.

If you give your reason in a subordinate clause (e.g. after *weil*), remember that the verb goes at the end.

This task requires you to use a past tense. The two details could be a programme type and an opinion, or you could say what you watched on two different days.

Listen carefully to the words used in the question and try to use a similar construction in your answer.

This question is in the present tense, so you don't need to ask about last or next weekend.

 2 Practise what you have prepared. Then, using your notes, listen and respond to the teacher.

 3 Listen to Leah's answers. Make a note of:
a how she answers the questions for points 1–4
b what question she asks for point 5.

Reading aloud

 4 Look at this task. With a partner, read the sentences aloud, paying attention to the underlined letters. Then listen and check your pronunciation.

> N<u>eu</u>lich <u>si</u>nd m<u>ei</u>n Bruder und <u>sei</u>ne Fr<u>eu</u>ndin <u>i</u>ns K<u>i</u>no gegangen.
>
> D<u>ie</u>ses W<u>o</u>chenende werde <u>i</u>ch <u>schl</u>ießl<u>i</u>ch m<u>i</u>t m<u>ei</u>ner <u>St</u>iefmutter <u>sch</u>wimmen gehen.
>
> <u>A</u>m <u>S</u>amstagmorgen m<u>ö</u>chte <u>i</u>ch m<u>ei</u>n H<u>a</u>ndy benutzen und v<u>ie</u>le F<u>o</u>tos h<u>o</u>chladen.
>
> M<u>ei</u>ne Eltern müssen sp<u>ä</u>ter in der <u>St</u>adt <u>ei</u>nkaufen gehen, <u>a</u>ber das m<u>a</u>chen sie nicht gern – das <u>i</u>st <u>ei</u>n Pr<u>o</u>blem!

 Think carefully about how to pronounce these sounds:
a, ä
o, ö
ie, ei, i
eu
sp, st, sch

 5 The teacher will ask four follow-up questions. Before you hear them, discuss with a partner what you think they might be. The start of each sentence is given below. Then listen and write down the questions.

1 Wie oft ...?   2 Beschreib ...   3 Wie findest du ...?   4 Warum ...?

 6 Prepare your own answers to the questions. Then listen again and respond to the teacher.

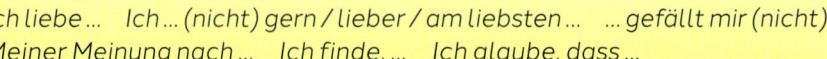 Include likes, dislikes and preferences in your opinions. Try using some of these phrases:
*Ich liebe ...   Ich ... (nicht) gern / lieber / am liebsten ...   ... gefällt mir (nicht)
Meiner Meinung nach ...   Ich finde, ...   Ich glaube, dass ...*

Photo card

 7 Look at the photos and listen to Leah describing them. Answer the questions in English.
1 Where does Leah say the young woman in the first photo is sitting?
2 What does Leah think she is doing?
3 Which adjective does Leah use to describe the man in the second photo?
4 What does she think he might do for a living?

You will be asked to talk about the content of these photos. You must say at least one thing about each photo.

After you have spoken about the content of the photos, you will be asked questions related to any of the topics within the theme of **Popular culture**.

Your responses should be as **full and detailed** as possible.

 8 Prepare your own description of the photos. Then, with a partner, take turns describing them.

> Auf dem ersten Foto gibt es …

 9 Listen to the teacher's first follow-up question, *Was machst du gern in deiner Freizeit?*, and Leah's response. Answer the questions in English.
1 Which **two** hobbies does Leah mention?
2 Which country does her favourite author come from?
3 Give **two** details about the sort of books this author writes.
4 What did Leah do yesterday? Why?

 10 The teacher then asks Leah, *Siehst du gern fern?* Listen to Leah's response and write down the missing word(s) for each gap.

Ich sehe **1** fern, vielleicht **2** in der Woche. Am Wochenende sehe ich **3** eine Sportsendung. Ich höre **4** Musik mit meinem Freund in meinem **5** . Am liebsten höre ich **6** Musik wie Rock, aber ich finde alte Musik wirklich **7** .

 11 Listen to two more follow-up questions and prepare your answers. Then respond to the recording. Make your answers as full as possible, including opinions and reasons.

> In this part of the speaking exam, you can really develop your answers. This is your opportunity to show off how well you can speak German by using a greater variety of vocabulary, structures and tenses. Try to include some of the structures and vocabulary you have learned in this module:
> - separable verbs: *Ich **sehe** jeden Tag **fern**.*
> - gern, lieber, am liebsten: ***Am liebsten** spiele ich Basketball.*
> - frequency phrases and subject–verb inversion: ***Zweimal in der Woche höre ich** Musik.*
> - the perfect and imperfect tenses together: *Ich **habe** einen Film **gesehen**, aber er **war** zu lang.*

 12 Prepare your own answers to as many of the Module 2 questions on page 226 as you can. Then practise with your partner.

neunundvierzig 49

Kapitel 2 Schreibtest

Translation

Look at this translation task and Alfie's translation of the sentences. Fill in the missing verbs.

1. They play basketball three times a week.
2. In my opinion music is often very relaxing.
3. I don't want to be sporty.
4. She likes cooking but she prefers shopping in town.
5. When you were younger, you always played on the computer.

1. Sie ___ dreimal in der Woche Basketball.
2. Meiner Meinung nach ___ Musik häufig sehr entspannend.
3. Ich ___ nicht sportlich ___ .
4. Sie ___ gern, aber sie ___ lieber in der Stadt ___ .
5. Als du jünger ___ , ___ du immer am Computer ___ .

Check carefully that you are using the correct tense and look out for word order after time phrases and subordinating conjunctions. Remember that the prefix of separable verbs goes to the end of the clause.

Translate these sentences into German.

1. We play football twice a week.
2. In my opinion money is not always important.
3. He doesn't want to be famous.
4. I like reading, but I prefer watching TV.
5. When I was younger, I often listened to music.

90-word writing task

Look at this writing exam task and then, for each bullet point:

1. think about the vocabulary and structures you have learned, which you could use in your answers. For example:
   - **nouns**, **verbs** and **adjectives** to write about music and other hobbies
   - language for **narrating a story** about a sport you did
   - how to explain what you **will do** and **why**
   - **connectives**, **intensifiers** and **sequencers** you would like to use.
2. write down three or four ideas for what you could write about
3. identify which tense(s) you will need to use in your answer.

You are writing to your friend about your free-time activities.

Write approximately **90** words in **German**.

You must write something about each bullet point.

Describe:
- which musical activities you like
- what sport you did last week
- what you will do next weekend.

Remember that what you write for the exam doesn't have to be true! You may not like music and you may not have done any sport last week, but you need to demonstrate that you can use the various tenses and know the relevant vocabulary. Similarly, if you don't have any plans for next weekend, make something up, using language you are sure of.

Kapitel 2

Lesen 4 Read Alfie's answer to the exam task. Answer the questions in the coloured boxes (1–5).

1 This is an example of **complex language**. What does it mean? Find three more examples of complex language in the text.

2 Alfie uses a **variety of time phrases**. What do these words mean? Find two more examples.

3 Which **tense** is this? What other examples can you find? Does Alfie use any other tenses?

> Jeden Tag höre ich gern Musik und ich lade sie oft herunter. Ab und zu gehe ich mit Freunden auf ein Konzert, weil wir das spannend finden. Ich spiele häufig Gitarre. Einmal im Monat spiele ich mit meinen Freunden in einer Band. Ich finde das meistens lustig. Es kann auch ganz laut sein!
>
> Letzte Woche bin ich mit Freunden schwimmen gegangen. Das hat viel Spaß gemacht. Danach sind wir Fahrrad gefahren.
>
> Nächstes Wochenende möchte ich eine Ausstellung mit meiner Familie in der Stadt besuchen. Leider muss ich auch meine Hausaufgaben machen. Das wird nicht so spannend sein!

4 How could Alfie **avoid repetition** by using a synonym or substituting a different word?

5 Which connective could you use here to form an **extended sentence**? What other connectives does Alfie use?

Lesen 5 Read Alfie's answer again and answer the questions in English.
1 How often does Alfie go to concerts?
2 What does he do once a month?
3 How do you know that Alfie is sporty? (Give **one** detail.)
4 When and where is Alfie going to the exhibition?
5 According to Alfie, what is not going to be fun?

Schreiben 6 Prepare your own answer to the task.
- Think about how you can develop your answer for each bullet point.
- Look back at your notes from exercises 3 and 4.
- Look at the 'Challenge checklist' and consider how you can show off your German!
- Write a brief plan and organise your answer into paragraphs.
- Write your answer and then carefully check for accuracy.

How do **you** check for accuracy? Is your approach effective or do you end up missing many of your own mistakes? Have a discussion with your partner about the different strategies you could adopt for checking your work. Which one do you think will be the most effective?
Here are some ideas for you to consider:
- read your work aloud
- ask a partner to check your work
- read through several times, checking for different things each time: verb endings, cases, word order, etc.

Challenge checklist

- ✓ Past, present and future time frames
- ✓ Connectives (*und, aber*) and time phrases (*gestern, später*)
- ✓ Some extended sentences
- ✓ An opinion verb (*ich liebe/mag/finde*) and simple adjectives (*toll, lustig*)

- ✓ A wider range of tenses and different verbs
- ✓ Different persons of the verb (*ich, wir, man, meine Familie*)
- ✓ More varied opinion verbs (*gefällt mir*) and phrases (*meiner Meinung nach*)
- ✓ Intensifiers and qualifiers (*zu, wirklich, besonders*)
- ✓ A wider range of interesting vocabulary (*Lieder, Geräte*)

- ✓ Phrases with more than one verb or one tense
- ✓ Different future time frames (future tense, present + future time phrase)
- ✓ Complex language (separable verbs, word order changes)
- ✓ Use of sequencing words (*nachdem, danach, schließlich*)
- ✓ More varied conjunctions (*weil, dass, obwohl*)

einundfünfzig 51

Kapitel 2 Wörter

Key:
bold = this word will appear in higher exams only
* = this word is not on the vocabulary list but you may use it in your own sentences

Kennst du diese *Musiker? (pages 30–31):

Musik	Music
Wie findest du (Rockmusik)?	What do you think of (rock music)?
Magst du die Musik von (Helene Fischer)?	Do you like (Helene Fischer's) music?
Was ist deine Lieblingsmusik?	What is your favourite music?
Ich liebe / mag ... (nicht) / hasse ...	I love / (don't) like / hate ...
Rock	rock
die Musik von (Mozart)	the music of (Mozart)
*elektronische Musik	electronic music
klassische Musik	classical music
Popmusik	pop music
Tanzmusik	dance music
denn er/sie/es ist ...	because it is ...
besonders	particularly
extrem	extremely
ganz	quite
nicht	not
sehr	very
wirklich	really
ziemlich	rather
zu	too
aufregend	exciting
interessant	interesting
komisch	funny, strange
langsam	slow
langweilig	boring
laut	loud
modern	modern
schnell	fast, quick
spannend	exciting

Was machst du gern in deiner Freizeit? (pages 32–33):

Freizeitaktivitäten	Free time activities
Was machst du gern in deiner Freizeit?	What do you like to do / doing in your free time?
Mein *Lieblingshobby ist ...	My favourite hobby is ...
Meine Lieblingsfreizeitaktivität ist ...	My favourite free time activity is ...
Ich interessiere mich (sehr/nicht) für ...	I'm (very/not) interested in ...
Einkaufen	shopping
Fahrradfahren	cycling
Fernsehen	TV
*Gaming	gaming
Lesen	reading
Sport	sport
Ich spiele am Computer.	I play on the computer.
Ich gehe ...	I go ...
einkaufen.	shopping.
ins Kino.	to the cinema.
in die Stadt.	to town.
schwimmen.	swimming.
wandern.	hiking.
Ich besuche (**Ausstellungen**/Freunde).	I visit (exhibitions/friends).
Ich bleibe zu Hause.	I stay at home.
Ich tanze/koche/singe.	I dance/cook/sing.
Ich mache Fotos.	I take photos.
Ich lese Bücher/Romane.	I read books/novels.
Ich **male**/**zeichne** Bilder.	I paint/draw pictures.
Ich höre Musik.	I listen to music.
Ich sehe fern/Filme.	I watch TV/films.
Ich treffe mich mit meinen Freunden.	I meet my friends.
ab und zu	now and again
jeden Tag / täglich	every day
manchmal	sometimes
(fast) nie	(almost) never
oft	often
selten	rarely
am Wochenende	at the weekend

Was machst du online? (pages 34–35):

Technologie	Technology
Welche **Geräte** benutzt du?	Which appliances / pieces of equipment do you use?
Ich habe ... / Wir haben ...	I have ... / We have ...
Ich benutze ... / Wir benutzen ...	I use ... / We use ...
einen Computer	a computer
einen Laptop	a laptop
eine *Spielkonsole	a games console
ein Handy	a mobile phone
ein *Smartphone	a smart phone
ein *Tablet	a tablet
Was machst du online?	What do you do online?
Ich sehe mir (Filme/Videos) an.	I watch (films/videos).
Ich lade (Apps) herunter.	I download (apps).
Ich lade (Fotos) hoch.	I upload photos.
Ich **nehme** (Musik) **auf**.	I record (music).
Ich rufe (meine Freunde) an.	I call/phone (my friends).
Ich benutze soziale Medien.	I use social media.
Ich schreibe/lese/schicke ... (die) Nachrichten	I write/read/send ... news, messages
Ich folge berühmten Persönlichkeiten.	I follow famous people.
Ich streame (Musik/Serien).	I stream (music/series).
Und wie oft?	And how often?
häufig	frequently
immer	always
jeden Abend	every evening
jeden Nachmittag	every afternoon
jede Woche	every week
normalerweise	normally
Was sind die Vorteile/Nachteile von Technologie?	What are the advantages/disadvantages of technology?
Man kann ...	You can ...
*Computer-Viren bekommen.	get computer viruses.
falsche Informationen oder Nachrichten lesen.	read wrong/untrue information or news.
Filme und Musik herunterladen.	download films and music.
Informationen schnell finden.	find information quickly.
mit Freunden in Kontakt bleiben.	keep in touch with friends.
Probleme mit Mobbing bekommen.	have problems with bullying.

Das Leben als Star (pages 36–37):

Wer ist deine Lieblingspersönlichkeit?	Who is your favourite personality?
Was ist er/sie von Beruf?	What does he/she do?
Er/Sie ist *Fußballprofi/ Tennisspieler(in).	He/She is a footballer / tennis player.
Er/Sie ist *Musiker(in)/ Sänger(in).	He/She is a musician/singer.
Er/Sie kann sehr gut singen / Fußball spielen.	He/She can sing / play football really well.
Er/Sie ist sehr *talentiert / ein **Vorbild**.	He/She is very talented / a role model.
Was hat er/sie gemacht?	What has he/she done?
Er/Sie hat viele Spiele gewonnen.	He/She has won lots of matches.
Er/Sie hat viel Musik gemacht.	He/She has made a lot of music.
Ein Vorteil von ihrem/seinem Leben ist, …	One advantage of his/her life is (that) …
er/sie ist ein **Vorbild**.	he/she is a role model.
er/sie kann um die Welt reisen.	he/she can travel around the world.
Ein Nachteil ist, …	One disadvantage is (that) …
er/sie muss immer fit sein.	he/she always has to stay fit.
er/sie muss immer gut aussehen.	he/she always has to look good.
er/sie hat kein Privatleben.	he/she doesn't have any private life.
Möchtest du berühmt sein?	Would you like to be famous?

Wie war der Film? (pages 38–39):

Film und Fernsehen — Film and TV

Das war …	It was …
ein Film.	a film.
ein Krimi.	detective story, thriller.
eine Komödie.	a comedy.
eine Serie.	a series.
eine Seifenoper.	a soap (opera).
*Im Film ging es um …	The film was about …
einen Schüler / eine Schülerin.	a pupil, student.
eine Familie.	a family.
eine Reise.	a journey, trip.
Die Sendung fand in (Berlin) statt.	The programme took place in (Berlin).
Es gab …	There was/were …
(Der Film) hatte …	The film had …
keinen/keine/kein	no
(zu) viel	too much
wenig	little, few
(die) Gewalt	violence
(die) **Spannung**	suspense, tension
(die) **Stimmung**	mood, atmosphere
Der Film war …	The film was …
Die Schauspieler(innen) waren …	The actors/actresses were …
Ich habe den Film … gefunden	I found the film …
ein bisschen	a little, a bit
total	totally
völlig	completely
kompliziert	complicated
lang	long
lustig	funny
schwach	weak
super	super
toll	great, terrific
traurig	sad
Heute Abend sehe ich vielleicht …	Tonight, perhaps I'll watch …

Hast du Pläne? (pages 40–41):

Das Wochenende — The weekend

Was wirst du am Wochenende machen?	What will you do at the weekend?
Ich werde …	I will …
später	later
heute Nachmittag	this afternoon
heute Abend	this evening
heute Nacht	tonight
morgen (früh)	tomorrow (morning)
nächsten (Samstag)	next (Saturday)
nächstes Wochenende	next weekend
allein	alone
mit meinem Freund / meiner Freundin	with my friend
mit meinen Freunden / meinen Freundinnen	with my friends
mit meiner Familie	with my family
am Strand	at the beach
im Park	in the park
in der Stadt(mitte)	in the town (centre)
in (Stuttgart)	in (Stuttgart)
zu Hause	at home
(Bücher) lesen.	read (books).
(soziale Medien) benutzen.	use (social media).
(Videos) hochladen.	upload (videos).
Wie wird das sein?	What will it/that be like?
Ich werde das … finden.	I will find it/that …
Das wird … sein.	It/That will be …
aufregend	exciting
schlecht	bad
danach	afterwards
dann	then
nachdem	after
zuerst	firstly, first of all
schließlich	finally

Kapitel 1–2 Grammatik: Wiederholung

Identifying tenses

 Decide if these sentences are in the past, present or future tense. Copy and complete the table.

past	present	future
1, ...		

1 Ich hatte viele Freunde.
2 Sophie wird Musik herunterladen.
3 Wir sehen fern.
4 Meine Eltern sind online.
5 Tom war in der Stadt.
6 Meine Schwester hat Kleidung gekauft.
7 Wir haben keine Hausaufgaben.
8 Er wird nichts machen.
9 Es gab keine Schuluniform.
10 Wie oft hast du Sport in der Schule?

Word order with time phrases

 Rewrite sentences 1–9 from exercise 1, starting with a suitable time phrase from the word cloud.
Example: 1 *Letztes Jahr hatte ich viele Freunde.*

gestern   heute   nächste Woche   früher   in Zukunft   morgen   jeden Tag   später   am Wochenende   jetzt   letztes Jahr   letzten Samstag

> Remember: the conjugated verb must be the second idea in the sentence.

Plural verb forms

 Rewrite the sentences, changing the underlined nouns and verbs to plural forms.

Example: 1 *Die Männer hören jetzt Musik, aber später werden sie Gitarre spielen.*

1 Der Mann hört jetzt Musik, aber später wird er Gitarre spielen.
2 Meine Freundin spielt heute Basketball, aber morgen wird sie Fußball spielen.
3 Der Junge liest ein Buch, aber später wird er fernsehen.
4 Die Schülerin lernt jetzt Deutsch, aber später wird sie Geschichte lernen.
5 Mein Freund geht heute Abend ins Kino, aber morgen wird er zu Hause bleiben.

> Go back to page 42 to refresh your memory on the present tense of regular and irregular verbs, and pages 40–41 for a reminder on how to form the future tense. Then test a partner.

 Rewrite the sentences, changing the underlined plural forms to the singular form.

1 Die Frauen gehen nicht gern einkaufen, also werden sie ins Restaurant gehen.
2 Die Kinder essen Pizza und danach werden sie schwimmen gehen.
3 Meine Freundinnen fahren mit dem Bus zur Schule, aber morgen werden sie zu Fuß gehen.
4 Wir lieben Naturwissenschaften und wir werden in der Zukunft Biologie studieren.

54 *vierundfünfzig*

Grammatik: Wiederholung — Kapitel 1–2

Modal verbs

 Read the notice. Are the statements true or false?

Informationen für alle Schüler*innen
- Man darf im Klassenzimmer nicht essen!
- Ihr könnt in der Pause in den Computerraum gehen, aber ihr dürft keine Computerspiele spielen.
- Man muss keine Getränke kaufen – Wasser kostet nichts.
- Schüler*innen dürfen nicht im Gang laufen.

1 There are only female students at this school.
2 Students are not allowed to eat in the classrooms.
3 Students are allowed to play on the computers during break.
4 Students must not buy drinks.
5 You have to pay for water.
6 Students are not allowed to run in the corridor.

Subordinate clauses

 Copy and complete the sentences with phrases from the box. Remember to change the word order in the subordinate clause.

1 Ich schwimme gern, wenn das Wetter schön ist.
2 Ich lerne am liebsten Deutsch, da ▭.
3 Es ist wichtig, dass ▭.
4 Ich habe gestern Fußball gespielt, weil ▭.
5 Ich gehe nicht gern wandern, wenn ▭.
6 Mein Lieblingsfach ist Geschichte, obwohl ▭.

> *Obwohl* (although), *wenn* (when) and *da* (since, because) send the verb to the end of the sentence, like *weil* (because) and *dass* (that).

ich mache meine Hausaufgaben   ich finde es nützlich   das Wetter ist schön
es regnet   es ist schwer   das Wetter war sehr gut

 Answer the questions and include a subordinate clause beginning with *weil*, *dass*, *obwohl*, *da* or *wenn* in each response. Use ideas from the box in exercise 6 or your own phrases.

Example: Mein Lieblingsfach ist Mathe, weil ich es einfach finde.

1 Was ist dein Lieblingsfach? Warum?
2 Lernst du gern Deutsch?
3 Wann machst du gern Sport?
4 Wie findest du Hausaufgaben?

The perfect tense

 Write the correct letter (a–h) to match up the sentence halves.

1 Nach dem Film haben wir
2 Zuerst habe ich meine Freunde
3 Schließlich sind wir alle
4 Am Samstag habe ich den ganzen Tag
5 Dort haben wir etwas
6 Ich habe Kinokarten
7 Danach sind wir
8 Dann haben wir einen tollen

a nach Hause gefahren.
b gegessen und getrunken.
c vor dem Kino Selfies gemacht.
d und ein Getränk gekauft.
e ins Kino gegangen.
f Horrorfilm gesehen.
g in der Stadt verbracht.
h in einem Café getroffen.

 Write out the sentences from exercise 8 in a logical sequence to describe a day out. Start with sentence 4.

 Translate the text into German.

> Last week I went to a concert with my family. I love music, although it is sometimes very loud. Afterwards, we ate and drank something in the café. Next weekend we will go to the sports centre because my sister prefers playing basketball. My brother likes shopping most of all. Yesterday, he bought black trousers and a blue T-shirt.

fünfundfünfzig 55

Kapitel 3
Meine Welt, deine Welt

Feste in der deutschsprachigen Welt
- Describing festivals and cultural events
- Giving opinions and justifications

Wir feiern!

Im Winter gibt es …

1 Nikolaustag

Im Dezember feiert man Nikolaustag in jeder Stadt. Weißt du, an welchem Tag?

2 Eisfasching

Wenn das Wetter kalt ist, gibt es Eisfasching in Berlin. Machst du mit?

3 Rosenmontag

In Eupen, wie in anderen deutschsprachigen Städten, feiert man Rosenmontag. Eupen ist eine Kleinstadt in Belgien, wo man Deutsch spricht.

Im Frühling gibt es …

4 „Buskers" Straßenkunstfest

Vaduz ist die Hauptstadt von Liechtenstein, ein kleines Land zwischen der Schweiz und Österreich. Hast du Lust, an diesem Straßenkunstfest mitzumachen?

Im Sommer gibt es …

5 „Kärnten läuft"

Komm mit deinen Sportschuhen nach Österreich und mach mit! „Kärnten läuft" ist für alle Sportfans.

Im Herbst gibt es …

6 Oktoberfest

Das berühmteste deutsche Fest findet in München statt. Tanzt du gern?

a Schwimmst du gern? Wie wäre es mit Eisbaden oder Winterschwimmen? Im Winter kommen kostümierte Schwimmer aus allen Teilen Deutschlands und aus dem Ausland zum Orankesee und schwimmen zusammen im eiskalten Wasser. Willst du nächstes Jahr daran teilnehmen?

b Das ist ein Lauffest am Wörthersee in Österreich. Es dauert drei Tage und man kann an einem Hundelauf, an einem Halb- und einem Viertelmarathon oder an einem Nachtlauf teilnehmen. Es gibt auch besondere Veranstaltungen für Kinder und Familien. Nimm deine Laufschuhe mit!

c Das ist das größte Bierfest der Welt. Es dauert zwei Wochen und findet in der Hauptstadt von Bayern statt. In Bayern heißt das „Wiesn", und man trägt oft traditionelle Kleidung. Auf dem Fest gibt es viele Fahrten. Hier isst, trinkt und lacht man viel!

d Das ist der beste Tag des Karnevals. In dieser deutschsprachigen Stadt feiert man Karneval mit schönen Festwagen. Es gibt viele Musiker mit bunten Kostümen. Man kann immer etwas Leckeres auf der Kirmes essen.

e Am Anfang des Monats feiert man dieses Fest überall in der deutschsprachigen Welt. In der Nacht füllt man die Schuhe und die Socken der Kinder mit Geschenken und Schokolade. Früher war es Obst in den Schuhen vor der Haustür.

f Zwei Tage lang gibt es ein wunderbares Fest hier. Man kann Künstler aus diesem Land und aus aller Welt sehen: Tanz, Musik, Humor, Akrobaten und Tricks. Alles findet auf der Straße statt. Hier gibt es auch leckeres Essen und Getränke.

baden	to swim, bathe
der Fasching	another word for **Karneval** (carnival)
der Festwagen	float (in a parade/procession)
die Kirmes	fair

sechsundfünfzig

Kulturzone Kapitel 3

 1 Look at the photos and captions (1–6) and read the descriptions of the festivals (a–f). Write the letter of the correct festival for each photo.

 2 Listen and write down in English exactly when each festival takes place. (1–6)

 3 Find the German for the phrases below in the descriptions.
1 from every part of Germany
2 it lasts for three days
3 take your running shoes
4 it takes place
5 there are many rides
6 people celebrate
7 at the beginning of the month
8 you can see artists from this country

 4 Read the descriptions again and answer the questions in English.
1 Name <u>four</u> festivals at which you can get something to eat.
2 During which festival do children receive presents?
3 Which festival offers special events for participants?
4 Which festival lasts two weeks?

 5 Listen (1–5) and write the letter of the festival (a–e) that suits each person best.

a Thüringer Bachwochen

b Blumenfest Röthenbach

c Granfondo Radsportfest Vaduz

d Bad Dürkheimer Wurstmarkt

e Weihnachtsmarkt in Luxemburg

 6 In pairs, discuss the festivals in the photos above. Give your opinion of the festivals and explain why.
● Wie findest du den Weihnachtsmarkt in Luxemburg?
■ Ich finde den Markt schön, aber alles ist sehr teuer.
  Ich finde das Radsportfest toll, weil mir Sport gut gefällt.
  Das Blumenfest interessiert mich nicht, weil es langweilig ist. Und du?
● Ich finde …

Ich finde	den Markt das Fest	interessant, toll, schön, langweilig, teuer, schlecht, laut,	weil	mir das (nicht) gut gefällt. mir das (keinen) Spaß macht. (Radfahren) mein Lieblingshobby ist. es (zu) viele Menschen gibt. mich das (nicht) interessiert. ich Sport / die Natur (nicht) mag.
Meiner Meinung nach ist	der Markt das Fest			
Der Weihnachtsmarkt Das Blumenfest	interessiert mich (nicht),			er/es schön/toll ist. er/es teuer/laut ist. es eine Menge Leute gibt.

siebenundfünfzig 57

1 Wie ist deine Familie?

- Describing family members
- Using possessive adjectives
- Using relative pronouns

Hören 1
Listen and read. Write the correct letter to match each description to a family portrait (a–c).

1. Mein Name ist Eleanor und das sind meine Geschwister auf dem Foto! Ich habe einen Bruder, der Max heißt, und eine Schwester, die Sofie heißt. Mein Bruder hat kurze, braune Haare und blaue Augen und er ist ziemlich groß. Sofie ist ganz klein und hat lange schwarze Haare. Sie trägt eine Brille. Wir haben ein weißes Kätzchen, das sehr süß ist.

2. Ich heiße Alex und ich bin Einzelkind. Auf dem Foto sieht man meinen Großvater, meinen Onkel, meine Tante und meine Eltern. Meine Tante, die in der Schweiz wohnt, heißt Julia. Meine Väter, die Jonas und Felix heißen, interessieren sich für Tiere und haben viele Fische.

G **Possessive adjectives** follow the same pattern as the indefinite article *ein*.
Only the masculine form changes in the accusative.

	nominative (subject)	accusative (object)
masc	mein (klein**er**) Fisch	mein**en** (klein**en**) Fisch
fem	mein**e** (lustig**e**) Großmutter	mein**e** (lustig**e**) Großmutter
neut	mein (weiß**es**) Kätzchen	mein (weiß**es**) Kätzchen
pl	mein**e** (freundlich**en**) Eltern	mein**e** (freundlich**en**) Eltern

(**subject**) *Mein kleiner Fisch heißt Otto.*
Ich finde (**object**) *meinen kleinen Fisch süß.*

Remember that adjective endings need to agree with the noun they are describing.

Page 68

a

b

c

Lesen 2
Read the texts again and find examples of possessive adjectives. Then answer the questions in English.

Who …?
1. is called Max
2. wears glasses
3. is Julia
4. has brown hair
5. lives in Switzerland
6. has many fish

Schreiben 3
Translate the sentences into German.
1. My brother has short, black hair.
2. My mum is called Josie.
3. My dads live in Switzerland.
4. I like my little fish.

Hören 4
Listen to Jens, Maria and Mohammed talking about their families. Select the **three** correct statements.

a. Jens has a sister who is very active.
b. Jens has two pets.
c. Maria has a big family.
d. Maria has five stepsisters.
e. Mohammed wears glasses.
f. Mohammed has black hair.

achtundfünfzig

5 In pairs, take turns to read out the blog post. Pay attention to the **u**, **ü** and **y** sounds. Then listen and check.

Gibt es eine typische Familie in Deutschland? Meiner Meinung nach gibt es keine! Familien sind alle unterschiedlich. In meiner Familie zum Beispiel gibt es meinen Bruder, meine zwei Halbbrüder, meine Stiefschwester, meinen Stiefvater, meine Mutter, die grüne Haare hat, und mich. Jede Familie ist anders und das finde ich gut.

The **u** sound can be long or short.
ü and **y** sound similar.

Listen and repeat the words.
u   Mein**u**ng, Br**u**der
ü and **y**   s**ü**ß, Br**ü**der, t**y**pisch

Relative pronouns (who, which) refer back to someone or something. They send the <u>verb</u> to the end of the clause.

masc	*Mein Vater,* **der** …	My dad, who …
fem	*Meine Mutter,* **die** …	My mum, who …
neut	*Mein Kätzchen,* **das** …	My kitten, which …
pl	*Meine Eltern,* **die** …	My parents, who …

Der Mann, **der** *zwei Kinder und drei Katzen* <u>hat</u>, …
The man, who <u>has</u> two children and three cats, …

Meine Frau, **die** *Julia* <u>heißt</u>, …
My wife, who <u>is called</u> Julia, …

Ein Haus, **das** *modern* <u>ist</u>, …
A house, which <u>is</u> modern, …

Meine Großeltern, **die** *sehr großzügig* <u>sind</u>, …
My grandparents, who <u>are</u> very generous, …

Page 68

 6 Read the texts in exercise 1 again and find the sentences with relative pronouns. Then translate these sentences into English.

 7 Write a description of the final family in exercise 1, picture a, as if it were your family. Try to use relative pronouns and a variety of adjectives.

 8 Translate the text below into German.

In my family there are nine people. My dad, my two sisters, my stepbrother, my grandparents and I live here in Berlin. My mum lives in Hamburg and I have a half-sister, who is called Jana. I call my mum every day and we like to watch films online together.

Beschreib (mir) deine Familie!
In meiner Familie gibt es meinen (Bruder) / meine (Schwester) / meine (Eltern).
Das ist mein (Bruder) / meine (Schwester) / mein (Kätzchen).
Das sind meine Eltern/Mütter/Väter/Brüder/Schwestern.

Mein …,	der … heißt, der immer (böse) ist,	hat		lange/kurze braune/rote/blonde/schwarze	Haare.
				blaue/braune/grüne/graue	Augen.
Meine …, Mein …,	die … heißt, das … heißt,	ist		nicht ziemlich sehr total	groß. klein.
Meine …,	die … heißen, die nie geheiratet haben,	sind	ab und zu manchmal oft immer nie		lustig. glücklich. großzügig. freundlich. traurig.
Er/Sie/Es ist … Sie sind …					
Er/Sie trägt (k)eine Brille.					

2 Deine Beziehungen

- Saying how you get on with people and why
- Using pronouns and possessive adjectives in the dative
- Writing about a friend using three time frames

1 Listen to and read the online magazine posts about family relationships. Write down the <u>ten</u> missing qualifiers or intensifiers you hear and translate them into English.

Die Beziehungsecke

Hallo Leute!
Die Frage der Woche: Wie verstehst du dich **mit deiner Stieffamilie**?
Ohan und Maria haben uns geschrieben.

Meine Stiefschwester ist ein `1` sportliches Mädchen und ist jeden Tag aktiv. Wir spielen gern Tennis zusammen und lachen viel. Ich verstehe mich sehr gut **mit ihr**, weil sie immer lustig und nie gemein ist. Ich komme nicht so gut **mit meinem Stiefvater** aus, weil er oft `2` streng ist. Er ist `3` ernst und ist nicht `4` lieb. Er verbringt viel Zeit allein und kann ab und zu `5` ärgerlich sein, aber er ist nie böse.

Ohan

Maria

Also, mein Stiefvater? Ich verstehe mich gut **mit ihm**. Er ist `6` freundlich. Ich verstehe mich auch sehr gut **mit meiner Halbschwester**, weil sie `7` ehrlich und nett ist. Sie kann manchmal `8` laut sein, aber das ist `9` normal, finde ich. Ich komme aber nicht so gut **mit meinen Stiefbrüdern** aus. Sie wohnen normalerweise mit ihrer Mutter zusammen. Sie sind nicht nett und nie glücklich, und wir haben unterschiedliche Interessen. Das finde ich `10` schlecht. Ja, ich verstehe mich gar nicht gut **mit ihnen**.

2 Read the magazine posts again. Copy and complete the table for Ohan's and Maria's relatives in English.

family member	gets on well? Y/N	qualities	other details
Ohan's stepsister			

G Some prepositions, like *mit*, are always followed by **dative** pronouns or possessive adjectives.
Ich verstehe mich gut / nicht gut …
Ich komme gut / nicht gut … aus.

mit mein**em** Vater	mit **ihm**
mit mein**er** Schwester	mit **ihr**
mit mein**em** Kind	mit **ihm**
mit mein**en** Freund**en**	mit **ihnen**

Page 69

3 Copy the Venn diagram and write in the German adjectives from the box below. Can you justify your choices?

lustig	sportlich	ernst	böse	ehrlich
unabhängig	aktiv	laut	süß	
streng	glücklich	freundlich	komisch	
verantwortlich	gemein	lieb	ärgerlich	
faul	frech	geduldig	hilfsbereit	höflich

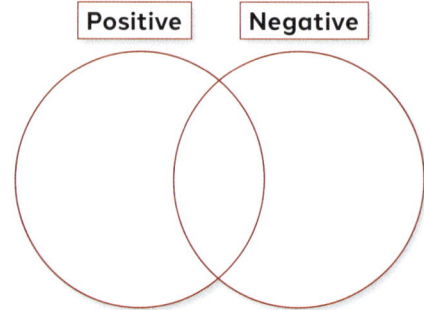
Positive   Negative

60 sechzig

Kapitel 3

 4 Listen to Elke, Axel and Gabi talking about who they get on with. Write down what they say about each family member.

Example: Elke: mostly gets on well with her parents. They're not too strict.

 5 Listen to Elke again and write down the words you hear.

- Kommst du gut mit **1** Familie aus, Elke?
- Ja, zu Hause gibt es nur meinen Vater, meine Mutter und mich. Ich komme meistens gut mit **2** Eltern aus, weil sie mit mir nicht so **3** sind. Meine Mutter kann manchmal ein bisschen **4** sein, aber normalerweise ist sie ziemlich **5** . Verstehst du dich auch gut mit **6** Familie, Axel?

 6 Look at the picture and imagine you are a member of the family. In pairs, take turns to ask and answer questions.

- *Wer bist du?*
- *Ich bin Luna.*
- *Hallo Luna. Kommst du gut mit deinem Bruder Theo aus?*
- *Ja, ich komme gut mit meinem Bruder aus, weil er immer so freundlich ist.*
- *Verstehst du dich gut mit deinem Vater?*
- *Nein, ich verstehe mich nicht so gut mit ihm, weil er oft gemein ist.*
- *Hast du eine gute Beziehung zu … ?*

Sohn: Theo
Vater: Kurt
Tochter: Luna
Opa: Martin
Mutter: Frida
Oma: Christel

Kommst du gut mit Verstehst du dich gut mit Hast du eine gute Beziehung zu	dein**em** (Vater) dein**er** (Tante) dein**en** (Großeltern)	aus? ?			
Ja, ich komme (sehr) gut mit Nein, ich komme nicht (so) gut mit	mein**em** (Bruder) / ihm mein**er** (Schwester) / ihr mein**en** (Eltern) / ihnen	aus,	weil er/ sie	nicht ziemlich ganz wirklich	lustig freundlich großzügig aktiv glücklich	ist.
Ja, ich verstehe mich gut mit Nein, ich verstehe mich nicht gut mit Ja, ich habe eine gute Beziehung zu Nein, ich habe eine schlechte Beziehung zu	mein**em** (Onkel) / ihm, mein**er** (Stiefmutter) / ihr, mein**en** (Geschwistern) / ihnen,		weil sie	so sehr total zu	lieb ernst streng gemein	sind.

 7 Listen to Lena talking about her friend Mikel. Answer the questions in English, giving as much detail as you can.

a How does Lena describe her friend?
b Why does Lena get on well with him?
c What did Lena and Mikel do together last weekend?
d What are Lena and Mikel going to do this evening?

 8 Write approximately 90 words in German about your friend(s). Include the following points:

- a description of a friend and why you get on well
- an activity you did together recently
- what you will do next weekend with your friend(s).

Mein Freund, der … heißt, ist … und er hat …
Meine Freundin, die … heißt, ist … und sie hat …
Ich verstehe mich gut mit ihm/ihr, weil …
Neulich haben/sind wir …
Nächstes Wochenende werden/möchten wir …

einundsechzig 61

3 Wer ist dir wichtig?

- Discussing role models
- Using two time frames together: past and present
- Using qualifiers and intensifiers

Lesen 1
Read what Simon, Aisha and Lena say about their role models. Find the German for the phrases below.

Simon

Aisha

Lena

Ich finde Vorbilder hilfreich, aber ich habe kein berühmtes Vorbild – das ist nicht nötig für mich. Meine Oma ist mein Vorbild. Sie war Lehrerin und hat ihr ganzes Leben Kindern geholfen. Sie hat aber auch immer Zeit für mich gehabt und sie akzeptiert mich und meine Entscheidungen. Bei ihrer Arbeit hat sie immer das Beste für junge Leute gewollt. Manchmal waren einige Kinder ein bisschen faul oder frech, aber meine Oma ist eine sehr geduldige Frau und sie hat sie immer unterstützt!

Für mich sind Vorbilder unwichtig. Ich brauche andere als Inspiration einfach nicht. Ich habe Stars immer total langweilig gefunden und sie interessieren mich überhaupt nicht. Ich finde, dass die Persönlichkeiten, die ständig in den sozialen Medien posten, nichts Neues zu sagen haben. Meiner Meinung nach haben sie einen negativen Einfluss auf uns Jugendliche. Ihre Welt ist nicht echt und wir sollen gegen diese „Vorbilder" kämpfen!

Ich habe die Sängerin Lena Meyer-Landrut immer geliebt. Ja, sie ist schon ein bisschen älter, aber sie hat so viele tolle Sachen in ihrem Leben gemacht. Sie hat im Jahr 2010 Eurovision für Deutschland gewonnen, aber singt heute immer noch neue Lieder. Sie ist sehr erfolgreich gewesen, aber sie unterstützt auch junge Musiker*innen und arbeitet viel mit Wohltätigkeitsorganisationen, vor allem für Kinder, in Deutschland und in der ganzen Welt.

die Wohltätigkeitsorganisation (-en) — charitable organisation

1 I think role models are helpful.
2 I don't have a famous role model.
3 She accepts me and my decisions.
4 She has always supported them.
5 Role models are unimportant for me.
6 I don't need other people for inspiration.
7 They have a negative influence on us.
8 Their world is not real.
9 She has done so many great things in her life.
10 She has been very successful.

Hören 2
Listen to Klara, Rainer and Sibylle talking about role models. Are they in favour of role models, against, or both, and why?

	for or against role models, or both?	reasons
Klara		

G Use the **present** and past tenses alongside each other to add interest and complexity to your German.
*Sie hat immer Zeit für mich gehabt und sie **akzeptiert** mich.*
*Ich habe Stars immer langweilig gefunden und sie **interessieren** mich überhaupt nicht.*

Page 70

zweiundsechzig

3 **Translate the sentences into German.**
1. Role models are very important for me.
2. He has never had time for me and he doesn't accept me.
3. In my opinion role models are not helpful.
4. Taylor Swift is my role model because she has made great music.
5. My dad is my role model because he supports me.
6. Role models have always helped young people.

4 **Read the text about Claudia Schiffer. Answer the questions in English.**

Claudia Schiffer ist im Jahr 1970 in Deutschland geboren. Als sie 17 Jahre alt war, hat man sie in einer Disco in Düsseldorf entdeckt und dann ist sie Model geworden.

Sie war extrem erfolgreich und hat überall auf der ganzen Welt gearbeitet. Sie ist auf dem Catwalk aufgetreten und war auch in sehr vielen Magazinen. Sie ist auch Schauspielerin und Geschäftsfrau. In ihrer Freizeit liebt sie Kunst und sie hat viele Bilder zu Hause.

Sie ist natürlich sehr reich, aber sie macht auch viel für Wohltätigkeitsorganisationen wie Unicef und arbeitet mit Organisationen, die gegen Armut kämpfen.

die Armut poverty

1. How did Claudia Schiffer become a model?
2. Where has she worked?
3. What other jobs does she have? (Give **two** details.)
4. What is her hobby?
5. What kind of charities does she work with? (Give **two** details.)

You can give emphasis to what you are saying by adding qualifiers and intensifiers:

sehr	very
völlig	completely
total	totally
besonders	especially
bestimmt	definitely
ziemlich	quite
überhaupt nicht	not at all

5 **Translate the second paragraph into English.**

6 **In pairs, discuss your opinions of role models.**
- *Ich finde, dass Vorbilder sehr wichtig sind, da…*
- *Nein! Meiner Meinung nach sind sie total nutzlos!*

Ich habe	keine Vorbilder,		da weil	ich sie nicht brauche.
Ich finde Meiner Meinung nach sind	Vorbilder	nützlich, wichtig, super,	da weil	sie mir Inspiration geben. sie hilfreich sind. sie mir helfen. sie für Rechte kämpfen. sie vielen Leuten helfen. sie hart arbeiten. sie erfolgreich sind.
		unwichtig, nutzlos, blöd,		sie nicht in der echten Welt leben. sie nicht interessant sind.
Mein Opa Roger Federer Meine Mutter Meine Schwester	ist mein Vorbild,		da weil	er mich unterstützt. er so viel gemacht hat. sie Zeit für mich hat. sie mich akzeptiert.

4 Wir haben gefeiert!

- Describing a family celebration in the past
- Practising word order
- Using time phrases

1 Hören
Listen to and read the online forum about celebrations. Write down in English what each person did, how or with whom and where they did it. (1–6)

Walda: Zu meinem letzten Geburtstag bin ich mit meiner ganzen Familie zu einem Freizeitpark gefahren.

Uwe: Am Samstag haben wir eine Party mit Freunden im Garten gemacht, weil mein Bruder einen neuen Job gefunden hat.

August: Weil meine Schwester ihre Prüfungen bestanden hat, haben wir am Wochenende mit ihren Freundinnen im Restaurant gefeiert.

Lise: Gestern bin ich mit meinen Geschwistern zum Fest gegangen, und wir haben Karneval gefeiert.

Samira: Letzten Monat hat meine Tante am Strand geheiratet. Wir haben eine Feier organisiert.

Milan: Am Samstag bin ich mit meiner Familie und meinem besten Freund ins Kino gegangen. Wir haben den Anfang der Schulferien gefeiert.

2 Sprechen
In pairs, take turns to select a person from exercise 1 and guess who your partner is.

- *Ich habe am Strand gefeiert.*
- *Bist du Samira?*
- *Ja, richtig!*

> **G** Remember the word order rule:
> **time** (when) – **manner** (how) – **place** (where).
>
> Ich bin **gestern mit dem Bus zum Fest** gefahren.
> **Im Juli** haben wir meinen Geburtstag **mit Freunden im Restaurant** gefeiert.
>
> Page 70

3 Hören
Listen to some young people talking about celebrations. Copy and complete the table in English. (1–5)

	reason for celebration	place
1		

4 Lesen
Read Torsten's blog about *Karneval*. Write down the <u>eight</u> missing past participles. Then listen and check your answers.

Letztes Jahr bin ich mit meinen Eltern zum berühmten Karneval in Düsseldorf gegangen. Die Feier hat in der Stadtmitte **1** und am Morgen haben wir viele bunte Festwagen **2** . Am Abend gab es ein großes Fest mit einem Feuerwerk. Die Menschen waren glücklich und haben laut **3** und viel gelacht. Die Stimmung war fantastisch! Viele Menschen haben lustige Kleider **4** . Die Feier hat mir wirklich gut **5** , weil wir dort viel Spaß **6** haben. Es war eine tolle Erfahrung. Ich habe den ganzen Tag mit meinen Geschwistern auf dem Fest **7** und wir haben dort nette Leute **8** .

gesungen gefallen verbracht gehabt
stattgefunden kennengelernt gesehen getragen

Karneval is known as *Fasching* in the south of Germany and Austria.

Kapitel 3

Hören 5 Listen and write down the missing words and phrases you hear to complete the sentences.

1 ▭ haben wir ▭ im Restaurant ▭.
2 ▭ ist Elke ▭ Karneval ▭.
3 ▭ wir mit der ▭ zum Musikfest ▭.
4 ▭ die ▭ wirklich ▭.

> **Time phrases** can give you a clue to the <u>tense</u> of a sentence:
> **Gestern** <u>haben</u> wir <u>gefeiert</u>. Yesterday we <u>celebrated</u>.
> Remember that the first <u>verb</u> still stays in second position.

Sprechen 6 In pairs, take turns to ask and answer the questions about a celebration.

- Hast du neulich ein Fest besucht?
- Wann hat es stattgefunden?
- Mit wem bist du gegangen?
- Was hast du gemacht?
- Was hast du gesehen?
- Wie war es?

Wer feiert was?

1 Ein Jude / eine Jüdin		a	Weihnachten
2 Ein(e) Sikh		b	Diwali
3 Ein Christ / eine Christin	feiert	c	Eid al-Fitr
4 Ein Muslim / eine Muslimin		d	Chanukka
5 Ein(e) Hindu		e	Hola Mohalla

Schreiben 7 Write approximately 90 words in German about a celebration in the past. Include the following points:
- when it was
- who you were with
- what you did or saw and your opinion of it.

Gestern Am Wochenende Letzte Woche	gab es	eine Party/Feier ein Fest	zu Hause. in der Stadt.
Neulich Letztes Jahr In den Ferien Im Winter Am (Musik-/Diwali-/Vesakh-)Fest Am Karneval An Neujahr	habe ich haben wir hat man	viel mit Freunden mit meiner Familie im Restaurant nette Leute	gefeiert. gelacht. gesungen. getanzt. Spaß gehabt. gegessen/getrunken. kennengelernt.
An Silvester Auf der Party/Feier An Chanukka/Eid al-Fitr/Hola Mohalla Zu Weihnachten/Ostern Zu meinem Geburtstag	bin ich sind wir	mit dem Bus mit dem Zug zu Fuß	ins Kino — gefahren. nach Berlin zum Fest — gegangen. zur Party

fünfundsechzig 65

5 Partyzeit!

- Discussing a party
- Using two time frames together: past and future
- Using *in* + accusative or dative

1 Listen to and read Zeynep's description of some celebrations. Decide whether she refers to each activity below in the past (**P**) or future (**F**).

Letzten Sommer habe ich eine Party für meine Tante organisiert. Vorher habe ich ihr nichts gesagt. Ich habe sie total überrascht, weil ich unsere Familie und zehn Freunde von ihr eingeladen habe. Es gab viel zu essen und zu trinken. Den ganzen Abend sind wir im Garten geblieben, weil das Wetter schön war. Wir haben viel gesungen, getanzt und gelacht.

An meinem nächsten Geburtstag werde ich mit vielen Freunden ins Kino gehen. Im Kino werden wir einen lustigen Film sehen. Danach werde ich meine Freunde zum Essen ins Restaurant einladen. Dann werde ich nach Hause fahren und mit meiner Familie feiern. Wir werden Musik hören, Computerspiele spielen und Kuchen essen. Das wird uns Spaß machen.

1 eating at a restaurant
2 enjoying nice weather
3 listening to music
4 going home
5 eating cake
6 organising party for aunt
7 going to the cinema
8 singing and dancing

2 Read out the text in exercise 1. Pay attention to the *v*, *w* and *z* sounds. Then listen again and check.

In German, the letters **v**, **w** and **z** are pronounced differently from English.

Listen and repeat the words.
- **v** like English 'f'   **v**orher, **v**on
- **w** like English 'v'   **w**eil, **w**ir
- **z** like English 'ts' **z**ehn, **z**u

3 Translate the six underlined sentences in exercise 1 into English.

4 Translate the sentences into German.
1 Next summer, I will organise a party for my friends.
2 There will be lots to eat and drink.
3 We will sing, dance and laugh.
4 Last week, we saw a funny film at the cinema.
5 After that we went home and celebrated.
6 That was fun.

To add interest and complexity to your German, use the past and future tenses in your work.

Past	Future
Ich **habe** eine Party **geplant**.	Ich **werde** eine Party **planen**.
Wir **sind** ins Kino **gegangen**.	Wir **werden** ins Kino **gehen**.
Sie **hat** viel Spaß **gehabt**.	Sie **wird** viel Spaß **haben**.
Das Fest **hat** im Park **stattgefunden**.	Das Fest **wird** im Park **stattfinden**.
Es **gab** viele Menschen dort.	Es **wird** viele Menschen dort **geben**.

Page 71

5 Listen. Copy and complete the table in English. (1–6)

	past, future or both?	type of celebration	extra details
1			

6 Read Julian's post on an online forum and find the phrases with *in*. Decide if they take the accusative or the dative and why. Then answer the questions in English.

Im Juli haben wir eine Abschlussfeier in der Schule gehabt, weil wir das Abitur bestanden haben. Die Feier hat in der Turnhalle stattgefunden und das war wirklich wunderbar, weil wir zusammen viel Spaß gehabt haben. Es gab Spiele, Musik und Sport, und wir haben auch die Schule geschmückt. Danach sind wir in den Park gegangen und haben dort ein Picknick genossen. Das war ein wunderbarer Tag und ich werde mich immer daran erinnern.

In den Sommerferien haben wir vor, wieder ins Kino oder an den Strand zu gehen. Ich glaube, dass es am Strand besser sein wird, weil wir dort schwimmen können. Ich möchte auch in den kleinen Geschäften in der Stadtmitte kleine Geschenke für meine Freunde kaufen. Das wird Spaß machen!

geschmückt — decorated

1 What type of party did Julian attend?
2 What were Julian and his friends celebrating?
3 What does Julian say about the picnic?
4 What would be the best translation of 'ich werde mich immer daran erinnern'?
5 Where does he want to go in the summer and why?
6 What would Julian also like to do?

G Some prepositions such as *in* can be followed by either the accusative or the dative case, depending on whether movement is involved.

		masc	fem	neut	pl
accusative (indicating movement)	ich gehe	in **den** Laden	in **die** Stadt	in **das** Kino	in **die** Geschäfte
dative (indicating position)	ich bin	in **dem** Laden	in **der** Stadt	in **dem** Kino	in **den** Geschäfte**n**

in dem is often abbreviated to *im*.
in das is often abbreviated to *ins*.
In the dative plural, remember to add an **-n** to the noun.

Page 71

7 In pairs, take turns to ask and answer the questions about celebrations in the past and future.
- Was hast du <u>an Silvester</u> gemacht?
- Ich habe <u>Kuchen gegessen</u> und <u>Cola getrunken</u>.
- Was wirst du <u>zu deinem Geburtstag</u> machen?
- Ich werde <u>tanzen</u> und <u>singen</u>.

8 Write approximately 150 words in German about celebrations and festivals. Describe:
- why you like or dislike festivals and celebrations
- what you did at a recent celebration.

Ich mag Silvester, weil …

Letztes Jahr haben wir … gefeiert. Wir haben …

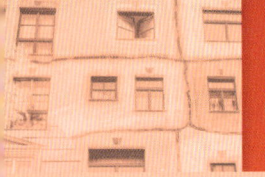

Grammatik 1

Possessive adjectives (Unit 1, page 58)

1 Write down the correct possessive adjectives (*mein, meine* or *meinen*) to complete the text.

Hallo, ich bin Michaela und **1** meine Familie ist ganz klein, aber ich habe Verwandte in der Schweiz und auch in Österreich. **2** Onkel, der in Wien wohnt, sehe ich nicht sehr oft, aber ich sehe **3** Onkel, der in Bern wohnt, wenigstens dreimal im Jahr. **4** Tanten wohnen in Vaduz. **5** Bruder, der acht Jahre alt ist, ist **6** bester Freund, aber **7** ältere Schwester, die Gerthi heißt, ist sehr oft gemein. Tiere habe ich auch. Ich mag **8** Kätzchen, **9** Hund und **10** Fische.

	masc	fem	neut	pl
nom (subject)	mein	meine	mein	meine
acc (object)	mein**en**	meine	mein	meine

Nom: *Mein Bruder ist sportlich.*
Acc: *Ich treffe meinen Bruder.*

These possessive adjectives also follow the same pattern:
dein (your – familiar, sg), **sein** (his), **ihr** (her), **unser** (our), **euer** (your – familiar, pl), **Ihr** (your – formal), **ihr** (their)

 Remember that the endings must agree with the noun that follows.

2 Copy and complete the sentences with the correct possessive adjectives.
1 **Sein** (*his*) Vater ist ziemlich jung, aber ____ (*his*) Mutter ist älter.
2 ____ (*her*) Kätzchen ist süß, aber ich finde ____ (*their*) Kätzchen noch süßer.
3 ____ (*my*) Geburtstag war langweilig, aber ____ (*your, formal*) Geburtstag war einfach toll.
4 ____ (*her*) Eltern sind nett, aber ich finde ____ (*our*) Eltern zu streng.
5 ____ (*your, familiar, sg*) Partner heißt Olek, und ich finde ____ (*his*) Namen super.
6 Oft sehe ich ____ (*your, familiar, pl*) Freunde im Park. ____ (*your, familiar, pl*) Freund spielt mit seinen Freunden dort Fußball.

Relative pronouns (Unit 1, page 59)

3 Select the correct relative pronoun to complete each sentence. Then translate the sentences into English.
1 Mein Onkel, **der / die / das** Bruno heißt, schwimmt nicht gern.
2 Seine Tochter, **der / die / das** gern Musik hört, heißt Laya.
3 Steffi Jones, **der / die / das** mein Vorbild ist, war Fußballspielerin.
4 Sie hat Freunde, **der / die / das** sehr sportlich sind.
5 Dieses Fest, **der / die / das** in Köln stattfindet, ist sehr groß.
6 Ihr (*your*) Bruder, **der / die / das** Bernd heißt, ist sehr ernst.

	masc	fem	neut	pl
nom	der	die	das	die
acc	den	die	das	die

Relative pronouns must be used in the same case as the noun to which they refer.

Subject (nom): *Dein Vater, **der** Jan heißt, ist sehr freundlich.*
(here, **der** – referring back to **dein Vater** – is the subject of the relative clause)

Object (acc): *Dein Vater, **den** ich gut kenne, ist sehr freundlich.*
(here, **ich** is the subject and **den** is the object of the relative clause)

4 Read out these sentences. Then decide whether each relative pronoun is in the nominative (**N**) or accusative (**A**) case.
1 Es gibt viele Leute, <u>die</u> auf der Straße tanzen.
2 Das Geschenk, <u>das</u> du mir gegeben hast, war toll.
3 Der Karneval, <u>den</u> wir nie gesehen haben, ist in Mainz.
4 Sie sprechen nicht mit Leuten, <u>die</u> sie nicht kennen.
5 Das Essen, <u>das</u> wir auf dem Fest probiert haben, war lecker.
6 Das Fest, <u>das</u> im Park stattfindet und <u>das</u> sehr berühmt ist, hatte eine gute Stimmung.

Kapitel 3

Pronouns and possessive adjectives in the dative case (Unit 2, page 60)

 Copy and complete the sentences with the correct form of *meinem*, *meiner* **or** *meinen*.

1 Letztes Jahr bin ich mit **meinen** Eltern (*pl*) nach Österreich gefahren.
2 Ich gehe immer mit ___ Schwestern (*pl*) zum Musikfest.
3 Ich war mit ___ Geburtstagsgeschenk (*n*) von ___ Familie (*f*) sehr zufrieden.
4 Ich bin mit ___ Hund (*m*) spazieren gegangen.
5 Ich gehe oft mit ___ Freundinnen (*pl*) aus.
6 Ich verstehe mich gut mit ___ Mutter (*f*), mit ___ Vater (*m*) und auch mit ___ Brüdern (*pl*).

 Write the correct letter to match the dative nouns (1–6) with their pronouns a–f. Then select the correct English translation.

Example: 1 d, with them

1 mit **meinen** Freunden	a	euch
2 mit **meinem** Kätzchen	b	ihm
3 mit **meinem** Bruder	c	ihr
4 mit **meiner** Familie und mir	d	ihnen
5 mit **dir und deinem** Bruder	e	ihm
6 mit **meiner** Schwester	f	uns

with her   with us   with it
with you   with them   with him

nom	acc	dat
ich	mich	**mir**
du	dich	**dir**
er	ihn	**ihm**
sie	sie	**ihr**
es	es	**ihm**
wir	uns	**uns**
ihr	euch	**euch**
sie	sie	**ihnen**
Sie	Sie	**Ihnen**

Remember that **mit** is followed by the dative.
Sie geht mit **mir**.
Wir sprechen mit **euch**.

mit mein**em** Vater	mit **ihm**
mit mein**er** Schwester	mit **ihr**
mit mein**em** Kind	mit **ihm**
mit mein**en** Freunden	mit **ihnen**

 Listen. Copy and complete the sentences with the correct noun and dative pronoun.

1 Meine **Stiefschwester** ist so freundlich! Ich komme gut mit **ihr** aus.
2 Meine ___ sind immer sehr lieb. Ich komme sehr gut mit ___ aus.
3 Meine ___ ist aber zu ernst. Ich verstehe mich nicht so gut mit ___.
4 Mein ___ ist auch lustig. Ich verstehe mich ziemlich gut mit ___.
5 Mein ___ ist so laut. Er kommt nicht so gut mit ___ aus.
6 Du bist mein bester ___! Ich verstehe mich wirklich gut mit ___.

ihm
Bruder
ihr
ihnen
dir
~~ihr~~
Cousin
Oma
uns
~~Stiefschwester~~
Eltern
Freund

Grammatik 2

Using two time frames: past and present (Unit 3, page 62)

1 Listen and write down the verbs you hear. Then decide if the verb is in the past or present tense.

1 Meine Oma ist mein Vorbild.
2 Vor sieben Tagen ___ ich meinen Geburtstag ___.
3 Letzten Samstag ___ ich eine Party ___.
4 Ich ___ Stars immer langweilig ___.
5 Wenn ich Zeit ___, ___ ich in die Stadt.
6 Glaubst du, dass Vorbilder nützlich ___?

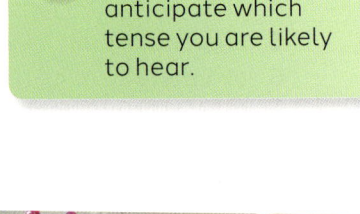

Look at any time phrases to help you anticipate which tense you are likely to hear.

2 Copy and complete the sentences with the correct tense of the verb in brackets.

1 Heute feiern wir meinen Geburtstag. (*feiern*)
2 Meine Oma ___ ein Vorbild für mich. (*sein*)
3 Sie ___ mich immer ___. (*akzeptieren*)
4 Früher ___ meine Schwester eine Brille ___. (*tragen*)
5 Normalerweise ___ ich nicht gern auf Partys. (*gehen*)
6 Als Kind ___ Julia viele Geschenke ___. (*bekommen*)
7 Ich ___ immer viel Kontakt mit meiner Tante. (*haben*)
8 Neulich ___ wir zusammen auf ein Fest ___. (*gehen*)

3 Write sentences using both the past and present tenses, with *früher* and *jetzt*. Then read them out.

Example: 1 *Früher hatte er schwarze Haare, aber jetzt hat er grüne Haare.*

1 er | haben | schwarze | grüne Haare
2 mein Bruder | machen | keinen | viel Sport
3 ich | tragen | eine Brille | keine Brille
4 es | geben | wenige Vorbilder | viele Vorbilder
5 meine Halbschwester | sein | klein | groß
6 ich | feiern Silvester | mit der Familie | mit Freunden

Word order: time – manner – place (Unit 4, page 64)

4 Put the words in the correct order to make sentences.

1 gehe jedes Jahr Ich mit meinen zum Karneval Freunden
2 zu Hause Ich gefeiert habe Jahr Silvester mit letztes meiner Familie
3 Eltern Max zu seinem ist Geburtstag seinen ins mit gegangen Restaurant
4 dem fahren werde Bus zur Party später Ich mit
5 Berlin Wir dem sind mit Zug nach gefahren gestern
6 haben gefeiert in Abend einem Restaurant Wir heute

70 siebzig

Kapitel 3

Using two time frames: past and future (Unit 5, page 66)

 Copy and complete the sentences with the correct verbs in the past and future tenses.

1. Letzte Woche **hatte** er braune Haare, aber nächste Woche **wird** er grüne Haare **haben**. (*had, will have*)
2. Früher ___ wir das nicht ___, aber nächstes Jahr ___ wir das ___. (*celebrated, will celebrate*)
3. Gestern ___ wir zum Fest ___, aber morgen ___ wir zu einer Feier ___. (*went, will go*)
4. Meine Freundin, die traurig ___, ___ sicher lockerer und ruhiger ___. (*was, will be*)
5. Letztes Jahr ___ es keine Party, aber nächste Woche ___ es eine große Feier ___. (*there was, there will be*)
6. Gestern ___ ich auf einer Party Spaß ___, aber morgen ___ wir zu Hause ___. (*had, will stay*)

In pairs, take turns to read out the questions in the perfect tense and change them into the future tense.

Example: 1 Was hast du an Silvester gemacht? Was wirst du an Silvester machen?

1. Was hast du an Silvester gemacht?
2. Wie hast du deinen letzten Geburtstag gefeiert?
3. Was für Geschenke hast du bekommen?
4. Was hast du im Kino gesehen?
5. Was hast du auf der Party gegessen und getrunken?
6. Wohin bist du am Wochenende mit deinen Freunden gegangen?

in + accusative or dative (Unit 5, page 67)

 Listen. Copy and complete the sentences with *in* + the article in the accusative or dative case.

1. Ich fahre **in die** Stadt (*f*).
2. Ich kaufe Geschenke ___ Stadtmitte (*f*).
3. Ich möchte ___ Geschäfte (*pl*) gehen.
4. ___ Geschäften (*pl*) gibt es Kostüme für Fasching.
5. Er hat sein Kostüm ___ Internet (*n*) gekauft.
6. In den Ferien spiele ich immer ___ Park (*m*) Fußball.
7. Ich treffe sie ___ Restaurant (*n*).
8. Ich gehe ___ Kino (*n*).

	masc	fem	neut	pl
accusative	in den	in die	in das	in die
dative	in dem	in der	in dem	in den

in + das → ins
in + dem → im

Remember to use the accusative when there is movement involved and the dative when there is no movement.

Los geht's!

 Translate the sentences into German.

1. I get on very well with my brother, who is very friendly.
2. For my birthday, I am going to the cinema with my friends.
3. Last year, we went to a New Year's Eve party, but this year we will stay at home.
4. Before, my mother was very strict but now she is always funny.

- Remember *mit* is followed by the dative.
- Think about word order here.
- Make sure you use the right tense with each time phrase.

Kapitel 3 Lese- und Hörtest

Reading

 Lesen 1

Birthday celebrations. You read Mika's blog about his birthday. Read the statements and write **A** if only statement **A** is correct, **B** if only statement **B** is correct, or **A + B** if both statements **A** and **B** are correct.

> Letztes Wochenende habe ich meinen achtzehnten Geburtstag mit meiner Familie und meiner Freundin gefeiert. Normalerweise mache ich eine Party zu Hause oder bei einem Freund aus meiner Schule, aber dieses Jahr haben wir in einem türkischen Restaurant in der Stadt gegessen. Türkisches Essen schmeckt mir, obwohl meine Schwester lieber Pizza isst.
>
> Die Feier hat uns wirklich Spaß gemacht, weil die Stimmung toll war und das Essen einfach lecker war. Fast die ganze Familie war da. Wir haben alle viel gelacht und getanzt. Ich habe auch schöne Geschenke bekommen: neue Geräte und Geld, das ich für meine Sommerferien in der Türkei benutzen kann.

1 **A** Mika celebrated his birthday with family members and his school friends.
  B Mika has a girlfriend.
2 **A** Mika celebrated his birthday with a party at home.
  B Mika went out for a special meal for his birthday.
3 **A** Mika and his guests ate Turkish food.
  B Mika's sister ate pizza.
4 **A** Mika enjoyed his birthday because of the atmosphere.
  B Mika enjoyed his birthday because of the food.
5 **A** Mika's presents included a flight to Turkey for the holidays.
  B Mika's presents included some gadgets.

 Lesen 2

Carnival. You read an extract from Alina's diary.

> Gestern sind meine Familie und ich zum Karneval in Köln gegangen. Das Fest hat am Marktplatz in der Stadt stattgefunden und da gab es eine Menge Leute mit bunter Kleidung. Es gab viel Musik und wir haben in den Straßen laut gesungen und viel getanzt. Später am Nachmittag habe ich ein Stück **Torte** gekauft und das hat sehr gut geschmeckt. Das war ein spannender Tag, den ich nie vergessen werde!

> ⭐ Use the context of the text and the surrounding language to help you work out what the unknown word might mean. Here, Alina uses the verb *schmecken* to give her opinion about the noun. Can you remember what this means?

1 Answer the following questions in **English**.
  a Where was the carnival? Give **two** details.
  b What did Alina do at the carnival? Give **two** details.
2 Read the last two sentences again. What is **Torte**?
  A a type of food
  B a type of drink
  C a type of music

Translate these sentences into English.

Be careful as this sentence is in a different tense from the others.

Do you remember what these possessive adjectives mean?

These are both negatives, but they have different translations.

In this sentence the word der is a relative pronoun.

There are two examples of the verb finden. Think about how they can be translated.

Read to the end of the sentence before starting to translate: this is a separable verb.

1 Murat hat seine Großeltern nie kennengelernt.
2 Dein Bruder, der Thomas heißt, findet Weihnachten spannend.
3 Ich finde es wichtig, dass die Gesellschaft Unterschiede feiert.
4 Berühmte Persönlichkeiten können einen negativen Einfluss haben.
5 Meine Stiefmutter kommt überhaupt nicht gut mit ihrem Vater aus.

Listening

Best friends. Hanna is talking about her best friend, Charlotte. What does she say? Listen to the recording and write **A**, **B** or **C** for each question.

1 Charlotte …
 A is very tall.   B likes swimming.   C is sporty.
2 Both Hanna and Charlotte have …
 A green eyes.   B short hair.   C long, brown hair.
3 a Charlotte is …
 A serious.   B independent.   C just like Hanna.
 b Hanna and Charlotte …
 A get on well.   B spend the weekend at home.   C always talk.

Remember that in this type of task, all the answer options might be mentioned in the recording. There are a lot of adjectives in this recording, so listen carefully to check who they relate to.

Role models. Jan and Mia are talking about their role models. Answer the questions in English. You do not have to answer in full sentences.

1 Why are role models important to Mia?
2 Who is her role model and why?
3 What does Jan say about role models in his life?
4 What is a good role model, according to Jan?

Remember that your answers need to be precise, but you don't have to write in full sentences.

Dictation

You will hear five short sentences. Write down exactly what you hear in German.

Think carefully about how these sounds are pronounced when you write down what you hear:
v, w, z
u, ü, y

There will be some words in the dictation task that are not on the vocabulary list, but don't panic: use your knowledge of sound-spelling links to help you transcribe these words accurately.

Kapitel 3 — Mündlicher Test

Role-play

1 Look at the role-play card and prepare what you are going to say.

You can choose anyone such as a sportsperson, actor, politician, or just someone from your family or friends.

Find any two positive adjectives. Even if it's a famous person, they won't be fact-checked!

You are talking to your Swiss friend about role models.
1 Say **who** your favourite role model is.
2 Say **where** and **how often** you have seen them.
3 Say **two** things you like about them. (Give **two** details.)
4 Say whether you think role models are important and **why (not)**. (Give **one** opinion and **one** reason.)
5 **?** Ask your friend a question about role models.

This point requires you to use a past tense.

Remember to put the verb at the end if you use a subordinate clause.

This can be any question, but just saying 'Do you have a role model?' could be the simplest.

2 Practise what you have prepared. Then, using your notes, listen and respond to the teacher.

3 Listen to Alex's answers. Make a note of:
  a how he answers the questions for points 1–4
  b what question he asks for point 5.

Reading aloud

4 Look at this task. With a partner, read the sentences aloud, paying attention to the underlined letters.

Zu meinem Geburtstag mache ich normalerweise eine Party zu Hause.

Ich lade meine Freunde ein, wir essen Kuchen und wir singen und tanzen im Garten.

Dieses Jahr werde ich Zeit mit meinen Verwandten verbringen. Wir werden zuerst ins Kino gehen.

Später werden wir ins Restaurant gehen und viel typisches türkisches Essen probieren.

Think carefully about how to pronounce these sounds:
v, w, z
u, ü, y

5 Listen and check your pronunciation.

6 Listen to the teacher asking the four follow-up questions. Translate each question into English and prepare your own answer to each one. Then listen again and respond to the teacher.

Photo card

7 Look at the photos and listen to Alex describing them. Write the letters (a–f) in the order in which Alex mentions these points.

a weather   c food and drinks   e friends
b clothing   d presents   f smiling

You will be asked to talk about the content of these photos. You must say at least one thing about each photo.

After you have spoken about the content of the photos, you will be asked questions related to any of the topics within the theme of **Popular culture**.

Your responses should be as **full and detailed** as possible.

8 Prepare your own description of the photos. Then, with a partner, take turns describing them.

> Auf dem ersten Foto gibt es …

9 Listen to the teacher's first follow-up question, *Wie hast du Silvester gefeiert?*, and Alex's response. Write down the <u>eight</u> missing past participles to complete the text.

Ich habe Silvester mit meiner Familie zu Hause **1** . Wir hatten eine wunderbare Party im Garten und ich habe meine Freunde **2** . Wir haben Musik **3** und viel **4** . Ich habe auch mit meinen Freunden **5** und um vierundzwanzig Uhr haben wir zusammen **6** und **7** . Das hat uns wirklich Spaß **8** .

The past participles are a mixture of regular and irregular verbs. One of them is a separable verb.

10 The teacher then asks Alex, *Wie feierst du normalerweise deinen Geburtstag?* Listen to his response and answer the questions.

1 What is the date of his birthday?
2 When does he usually celebrate it?
3 What does he do in the morning? Give **two** details.
4 Who does he meet at lunchtime?
5 Where does he like going in the evening? Why?

11 Listen to two more follow-up questions and prepare your answers. Then respond to the recording. Make your answers as full as possible, including opinions and reasons.

12 Prepare your own answers to as many of the Module 3 questions on page 226 as you can. Then practise with your partner.

fünfundsiebzig **75**

Kapitel 3 Schreibtest

Translation

 Reorder the German words to make correct translations of the English sentences. Add punctuation and make the first word start with a capital letter.

1. I have a brother who is tall.
2. She gets on well with her father.
3. She is a footballer and she has won quite often.
4. Yesterday I went to the party by bus.
5. Next month I will celebrate my birthday at home.

1. Bruder ist ich groß der habe einen
2. mit versteht sie ihrem gut Vater sich
3. ziemlich hat sie Fußballspielerin und gewonnen ist oft sie
4. dem mit gefahren ich zur gestern Feier Bus bin
5. feiern Hause zu werde Geburtstag meinen ich Monat nächsten

> Word order is very important in each of these sentences. Don't forget the 'time – manner – place' rule.

 Translate these sentences into German.
1. I have a sister who is short.
2. He gets on well with his mother.
3. He is a singer, but he has sung very rarely.
4. Last weekend I went to the festival by car.
5. Next year I will celebrate my birthday at the cinema.

90-word writing task

 Look at this writing exam task and then, for each bullet point:
1. think about the vocabulary and structures you have learned, which you could use in your answers. For example:
   - **nouns**, **verbs** and **adjectives** to write about celebrations and the **names** of festivals you might want to mention. Consider including **nouns** for **food and drink.**
   - language for **narrating a story** about how you celebrated
   - how to explain what you **will do** and **why**
2. write down three or four ideas for what you could write about
3. identify which tense(s) you could use in your answer
4. make a list of verbs, connectives, intensifiers and sequencing words you would like to use.

> You are writing to your friend about celebrations.
>
> Write approximately **90** words in **German**.
>
> You must write something about each bullet point.
>
> Describe:
> - the type of celebration you like
> - what you did to celebrate your best friend's birthday
> - what activity you will do after your exams.

> You can use any language you are familiar with and secure about using in your written work, but always make sure that what you write answers the question. Don't be tempted to bring in other language just to 'showcase' what you know if it causes your response to stray off-topic.

Kapitel 3

Lesen 4 Read Jenna's answer to the exam task. Answer the questions in the coloured boxes (1–5).

1. This is an example of **complex language**. What does it mean? Find <u>three</u> more examples of complex language in the text.

2. Jenna uses a **variety of nouns**. What do these words mean? Find <u>two</u> more examples.

3. Which **tense** is this? Find another example of this tense. Does Jenna use any other tenses?

> Ich finde Feste toll, aber mein Geburtstag gefällt mir am besten. Ich bekomme viele Geschenke. Auch darf ich immer einen großen Kuchen haben.
>
> Petra ist meine beste Freundin und wir sind zu ihrem Geburtstag schwimmen gegangen, weil sie Sportfan ist. Danach gab es ein Fußballspiel. Das hat uns sehr gut gefallen. Wir haben Würste und Pommes gegessen und Cola getrunken. Das war lecker! Die ganze Feier war wunderbar.
>
> Nach den Prüfungen werden wir eine Fahrradfahrt machen und dann am Abend wird es eine Feier am Strand geben. Das wird Spaß machen.

4. To **avoid repetition**, Jenna has used these synonyms. Can you find any more examples?

5. Which connective could you use here to form an **extended sentence**? What other connectives does Jenna use?

Lesen 5 Read Jenna's answer again and answer the questions.

1. Why does Jenna like her birthday?
2. What activities did Petra do on her birthday, and why?
3. What did they eat and drink on Petra's birthday?
4. What sporting activity will they do after the exams?
5. Where will the party take place?

Schreiben 6 Prepare your own answer to the task.

- Think about how you can develop your answer for each bullet point.
- Look back at your notes from exercises 3 and 4.
- Look at the 'Challenge checklist' and consider how you can show off your German!
- Write a **brief** plan and organise your answer into paragraphs.
- Write your answer and then carefully check for accuracy.

Challenge checklist

	✓ Past, present and future time frames
	✓ Connectives (*und, aber*) and time phrases (*nächstes Jahr, letzte Woche*)
	✓ Some extended sentences
	✓ An opinion verb (*ich liebe, ich mag*) and simple adjectives (*interessant, gut*)
	✓ A wider range of tenses and different verbs
	✓ Different persons of the verb (*meine Klasse, die Menschen, meine Freunde und ich*)
	✓ More varied opinion phrases (*ich finde, … gefällt mir eigentlich nicht, das interessiert mich*)
	✓ Intensifiers and qualifiers (*so, ganz, total*)
	✓ A wider range of interesting vocabulary (*die Stimmung, eine Menge, danach, eine Feier*)
	✓ Sentences with more than one tense (*Mein Bruder heißt Ben und er hatte … Geburtstag*)
	✓ Relative clauses (*Meine Freundin, die Petra heißt, ist …*)
	✓ Complex language: separable verbs (*ich lade … ein, wir gehen … aus*), time – manner – place, subject–verb inversion (*Natürlich gehe ich …*), use of the dative case (*mit meinen Freunden, mit ihr*)
	✓ Use of sequencing words (*dann, endlich*)
	✓ More varied conjunctions (*weil, dass*)

siebenundsiebzig

Kapitel 3 Wörter

Key:
bold = this word will appear in higher exams only
* = this word is not on the vocabulary list but you may use it in your own sentences

Feste in der deutschsprachigen Welt (pages 56–57):

Feste	Festivals/celebrations
Ich finde …	I find/think …
den Markt	the market
Meiner Meinung nach ist …	In my opinion, … is
das Fest	the festival, celebration
interessant, …	interesting, …
langweilig, …	boring, …
laut, …	loud, …
schlecht, …	bad, …
schön, …	beautiful, …
teuer, …	expensive, …
toll, …	great, terrific, …
weil …	because …
mir das (nicht) gut gefällt.	I (don't) like it.
mir das (keinen) Spaß macht.	it's (not) fun for me.
das mein *Lieblingshobby ist.	it's my favourite hobby.
es (zu) viele Menschen gibt.	there are (too) many people.
mich das (nicht) interessiert.	it interests (doesn't interest) me.
ich es (nicht) mag.	I (don't) like it.
Der Weihnachtsmarkt	The Christmas market
Das *Radsportfest	The cycling festival
Das *Blumenfest	The flower festival
… interessiert mich (nicht), …	… interests / doesn't interest me …
weil er/es … ist.	because it is …
laut	loud/noisy.
schön	lovely/beautiful.
teuer	expensive.
toll	great/terrific/amazing.
weil es eine Menge Leute gibt.	because there are a lot of people.

Wie ist deine Familie? (pages 58–59):

Familie	Family
Beschreib (mir) deine Familie!	Describe your family (to me)!
In meiner Familie gibt es meinen (Bruder) / meine (Schwester) / meine (Eltern).	In my family, there are my (brother/sister/parents).
Das ist mein (Bruder) / meine (Schwester) / mein (Kätzchen).	That is my (brother/sister/kitten).
Das sind meine (Eltern/Mütter/Väter/Brüder/Schwestern/Geschwister).	These are my (parents/mothers/fathers/brothers/sisters/siblings).
Ich bin Einzelkind.	I am an only child.
Mein/Meine …, der/die/das … heißt, …	My … , who is called …, …
hat … Haare/Augen.	has … hair/eyes.
blaue	blue
*blonde	blond(e)
braune	brown
graue	grey
grüne	green
kurze	short
lange	long
rote	red
schwarze	black
ist …	is …
groß	big/tall
klein	small
Meine …, die … heißen, sind …	My … , who are called …, are …
Meine …, die nie geheiratet haben, sind …	My …, who never married, are …
Er/Sie/Es ist … / Sie sind …	He/She/It is … / They are …
ab und zu	now and again
immer	always
manchmal	sometimes
nicht	not
nie	never
oft	often
sehr	very
total	completely
ziemlich	rather
freundlich	friendly
glücklich	happy
großzügig	generous
lustig	funny
traurig	sad
Er/Sie trägt (k)eine **Brille**.	He/She (doesn't) wear glasses.

Deine Beziehungen (pages 60–61):

Beziehungen	Relationships
Hast du eine gute Beziehung zu …?	Do you have a good relationship with …?
Kommst du gut mit … aus?	Do you get on well with …?
deinem (Vater)	your (father)
deiner (Tante)	your (aunt)
deinen (Großeltern)	your (grandparents)
Ja, ich komme gut mit … aus.	Yes, I get on well with …
Ich verstehe mich gut mit …	I get on well with …
meinem (Onkel) / ihm, weil er … ist.	my (uncle) / him, because he is …
meiner (Stiefmutter) / ihr, weil sie … ist.	my stepmother / her, because she is …
meinen (Eltern) / ihnen, weil sie … sind.	my parents / them, because they are …
aktiv	active
ärgerlich	annoying
böse	angry
ehrlich	honest
ernst	serious
gemein	mean
komisch	funny, strange
laut	loud
lieb	sweet, kind
sportlich	sporty
streng	strict
süß	sweet
unabhängig	independent
verantwortlich	responsible

Kapitel 3

Wer ist dir wichtig? (pages 62–63):

Wer ist dir wichtig?	Who is important to you?
Ich habe keine **Vorbilder**, da/weil …	I have no role models, because …
ich sie nicht brauche.	I don't need them.
Ich finde **Vorbilder** … nützlich/wichtig/super, da/weil …	I find role models … useful/important/great, because …
sie mir *Inspiration geben.	they give me inspiration.
sie mir helfen.	they help me.
sie vielen Leuten helfen.	they help a lot of people.
sie hart arbeiten.	they work hard.
sie erfolgreich sind.	they are successful.
sie **hilfreich** sind.	they are helpful.
sie für Rechte **kämpfen**.	they campaign for our rights.
Meiner Meinung nach sind **Vorbilder** … unwichtig/nutzlos, da/weil …	In my opinion, role models are … unimportant/useless, because …
sie nicht in der echten Welt leben.	they don't live in the real world.
sie nicht interessant sind.	they are not interesting.
Mein/Meine … ist mein **Vorbild**, da/weil …	My … is my role model, because …
er/sie Zeit für mich hat.	he/she has time for me.
er/sie mich akzeptiert.	he/she accepts me.
er/sie mich unterstützt.	he/she supports me.
er/sie so viel gemacht hat.	he/she has done so much.

Wir haben gefeiert! (pages 64–65):

Feste	Festivals/celebrations
Gestern …	Yesterday …
Am Wochenende …	At the weekend …
Letzte Woche …	Last week …
Neulich …	Recently, the other day …
Letztes Jahr …	Last year …
In den Ferien …	In the holidays …
Im Winter …	In winter …
der Christ / die Christin	Christian
der/die Hindu	Hindu
der Jude / die Jüdin	Jew
der Muslim / die Muslimin	Muslim
der/die *Sikh	Sikh
Am Musikfest …	At a music festival …
Am Karneval …	At Carnival …
An Neujahr …	At New Year …
An Silvester …	On New Year's Eve …
Auf einer Party/Feier …	At a party/festival/celebration …
An *Chanukka / *Eid al-Fitr / *Hola Mohalla …	At Hanakkah / Eid al-Fitr / Hola Mohalla …
Zu meinem Geburtstag …	On my birthday …
Zu Weihnachten/Ostern …	At Christmas/Easter…

gab es eine Party / eine Feier / ein Fest.	there was a party / a celebration / a festival.
habe ich … / haben wir …	I/we …
viel (mit Freunden / mit meiner Familie / im Restaurant) …	… a lot (with friends / with my family / in a restaurant).
gefeiert.	celebrated
gelacht.	laughed
gesungen.	sang
getanzt.	danced
gegessen.	ate
getrunken.	drank
nette Leute kennengelernt.	got to know nice/kind people.
Spaß gehabt.	had fun.
bin ich / sind wir … gefahren/gegangen.	I / we went …
mit dem Bus / mit dem Zug / zu Fuß	by bus / by train / on foot.
ins Kino / nach Berlin	to the cinema / to Berlin.
zum Fest / zur Party	to a festival/party.

Partyzeit! (pages 66–67):

Partys	Parties
der Anfang	start, beginning
der Film	film
der Geburtstag	birthday
der Kuchen	cake
der Silvester	New Year's Eve
der Sommer	summer
die Musik	music
die Party	party
das Fest	festival
das Jahr	year
das Kino	cinema
die Ferien	holidays
der Spaß	fun
das Neujahr	New Year, New Year's Day
das Weihnachten	Christmas
einladen	to invite
essen	to eat
feiern	to celebrate
gehen	to go
hören	to hear, listen
lachen	to laugh
organisieren	to organise
planen	to plan
singen	to sing
tanzen	to dance
trinken	to drink
stattfinden	to take place
danach	afterwards
letzt	last
nächst	next
normalerweise	normally
Es gibt …	There is/are …
Es gab …	There was/were …
Es wird … geben	There will be …
Ich mag (Silvester) weil …	I like (New Year) because …
Letztes Jahr haben wir (*Diwali) gefeiert.	Last year we celebrated (Diwali).

neunundsiebzig

Kapitel 4 — Bleib gesund!

Ich liebe Sport
- Learning about favourite sports in the German-speaking world
- Using comparative and superlative adjectives and adverbs

A Weißt du was …?

1. In der Schweiz waren die beliebtesten Sportarten in den letzten Jahren: Wandern (56,9%), Fahrradfahren (42%), Schwimmen (38,6%) und Skifahren (34,9%).

2. In Österreich ist der häufigste Sport Fahrradfahren. 38% der Österreicher fahren regelmäßig Fahrrad.

3. In Deutschland gibt es fast so viele Fahrräder wie Menschen: Es gibt 83,2 Millionen Einwohner und 82,8 Millionen Fahrräder!

4. Schwimmen im Freien ist in Österreich beliebter als Schwimmen im Hallenbad: Es gibt über 300 Freibäder, aber nur ungefähr 100 Hallenbäder, und es gibt auch über 400 Badeseen.

5. Der Bodensee ist nicht nur der größte Badesee im deutschsprachigen Raum, sondern auch ein Dreiländersee: er gehört zu Deutschland, Österreich und der Schweiz.

6. In der Schweiz treiben 59% der Jugendlichen zwischen 15 und 24 Jahren mindestens drei Stunden pro Woche Sport.

7. Deutschland ist die zweitgrößte Ski-Nation der Welt (nach den USA und vor China). 38% der Deutschen machen gerne Wintersport.

8. Die Schweiz hat 38 Berge, die höher als 4 000 Meter sind. Der höchste Berg in der Schweiz ist die Dufourspitze mit 4 634 Metern.

das Hallenbad (¨er)	indoor swimming pool
das Freibad (¨er)	outdoor swimming pool
der Badesee (-n)	lake for swimming
der Bodensee	Lake Constance

B

1 Aïsha

Welchen Sport treibst du regelmäßig?
Ich gehe gern laufen und ich spiele einmal pro Woche Tennis.

Was ist dein Lieblingssport?
Mein Lieblingssport ist Fußball, aber im Winter gehe ich am liebsten Skifahren.

2 Mia

Welche Sportart treibst du regelmäßig?
Ich mache regelmäßig Fitnesstraining und ich spiele auch gern Basketball.

Und welche Sportart machst du nicht so gern?
Ich gehe nicht gern wandern, weil es meistens langweilig ist. Ich finde Klettern viel interessanter!

3 Leon

Treibst du regelmäßig Sport?
Ja, ich treibe normalerweise viel Sport. Ich spiele zweimal pro Woche Fußball und am Wochenende fahre ich oft mit meiner Familie Fahrrad.

Was war deine beste Leistung?
Letztes Jahr bin ich 65km an einem Tag Fahrrad gefahren! Es war super und ich möchte das öfter tun.

Kulturzone Kapitel 4

 Lesen 1 Read the article (A). Is each statement below true or false?
1. The most popular sport in Switzerland is hiking.
2. Cycling is the most common sport in Austria.
3. There are more bikes than people in Germany.
4. Austrians prefer to swim outside.
5. The *Bodensee* borders two countries.
6. Over half of the young people in Austria do at least three hours of sport per week.
7. Germany is the biggest skiing nation in the world.
8. A total of 38 mountains in Switzerland are higher than 4000 metres.

The **comparative** is used to **compare** two things: just add **-er** to the adjective and use **als** to mean 'than'.
klein small   klein**er** small**er**
beliebt popular   beliebt**er more** popular

Die Schweiz ist kleiner als Österreich.
Switzerland is smaller **than** Austria.

If the adjective comes **before a noun**, it needs to agree in gender, number and case:
Skifahren ist ein gefährlicherer Sport als Tennis.
Skiing is a **more dangerous** sport than tennis.

The **superlative** is used to say something is 'the most ...': add **-(e)st** at the end of the adjective and make sure it agrees with the noun.
Skifahren ist der gefährlichste Sport.
Skiing is the **most dangerous** sport.

Some adjectives are **irregular**:
gut – besser – der/die/das beste
nah – näher – der/die/das nächste
viel(e) – mehr – die/die/das meiste

One-syllable adjectives often add an umlaut:
groß – gr**ö**ßer – der/die/das gr**ö**ßte

Page 92

sondern is used to contrast two ideas in a sentence and means 'but rather' or 'on the contrary'.

It is also used in the phrase *nicht nur ... sondern auch*, which means 'not only ..., but also':

Ich schwimme nicht im Hallenbad, sondern im Meer.
I don't swim in the swimming pool, **but rather** in the sea.

Ich spiele nicht nur Tennis, sondern auch Tischtennis.
I **not only** play tennis, **but also** table tennis.

 Lesen 2 Read the article again. Find and write down **five** superlative phrases and **two** comparative adjectives.
Example: 1 *die beliebtesten Sportarten*

Ski is pronounced like the English 'she'.
*Ski*fahren can also be spelled *Schi*fahren.
The letter combination **schw** is pronounced like 'shv'.
Listen and repeat the sentence.
*Die **Schw**eizer gehen gern **schw**immen, aber am liebsten fahren sie **Ski**.*

 Hören 3 Listen to and read the interviews with Aïsha, Mia and Leon (B). Translate the underlined sentences into English.

 Schreiben 4 Translate the sentences into German.
1. Germany is bigger than Austria.
2. I find climbing more interesting than hiking.
3. Winter sports are more popular in Switzerland than in Great Britain.
4. Mont Blanc is the highest mountain in Europe.
5. Football is the most popular sport in Germany.
6. Swimming was my best achievement.

Ich	treibe	regelmäßig häufig ab und zu selten	Sport.
	spiele		Fußball. Tennis. Basketball.
	mache		Fitnesstraining.
	fahre		Fahrrad. Ski.
	gehe		klettern. schwimmen. wandern.

Mein Lieblingssport ist ..., aber ich ... auch gern ...
Ich ... nicht gern ..., weil ...
Im Sommer ... ich lieber ...
Im Winter ... am liebsten ...

 Sprechen 5 In pairs, take turns to ask and answer the following questions.
- Welchen Sport treibst du regelmäßig?
- Was ist dein Lieblingssport?
- Welchen Sport machst du nicht so gern?

 Schreiben 6 Write down your answers to exercise 5, adding more information where possible.

einundachtzig

1 Willst du fit und gesund sein?

- Talking about healthy lifestyles
- Using *um ... zu*
- Practising an extended conversation

1 Listen and read the texts. Then answer the questions.

Meine Gesundheit ist sehr wichtig für mich. Ich will später Profi-Fußballspielerin werden und deshalb esse ich gesund: wenig Zucker, aber viel Obst und Gemüse. <u>Ich trinke die ganze Zeit Wasser, um gesund zu sein</u>, und weder rauche ich noch nehme ich Drogen. Ich gehe jeden Tag ins Fitness-Studio, weil ich in Form sein will, und natürlich trinke ich keinen Alkohol.
Sophia

Für mich ist es schwer, gesund zu leben. Wasser schmeckt mir nicht und ich trinke viel lieber Cola. Ich mag auch nur sehr wenig Gemüse und deshalb esse ich oft Pasta mit Butter oder sogar Hamburger mit Pommes. Außerdem rauchen meine Freunde alle und es gibt viel Gruppendruck, aber ich werde nie rauchen. <u>Ich treibe auch viel Sport und schwimme jede Woche, um fit zu bleiben</u> und nicht übergewichtig zu werden.
Florian

Gesund leben ist kein Problem für mich! Ich bin noch jung und mein Körper ist stark. Jedes Wochenende gehe ich mit meinen Freunden feiern. Ich spreche mit Freunden and tanze viel! Einige Freunde trinken aber viel Alkohol (Wein, Bier und so weiter) und rauchen E-Zigaretten. <u>Sie denken, dass sie betrunken sein müssen, um Spaß zu haben</u>. Manchmal nehmen sie auch Drogen, aber das finde ich wirklich blöd. Ich will nicht süchtig sein! Ich weiß, dass ich nicht genug schlafe, aber ich kann natürlich schlafen, wenn ich älter bin!
Marlene

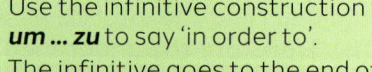
die E-Zigarette vape

1 Why does Sophia eat healthily?
2 What <u>three</u> things does Sophia **not** do?
3 Why is it difficult for Florian to live healthily? (Give <u>two</u> reasons.)
4 What is Florian under pressure to do?
5 Name the <u>three</u> unhealthy things that Marlene's friends do.
6 What does Marlene say she can do when she is older?

> **G**
> Use the infinitive construction **um ... zu** to say 'in order to'.
> The <u>infinitive</u> goes to the end of the clause and there is a comma before *um*:
> *Ich esse viel Obst, **um** gesund **zu** <u>sein</u>.*
> I eat lots of fruit (in order) to be healthy.
> *Ich mache viel Sport, **um** fit **zu** <u>bleiben</u>.*
> I do lots of sport (in order) to keep fit.
>
> **ohne ... zu** (without) and **statt ... zu** (instead of) are used in the same way:
> *Ich esse gesund, **ohne** leckeres Essen auf**zu**geben.*
> I eat healthily without giving up tasty food.
> ***Statt** Kaffee **zu** trinken, trinke ich Wasser.*
> Instead of drinking coffee, I drink water.
> Page 93

2 Translate the <u>underlined</u> phrases in exercise 1 into English.

3 Translate the sentences into German.

> Where should adverbs of time be positioned?

> Remember that *weil* and *dass* send the verb to the end of the clause.

1 My sister never drinks alcohol, because it is unhealthy.
2 I know that I don't eat enough fruit and vegetables.
3 We do lots of sports in order to stay healthy. — Use *um ... zu* + infinitive.
4 They neither smoke nor take drugs. — Use *weder ... noch*.
5 I celebrate with friends, in order to have fun.

4 Listen to Aisha and Fred talking about their daily lives. What do they say is healthy or unhealthy about their lifestyle? Copy and complete the table in English with two details for each box.

	healthy	unhealthy
Aisha		
Fred		

 5 Read Detlev's blog post and select the three correct statements.

Hallo, ich bin Detlev und ich komme aus Leipzig. Meiner Meinung nach ist es sehr wichtig, ein gesundes Leben zu führen. Ich finde, man soll jeden Tag mindestens zwei Liter Wasser trinken und auch mehr als fünf Portionen Obst und Gemüse essen. Ich esse oft Salat mit Hähnchen statt Fastfood. Protein ist wichtig! Dazu glaube ich auch, dass wir keinen Alkohol trinken sollen. Er ist sehr schlecht für die Gesundheit und außerdem schmeckt er mir überhaupt nicht.

Aber ich habe einige Freunde, die ab und zu auf Partys rauchen. Ich glaube, dass es sehr ungesund ist. Ich muss sagen, dass ich zu wenig schlafe und viel zu lange auf dem Computer spiele. Nächstes Jahr, wenn ich Prüfungen habe, werde ich versuchen, jede Nacht acht Stunden zu schlafen.

1 Detlev thinks it's important to lead a healthy life.
2 He drinks at least two litres of water a day.
3 He likes the taste of alcohol.
4 His friends sometimes smoke at parties.
5 He chats to his friends on his computer.
6 He wants to sleep eight hours a night.

 6 Translate the second paragraph of Detlev's blog post into English.

 7 Listen to the dialogue, then read it aloud with a partner.

- *Wie isst oder trinkst du gesund?*
- *Ich esse viel Gemüse und ich trinke viel Wasser.*
- *Was machst du, um fit zu bleiben?*
- *Ich spiele jeden Tag Fußball.*
- *Was hast du in letzter Zeit gemacht, um fit zu bleiben?*
- *Ich habe im Park Tennis gespielt und ich bin ins Fitness-Studio gegangen.*
- *Wie findest du Rauchen? Warum?*
- *Ich finde Rauchen schlecht, weil es ungesund ist.*
- *Ah, interessant!*
- *Was machst du, um fit zu bleiben?*
- *Ich trinke viel Wasser und ich laufe jeden Tag.*

 8 Prepare your own answers using the key language box and practise with your partner.

Ich	treibe		Sport.
	spiele	viel jeden Tag (sehr) oft	Tennis. Fußball. Basketball.
	gehe	jede Woche regelmäßig immer	schwimmen. laufen. ins Fitness-Studio.
	esse	kaum nie (nicht) genug	viel Obst. viel Gemüse. Fastfood.
	trinke		Wasser. Alkohol.
Ich habe	Tennis/Fußball		gespielt.
Ich bin	ins Fitness-Studio / laufen		gegangen.
Ich finde Meiner Meinung nach ist	Rauchen	sehr ziemlich extrem total	schlecht, ... blöd, ...
..., weil es		ungesund langweilig gefährlich	ist.

2 Es geht mir nicht gut

- Talking about accidents and illnesses
- Using modal verbs in the imperfect tense
- Using *seit*

 1 Listen (1–15) and write the letters (a–r) for the parts of the body mentioned.

 2 Select <u>six</u> parts of the body from exercise 1 and write sentences describing what's wrong.

 3 In pairs, create dialogues. Take turns to read out a question from the key language box, point to a part of the body and respond.
- *Wie geht es dir?*
- *Nicht so gut. Ich habe <u>Kopfschmerzen</u>.*

 4 Read the forum posts and find the German for the phrases.
1 while playing football
2 since yesterday
3 I couldn't move my arm for three days.
4 three years ago
5 I broke my leg while skiing.
6 I had to go to hospital in Austria.
7 I had an accident while cycling.
8 I injured my shoulder.

Wie geht es dir?	Ich habe (Zahn)schmerzen.
Was ist los?	Ich habe mir (den Finger / die Nase /
Was hast du?	das Bein) verletzt/gebrochen.

a das Gesicht
b das Ohr (-en)
c der Mund
d der Kopf
e die Schulter (-n)
f der Rücken
g der Bauch
h das Bein (-e)
i das Auge (-n)
j die Nase
k der Zahn (¨e)
l die Haut
m das Herz
n der Arm (-e)
o die Hand (¨e)
p der Finger (-)
q das Knie (-)
r der Fuß (¨e)

 Letzten Monat habe ich mir beim Fußballspielen das Knie verletzt. Ich konnte zwei Wochen lang nicht gehen, aber jetzt ist mein Knie wieder okay und ich kann seit gestern wieder Fußball spielen.

 Ich habe mir letzte Woche beim Fitnesstraining einen Muskel im Arm verletzt. Ich konnte den Arm drei Tage lang nicht bewegen, aber gestern hatte ich einen Termin bei der Ärztin. Sie hat mich untersucht und mir ein Medikament gegeben.

 Vor drei Jahren habe ich mir beim Skifahren das Bein gebrochen. Es gab so viel Blut! Ich hatte viele Schmerzen und ich musste in Österreich ins Krankenhaus gehen, aber jetzt ist mein Bein wieder gut.

 Vor zwei Jahren hatte ich beim Fahrradfahren einen Unfall. Ich habe mir die Schulter verletzt und ich durfte drei Wochen lang keinen Sport treiben. Seitdem bin ich viel vorsichtiger.

G Use **beim** + <u>noun</u> to say 'while doing something':
*Ich hatte einen Unfall **beim** <u>Fahrradfahren</u>.*
I had an accident **while** cycling.

Remember: in German you can change any verb into a <u>noun</u> simply by using a capital letter. The noun is always neuter:
*Ich habe mir den Arm **beim** <u>Schwimmen</u> verletzt.*
I injured my arm **while** swimming.

Page 93

Kapitel 4

Lesen 5 Read the forum posts in exercise 4 again and find the modal verbs in the imperfect tense.

Schreiben 6 Translate the sentences into German.
1. I was not allowed to play football.
2. He could not sleep.
3. You (informal, sg) had to stay in bed.
4. We did not have to go to school.

> **G** Modal verbs in the **imperfect tense** have these endings:
>
> | **können** (can, be able) | **dürfen** (may, be allowed) | **müssen** (must, have to) |
> |---|---|---|
> | ich kon**nte** | ich dur**fte** | ich muss**te** |
> | du konn**test** | du durf**test** | du muss**test** |
> | er/sie/es/man konn**te** | er/sie/es/man durf**te** | er/sie/es/man muss**te** |
>
> Page 94

Hören 7 Listen. Copy and complete the table in English. (1–4)

	invitation to …	problem/excuse	since when? when did it happen?	any extra information
1				

Schreiben 8 Look at the role-play card and write your own responses using the key language box below.

> You are talking to your German friend.
> You should address your friend as *du*.
>
> - *Hallo! Wie geht's?*
> - Say you don't feel well.
> - *Was ist los?*
> - Say what's wrong.
> - *Seit wann hast du das?*
> - Say since when you've had the problem.
> - *Wie ist das passiert?*
> - Say how it happened.
> - *Ask how your friend is.*
> - *Gut, danke!*

> **G** *Seit* ('since' or 'for') is used with the present tense in German and is always followed by the dative case. It indicates something that started in the past and is still ongoing.
>
> *Seit* wann **hast** du Rückenschmerzen?
> **Since** when have you had backache?
>
> Ich **habe** **seit** Montag Rückenschmerzen.
> I have had backache **since** Monday.
>
> Ich **habe** **seit** zwei Tag**en** / ein**er** Woche / ein**em** Jahr Rückenschmerzen.
> I have had backache **for** two days / a week / a year.
>
> Page 94

> The German letter **s** at the beginning of a word or before a vowel is pronounced like the English 'z'. Listen and repeat the words.
> Ge**s**icht Na**s**e **s**ehr vor**s**ichtig **s**eit **S**ie

Sprechen 9 In pairs, take turns to practise the role-play, giving your own answers. Pay attention to the *s* sound.

Wie geht es dir?	Mir geht es nicht gut.
Was ist los?	Ich habe …schmerzen. Ich habe mir … gebrochen/verletzt.
Seit wann hast du das?	Seit gestern. Seit drei Tagen. Seit einer Woche.
Wann ist das passiert?	Gestern / Am Wochenende. Vor zwei Tagen / Vor einer Woche.
Wie ist das passiert?	Beim Laufen. Ich bin schwimmen gegangen.

fünfundachtzig 85

3 Was möchte ich verbessern?

- Talking about good and bad habits
- Revising present, past and future tenses
- Using infinitive constructions with *zu*

 1 Listen to and read Sandro's diary entry for 20 April. Copy and complete the table in English.

	issue	reason
1	can't concentrate	sits in front of a computer too much

Liebes Tagebuch!

20. April

Das Problem:
1 Ich kann mich nicht gut konzentrieren, weil ich zu viel vor dem Computer sitze.
2 Ich habe nicht genug Zeit für die Schule, weil ich zu viel Zeit auf meinem Handy verbringe.
3 Ich bin nicht fit, weil ich mich nicht genug bewege.
4 Meine Ernährung ist nicht so gut. Ich esse nicht genug Obst und Gemüse.
5 Ich fühle mich nicht wohl, weil ich nicht genug schlafe. Ich bin so müde!
6 Wenn ich nichts mache, werde ich bald nicht mehr gesund sein! Ich muss mein Leben verbessern!

 2 Now read Sandro's diary entry for 21 April. Match the resolutions to the issues in the 20 April entry. There is more than one possible option for some issues.

Example: 1 b, …

 3 Write Sandro's diary entry for 28 April, imagining that he achieved all his resolutions successfully. Rewrite the sentences in exercise 2 (a–h) in the perfect tense.

21. April

Die Lösung:

Ich werde …
a jeden Tag zu Fuß in die Schule gehen.
b die Zeit vor dem Computer reduzieren.
c weniger Zeit auf meinem Handy verbringen.
d fast jeden Tag ein Stück Obst und fünf Portionen Gemüse essen.
e jeden Tag früher ins Bett gehen.
f zweimal pro Woche schwimmen gehen.
g einmal pro Woche laufen gehen.
h nicht aufgeben!

28. April

a Ich bin jeden Tag zu Fuß in die Schule gegangen.

Remember that the **perfect tense** is formed with *haben* or *sein* and the past participle. Some of these past participles are irregular.

The **future tense** is formed with *werden* and the infinitive.

infinitive	present tense	perfect tense	future tense
schlafen	ich schlafe	ich habe … geschlafen	ich werde … schlafen
planen	ich plane	ich habe … geplant	ich werde … planen
gehen	ich gehe	ich bin … gegangen	ich werde … gehen
verbringen	ich verbringe	ich habe … verbracht	ich werde … verbringen
reduzieren	ich reduziere	ich habe … reduziert	ich werde … reduzieren
aufgeben	ich gebe … auf	ich habe … aufgegeben	ich werde … aufgeben

Page 95

4 Listen and write down in English what Sandro actually achieved in the last week. (1–4)

 5 Listen to and read about what Sandro still needs to improve on. Copy and complete the table in English.

30. April

- Ich habe mich entschieden, mehr zu schlafen, aber leider habe ich nicht genug geschlafen, weil ich immer spät ins Bett gegangen bin. Ich werde versuchen, früher ins Bett zu gehen.
- Mein Plan war auch, häufiger laufen zu gehen, aber ich hatte diese Woche leider keine Zeit. Ich werde versuchen, das nächste Woche zu machen.
- Außerdem habe ich es nicht geschafft, weniger Zeit auf dem Handy zu verbringen. Die Lösung? Ich plane, nächste Woche einen handyfreien Tag zu haben!
- Ich habe zumindest mehr Obst gegessen und ich habe vor, auf Schokolade zu verzichten.

He didn't manage to …	He plans to …
sleep enough	go to bed earlier

Remember that an umlaut acts as a 'sound changer'. In German, only **a**, **o** and **u** can have an umlaut.
Listen and repeat the words.

a	H**a**nd	ä	H**ä**nde
au	B**au**m	äu	B**äu**me
o	r**o**t	ö	r**ö**ter
u	Br**u**der	ü	Br**ü**der

 6 Read out the text in exercise 5, paying attention to the sounds with umlauts.

 7 Listen to two teenagers talking about their health and make notes on the following points: what's wrong, what they've tried and their future intentions.

 Some verbs require the addition of **zu** before the infinitive.

In the same way as for the **um** … **zu** construction, you need to use a comma before the infinitive construction:
*Ich beginne, mehr Obst **zu** essen.*

Ich beginne, … zu …	I begin to …
Ich beschließe, … zu …	I decide to …
Ich entscheide (mich), … zu …	I decide to …
Ich habe vor, … zu …	I intend to / plan to …
Ich plane, … zu …	I plan to …
Ich versuche, … zu …	I try to …

Modal verbs do not follow this pattern and do not need **zu** before the infinitive.
*Ich **muss** mehr Obst **essen**.*

Page 93

8 In pairs, take turns to discuss problems and resolutions to improve your wellbeing.

- Was ist das Problem?
- Ich bin nicht fit.
- Was hast du schon gemacht, um das Problem zu lösen?
- Ich bin einmal pro Woche schwimmen gegangen.
- Was wirst du in der Zukunft machen?
- Ich werde dreimal pro Woche schwimmen gehen.

 9 Translate the text into German.

I can't concentrate because I don't sleep enough. I also spend too much time in front of the computer and I don't exercise regularly. I have tried to be fit and healthy, but I don't like going to the gym. I have decided to go swimming with my friend twice a week. I also plan to spend more time outside.

siebenundachtzig

4 Gute Tage, schlechte Tage

- Talking about wellbeing
- Using *wenn*
- Using set phrases with *zu*

Lesen 1 Read the problems and match them to the correct photos (a–d).

Probleme der Woche

1 Mein Bruder ist so gemein! Er ist immer sehr laut und das stört mich, wenn ich meine Hausaufgaben mache. Er ist so ärgerlich und das geht mir auf die Nerven! Wir streiten oft!

<u>Wenn mein Bruder so laut wäre</u>, würde ich mit meinen Eltern darüber sprechen.

2 Ich habe meine letzte Prüfung geschrieben und jetzt habe ich zu viel Freizeit! Ja, wirklich, zu viel!

<u>Wenn ich zu viel Freizeit hätte</u>, würde ich mehr Sport treiben und mit meinen Freunden regelmäßig ausgehen.

3 Ich bin immer so müde und habe wenig Energie. Ich fühle mich immer so faul!

<u>Wenn ich immer so müde wäre und wenig Energie hätte</u>, würde ich regelmäßig spazieren gehen.

4 Nächste Woche habe ich eine Matheprüfung, die sehr wichtig ist, aber ich finde Mathe so schwierig und auch ziemlich langweilig!

<u>Wenn ich eine Matheprüfung hätte</u>, würde ich mit meinen Freunden dafür lernen! Das würde mehr Spaß machen!

> **G** The conjunction **wenn** is often used together with the **imperfect subjunctive** (*hätte*, *wäre*) and **conditional** (*würde*) to express what you **would** do if you **had** … or if you **were** …
>
> **Wenn** ich mehr Zeit **hätte**, <u>würde</u> ich mehr Sport <u>treiben</u>.
> **If I had** more time, I **would** do more sport.
>
> **Wenn** ich nicht so müde **wäre**, <u>würde</u> ich mich besser <u>konzentrieren</u>.
> **If I were** not so tired, I **would** concentrate better.
>
> Note the **verb**-**comma**-**verb** structure and the <u>infinitive</u> at the end of the sentence.
>
> Page 95

Lesen 2 Read the problems in exercise 1 again and translate the <u>four</u> <u>underlined</u> phrases into English.

Sprechen 3 Read out problems 3 and 4 in exercise 1. Pay attention to the *-ig* sounds. Then listen and check.

Hören 4 Listen. Copy and complete the table in English. (1–6)

	If …	I would …
1	I had more time	do sport regularly

> The letter combination **-ig** at the end of a word is pronounced like the German word **ich** (meaning 'I').
>
> Listen and repeat the words.
> langweil**ig**   wicht**ig**   regelmäß**ig**
> schwier**ig**   wen**ig**   zwanz**ig**

88 achtundachtzig

5 In pairs, take turns to complete the sentences with your own ideas.

1 Wenn ich mehr Zeit hätte, würde ich …
2 Wenn ich weniger Hausaufgaben hätte, würde ich …
3 Wenn ich ein Problem hätte, würde ich …
4 Wenn ich nicht so müde wäre, würde ich …
5 Wenn das Wetter besser wäre, würde ich …
6 Wenn ich berühmt wäre, würde ich …

Wenn ich … hätte/wäre,	würde ich	regelmäßig Sport treiben.
		ein Instrument lernen.
		öfter ins Kino gehen.
		mit meinen Eltern (darüber) sprechen.
		nicht so viel Stress haben.
		mich besser konzentrieren können.
		glücklicher sein.
		mich besser fühlen.
		mehr Energie haben.
		draußen Fußball spielen.

6 Listen to and read the article. Answer the questions below in English.

Was ist gut für die geistige Gesundheit?

<u>Es ist wichtig, aktiv zu sein</u>. Das heißt: sich regelmäßig bewegen, viel draußen in der Natur sein, öfter Veranstaltungen besuchen (Kino, Theater, Konzerte, Ausstellungen usw.). <u>Natürlich ist es auch wichtig, gute Freunde zu haben</u> und gute Kommunikation zu pflegen. <u>Es ist sinnvoll, über Probleme zu sprechen</u>. Ein Haustier kann auch vielen Menschen Freude bringen.

<u>Es ist auch nötig, gesund zu essen</u> und genug zu schlafen. <u>Es ist oft schwierig, eine positive Einstellung zu haben</u>. Man muss akzeptieren, dass man manchmal traurig ist und dass Konflikte ein Teil des Lebens sind. Weinen kann gut sein.

<u>Wenn es Probleme gibt, ist es wichtig, ruhig zu bleiben</u> und die Hoffnung nicht aufzugeben.

geistig mental
Einstellung attitude

1 What examples are given for 'being active'? (Give <u>three</u> details.)
2 What is it useful to do?
3 What can a pet provide?
4 What is it necessary to do? (Give <u>two</u> details.)
5 What should we accept? (Give <u>two</u> details.)
6 What can be good for you?
7 What is it important to do when there are problems?
8 What should we not give up?

> **zu** + infinitive is used with a number of phrases containing an <u>adjective</u> and the verb *sein*:
>
> Es ist <u>wichtig</u>, aktiv **zu** sein.
> It is important to be active.
>
> Es ist <u>sinnvoll</u>, … (useful)
> Es ist <u>nötig</u>, … (necessary)
> Es ist <u>schwierig</u>, … (difficult)
>
> Remember to use a comma before the *zu* phrase.

7 Translate the <u>six underlined</u> phrases in exercise 6 into English.

8 Translate the sentences into German.

> Use *wenn* + imperfect subjunctive.

> Use an infinitive structure with *zu*.

1 If the weather were good, I would go cycling.
2 If I had more energy, I would be happier.
3 It is important to sleep well.
4 It is good to talk to a friend.

> Remember the umlauts here.

> Use talk 'with' + dative.

5 Das finde ich wichtig!

- Talking about what is important to you
- Asking questions in different tenses
- Writing about lifestyle and wellbeing

1 Read an interview with Noah. Write the correct letter to match each answer (a–h) to a question. Then write which tense each question is in: past, present or future.

1. Wie fühlst du dich normalerweise?
2. Wie oft treibst du Sport?
3. Welchen Sport hast du letztes Wochenende gemacht?
4. Isst du gesund?
5. Welche Situation macht dir Stress?
6. Was machst du, wenn du traurig bist?
7. Was wirst du nächstes Wochenende machen?
8. Was ist für dich wichtig im Leben?

Noah

a. Die Schule kann mir viel Stress machen.
b. Wenn ich traurig bin, simse ich meinem besten Freund.
c. Nächstes Wochenende werde ich Basketball spielen.
d. Ich würde sagen, dass ich ziemlich gesund esse.
e. Ich treibe dreimal pro Woche Sport.
f. Für mich sind gute Beziehungen wichtig.
g. Ich fühle mich normalerweise ziemlich gut und glücklich.
h. Letztes Wochenende habe ich mit Freunden Basketball gespielt.

2 Listen to Noah's interview and check your answers to exercise 1. Write down <u>one</u> additional detail he gives in response to each question in English. (1–8)

Example: 1 He is fit and healthy.

3 Look at the diagram and find the German for the phrases.

Was ist für mich wichtig im Leben?

1. to have a goal in life
2. working together with others, cooperation
3. to exercise daily
4. to develop one's potential
5. enough sleep
6. success

persönliche Werte
- Sinn finden
- Vorbilder haben
- ein Lebensziel haben
- eine positive Einstellung zum Leben haben

Gesundheit	Freizeit	Beziehungen	Karriere
• sich täglich bewegen • gesundes Essen • genug Schlaf	• Sport • Spaß • Abenteuer • Work-Life-Balance	• Familie • Freunde • anderen helfen • Zusammenarbeit • einen Partner finden	• Erfolg • interessante Arbeit • Intelligenz • sein Potential entwickeln

4 Listen to what Samira says is important in her life and answer the questions.

1. Why are relationships important to Samira?
2. How does she try to stay healthy?
3. Why does she find role models important?
4. Why does she like to help others?
5. Why is money not so important to her?
6. What does she say about success?

5 In pairs, ask and answer the questions in exercise 1.

6 Listen to and read the article. Translate the quotation and the six underlined phrases into English.

Anna-Lena – Skifahrerin und Studentin

Anna-Lena Forster <u>begann mit sechs Jahren, Ski zu fahren</u>, und hat die Freiheit auf dem Schnee sofort geliebt. Seit 2013 hat sie viele Medaillen in dieser spannenden Sportart gewonnen. In ihrer Freizeit hört Anna-Lena gerne Musik. Sie liest auch oft mal ein Buch, trifft sich mit Freunden und verbringt Zeit mit ihrem Familienhund.

Anna-Lena <u>ist Rollstuhlfahrerin</u>. Ihre Eltern und ihr Bruder waren gute Skifahrer und sie wollten gemeinsam Urlaub machen. <u>Daher hat Anna-Lena Monoski probiert</u>. <u>Sie machte schnell große Fortschritte</u> und <u>dazu braucht man Talent und Motivation</u>. 2014 hat sie bei den Paralympischen Spielen in Sotschi Silber im Slalom und in der Super-Kombination gewonnen. 2018 hat sie zwei Goldmedaillen in China gewonnen, aber <u>mit dem Erfolg steigt auch der Druck</u>. Deshalb arbeitet Anna-Lena seit ein paar Jahren mit einer Mentaltrainerin. Sie entwickeln Strategien, wie Anna-Lena ihre Angst vor einem Wettbewerb kontrollieren kann. Außerdem interessiert Anna-Lena sich sehr für Psychologie. Sie studiert Psychologie an der Universität und möchte in der Zukunft Sport mit Psychologie verbinden.

„Auf dem Ski fühle ich mich frei."

| *die Medaille (-n)* | medal |
| *ein paar* | a few |

 7 Read the article again and answer the questions in English.
1. What does Anna-Lena love about being on the snow?
2. When did she start winning medals?
3. What enabled her to make great progress? (Give two details.)
4. Why is she working with a mental coach?
5. What does the mental coach help her with?
6. What would Anna-Lena like to do in the future?

 8 Write approximately 150 words about lifestyle and wellbeing. Include the following points:
- what is important to you in life
- what you will do in the future to improve your wellbeing.

Für mich	ist	Gesundheit Freizeit Karriere	das Wichtigste. sehr wichtig.
	sind	persönliche Werte Beziehungen	
Neulich habe ich	beschlossen, mich entschieden, versucht,	gesünder zu essen. öfter Sport zu machen. früher ins Bett zu gehen.	
In der Zukunft	habe ich vor, plane ich,		
Ich hoffe,		mehr Energie zu haben. mehr Zeit mit meiner Familie zu verbringen. weniger Stress im Leben zu haben.	

Grammatik 1

Comparative and superlative adjectives and adverbs (Culture, page 81)

 1 Read the comparative sentences and translate the underlined words into English.

1 Ich finde Tennis <u>interessanter als</u> Wandern.
2 Fahrradfahren ist <u>beliebter als</u> Laufen.
3 Die Dufourspitze finde ich <u>schöner als</u> den Ben Nevis.
4 Fahrradfahren ist in Deutschland <u>wichtiger als</u> Skifahren, denke ich.
5 Treibst du <u>regelmäßiger</u> Sport <u>als</u> deine Schwester?
6 Ist Tennis <u>genauso schwierig wie</u> Badminton? Nein, ich finde Tennis <u>einfacher als</u> Badminton.

 2 Copy and complete the table with the correct forms of the irregular adjectives.

kalt	kälter	am kältesten
1 warm	wärmer	**2**
jung	**3**	am jüngsten
4	älter	**5**
gut	**6**	**7**
8	**9**	am kürzesten
10	**11**	am stärksten
12	schwächer	**13**

 If the comparative adds an umlaut to the vowel, the superlative does too.

 3 Listen and write down the superlative adjectives you hear.

1 Badminton ist die ___ Aktivität.
2 Ich nehme immer den ___ Weg.
3 Tennis ist der ___ Sport.
4 Ich möchte das ___ Eis, bitte.
5 Möchtest du den ___ Sport probieren?
6 Meine ___ Leistung war ein Marathon.

 4 Translate the sentences into German.

1 Football is as difficult as basketball.
2 He cycles more quickly.
3 She eats most quickly.
4 What is your biggest achievement?
5 I like playing tennis most of all.

 Remember that to compare two things in German, you add **-er** to the adjective and use **als** to mean 'than'.

Großbritannien ist **kleiner als** *Deutschland.*
Great Britain is **smaller than** Germany.
Unlike in English, you never add **mehr** to comparatives.
Ich finde Wandern **interessanter als** *Basketball.*
I think hiking is **more interesting than** basketball.

Some shorter adjectives that add an umlaut:
lang – l**ä**nger – der/die/das l**ä**ngste
hoch – h**öh**er – der/die/das h**ö**chste

To say something is the same as something else, use **(genau)so ... wie**:
Fahrradfahren ist **(genau)so** *beliebt* **wie** *Wandern.*
Cycling is **(just) as** popular **as** hiking.

For **superlatives** on their own, without a noun after them, use **am** before the adjective and add **-(e)sten** at the end.
Wandern ist **am** *beliebt***esten**.
Hiking is **the most** popular.

It is also common to form the superlative by adding **-(e)st** to the adjective. Remember that adjectives need to agree with the noun they are describing; this is also true for superlative adjectives.

	nominative	accusative	dative
masc	**der** höchst**e** Berg	**den** höchst**en** Berg	**dem** höchst**en** Berg
fem	**die** längst**e** Pause	**die** längst**e** Pause	**der** längst**en** Pause
neut	**das** größt**e** Land	**das** größt**e** Land	**dem** größt**en** Land
pl	**die** jüngst**en** Kinder	**die** jüngst**en** Kinder	**den** jüngst**en** Kinder**n**

Comparative and superlative **adjectives** can be used as **adverbs** to describe verbs in German.

Sie läuft **schneller**. She runs **more quickly**.
Er springt **am höchsten**. He jumps **the highest**.

These common adverbs are very useful:
mehr – am meisten
weniger – am wenigsten
gern – lieber – am liebsten

Infinitive constructions (Unit 1, page 82; Unit 3, page 87)

 5 Copy and complete the sentences with *zu* + infinitive or *um ... zu* + infinitive.

Example: 1 *Ich habe keine Zeit, Fußball zu spielen.*

1 Ich habe keine Zeit, (*Fußball spielen*).
2 Ich gehe ins Café, (*etwas essen*).
3 Ich habe beschlossen, weniger (*fernsehen*).
4 Es ist wichtig, (*viel Wasser trinken*).
5 Ich mache eine Pause, (*mich entspannen*).
6 Ich gehe ins Fitness-Studio, (*schwimmen*).

 With separable verbs, **zu** comes in the middle of the word, **after** the separable prefix.

*aufstehen: Ich plane, früher auf**zu**stehen.*
I plan **to** get up earlier.

You can also use **zu** + infinitive after adjectives.
*Es ist wichtig, gesund **zu** essen.*
It is important **to** eat healthily.

If you are not sure whether to use **zu** on its own or **um ... zu**, check whether the English sentence makes sense with 'in order to'.

 6 In pairs, take turns to read out the first part of each sentence in exercise 5 and finish it off with your own information.

 7 Translate the diary entry into English.

> Früher war ich nicht so fit wie meine Freunde. Dann habe ich beschlossen, mein Leben zu verbessern. Ich habe mich entschieden, jeden Tag zu Fuß zur Schule zu gehen. Ich habe auch versucht, weniger Zeit vor dem Computer zu verbringen. Ich habe begonnen, zweimal pro Woche schwimmen zu gehen. Jetzt fühle ich mich viel besser und ich bin fitter und gesünder!

 8 Translate the sentences into German.

1 I play tennis to stay fit.
2 My sister plans to play football once a week.
3 We have started to do more sport.
4 My mother goes to the supermarket to buy milk.
5 My brother tries to eat more healthily.
6 It is important to have a positive attitude.

beim + noun (Unit 2, page 84)

 9 Copy and complete the sentences with the correct noun.

1 Letzte Woche habe ich mir beim Tennisspielen den Arm verletzt. (*playing tennis*)
2 Ich habe mir gestern beim ___ die Schulter verletzt. (*swimming*)
3 Vor drei Jahren habe ich mir beim ___ den Arm gebrochen. (*skiing*)
4 Vor zwei Monaten hatte ich beim ___ einen Unfall. (*cycling*)
5 Heute möchte ich mich beim ___ viel bewegen. (*fitness training*)
6 Morgen werde ich mich beim ___ entspannen. (*watching TV*)

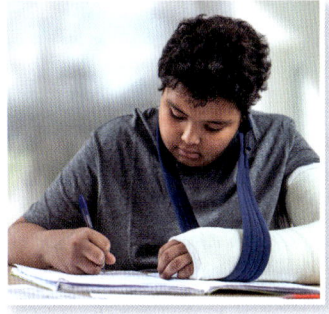

Remember, you can turn any verb into a noun by adding a capital letter:
wandern → *beim Wandern*
laufen → *beim Laufen*

Grammatik 2

Modal verbs in the imperfect tense (Unit 2, page 85)

 1 Write the correct letter (a–f) to match each German sentence to an English translation.

1. He had to go to the hospital.
2. I couldn't walk for two weeks.
3. She was supposed to stay in bed.
4. We didn't want to have an accident.
5. They weren't allowed to eat anything.
6. I didn't like listening to music.

a Wir wollten keinen Unfall haben.
b Ich mochte nicht Musik hören.
c Sie sollte im Bett bleiben.
d Ich konnte zwei Wochen lang nicht gehen.
e Er musste ins Krankenhaus gehen.
f Sie durften nichts essen.

 2 Read out the message. Then listen and check your pronunciation.

> Ich wollte am Wochenende ins Kino gehen, aber ich konnte nicht, weil ich für eine Prüfung lernen musste. Ich sollte auch mein Zimmer sauber machen, aber ich mochte nicht und deswegen durfte ich auch nicht fernsehen. Das Leben kann so unfair sein!

 All modal verbs follow the same pattern of endings in the imperfect tense:

können (to be able to)	
ich konn**te**	wir konn**ten**
du konn**test**	ihr konn**tet**
er/sie/es/man konn**te**	Sie konn**ten**
	sie konn**ten**

müssen (to have to) — ich muss**te**
wollen (to want to) — ich woll**te**
dürfen (to be allowed to) — ich durf**te**
sollen (to be supposed to) — ich soll**te**
mögen (to like to) — ich moch**te**

Note that there is no umlaut on modal verbs in the imperfect tense.

 3 Translate the sentences into German.

1. I couldn't eat because I had toothache.
2. He had to go to hospital because he was ill.
3. I wasn't able to visit my friend because I didn't have time.
4. She wanted to play tennis, but she had to do her homework.
5. I was supposed to stay in bed, but I didn't want to do that.

seit (Unit 2, page 85)

 4 Translate the sentences into English.

1. Ich bin seit gestern krank.
2. Karin hat seit zwei Stunden Kopfschmerzen.
3. Ich spiele seit einem Jahr Tennis.
4. Hast du seit letzter Woche Rückenschmerzen?
5. Ich lerne seit einer Woche, Tennis zu spielen.
6. Ich warte seit zehn Minuten vor dem Krankenhaus.

 Remember that *seit* can mean 'for' as well as 'since' in English and is always followed by the dative case.

 5 Translate the phrases into German using *seit*.

1 for a month
2 since Saturday
3 for an hour
4 for a week
5 since January
6 since last year

Irregular past participles (Unit 3, page 86)

 6 Copy and complete the sentences with the correct irregular past participle.

1. Ich habe Zeit mit Freunden ___verbracht___. (*verbringen*)
2. Warum hast du Tennis ___? (*aufgeben*)
3. Mein Bruder hat eine Party ___. (*organisieren*)
4. Ich habe ___, gesünder zu essen. (*beginnen*)
5. Hast du ___, häufiger Sport zu treiben? (*beschließen*)
6. Max hat ___, Fernsehen aufzugeben. (*sich entscheiden*)

 Most verbs form their past participles by adding **ge-** to the stem of the verb and adding **-t** or **-en** to the end. Those that end *-en* often have a spelling change in their stem, e.g. *trinken – getrunken*. Some verbs form their past participles differently:

type of verb	perfect tense form	infinitive	past participle
-ieren	no ge- add -iert to the stem	telefonieren	telefoniert
verbs with inseparable prefixes: be-, ent-, er-, ge-, über-, ver-	no ge-	besuchen entscheiden	besucht entschieden
verbs with separable prefixes	add ge- after the prefix	aufstehen	aufgestanden

wenn (Unit 4, page 88)

 7 Listen and write whether you hear the present tense (P) or the conditional (C) with wenn. (1–8)
Example: 1 P

 8 Read out the sentences. Then listen and check your pronunciation.

1. Wenn ich mich regelmäßig bewege, schlafe ich besser.
2. Wenn ich genug schlafe, fühle ich mich viel besser.
3. Wenn ich nicht so müde wäre, würde ich laufen gehen.
4. Wenn ich mehr Zeit hätte, würde ich mehr schlafen.

 Remember: **wenn** also means 'when' and can be used with the present tense to talk about things which are generally true.
Wenn das Wetter schlecht ist, bleibe ich zu Hause.
When the weather is bad, I stay at home.

But when **wenn** is used with the imperfect subjunctive and conditional, it means 'if'.
Wenn das Wetter schlecht wäre, würde ich zu Hause bleiben.
If the weather were bad, I would stay at home.

 9 Translate the sentences into German.

1. If the weather were good, I would go to the park.
2. If I were tired, I would go to bed.
3. If I had a problem, I would speak to my parents.
4. If I had more time, I would read more.
5. If the weather were better, I would play tennis.
6. If I had lots of stress, I would stay positive.

Los geht's!

 10 Listen and write down the words or sentences you hear.

1. ___ ist ___ Sport.
2. Ich habe ___.
3. Ich ___ ins ___.
4. ___.
5. ___.
6. ___.

fünfundneunzig

Kapitel 4 Lese- und Hörtest

Reading

Wellbeing. Two German teenagers are discussing their lifestyles.
Answer the following questions. Write **A** for **Anton**, **E** for **Elise**, **A + E** for **Anton and Elise**.

Anton
Es gibt viele wichtige Sachen in meinem Leben, zum Beispiel Sport und gute Beziehungen. Jeder Mensch hat Probleme, aber das Wichtigste für mich ist, dass man immer eine praktische Lösung sucht. Es hilft niemandem, immer traurig zu sein. Ich finde, der Mensch braucht ein Lebensziel, um glücklich und gesund zu bleiben. Meine Familie ist mir genauso wichtig wie meine Freunde, meine Karriere, meine Gesundheit oder meine Freizeitaktivitäten. Ich brauche all diese Dinge, um ein sinnvolles Leben zu haben.

Elise
Ich soll aktiver sein, aber im Moment muss ich viel in der Schule lernen. Wenn ich mehr Zeit hätte, würde ich mit meinem **Zwilling** spazieren gehen. Wir verstehen uns sehr gut miteinander. Ich soll auch früher ins Bett gehen. Wenn ich nicht so müde wäre, würde ich mehr Energie haben. Bewegung ist gut für die Gesundheit, aber Beziehungen sind auch wichtig: Man muss Freunde haben und gute Kommunikation mit ihnen pflegen. Meine Freunde bringen mir viel Freude. Ich versuche, Streit mit ihnen zu vermeiden, und es hilft mir, über Probleme sprechen zu können.

1 Who tries to avoid arguments?
2 Who thinks both relationships and exercise are important?
3 Who thinks more sleep would help their wellbeing?
4 Who thinks that people need a goal in life to be happy and healthy?
5 Read Elise's second sentence again. What is a **Zwilling**?
   A a means of transport   **B** an activity   **C** a person

Translate these sentences into English.

You can't translate this literally. How would this be phrased best?

Make sure you account for the incidental words that are easy to forget.

The ending -er makes this word a comparative. You need to include the English word 'more'.

1 Frühstück ist mir wichtig, weil ich immer großen Hunger habe.
2 In der Schweiz ist Klettern beliebter als Basketball.
3 Leider hat er seit drei Monaten Rückenschmerzen.
4 Gestern hatte ich nur wenig Freizeit, weil ich arbeiten musste.
5 Wenn ich mehr Energie hätte, würde ich häufiger wandern.

Is this translated as 'since' or 'for' here? The tense is different in English.

Which tense do you need in your English translation, to match this form of müssen?

Looking at the form of the verbs, would you translate wenn as 'when' or 'if'?

Listening

Sport. Sascha is talking about her sporting activities. Write the **two** correct letters to answer each question.

1. Which **two** activities did she do **in the past**?
2. Which **two** activities does she do **now**?

A	cycling
B	running
C	hiking
D	swimming
E	football
F	basketball

Listen carefully for the tenses used when you hear the activity. Also listen out for negatives: you might hear some of the incorrect answers mentioned, but the speaker might be saying that this is an activity which they **didn't** or **don't** do.

Bad habits. Lukas, Mia and Felix are talking about their bad habits. Answer the questions in English.

1. How should Lukas improve his concentration?
2. What is a remedy for Mia feeling unwell?
3. Why did Felix do no homework yesterday?

In this task, you will need to pick out the details that are relevant to the questions. There is more information than you need, so listen carefully.

Dictation

You will hear five short sentences. Write down exactly what you hear in German.

You will hear each sentence three times: the first time as a full sentence, the second time in short sections and the third time as a full sentence again.

Think carefully about spelling and use your knowledge of grammar to ensure you add the correct verb, adjective and article endings. Remember that all nouns need a capital letter.

The sentences will include some words that are not on the AQA vocabulary list. Use your knowledge of sound–spelling links to work out how to spell them.

Think carefully about how these sounds are pronounced when you write down what you hear:
s, ski, schw
a, ä
au, äu
o, ö
u, ü
-ig

siebenundneunzig

Kapitel 4 Mündlicher Test

Role-play

 1 Look at the role-play card and prepare what you are going to say.

Use an opinion phrase such as *Meiner Meinung nach*. Remember, you can make something up if you wish.

You are talking to your Austrian friend about healthy lifestyles.
1 Say how healthy you think your lifestyle is. (Give **one** detail.)
2 Say **two** things people can do to stay healthy.
3 Describe **one** thing which is bad for your health and why. (Give **one** detail and **one** reason.)
4 Say what you will do in future to be more fit and healthy. (Give **two** details.)
5 ? Ask your friend a question about their lifestyle.

Use the pronoun *man* to make a general point and choose a modal verb such as *kann* or *soll*.

Remember to put the verb at the end if you give your reason using *weil*.

Use the future tense and remember to use subject–verb inversion if you begin with the words *In der Zukunft …*

You could ask your friend their opinion of smoking or which sports they do.

 2 Practise what you have prepared. Then, using your notes, listen and respond to the teacher.

 3 Listen to Toni's response. Write down the phrases you hear to complete each sentence.
1 Meiner Meinung nach …
2 Man kann …
3 Man soll nicht …
4 In der Zukunft …
5 …?

Reading aloud

 4 Look at this task. With a partner, read the sentences aloud, paying attention to the <u>underlined</u> letters.

Meine größeren Brüder schwimmen gern in einem See.

Im Sommer besuchen sie oft unser Haus in der Schweiz und laufen in der Nähe.

Nächste Woche möchte ich öfter und länger Sport treiben, um nicht so müde zu sein.

Zusammen essen ist wichtig und wir nehmen häufig etwas Süßes, aber kein Gemüse.

Think carefully about how to pronounce these sounds:
s, schw
a, ä
au, äu
o, ö
u, ü
-ig

 5 Listen and check your pronunciation.

 6 Listen to the teacher asking four follow-up questions. Translate each question into English and prepare your own answer for each one. Then listen again and respond to the teacher.

achtundneunzig

Kapitel 4

Photo card

7 Look at the photos and listen to Toni describing them. Which of these statements does she say? Select the **three** you hear.

- a There are seven friends.
- b I see trees and grass.
- c They are happy.
- d I think it is summer.
- e They are keeping fit.
- f She is unhealthy.
- g She might be a student.
- h There are crisps and sweets on the table.

You will be asked to talk about the content of these photos. You must say at least one thing about each photo.

After you have spoken about the content of the photos, you will be asked questions related to any of the topics within the theme of **People and lifestyle**.

Your responses should be as **full and detailed** as possible.

8 Prepare your own description of the photos. Then, with a partner, take turns describing them.

> Auf dem ersten Foto gibt es …

9 Listen to the teacher's first follow-up question, *Was machst du, um gesund zu bleiben?*, and Toni's response. Write the letters (a–e) in the order in which Toni mentions these points.

- a swimming
- b sleep
- c food
- d gym
- e drink

10 The teacher then asks Toni, *Findest du es schwer, gesund zu leben?* Listen to her response and answer the questions.

1 Which **two** things does Toni say that her friends do?
2 Why is this a problem for her?
3 Which **two** things does Toni say are expensive?
4 Which **two** things does she suggest for people who don't have much money?

11 Listen to two more follow-up questions and prepare your answers. Then respond to the recording. Make your answers as full as possible, including opinions and reasons.

12 Prepare your own answers to as many of the Module 4 questions on page 226 as you can. Then practise with your partner.

> Think about ways in which you can extend your answers. As long as you are speaking, you are in control of the conversation. Think about how you could include:
> - tenses other than the one required by the question; for example, add what you did in the past and what you will do in the future. If you are asked about lessons, say what you had yesterday and what you will have later or tomorrow: *Gestern hatte ich … und morgen werde ich … haben.*
> - opinions, even when the teacher doesn't ask for them: *ich finde das … / und das gefällt mir (nicht).*
> - reasons for your opinions: *Ich finde Sport toll, weil der Lehrer sehr lustig ist.*

neunundneunzig

Kapitel 4 Schreibtest

Translation

 1 Look at the translation task and match the sentence halves to form the correct German translation for each sentence.

1 He doesn't like playing football because he prefers cycling.
2 We would like to eat more healthily in the future.
3 The pupils are trying to drink more water.
4 Last week you went to bed later.
5 When we were younger, we ate less fruit.

i Wir möchten in der
ii Letzte Woche bist du
iii Er spielt nicht gern Fußball,
iv Als wir jünger waren,
v Die Schüler*innen versuchen,

a haben wir weniger Obst gegessen.
b Zukunft gesünder essen.
c mehr Wasser zu trinken.
d später ins Bett gegangen.
e weil er lieber Fahrrad fährt.

 2 Translate these sentences into German.
1 I do not like running, because I prefer swimming.
2 She would like to be healthier in the future.
3 The children are trying to eat more fruit and vegetables.
4 Yesterday I went to bed earlier.
5 When I was younger, I did less sport.

150-word writing task

 3 Look at this writing exam task and then, for each bullet point:
1 think about the vocabulary and structures you have learned, which you could use in your answer. For example:
  - **nouns**, **verbs** and **adjectives** to write about healthy lifestyles
  - **verbs of opinion** and **adjectives** to give reasons
  - how to explain **what your plans are** and **why**
  - connectives and intensifiers you would like to use
2 write down three or four ideas for what you could write about
3 identify which tense(s) you could use in your answer.

> You are writing an article about healthy lifestyle.
>
> You **must** write approximately 150 words in **German**.
>
> You must write something about both bullet points.
>
> Describe:
> - what makes a healthy lifestyle
> - your plans for staying healthy in the future

> Try to stay within the word count and use language that you are sure of. You need to demonstrate that you can use two time frames and you will gain marks for showing knowledge of more complex structures. Make sure you answer the question and write something about both bullet points.

Read Theo's answer to the exam task. Answer the questions in the coloured boxes (1–5).

1 This is an example of **complex language**. What does it mean? Find <u>three</u> more examples of complex language in the text.

2 Theo uses a **variety of compound nouns**. What do these words mean? Find <u>two</u> more examples.

3 What type of **grammatical structure** is this? What other examples can you find?

Sport ist mir sehr wichtig und ich spiele oft mit meinen Freunden Fußball. Ich finde Sport gesund. Das macht fit. Aber es kann auch negativ sein. Manchmal kann man sich verletzen, wenn man Sport treibt. Zum Beispiel habe ich mir letztes Wochenende beim Fußballspielen das Bein verletzt. Einmal in der Woche gehe ich ins Fitness-Studio. Es ist auch wichtig, gesund zu essen. Ich esse gern Pommes und Wurst. Das ist nicht so gesund. Man soll auch nicht zu viel Süßes essen.

In der Zukunft möchte ich öfter Obst und Gemüse essen und mehr Wasser trinken, um gesünder zu sein. Es ist genauso wichtig in Ruhe zu essen, um nicht so viel Stress zu haben. Ich verbringe ungefähr vier Stunden pro Tag am Computer. Ich werde versuchen, die Zeit vor dem Computer zu reduzieren. Ich habe vor, an Wochentagen früher ins Bett zu gehen, um mehr Energie zu haben. Wenn ich älter bin, werde ich weder rauchen noch Drogen nehmen.

4 Which connective could you use here to form an **extended sentence**? What other connectives does Theo use?

5 This is one way of expressing a **future** intention. Find <u>two</u> more verbs which Theo uses to express the future.

Read Theo's answer again and answer the questions.

1 What happened to Theo last weekend?
2 What does Theo like to eat?
3 How does he intend to improve his diet?
4 What will help him feel more energetic?
5 What will he not do when he is older?

Prepare your own answer to the task.

- Think about how you can develop your answer for each bullet point.
- Look back at your notes from exercises 3 and 4.
- Look at the 'Challenge checklist' and consider how you can show off your German!
- Write a **brief** plan and organise your answer into paragraphs.
- Write your answer and then carefully check for accuracy.

Challenge checklist

✓ Past and future time frames
✓ Connectives (*und, aber*) and time phrases (*in der Woche*)
✓ Some extended sentences (*Schwimmen ist hart, aber macht Spaß.*)
✓ An opinion (*Ich finde das gesund.*)

✓ A wider range of tenses
✓ Different persons of the verb
✓ Varied sentence openers (*In der Zukunft möchte ich*)
✓ Intensifiers and qualifiers (*besonders, meistens*)
✓ A wider range of interesting vocabulary (*Sinn finden, genug Schlaf, Vorbilder haben*)

✓ Use of *ich würde, ich hätte, ich möchte*
✓ Complex language: infinitive constructions, comparatives, superlatives, um … zu, beim
✓ Modal verbs (*ich muss, kann, darf, will, soll, mag*)
✓ Varied time phrases (*später, in der Zukunft, neulich, regelmäßig, seit + present tense*)
✓ More varied conjunctions (*außerdem, wenn*)
✓ Subordinate clause at start of sentence and verb, comma, verb rule (*Wenn ich älter bin, werde ich …*)

Kapitel 4 — Wörter

Key:
bold = this word will appear in higher exams only
* = this word is not on the vocabulary list, but you may use it in your own sentences

Ich liebe Sport (pages 80–81):

Gesundheit und Fitness — *Health and fitness*

Ich ... / I ...
- treibe ... Sport. — do sport.
- spiele ... (Fußball/Tennis/Basketball). — play ... (football/tennis/basketball).
- mache ... (Fitnesstraining). — do ... (fitness training).
- fahre ... (Fahrrad/*Ski). — (ride a bike/ski).
- gehe ... (**klettern**/laufen/schwimmen/wandern). — go (climbing/running/swimming/hiking).

regelmäßig	regularly
häufig	frequently
ab und zu	now and again
selten	rarely

Mein Lieblingssport ist ..., aber ich ... auch gern ... — My favourite sport is ..., but I also like ...
Ich ... nicht gern ..., weil ... — I don't like ..., because ...
Im Sommer/Winter ... ich lieber / **am liebsten** ... — In summer/winter ... I prefer/like ... the best.

Willst du fit und gesund sein? (pages 82–83):

Gesundes Leben — *Healthy living*

Wie isst oder trinkst du gesund? — How do you eat or drink healthily?
Was machst du, um *fit zu bleiben? — What do you do to keep fit?
Was hast du in letzter Zeit gemacht, um fit zu bleiben? — What have you done recently to keep fit?
Wie findest du (Rauchen)? — What do you think of (smoking)?

Ich ... / I ...
- gehe ... (schwimmen / ins Fitness-Studio). — go (swimming / to the gym).
- esse ... (viel Obst und Gemüse / Fastfood). — eat (lots of fruit and vegetables / fast-food).
- trinke ... (Wasser / keinen Alkohol). — drink (water / no alcohol).
    - viel — lots / a lot of
    - jeden Tag — every day
    - (sehr) oft — (very) often
    - jede Woche — every week
    - regelmäßig — regularly
    - immer — always
    - **kaum** — hardly (ever)
    - nie — never
    - (nicht) genug — (not) enough

Ich ... / I ...
- habe (Tennis) gespielt. — played (tennis).
- bin (laufen) gegangen. — went (running).
- finde Rauchen ..., weil es ... ist. — find smoking ... because it is ...

schlecht	bad
unwichtig	unimportant
gut	good
sehr	very
ziemlich	quite
extrem	extremely
total	totally
(**überhaupt**) nicht	not (at all)
ungesund	unhealthy
langweilig	boring
gefährlich	dangerous
entspannend	relaxing

Es geht mir nicht gut (pages 84–85):

Unfälle und Krankheiten — *Accidents and illnesses*

der Arm	arm
der **Bauch**	stomach, belly
der **Finger**	finger
der Fuß	foot
der Kopf	head
der Mund	mouth
der Rücken	back
der **Zahn**	tooth
die Hand	hand
die **Haut**	skin
die **Nase**	nose
die **Schulter**	shoulder
das Auge	eye
das Bein	leg
das Gesicht	face
das Herz	heart
das **Knie**	knee
das Ohr	ear

Wie geht es dir? — How are you?
Mir geht es nicht gut. — I'm not well.
Was ist los? — What's the matter? / What's wrong?

Was hast du? — What's the matter?
Ich habe ...schmerzen. — I have ... ache.
Ich habe mir ... gebrochen/verletzt. — I have broken/injured my ...

Seit wann hast du das? — How long have you had it?
- Seit gestern. — Since yesterday.
- Seit drei Tagen. — For three days.
- Seit einer Woche. — For a week.

Wann ist das passiert? — When did it happen?
- Gestern. — Yesterday.
- Vor zwei Tagen. / Vor einer Woche. — Two days ago. / A week ago.

Wie ist das passiert? — How did it happen?
- **Beim** Laufen. — While running.
- Ich bin schwimmen gegangen. — I went swimming.

Was möchte ich verbessern? (pages 86–87):

Probleme und Lösungen	Problems and solutions
ändern	to change, alter
aufgeben	to give up
essen	to eat
(sich) fühlen	to feel
gehen	to go, walk
hoffen	to hope
laufen	to run
lösen	to solve
planen	to plan
reduzieren	to reduce
schlafen	to sleep
schwimmen	to swim
verbringen	to spend (time)
versuchen	to try
werden	to become

der Computer	computer
der Freund	friend, ally, boyfriend
die Freundin	female friend, girlfriend
die *Portion	portion, helping, serving
die Schule	school
die Woche	week
die Zeit	time
das Bett	bed
das Fitness-Studio	gym
das Gemüse	vegetable
das Handy	mobile phone
das Obst	fruit
das Problem	problem
das Stück	piece

Gute Tage, schlechte Tage (pages 88–89):

Das *Wohlbefinden	Wellbeing
ärgerlich	annoying
gemein	mean
schwierig	difficult
das stört mich	that bothers me
das geht mir auf die Nerven	that gets on my nerves
Wenn ich … **hätte**, … **würde** ich …	If I had …, I would …
viel Freizeit	a lot of free time
wenig Energie	little energy
Wenn ich … **wäre**, **würde** ich …	If I were …, I would …
zu müde	too tired
nicht so faul	not so lazy
berühmt	famous

… regelmäßig Sport treiben.	do sport regularly.
… ein Instrument lernen.	learn (to play) an instrument.
… öfter ins Kino gehen.	go to the cinema more often.
… mit meinen Eltern (**darüber**) sprechen.	talk to my parents (about it).
… nicht so viel *Stress haben.	have less stress.
… **mich** besser **konzentrieren** können.	be able to concentrate better.
… glücklicher sein.	be happier.
… mich besser fühlen.	feel better.
… mehr Energie haben.	have more energy.
… spazieren gehen.	go for a walk, stroll.
… draußen Fußball spielen.	play football outside.

Das finde ich wichtig! (pages 90–91):

Das **Wichtigste** im Leben	The most important thing in life
Für mich ist/sind … sehr wichtig / das **Wichtigste**.	For me … is/are very important / the most important.
(die) Gesundheit	health
(die) Freizeit	free time
(die) Karriere	career
persönliche **Werte**	personal values
Beziehungen	relationships
In der Zukunft **habe** ich **vor**, … / plane ich, …	In the future I intend/plan to …
Neulich habe ich …	Recently I have …
beschlossen, …	decided, …
mich entschieden, …	decided, …
versucht, …	tried, …
gesünder zu essen.	to eat more healthily.
öfter Sport zu machen.	to do sport more often.
früher ins Bett zu gehen.	to go to bed earlier.

Ich hoffe, …	I hope …
mehr Energie zu haben.	to have more energy.
mehr Zeit mit meiner Familie zu verbringen.	to spend more time with my family.
weniger *Stress im Leben zu haben.	to have less stress in my life.
entwickeln	to develop
der Erfolg	success
der **Sinn**	meaning
die Einstellung	attitude
das **Vorbild**	role model
das Lebensziel	life goal

hundertdrei

Kapitel 5 — Meine Gegend

Wo spricht man Deutsch?
- Learning key facts about German-speaking countries
- Revising the superlative

A

Belgien
- Hauptstadt: Brüssel
- Nationalfeiertag: 21. Juli
- Fläche: 30 528km²
- Höchster Punkt: 694m
- Längster Fluss: die Maas
- Einwohner: 11 715 744

Deutschland
- Hauptstadt: Berlin
- Nationalfeiertag: 3. Oktober
- Fläche: 358 000km²
- Höchster Punkt: 2 962m
- Längster Fluss: der Main
- Einwohner: 83 294 633

Österreich
- Hauptstadt: Wien
- Nationalfeiertag: 26. Oktober
- Fläche: 83 871km²
- Höchster Punkt: 3 798m
- Längster Fluss: die Enns
- Einwohner: 8 958 960

Namibia
- Hauptstadt: Windhoek
- Nationalfeiertag: 21. März
- Fläche: 824 292km²
- Höchster Punkt: 2 573m
- Längster Fluss: der Fischfluss
- Einwohner: 2 604 172

Luxemburg
- Hauptstadt: Luxemburg
- Nationalfeiertag: 23. Juni
- Fläche: 2 586km²
- Höchster Punkt: 560m
- Längster Fluss: die Sauer
- Einwohner: 654 768

Die Schweiz
- Hauptstadt: Bern
- Nationalfeiertag: 1. August
- Fläche: 41 284km²
- Höchster Punkt: 4 634m
- Längster Fluss: die Aare
- Einwohner: 8 796 669

die Fläche	surface area
der Quadratkilometer (km²)	square kilometre

B

Vaduz, Liechtenstein

Weißt du was?

Deutsch ist die einzige offizielle Sprache in drei Ländern: Deutschland, Österreich und Liechtenstein.

In der Schweiz, Luxemburg und Belgien ist Deutsch eine der offiziellen Sprachen. In Luxemburg spricht man auch Luxemburgisch und Französisch. In Belgien spricht man auch Niederländisch und Französisch. In der Schweiz spricht man auch Französisch, Italienisch und Rätoromanisch.

Deutsch ist eine regionale offizielle Sprache in Südtirol in Italien. Man spricht auch Deutsch in anderen Ländern, zum Beispiel Namibia und Südafrika (Afrika), Paraguay und Brasilien (Südamerika).

Kulturzone — Kapitel 5

Lesen 1 Read the information cards (A). Is each statement below true or false?
1. Der Nationalfeiertag von Belgien ist im Juli.
2. Der höchste Punkt liegt in Deutschland.
3. Luxemburg ist das kleinste Land.
4. Der längste Fluss in Namibia ist der Fischfluss.
5. Die Schweiz hat die meisten Einwohner.
6. Bern ist die Hauptstadt von Österreich.

Hören 2 Listen to a description of South Tyrol. Copy and complete the final information card.

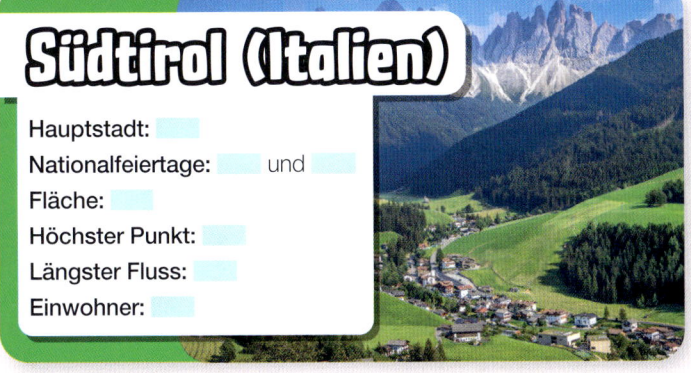

Südtirol (Italien)
- Hauptstadt:
- Nationalfeiertage: ___ und ___
- Fläche:
- Höchster Punkt:
- Längster Fluss:
- Einwohner:

Practise saying these higher numbers:

8 256 000 – *acht Millionen zweihundertsechsundfünfzigtausend*

2.606,02 – *zweitausendsechshundertsechs Komma null zwei*

German uses small spaces or a full stop to separate thousands and a comma as a decimal point – the opposite of the format used in English!

G Remember that the **superlative** form of an adjective describes something as the most or the least, and is formed by adding **-(e)ste** to the adjective.

The adjective needs to agree with the noun it is describing, and many adjectives with one syllable also add an umlaut to the vowel.

hoch: *Das ist der **höchste** Berg.*
alt: *Ich habe das **älteste** Schloss gesehen.*

Lesen 3 Read the article (B). Copy and complete the table in English with the names of the countries where German is (the):

only official language	one of the official languages	regional official language

Sprechen 4 In pairs, take turns to give <u>three</u> details about one of the countries and guess which one it is.
- Welches Land ist das?
- Der Nationalfeiertag ist am …
- Die Fläche ist …
- Der höchste Punkt liegt bei …
- Der längste Fluss heißt …
- Es gibt … Einwohner.

Schreiben 5 Translate the sentences into German.
1. The longest river in Austria is the Enns.
2. The highest point in Switzerland is 4 634m.
3. Namibia has the largest surface area.
4. Luxemburg has the smallest surface area.
5. Germany has the most inhabitants.
6. Namibia has the earliest national holiday.

Schreiben 6 Use the information on the cards to write a short description of one of the German-speaking countries.

> Die Hauptstadt von Belgien heißt Brüssel. Der Nationalfeiertag ist am 21. Juli. Die Fläche ist 30 528 Quadratkilometer. Der höchste Punkt liegt bei 694 Metern. Der längste Fluss heißt die Maas. Belgien hat 11 715 744 Einwohner.

Brüssel

hundertfünf

1 Wo wohnst du?

- Describing where you live
- Using prepositions followed by the dative
- Using a variety of adjectives with intensifiers and qualifiers

1 Listen (1–5) and write the correct letters for where the people live and the facilities they have (a–l).

Wo wohnst du?   Wo liegt das?   Was gibt es dort?

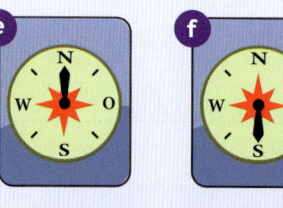

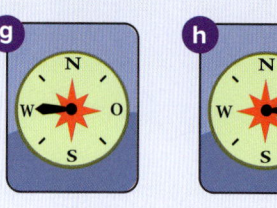

a – in einer Kleinstadt
b – in einem Dorf
c – in einer Großstadt
d – auf dem Land

2 Translate the text into English.

Ich wohne in einem Dorf auf dem Land. Das liegt im Osten von der Schweiz. Meine Gegend ist echt sauber und relativ ruhig. Es gibt eine Schule, aber kein Krankenhaus und kein Fitness-Studio. Früher gab es eine Post und eine Bank. Ich liebe mein Dorf!

Es gibt (there is / there are) is followed by the accusative.
Masc: Es gibt **einen** Flughafen.   There is **an** airport.
Fem: Es gibt **keine** Universität.   There is **no** university.
Neut: Es gibt **kein** Kino.   There is **no** cinema.

Check the gender of the noun you are using and remember to use the correct form of the indefinite article.

Es gab (there was / there were) works in exactly the same way.
Es gab **keinen** Flughafen.   There was **no** airport.

3 Listen to Arda talking about where he lives and write down his answers in English. (1–6) What is the meaning of the final two questions he is asked?

4 Select an option from each highlighted box and write down your choices in secret. Ask your partner the questions. Your partner has to answer, guessing which options you selected. If your partner goes wrong, start again.

- *Wo wohnst du?*
- *Ich wohne* **in einem Dorf / im Stadtzentrum / am Stadtrand** .
- *Wo liegt das?*
- *Das liegt im* **Norden / Süden / Osten / Westen** *von Großbritannien.*
- *Wie ist deine Region?*
- **Mein Bereich / Meine Umgebung / Mein Ort** *ist sehr* **schmutzig / ruhig / sicher** .
- *Was gibt es dort?*
- *Es gibt* **ein Stadion / viel Verkehr / viele Geschäfte** *, aber* **keine Kirche / keine Synagoge / keine Moschee** .
- *Was gab es früher?*
- *Früher gab es* **eine Bank / einen Tempel / ein Museum** .
- *Was wird man in der Zukunft bauen?*
- *In der Zukunft wird man* **eine Schule / ein Krankenhaus / ein Fitness-Studio** *bauen.*

106 hundertsechs

5 Listen to and read the descriptions. Copy and complete the table below in English.

Hier wohne ich!

Ich wohne mit meiner Mutter und meinen Schwestern in Vaduz. Das ist die Hauptstadt von Liechtenstein. Meine Wohnung liegt in der Nähe von der Altstadt und von meinem Fenster aus hat man einen echt schönen Blick. Die Stadt ist manchmal wirklich ruhig, aber die Gegend ist relativ grün und sauber. In der Vergangenheit gab es viele kleine Läden, aber seit zwei Jahren ist mein Lieblingsgeschäft geschlossen. Schade! Deswegen gehe ich jetzt zum Einkaufszentrum. In der Zukunft wird man hier einen neuen Supermarkt bauen.

Bente

Meine Eltern, meine Geschwister und ich wohnen seit sechs Jahren in Windhoek. Das ist die Hauptstadt von Namibia. Unser Haus ist besonders groß und extrem modern. Ich wohne gern hier. Das Stadtzentrum ist oft ein bisschen laut, weil es viel Verkehr gibt, aber ich denke, dass es sicher und sauber ist. Bei uns sind die Leute auch total freundlich und die Umgebung ist nie langweilig! Früher gab es ein altes Stadion, aber vor einigen Jahren hat man ein neues Stadion gebaut. In der Zukunft wird man ein neues Einkaufszentrum bauen.

Mika

Ich wohne mit meiner Familie in Vila Velha in Brasilien, aber ich komme aus der Schweiz. Das ist eine sehr alte, historische Stadt. Die Stadt ist ziemlich groß und ziemlich schmutzig, aber generell ist die Gegend schön und es gibt viele Blumen, Pflanzen und Bäume. Nach der Schule gehe ich an den Strand, weil das Wetter immer schön und es ganz heiß ist. Wir wohnen in einer kleinen Wohnung nicht weit vom Meer. Es ist wirklich wunderbar! Früher gab es hier zu viel Verkehr, aber jetzt gibt es autofreie Tage. In der Zukunft wird man ein neues Theater bauen.

Katharina

	advantages	disadvantages	there used to be ...	future improvements
1				

6 Write a list of the qualifiers and intensifiers used in the texts in exercise 5.

Example: echt

Remember to use qualifiers and intensifiers in front of adjectives or adverbs to add detail to your descriptions.
*Von meinem Fenster aus hat man einen **echt** schönen Blick.*
From my window there is a **really** nice view.

7 Translate the eight underlined sentences in the texts in exercise 5 into English. Find the dative preposition in each one.

Some **prepositions** in German are always followed by the **dative**:

außer	except	**nach**	after, to, according to
aus	from, out of	**seit**	since, for
bei	at, near, by	**von**	from, by, of, about
gegenüber	opposite	**zu**	to
mit	with, by means of		

*Er geht **aus dem** Zimmer.*
*Es gibt einen Park in der Nähe **von meinem** Haus.*

Remember:
- zu + dem → zum
  zu + der → zur
  von + dem → vom
- *in* can take the accusative or the dative, depending on whether it indicates movement or position.

Page 116

8 Write approximately 90 words describing where you live. Include the following points:
- the positive and negative aspects of where you live
- what your town/village did not have in the past that it has now
- what improvements there will be in the future.

hundertsieben **107**

2 Wie fährst du?

- Discussing transport in your local area
- Using prepositions with the accusative
- Using the correct word order with modal verbs and *weil*

1 Listen (1–8) and write the letter(s) of the modes of transport that are mentioned (a–i).

Der Bahnhof am Jungfraujoch in der Schweiz ist der höchste Bahnhof in Europa. Er liegt auf einer Höhe von 3 454 Metern. Die Jungfraubahn fährt 365 Tage im Jahr. Die Fahrt ist echt toll und das Gebiet sieht von oben sehr schön aus.

2 Listen again. Is each statement below true or false?

1 You can travel to the airport by train in 20 minutes.
2 You can walk to the station.
3 You can't go on an excursion by train.
4 You can't take a bike on a tram.
5 You can charge your electric car in the town centre.
6 You can't cycle to Lake Thun to catch a boat.
7 You can travel on the underground in Bern.
8 You can travel to Ostermundigen by bus number 10.

3 Translate the text in the culture box into English.

4 Listen and write down the words you hear to complete the sentences. Be careful with the **s** sound.

1 Ich fahre ▒▒▒ ▒▒▒ ▒▒▒ zur Schule, weil ich um die Ecke wohne.
2 Wir ▒▒▒ ▒▒▒, weil wir weit weg von der Schule wohnen.
3 Ich ▒▒▒ ▒▒▒ ▒▒▒, weil man damit am schnellsten fahren kann. Es ist eine lange Fahrt!
4 ▒▒▒ ▒▒▒, ▒▒▒ ▒▒▒ weit ist. Die Schule ist neben dem Spielplatz.
5 Wenn man ▒▒▒ ▒▒▒ fährt, ▒▒▒ ▒▒▒ nur zehn Minuten.
6 ▒▒▒ ▒▒▒ mit dem Bus, weil es ▒▒▒ ▒▒▒.

s, ss/ß, st, sp and **sch** are pronounced differently. Listen and repeat the words.

s like 'z'	**R**e**is**e	**S**ee	**S**onntag
ss/ß like 's'	ein bi**ss**chen	ge**s**chlo**ss**en	zu Fu**ß**
st like 'sht'	**St**rand	**St**uhl	**St**recke
sp like 'shp'	**Sp**anien	**sp**rechen	**Sp**ielplatz
sch like 'sh'	**Sch**ule	am **sch**nellsten	**Sch**nee

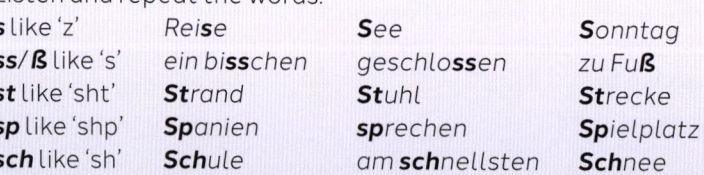

- Remember: Time – Manner – Place:
  Im Winter fahre ich mit dem Auto in die Stadt.
  Time   Manner   Place

- Remember also that **modal verbs** send the infinitive to the end of the sentence.
  Man **kann** *mit dem Auto in die Stadt* fahren.

- If you are giving reasons, remember that **weil** sends the verb to the end of the sentence.
  Ich gehe zu Fuß in die Stadt. Ich wohne um die Ecke.
  Ich gehe zu Fuß in die Stadt, **weil** *ich um die Ecke* wohne.

- If there is also a **modal verb** in the sentence with *weil*, this goes after the infinitive:
  Ich fahre mit dem Zug in die Stadt, **weil** *man im Zug* schlafen **kann**.

Page 119

hundertacht

5 In pairs, ask and answer the questions about using transport where you live.

- Wie fährst du zur Schule? Warum?
- Wie fährst du ins Stadtzentrum? Warum?
- Wie fährst du nach Hause von der Schule? Warum?
- Wie kann man zum Bahnhof fahren?
- Wie kann man zum nächsten Flughafen fahren?
- Wie kann man in die USA reisen?

Man kann Man muss Man soll	mit dem (Elektro)auto mit dem Boot/Schiff mit dem Bus mit dem Fahrrad	nach Frankreich ins Stadtzentrum nach Hause	fahren, reisen,	weil	ich um die Ecke wohne. wir weit weg von der Schule wohnen. die Schule ganz in der Nähe ist. es eine lange Fahrt ist.
Ich fahre Wir fahren	mit dem Fahrzeug mit dem Zug mit der Bahn mit der Straßenbahn	zum Bahnhof zum Flughafen zur Schule		..., weil	die Fahrt nur zehn Minuten dauert. die Reise sehr lange dauert. es am schnellsten geht.
Ich fliege Wir fliegen	mit dem Flugzeug	in die USA nach Griechenland			

6 Read the text about Karla's visit to the Swiss Steam Park and answer the questions below in English.

der Dampf	steam
der Genfer See	Lake Geneva
der Hafen	harbour
der Eintritt	entrance

Besuchen Sie den Schweizer Dampfpark!

Letzten Sommer habe ich den Schweizer Dampfpark besucht. Meine Geschwister sind große Fans von Zügen, aber Züge interessieren mich nicht und ich war gegen den Vorschlag. Der Schweizer Dampfpark liegt am Genfer See und hat eine Fläche von mehr als 19 000m². Wir sind ohne das Auto dorthin gefahren. Wir sind mit dem Boot nach Saint-Gingolph gefahren und wir haben Fahrräder mitgenommen, weil der Park um die Ecke vom Hafen liegt. Die Eintrittskarten waren nicht teuer – für meine Geschwister kosteten sie nur CHF15 und für mich kostete die Karte CHF19. Wir sind mit einem kleinen Dampfzug durch den Park gefahren. Wir sind auch zu Fuß den See entlang gegangen. Dann sind wir vom See zum Picknickplatz gegangen und haben dort gegessen. Im Park kann man mehr als 135 Pflanzen- und Baumarten entdecken. Der Besuch war toll, weil der Park sehr grün und ruhig war. Im Großen und Ganzen hat mir der Park gut gefallen.

1. How did Karla get to Saint-Gingolph?
2. What did they take with them?
3. How did they travel through the park?
4. How did they travel along the lake?
5. Where did they eat?
6. What did Karla think of the visit and why?

7 Find **six** phrases in the text in exercise 6 containing prepositions followed by the accusative and translate them into English.

These **prepositions** are always followed by the **accusative**:

für for	**entlang** along
um around, about	**bis** until
durch through	**ohne** without
gegen against	**wider** against

*Ich gehe **den** Fluss **entlang**.*
*Ich gehe **um die** Ecke.*
*Ich gehe **durch das** Stadtzentrum.*

Note that *entlang* comes after the noun rather than before it.

Remember that *mit* and *zu* are always followed by the dative. Can you find some examples in the key language box?

Page 116

8 Write a short paragraph about how you travel to the following places and why.

- school
- town
- a friend's house
- on holiday

3 Wo gehst du gern einkaufen?

- Discussing shopping habits
- Using dual-case prepositions followed by the dative
- Using plurals of nouns

Lesen 1 Read the brochure about shopping in Bern. Find <u>one</u> example of each type of shop below in the brochure and write the name.

| der Brunnen | fountain |
| der Zeitglockenturm | clock tower |

Was für Geschäfte gibt es in Bern?

In der oberen Altstadt gibt es große Kleidungsgeschäfte, wo man internationale Markenkleidung kaufen kann.

<u>Zwischen den Brunnen</u> in der unteren Altstadt gibt es viele kleine Läden. Diese Läden findet man nur in Bern. <u>Im Geschäft</u> „Feines" verkauft man buntes Papier und Bücher. Im Geschäft „Die Schwarze Katze" findet man Souvenirs und Geschenke. <u>Auf den Tischen</u> im Geschäft „Stoor" liegen T-Shirts und Jeans. <u>Im Familiengeschäft</u> „Bucherer" findet man Schweizer Uhren. Bei „Chäsbueb" kann man viele verschiedene Käsesorten probieren – ideal, wenn man etwas Leckeres sucht! <u>Im Laden</u> „Sterchi" kann man 15 verschiedene handgemachte Brote kaufen. Der Supermarkt liegt <u>vor dem Zeitglockenturm</u> „Zytglogge", wenn man Medikamente braucht.

Der Glockenturm liegt <u>hinter dem Supermarkt</u>. Vom Glockenturm aus hat man einen schönen Blick über die Stadt. <u>Neben dem Fluss</u> findet man viele Cafés und es gibt ein Restaurant <u>unter der Brücke</u>.

die Zytglogge

1 ein Kleidungsgeschäft/Modegeschäft
2 ein Geschäft, das Papierprodukte verkauft
3 drei Geschäfte, wo man Essen kaufen kann
4 ein Uhrengeschäft
5 ein Souvenirgeschäft

Lesen 2 Translate the <u>nine underlined</u> phrases in the brochure into English.

Hören 3 Listen to the advert for a shopping centre and answer the questions in English.

1 At what time does the centre open and close on a Saturday?
2 How many shops are there?
3 Name <u>three</u> modes of public transport you can use to get to the centre.
4 Which advantage can electric car drivers enjoy?
5 Which activities are there for adults? (Give <u>two</u> details.)
6 What can children do? (Give <u>two</u> details.)

Schreiben 4 Translate the sentences into German.

1 In the old town, there are a lot of small shops.
2 Between the cinema and the church there is a clothes shop.
3 The theatre is behind the cheese shop.
4 There are three banks.
5 The station is next to the river.
6 The hotel is behind the supermarket.

G Some **prepositions** are followed by the **accusative** when there is movement towards an object, or by the **dative** when there is no movement:

an on (a vertical surface)	**über** over, above
auf on (a horizontal surface)	**unter** under
hinter behind	**vor** in front of
in in	**zwischen** between
neben next to	

Acc: Ich lege es **auf den** Tisch. — I put it **on the** table.
Dat: Es liegt **auf dem** Tisch. — It is **on the** table.

Page 117

Remember that there are lots of ways to form **plurals of nouns**, but there are patterns you can follow:

	singular	plural
(-e) (¨e)	Geschäft, Supermarkt	Geschäft**e**, Superm**ä**rkt**e**
(-n) (-en)	Kirche, Bank	Kirche**n**, Bank**en**
(-)	Theater	Theater
(¨er)	Krankenhaus	Krankenh**ä**us**er**
(-s)	Hotel	Hotel**s**

Note: the plural of *Museum* is *Museen*.

5 Hören
Listen and write down the words you hear to complete the sentences with *was*, *wer* or *wo*.

1 Gibt es ein Geschäft, ___ ich eine Uhr kaufen kann?
2 Gibt es ein Kino, ___ ich einen Film sehen kann?
3 Wissen Sie, ___ es in der Stadt für Touristen gibt?
4 Gibt es ein Café, ___ wir etwas essen können?
5 Weißt du, ___ mir helfen kann?
6 Gibt es einen Supermarkt, ___ ich Käse kaufen kann?

> **G** *was*, *wer* and *wo* can be used as relative pronouns when you are referring to something non-specific. They send the verb to the end.
>
> *Ich habe alles, **was** ich brauche.*
> I have everything **that** I need.
> *Ich weiß nicht, **wer** kommen wird.*
> I don't know **who** will come.
>
> If there is a modal verb in the relative clause, it goes at the end, after the infinitive.
> *Gibt es ein Café, **wo** wir etwas trinken können?*
> Is there a café **where** we can drink something?
>
> Page 117

6 Hören
Listen to some people explaining why they shop online. Write the correct letters to match the reasons (a–j) to a speaker. (1–5)

Warum shoppst du online?

a Unabhängig von Öffnungszeiten
b Lieferung nach Hause
c Zeitsparend
d Große Auswahl
e Produkte, die es nur online gibt
f Niedrige Preise
g Mehr Produktinformationen
h Rabatte
i Einfach, Produkte zurückzuschicken
j Keine Geschäfte im Wohnort

die Öffnungszeiten (pl)	opening hours
die Lieferung	delivery
die Auswahl	choice, selection
der Rabatt (-e)	reduction, discount

7 Sprechen
In pairs, take turns to ask and answer the questions.

- Was für Geschäfte gibt es in deiner Stadt / in deinem Dorf?
- Wo gehst du gern einkaufen und warum?
- Kaufst du lieber im Einkaufszentrum oder online ein und warum?

In meinem Dorf In meiner Stadt	gibt es	keine Geschäfte. einige Secondhandläden. viele Cafés. einen großen Supermarkt. ein großes Einkaufszentrum.
Ich kaufe gern	im Einkaufszentrum mit einer Einkaufs-App online	ein, …
…, weil das	einfach(er) billig(er) praktisch(er)	ist.
Man kann	Zeit schöne Sachen ungewöhnliche Produkte	sparen. finden.
Man kann Produkte	einfach sofort	zurückschicken.
Man bekommt	bessere	Informationen. Rabatte. Preise.
Die Produkte	kommen	direkt nach Hause.
Die Preise	sind	reduziert.
Die Beschreibungen	sind	nicht so klar.

4 Mein idealer Wohnort

- Describing an ideal place to live
- Using the imperfect tense
- Revising the conditional

 1 Listen to and read the article about Roger Federer, Switzerland's most successful tennis player. Answer the questions in English.

Als er klein war ...

Roger Federer wurde in Basel, in der Schweiz, geboren. Seine Mutter kommt aus Südafrika und sein Vater kommt aus der Schweiz. Er sagt oft, dass er sich in zwei Ländern zu Hause fühlt: in der Schweiz und in Südafrika. Als er klein war, wohnte die Familie in der Nähe von Basel. Später sind sie nach Wasserhaus gezogen.

In den Schulferien besuchte die Familie oft Südafrika. In der Schweiz machten sie viele Ausflüge im ganzen Land. Im Sommer wanderten sie viel und im Winter gingen sie Skifahren. Roger spielte natürlich auch oft Tennis.

Roger fand die Schweiz toll als Kind. Die Leute waren immer sehr freundlich und das Leben war sehr einfach und ganz normal – und natürlich fand er die Schokolade sehr lecker!

Laut Roger ist die Schweiz ein unglaubliches Land mit einer sauberen und wunderbaren Landschaft. Man kann in 15 Minuten am See, in den Bergen oder ebenfalls an einem Fluss sein. Er glaubt, dass die Schweiz das schönste Land der Welt ist!

1 Where was Roger Federer born?
2 Where did he live when he was young?
3 What did he do in the summer?
4 What did he do in the winter?
5 What was his opinion of the people?
6 What does he think of Switzerland today?

 2 Find the German for the phrases below in the text in exercise 1.

1 The family lived near the town of Basel.
2 In the school holidays the family often visited South Africa.
3 Roger also naturally often played tennis.
4 As a child, Roger found Switzerland great.
5 He found the chocolate very delicious.

 3 Listen to the biography of Tama Vakeesan, a Swiss journalist. Write down the sentences you hear. Be careful with the *w* sounds. (1–5)

The German **w** is pronounced like the English 'v'.

Listen and repeat the words.
wohnt **w**ar **w**urde
Wohnung **W**ohnort **w**enig

The **imperfect tense** is used mainly in written narrative accounts and stories.
To form regular verbs in the imperfect tense, add the **endings** to the stem (the infinitive with **-en** removed).
Haben has an irregular stem but uses the regular endings.

	wohnen (to live) (regular verb)	**haben** (to have)
ich	wohn**te**	hat**te**
du	wohn**test**	hat**test**
er/sie/es/man	wohn**te**	hat**te**
wir	wohn**ten**	hat**ten**
ihr	wohn**tet**	hat**tet**
Sie	wohn**ten**	hat**ten**
sie	wohn**ten**	hat**ten**

Some verbs are completely irregular and have the following endings:

	sein (to be)	**gehen** (to go)
ich	war	ging
du	war**st**	ging**st**
er/sie/es/man	war	ging
wir	war**en**	ging**en**
ihr	war**t**	ging**t**
Sie	war**en**	ging**en**
sie	war**en**	ging**en**

Remember:
es gibt (there is/are) → *es gab* (there was/were).

Page 118

4 Listen to Yasmin answering the quiz questions below and write down the letter she gives for each answer.

 5 In pairs, ask and answer the quiz questions. Then read the answers and discuss if they are true for you.

Wie wäre dein idealer Wohnort?

1 Wo würdest du gern leben?
- A Ich würde gern in einem Dorf in Amerika leben.
- B Ich würde gern in einer Kleinstadt in Europa leben.
- C Ich würde gern in einer Hauptstadt in Asien wohnen.

2 Was würdest du gern dort machen?
- A Ich würde gern spazieren gehen.
- B Ich würde gern mit Freunden ins Café gehen.
- C Ich würde gern einkaufen gehen.

3 Wie wäre deine Umgebung?
- A Sie wäre sehr grün mit vielen Bäumen.
- B Sie wäre ziemlich ruhig, aber nicht langweilig.
- C Sie hätte viele interessante Gebäude.

4 Wie wäre dein Haus oder deine Wohnung?
- A Es/Sie wäre ziemlich groß und alt.
- B Es/Sie wäre hell und modern.
- C Es/Sie wäre klein und sauber.

5 Was hätte dein idealer Wohnort?
- A Er hätte viele Bäume und Pflanzen.
- B Er hätte ein Kino und ein Restaurant.
- C Er hätte einen Bahnhof und ein Stadion.

6 Was für Einkaufsmöglichkeiten hätte dein idealer Wohnort?
- A Er hätte eine Bäckerei und einen Markt.
- B Er hätte einen Supermarkt und viele kleine Geschäfte.
- C Er hätte ein riesiges Einkaufszentrum.

Asien Asia

Hast du mehr As, Bs oder Cs?
- **As** Du liebst die Natur und die frische Luft. Dein idealer Wohnort wäre auf dem Land.
- **Bs** Du liebst die Ruhe sowohl als auch das Stadtleben. Dein idealer Wohnort wäre am Stadtrand.
- **Cs** Du liebst ein aktives Leben. Dein idealer Wohnort wäre im Stadtzentrum.

 6 Listen to Anna describing how she would improve her town and where she would like to live in the future. Is each statement below true or false?
1. Anna thinks it would be good to have a new hospital and a new school.
2. She thinks people should protect nature.
3. Her perfect place to live would be in Asia.
4. She would live by the sea.
5. Her ideal town would have a theatre.
6. There wouldn't be lots of houses.

 7 Imagine you are a famous person.
Write approximately 150 words about your area. Include the following points:
- what you like about where you live
- what your ideal place to live would be like.

You have already met **wäre**, **hätte** and **würde** in sentences like these:

Wenn ich Zeit hätte, würde ich mehr Sport machen.
If I **had** more time, I **would** do more sport.

Wenn ich müde wäre, würde ich früher ins Bett gehen.
If I **were** tired, I **would** go to bed earlier.

wäre can also mean 'would be':

Mein idealer Wohnort wäre sehr grün.
My ideal place to live **would be** very green.

hätte can also mean 'would have':

Mein idealer Wohnort hätte ein Einkaufszentrum.
My ideal place to live **would have** a shopping centre.

würde can be used with **gern** to mean 'would like' and can be a synonym for **möchte**.

Ich würde gern in Amerika leben.
I **would like** to live in America.

Page 118

hundertdreizehn **113**

5 Bei mir zu Hause

- Describing your home
- Using dual-case prepositions with the accusative
- Working out the meaning of compound nouns

Hören 1 Listen to Jonas describing his house. Write the correct letter to match each activity (a–g) to the correct room.

- Im Badezimmer
- In der Küche
- Im Wohnzimmer
- In meinem Schlafzimmer
- Im Büro
- Im Esszimmer
- Im Garten

a mache ich meine Hausaufgaben.
b sehe ich fern und ich spiele auf dem Computer.
c höre ich Musik und ich lese auch Bücher.
d frühstücke ich.
e essen wir im Sommer.
f arbeitet meine Mutter.
g dusche ich.

duschen — *to shower*

Lesen 2 Work out the meaning of the following compound nouns in English.

1 das Arbeitszimmer
2 die Essecke
3 der Dachboden
4 das Schlafzimmer
5 die Haustür
6 das Spielzimmer

German often combines two or more words to form new compound nouns. The two words could be:

- two nouns
  Wein (wine) + *Keller* (cellar) ⟶
  der Weinkeller (wine cellar)

- a verb and a noun
  schlafen (to sleep) + *Zimmer* (room) ⟶
  das Schlafzimmer (bedroom)

- an adjective and a noun
  klein (small) + *Stadt* (town) ⟶
  die Kleinstadt (small town)

The gender of the compound noun is always determined by the gender of the **final** noun.
der Keller ⟶ **der** Wein**keller**
das Zimmer ⟶ **das** Schlaf**zimmer**
die Stadt ⟶ **die** Klein**stadt**

Sprechen 3 In pairs, ask each other what you do in each room at home.

- *Was machst du in der Küche?*
- *In der Küche …*
- *Was machst du im Wohnzimmer?*
- *Im Wohnzimmer …*

Im Badezimmer	dusche ich. wasche ich mir die Haare.
Im Büro Im Arbeitszimmer	arbeite ich. mache ich meine Hausaufgaben.
Im Esszimmer	esse ich (zu Mittag / zu Abend).
Im Schlafzimmer	schlafe ich. höre ich Musik.
Im Garten	lese ich.
Im Wohnzimmer	sehe ich fern. spiele ich auf dem Computer.
In der Essecke	frühstücke ich.
In der Küche	kochen wir.
In der Garage	parken wir das Auto.

- Remember that the **verb** must be the second idea if you put the room first:
  In der Küche **frühstücke** *ich.*

- Pay attention to the word order when using separable verbs:
  fernsehen: *Im Wohnzimmer* **sehe** *ich* **fern**.

- When using separable verbs after a subordinating conjunction (*weil, da, obwohl*), the verb comes back together again:
  Ich mag mein Zimmer. Ich **sehe** *dort* **fern**.
  Ich mag mein Zimmer, weil ich dort **fernsehe**.

Lesen 4 Martina is looking for a new flat in Bern. Read the adverts and write the correct letter to match the property (a–c) to each statement.

a Dachwohnung mit Garage und Keller
CHF1 700 im Monat
3 Zimmer, 65m² Wohnfläche

Diese schöne Wohnung hat eine Küche mit Waschmaschine. Unten gibt es einen Keller und eine Garage, wo man für CHF115 pro Monat parken kann.

b Schöne Wohnung mit kleinem Garten
CHF1 730 im Monat
3 Zimmer, 61m² Wohnfläche

Diese helle Wohnung hat ein großes Wohnzimmer mit Essecke und ein großes Schlafzimmer. In der Wohnung gibt es eine moderne Küche und ein neues Badezimmer. Hinter der Wohnung gibt es einen privaten Garten.

c Sonnige Wohnung mit großer Küche
CHF1 760 im Monat
3 Zimmer, 61m² Wohnfläche

Diese ruhige, sonnige Wohnung ist ab 1. August frei. Sie liegt oben im Gebäude und hat eine große Küche. Für die Kinder gibt es einen Spielplatz und man kann auch Hunde oder Katzen in der Wohnung haben.

1 There is a play area.
2 You can eat your meals in the living room.
3 There is a washing machine.
4 You can park there.
5 There is a private garden.
6 Pets are allowed.

> In Germany and Switzerland, it is more common to rent a house or flat than to buy.

Hören 5 Listen to Martina talking about where everything should go in her new flat. Write down the words you hear to complete the sentences.

1 Das Bett kommt _____ _____ Fenster.
2 Die Pflanze kommt _____ _____ Haustür.
3 Der Tisch kommt _____ _____ Küche.
4 Die Waschmaschine stellen wir _____ _____ Badezimmer.
5 Den Computer stellen wir _____ _____ Tisch.
6 Das Foto hängen wir _____ _____ Fenster.

Schreiben 6 Write a rental listing for a house or flat you would like to move into, using the examples in exercise 4.

> **G** Remember that some **prepositions** are followed by the **accusative** when there is movement towards an object, or by the **dative** when there is no movement:
>
> *an*, *auf*, *in*, *unter*, *über*, *hinter*, *vor*, *zwischen*, *neben*
>
> *Wir hängen das Bild **an die** Wand.*
> We are hanging the picture **on the** wall.
> *Das Bild ist **an der** Wand.*
> The picture is **on the** wall.
>
> Page 119

Grammatik 1

Prepositions followed by the dative (Unit 1, page 107)

Hören 1 Listen and write down the words you hear to complete each sentence.
1. Ich wohne seit vier Jahren hier.
2. Unsere Wohnung liegt _____ _____ Kirche.
3. Um 7:00 Uhr gehe ich _____ _____ Haus.
4. Ich fahre _____ _____ Bruder _____ Schule.
5. Der Park liegt direkt _____ _____ Wohnung.
6. _____ _____ Schule treibe ich Sport.
7. Ich verbringe das Wochenende _____ _____ Großeltern.
8. Am Sonntag gehen wir _____ Kirche.

> 💡 Remember that these prepositions always take the **dative**:
> **außer, aus, bei, gegenüber, mit, nach, seit, von, zu**
>
> Use the correct **dative** articles:
>
> | masc | fem | neut | pl |
> |---|---|---|---|
> | **definite article: the** | | | |
> | dem | der | dem | den + -n |
> | **indefinite article: a, an, negatives and possessive adjectives** | | | |
> | einem keinem meinem | einer keiner meiner | einem keinem meinem | keinen + -n meinen + -n |
>
> 💡 In the **dative**, remember to add **-n** to the plural noun:
> *Ich will mit meinen Freunde**n** wohnen.*

Sprechen 2 In pairs, ask and answer the questions, using a preposition + dative in your responses.
- *Seit wann wohnst du hier?*
- *Ich wohne seit …*
- *Wo liegt dein Haus / deine Wohnung?*
- *Es/Sie liegt gegenüber von …*
- *Um wie viel Uhr gehst du aus dem Haus?*
- *Ich gehe um 7:30 Uhr aus dem Haus.*
- *Und mit wem fährst du zur Schule?*
- *Ich fahre mit …*

Prepositions followed by the accusative (Unit 2, page 109)

Lesen 3 Copy and complete the text with the correct definite article in the accusative (*den, die, das*).

> Peter wollte nicht in *die* Schule gehen.
> - Er ist mit dem Rad durch **1** Stadt (f) gefahren.
> - Zuerst ist er **2** Fluss (m) entlanggefahren.
> - Danach ist er um **3** Park (m) gefahren.
> - Er hat im Supermarkt einen Kuchen für **4** Pause (f) gekauft.
> - Leider ist er ohne **5** Kuchen (m) in der Schule angekommen. Er hat ihn im Supermarkt vergessen!

> 💡 Remember that these prepositions always take the **accusative**:
> **bis, durch, entlang, für, gegen, ohne, um, wider**
>
> Use the correct **accusative** articles:
>
> | masc | fem | neut | pl |
> |---|---|---|---|
> | **definite article: the** | | | |
> | den | die | das | die |
> | **indefinite article: a, an, negatives and possessive adjectives** | | | |
> | einen/keinen/meinen | eine/keine/meine | ein/kein/mein | keine/meine |

Sprechen 4 Listen and check your answers to exercise 3. Then read out the sentences.

Dual-case prepositions followed by the dative (Unit 3, page 110)

Translate the sentences into English.
1. Das Kleidungsgeschäft liegt neben dem Krankenhaus.
2. Das Sportgeschäft liegt hinter dem Stadion.
3. Der Supermarkt liegt zwischen der Moschee und der Kirche.
4. Auf dem Fluss gibt es viele Boote.
5. Die Post liegt vor dem Bahnhof.
6. Das Café ist im Museum.
7. Unter der Brücke gibt es ein Theater.
8. Der Markt liegt auf dem Marktplatz.

> These prepositions take the **dative** when there is no movement:
>
> | | |
> |---|---|
> | an | on (a vertical surface) |
> | auf | on (a horizontal surface) |
> | hinter | behind |
> | in | in |
> | neben | next to |
> | über | over, above |
> | unter | under |
> | vor | in front of |
> | zwischen | between |
>
> Remember that *in + dem* is shortened to *im*.

In pairs, take turns to describe a location on the map and guess the place.

- *Das liegt neben der Bank.*
- *Das ist das Museum!*
- *Nein, das stimmt nicht. Das liegt zwischen der Bank und dem Café.*
- *Das ist das Kino.*
- *Ja, das stimmt.*

Relative pronouns (Unit 3, page 111)

Write the correct letter (a–d) to match the two sentence halves. Then translate the sentences into English.

Example: 1 d – There is a café where you can drink coffee.

1. Es gibt ein Café,
2. Ich weiß nicht,
3. Es gibt einen Supermarkt,
4. Entschuldigung, weißt du,

a. wo man Brot kaufen kann.
b. was man in dieser Stadt machen kann.
c. wo man Kaffee trinken kann.
d. wer mir helfen kann?

Translate the sentences into German.
1. There is a museum where you can buy presents.
2. Do you know what there is for tourists here?
3. There is a cinema where you can watch a film.
4. Do you know who is in the café today?

Grammatik 2

The imperfect tense and the conditional (Unit 4, pages 112–113)

 1 Copy and complete the account of Heidi's childhood with the correct imperfect tense form of the verbs in brackets.

> Als Heidi klein **1** (*sein*), **2** (*wohnen*) sie in Graubünden, im Osten von der Schweiz. Sie **3** (*wohnen*) mit ihrem Opa in einem kleinen Haus. Ihr Opa und sie **4** (*sein*) sehr glücklich.
>
> Heidi **5** (*haben*) zwei gute Freunde, Peter und Klara. Im Sommer **6** (*wandern*) die Freunde viel in den Bergen. Im Winter **7** (*spielen*) sie zusammen im Schnee. Es **8** (*geben*) oft viel Schnee!

 2 Write a description of your own childhood or the childhood of a famous fictional character you know. Use exercise 1 to help you.

 3 Listen (1–6) and decide if each sentence is in the imperfect tense (**I**) or the conditional (**C**).

Example: 1 I

 Remember that verbs in the conditional take umlauts, which act as a sound changer.

hatte	hätte
war	wäre
wurde	würde

 4 In pairs, read out the dialogue and select the correct option to complete each sentence in the conditional. Then listen and check your answers.

- Wie **wäre / war / ist** dein idealer Wohnort?
- Ich **werde / wurde / würde** gern am Meer wohnen.
- Was **wurdest / würdest / wirst** du gern dort machen?
- Ich **wurde / würde / werde** gern jeden Tag schwimmen gehen.
- Was **hätte / hatte / hättest** dein idealer Wohnort?
- Er **hatte / hätte / haben** einige Geschäfte und ein schönes Café.
- Wie **war / ist / wäre** deine ideale Wohnung?
- Sie **war / ist / wäre** sehr modern.

 5 In pairs, ask and answer the questions in exercise 4 again and give your own answers.

Word order (Unit 2, page 108)

Put the words in the correct order, starting with the word in bold.
1 Stadt / fahre / mit / **Ich** / Bus / in / am / dem / Samstag / die
2 **Wir** / mit / fliegen / USA / nächste / in / Woche / dem / Flugzeug / die
3 es / nicht / Fuß / gehe / zu / in / ist / **Ich** / Stadt, / die / weit / weil
4 dem / Flughafen, / so / teuer / fahre / nie / mit / ist / **Ich** / weil / Auto / zum / es
5 lieber / mit / **Ich** / im / Bus, / kann / lesen / dem / fahre / Bus / weil / man
6 nicht / schnell / Fahrrad, / fahren / kann / gern / mit / **Wir** / dem / weil / man / nicht / fahren
7 **Ich** / Montag / ich / am / wieder / Wochenende / Hause, / weil / am / arbeiten / nach / muss / fahre
8 kann / Frankreich, / fahre / **Ich** / die / weil / dem / Reise / lange / nie / mit / Boot / nach / so / dauern

Dual-case prepositions (Unit 5, page 115)

Translate into English the instructions for some friends who are helping you move.
Example: 1 The table goes under the window.

1 Der Tisch kommt unter das Fenster.
2 Das Bett kommt neben den Tisch.
3 Die Pflanze kommt auf den Tisch.
4 Der Stuhl kommt vor den Tisch.
5 Das Foto kommt über das Bett.
6 Die Tasche kommt unter das Bett.
7 Die Flaschen kommen in die Küche.
8 Der kleine Tisch kommt zwischen das Bett und den großen Tisch.

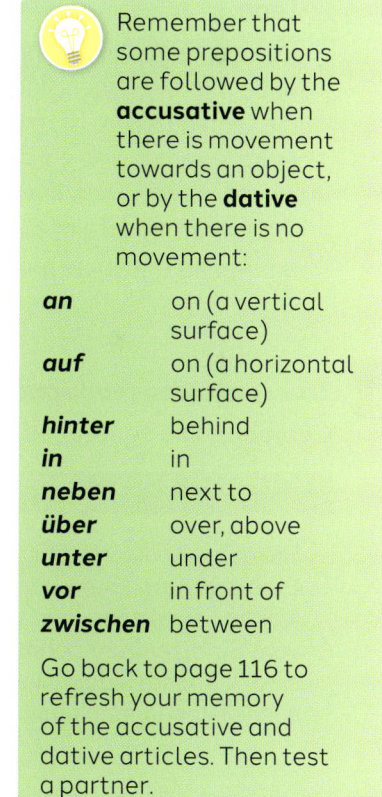

Remember that some prepositions are followed by the **accusative** when there is movement towards an object, or by the **dative** when there is no movement:

an	on (a vertical surface)
auf	on (a horizontal surface)
hinter	behind
in	in
neben	next to
über	over, above
unter	under
vor	in front of
zwischen	between

Go back to page 116 to refresh your memory of the accusative and dative articles. Then test a partner.

Draw a plan of a bedroom and tell your partner where to put the following items. Your partner has to draw the items in the correct place.
Example: Das Bett kommt neben den Tisch.

das Bett   der Tisch   das Poster   das Bild
das Foto   der Computer   das Handy

Write a description of the bedroom plan you drew in exercise 8, using as many different prepositions + dative as possible.
Example: Das Bett ist unter dem Fenster.

Los geht's!

Copy and complete the text with the correct word in each gap.
– **1** Wo gehst du normalerweise einkaufen, Leon?
– Ich gehe gern **2** Einkaufszentrum in **3** Stadtmitte **4** es viele unterschiedliche Geschäfte gibt. Ich muss heute ein Geschenk für **5** Stiefvater kaufen, aber ich weiß nicht, **6** ich kaufen **7** . Er hat morgen Geburtstag! Wenn ich ein bisschen mehr Zeit **8** , **9** ich etwas online kaufen. Also, nach **10** Schule gehe ich in **11** Stadt.

Kapitel 5 Lese- und Hörtest

Reading

My town. Two young Austrians are discussing their towns on social media. Who says what? Write **J** for **Jana**, **L** for **Leon**, or **J+L** for **Jana** and **Leon**.

> Read both blog posts carefully as it is likely that at least one statement will refer to both people.

Jana
Ich wohne in einer kleinen Stadt auf dem Land, die im Norden von Deutschland liegt. Die Landschaft ist besonders schön und die Umgebung, wo ich wohne, gefällt mir. Im Stadtzentrum gibt es einige Geschäfte, einen Supermarkt, eine Kirche, aber leider kein Kino oder Theater. Meine Wohnung liegt am Stadtrand, nicht weit von einem kleinen Park, wo ich mit meinem Hund spazieren gehe.

Leon
Ich wohne gern in meiner Stadt, weil ich viele Freunde habe. Die Menschen sind auch ziemlich freundlich. Obwohl die Gegend sicher ist, gibt es trotzdem viel Verkehr, weil es im Sommer viele Touristen gibt. Sie besuchen gern das alte Schloss am See und die historischen Gebäude im Stadtzentrum. Es gibt nicht viel zu tun für die Jugendlichen am Abend und manchmal kann es langweilig sein.

> You won't find these exact words in the text so you will have to infer meaning, i.e. use the information given to work out the answer.

1 Whose home town is popular with visitors?
2 Who feels there are not enough entertainment opportunities?
3 Who lives on the outskirts of town?
4 Who likes living in their town?

> Remember, there is more than one way to express liking something.

Transport. You read Jonas's blog post about transport in his town.
Complete the sentences below. Write the correct letter, **A**, **B** or **C**, for each question.

> Hier gibt es viel Verkehr, weil ich in einer Großstadt wohne. Man kann mit der Straßenbahn zum Stadtzentrum fahren oder mit dem Bus zum Sportzentrum und zum Hauptbahnhof. Am Stadtrand, wo ich wohne, ist es schneller und praktischer, mit der Bahn zum Flughafen zu fahren, obwohl man auch einen Bus vom Stadtzentrum nehmen kann. Es gibt auch für längere Fahrten billige **Reisebusse**, die sehr bequem sind. Ich fahre jedoch lieber mit dem Zug, wenn ich eine lange Reise machen will, weil man damit am schnellsten fahren kann.

1 You can take the tram to the …
   A station.   **B** town centre.   **C** leisure centre.

2 Jonas lives …
   A near the airport.   **B** in the town centre.   **C** on the edge of town.

3 You have a choice of two ways of getting to the …
   A town centre.   **B** edge of town.   **C** airport.

4 Jonas prefers to travel by train …
   A as it is cheaper.   **B** for long distances.   **C** because it's more comfortable.

5 What would you do with **Reisebusse**? Write the correct letter, **A**, **B** or **C**.
   A ride on them   **B** buy them   **C** avoid them

Kapitel 5

Lesen 3 Translate these sentences into English.

The preposition *um* is used for telling the time, but what does it mean when talking about a location?

Thinking about the case used here might help you find the correct meaning.

1 Gestern bin ich mit der Straßenbahn zur Schule gefahren.
2 Ich darf nicht mit dem Fahrrad fahren, weil ich zu weit weg wohne.
3 Mein bester Freund wohnt um die Ecke, was toll ist.
4 Die Fahrt in die Großstadt ist besonders lang.
5 Wenn wir Zeit hätten, wäre es besser, mit der Bahn zu fahren.

Remember that *was* can be a relative pronoun as well as a question word.

Which tense are these two verbs in?

Listening

Hören 4 *My home.* You hear Katharina talking about her home. What does she say? Listen to the recording and write A, B or C for each question.

1 Katharina lives ...
  A in a village.   B in a flat.   C on the edge of town.

2 Katharina and her family eat in the ...
  A dining room.   B living room.   C kitchen.

3 The family stores their bikes in the ...
  A garage.   B street.   C garden.

Hören 5 *Shopping.* You hear Felix talking about shopping in his town. What does he say? Complete the sentences in English.

1 Felix travels to the shopping centre by tram because ...
2 He finds it better than travelling by car because ...
3 Last week he wanted to ...
4 Normally he prefers ...

Dictation

Hören 6 You will hear five short sentences. Write down exactly what you hear in German.

Think carefully about how these sounds are pronounced when writing down what you hear:
s, ss and ß
sp, st and sch
w

In the dictation task, there will always be some words that are not on the vocabulary list. You may not have come across them before, so listen carefully and think about the sounds you hear when you transcribe (write down) these words.

hunderteinundzwanzig

Kapitel 5 Mündlicher Test

Role-play

 1 Look at the role-play card and prepare what you are going to say.

You can talk either about your house or about the area where you live.

You are talking to your German friend about where you live.
1 Say where you live. (Give **two** details.)
2 Say how long you have lived there.
3 Say whether you like your region and why. (Give **one** opinion and **one** reason.)
4 Say **two** things you did recently in your area.
5 **?** Ask your friend a question about their house.

You need to use the present tense if you use the word *seit* (since).

If you use *weil*, send the verb to the end.

Remember to use a past tense.

Say whatever is easiest for you: either use a question word (Where is your house?) or invert the verb and subject (Do you like your house?).

 2 Practise what you have prepared. Then, using your notes, listen and respond to the teacher.

 3 Listen to Sam's responses and write down the correct letter(s) for his answer to each of the first four questions. Then write down, in English, the question he asks at the end.

1 **A** house   **B** flat   **C** edge of town   **D** town centre
2 **A** 1 year   **B** 10 years   **C** 5 years   **D** 2 years
3 **A** likes it   **B** doesn't like it   **C** loves it   **D** hates it
4 **A** cinema   **B** shopping   **C** park   **D** football

Reading aloud

 4 Look at this task. With a partner, read the sentences aloud, paying attention to the underlined letters.

Regelmäßig fahre ich mit der Straßenbahn in die Stadt.

Am liebsten kaufe ich online ein, weil es praktischer ist.

Ich mag in meinem Wohnzimmer sitzen, was sehr bequem ist.

Ich suche schöne Sachen, die sofort nach Hause kommen.

Man spart Geld, bekommt bessere Preise und kann etwas zurückschicken, wenn es nicht passt.

Think carefully about how to pronounce these sounds:
s, ss and ß
sp, st and sch
w

 5 Listen and check your pronunciation.

 6 Listen to the teacher asking four follow-up questions. Translate each question into English and prepare your own answer to each one. Then listen again and respond to the teacher.

You don't need to give lots of details in your answers. Try instead to vary the structures you use, to add interest to your responses.

Photo card

7 Look at the photos and listen to Sam describing them. Answer the questions in English.
1 Which **three** items in the town does he mention in his description of the first photo?
2 What does he say about the two people in the first photo?
3 What details does he give about the man and woman in the second photo?

You will be asked to talk about the content of these photos. You must say at least one thing about each photo.

After you have spoken about the content of the photos, you will be asked questions related to any of the topics within the theme of **Communication and the world around us**.

Your responses should be as **full and detailed** as possible.

8 Prepare your own description of the photos. Then, with a partner, take turns describing them.

> Auf dem ersten Foto gibt es …

9 Listen to the teacher's first follow-up question, *Wie wichtig ist dir dein Handy?*, and Sam's response. Which **two** reasons does Sam give for his mobile phone being important? Give as much detail as possible.

10 The teacher then asks Sam, *Was machst du online?* Listen to his response and write down the missing word for each gap in the text.

> Viele Sachen! Ich **1** Filme und Videos, die ich in meinem **2** sehe. Mit meinen Eltern sehe ich fast nie **3** , weil ihre **4** immer so langweilig sind. Immer die Nachrichten! Natürlich mache ich auch meine **5** online. Ab und zu kaufe ich neue Kleidung oder **6** für meine Familie und Freunde, weil das so **7** ist. Ich liege im Bett, benutze mein Handy und muss nicht **8** . Super!

11 Listen to two more follow-up questions and prepare your answers. Then listen again and respond. Make your answers as full as possible, including opinions and reasons.

> Get into the habit of including an opinion and reason for every answer you give. Learn a variety of opinion adjectives which are more interesting than just *gut* or *schlecht*. For example, when talking about your area, you could use *angenehm* or *hässlich*.

12 Prepare your own answers to as many of the Module 5 questions on page 227 as you can. Then practise with your partner.

Kapitel 5: Schreibtest

Translation

 Look at the translation task and read Lisa's translation into German. Correct the two mistakes in each German sentence.

1. There are lots of shops where I live.
2. The hospital is between the park and the school.
3. We do not have a station in my village.
4. I went into town last weekend.
5. I buy lots of clothing online because it is quicker.

1. Es gibt keine Geschäfte, wo wir wohnen.
2. Das Krankenhaus ist neben dem Park und der Post.
3. Wir haben einen Flughafen in meinem Dorf.
4. Ich bin nächstes Wochenende in die Moschee gegangen.
5. Ich kaufe viel Musik online, weil es billiger ist.

 Translate the following sentences into German.

1. My region is particularly beautiful.
2. There are lots of trees and the countryside is quiet.
3. We have no shops in my village, but there is a station next to the park.
4. Last week I travelled to school by train.
5. I like living in a town, because it is more interesting.

150-word writing task

 Look at this writing exam task and then, for each bullet point:

1. think about the vocabulary and structures you have learned, which you could use in your answers. For example:
   - **nouns** and **verbs** to write about what there is and what you can do
   - **verbs of opinion** and **adjectives** to explain positive and negative aspects
   - how to explain where you **want** or **would like to live** and **why**
   - **connectives**, **intensifiers** and **sequencers** you would like to use.
2. write down three or four ideas for what you could write about.
3. identify which tense(s) you could use in your answer.

> You are writing an article about where you live.
> Write approximately **150** words in **German**.
> You **must** write something about both bullet points.
> Describe:
> - the positive and negative aspects of where you live
> - where you would like to live in the future.

Kapitel 5

Lesen 4
Read Lisa's answer to the exam task. Answer the questions in the coloured boxes (1–5).

1 This is an example of **complex language**. What does it mean? Find <u>three</u> more examples of complex language in the text.

2 Lisa uses a **variety of plural nouns**. What do these words mean? Find <u>two</u> more examples.

3 Which **tense** is this? When is it used? Which other tenses does Lisa use?

Ich wohne in einer Kleinstadt auf dem Land, wo es ruhig ist. Das ist mir lieber als eine Großstadt, denn es ist sehr laut und schmutzig dort. Hier ist die Landschaft schön und meine Umgebung ist sauber und sicher. In fünf Minuten bin ich am Fluss, wo ich im Sommer manchmal schwimme. Mein Haus ist klein, aber es ist sehr bequem. Obwohl es ziemlich alt ist, gibt es eine moderne Küche und einen großen Garten. Ich mag mein Haus. Wir haben leider keinen Bahnhof in meiner Stadt. Es gibt Busse, aber die sind teuer und sie fahren nur zweimal am Tag. Das finde ich nicht so gut. Wir haben einen kleinen Laden um die Ecke. Früher gab es viele Geschäfte, aber jetzt sind viele geschlossen.

Wenn ich älter bin, würde ich gern an der Küste wohnen. Ich würde ein Haus neben dem Strand kaufen. Ich möchte jeden Tag im Meer schwimmen oder am Strand spazieren gehen. Es hätte einen Garten mit Bäumen und die Umgebung wäre grün.

4 Which connective could you use here to form an **extended sentence**? What other connectives does Lisa use?

5 To **avoid repetition,** Lisa has used these synonyms. Can you find <u>two</u> more pairs of synonyms?

Lesen 5
Read Lisa's answer again. Copy and complete the sentences in English.

1 Lisa ▓▓ to live in the ▓▓.
2 Lisa does not like the ▓▓ because it is ▓▓ and ▓▓.
3 Not far from Lisa's house is a ▓▓ where she sometimes ▓▓.
4 There is no ▓▓ but there are occasional ▓▓.
5 Many of the ▓▓ have ▓▓ in her town.
6 Lisa would like to live ▓▓.

Schreiben 6
Prepare your own answer to the task in exercise 3.

- Think about how you can develop your answer for each bullet point.
- Look back at your notes from exercises 3 and 4.
- Look at the 'Challenge checklist' and consider how you can show off your German!
- Write a **brief** plan and organise your answer into paragraphs.
- Write your answer and then carefully check for accuracy.

Challenge checklist

- ✓ Past, present and future time frames
- ✓ Connectives, time phrases and sequencers
- ✓ Some extended sentences
- ✓ Different opinion phrases

- ✓ A wider range of tenses (imperfect: *gab*, perfect: *sind geschlossen*)
- ✓ Different persons of the verb (*es, wir*)
- ✓ Correct use of cases (*Es gibt kein**en** Bahnhof in mein**er** Stadt.*)
- ✓ A wider range of interesting vocabulary

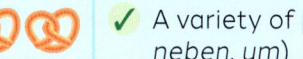
- ✓ Phrases with more than one tense (*Wenn ich älter bin, würde ich gern …*)
- ✓ Subordinating conjunctions (*wo, weil*)
- ✓ Complex language (*würde, hätte, wäre*)
- ✓ A variety of prepositions (*in, auf, an, neben, um*)
- ✓ Plural nouns (*Busse, Städte, Geschäfte*)
- ✓ Time – manner – place (*Im Sommer schwimme ich mit meinen Freunden im Fluss.*)
- ✓ Separable verbs (*ich kaufe ein, er fährt ab*)

hundertfünfundzwanzig **125**

Kapitel 5 Wörter

Key:
bold = this word will appear in higher exams only
* = this word is not on the vocabulary list, but you may use it in your own sentences

Wo spricht man Deutsch? (pages 104–105):

Die *deutschsprachigen Länder	German-speaking countries
*Belgien	Belgium
Deutschland	Germany
*Liechtenstein	Liechtenstein
*Luxemburg	Luxembourg
*Namibia	Namibia
Österreich	Austria
die Schweiz	Switzerland
*Südtirol	South Tyrol
der **Einwohner**	inhabitant, resident
der Fluss	river
der *Nationalfeiertag	national day
der **höchste** Punkt	the highest point
die *Fläche	surface area
die **Hauptstadt**	capital city
das Land	country, land, state

Wo wohnst du? (pages 106–107):

Wo ich wohne	Where I live
Ich wohne …	I live …
in einem Dorf.	in a village.
in einer Kleinstadt.	in a small town.
in einer *Großstadt.	in a city.
im Stadtzentrum.	in the town/city centre.
in den Bergen.	in the mountains.
am **Stadtrand**.	on the edge of town.
auf dem Land.	in the countryside.
an einem See.	by a lake.
an der Küste.	at the coast.
Das liegt …	It lies / is situated …
im Norden von …	in the north of …
im Osten von …	in the east of …
im Süden von …	in the south of …
im Westen von …	in the west of …
Mein Ort ist …	My place, location, town is …
Mein **Bereich** ist …	My area is …
Die Gegend ist …	The region, area is …
Die Landschaft ist …	The countryside, scenery, landscape is …
Die Region ist …	The region is …
Die Umgebung ist …	The surroundings are …
besonders	particularly, especially
echt/extrem	really/extremely
ganz/**relativ**	quite/relatively
sehr/so	very/so
total/wirklich	totally/really
ein bisschen / ziemlich	a little / rather
nicht	not
zu	too
alt/neu.	old/new.
sauber/schmutzig.	clean/dirty.
schön.	beautiful.
historisch/modern.	historic/modern.
ruhig/laut.	quiet/noisy.
sicher.	safe.
Es gibt …	There is …
(k)einen Flughafen.	no airport / an airport.
(k)eine Bank.	no bank / a bank.
(k)eine Kirche.	no church / a church
(k)eine Moschee.	no mosque / a mosque
(k)eine Post.	no post office / a post office.
(k)eine Schule.	no school / a school.
(keine) Universität.	no university / a university.
(k)ein Fitness-Studio.	no gym / a gym.
(k)ein Geschäft.	no shop / a shop.
(k)ein Kino.	no cinema / a cinema.
(k)ein Krankenhaus.	no hospital / a hospital.
(k)ein Museum.	no museum / a museum.
(k)ein Schloss.	no castle / a castle.
(k)ein Stadion.	no stadium / a stadium.
(k)ein Theater.	no theatre / a theatre.
viel Verkehr.	a lot of traffic.

Wie fährst du? (pages 108–109):

Das Verkehrsmittel	Means of transport
Man kann …	You can …
Man muss …	You have to, must …
Man soll …	You should, are supposed to, ought to …
fahren, …	go (by transport), drive
fliegen, …	fly
reisen, …	travel
Ich fahre / Wir fahren / Man fährt …, …	I/We/You go …, …
mit dem Auto …	by car
mit dem **Boot**/Schiff …	by boat/ship
mit dem Bus …	by bus
mit dem **Elektroauto** …	by electric car
mit dem Fahrrad …	by bicycle, bike
mit dem **Fahrzeug** …	by vehicle
mit dem Flugzeug …	by aeroplane
mit dem Zug …	by train
mit der Bahn …	by rail
mit der **Straßenbahn** …	by tram
in die **USA**	to the USA.
ins Stadtzentrum	to the town / city centre.
nach Hause	home.
zum Bahnhof	to the station.
zum Flughafen	to the airport.
zur Schule	to school.
weil …	because …
ich um die **Ecke** wohne.	I live around the corner.
wir weit weg von der Schule wohnen.	we live far / a long way from (the) school.
die Schule ganz in der Nähe ist.	the school is quite near/ close.
es eine lange Fahrt ist.	it is a long journey.
die Fahrt nur zehn Minuten dauert.	the journey only takes ten minutes.
die Reise sehr lange dauert.	the journey takes a long time.
es **am schnellsten** geht.	it is the quickest way.

Wo gehst du gern einkaufen? (pages 110–111):

Einkaufen	Shopping
die Bank	bank
das Käsegeschäft	cheese shop
das Kleidungsgeschäft	clothes shop
das **Modegeschäft**	fashion shop
das *Souvenirgeschäft	souvenir shop
der Supermarkt	supermarket
das Uhrengeschäft	watch shop

In meinem Dorf / In meiner Stadt gibt es … — *In my village/town there is/are …*
- keine Geschäfte. — *no shops.*
- einige Secondhand**läden**. — *some second-hand shops.*
- viele Cafés. — *a lot of cafés.*
- einen großen Supermarkt. — *a large supermarket.*
- ein großes Einkaufszentrum. — *a large shopping centre.*

Ich kaufe (nicht) gern … ein, — *I (don't) like shopping …*
- im Einkaufszentrum — *in the shopping centre,*
- mit einer Einkaufs-App — *with a shopping app,*
- online — *online,*

weil das … ist. — *because it is …*
- einfach(er). — *easy (easier).*
- billig(er). — *cheap(er).*
- praktisch(er). — *practical (more practical).*

Man kann Zeit sparen. — *You can save time.*
Man kann schöne Sachen finden. — *You can find beautiful things.*
Man kann **Produkte** einfach zurückschicken. — *You can simply/easily return products.*
Man kann **Produkte** sofort zurückschicken. — *You can return products immediately.*
Man bekommt bessere … — *You get better …*
- Informationen. — *Information.*
- *Rabatte. — *discounts.*
- Preise. — *prices.*

Die **Produkte** kommen direkt nach Hause. — *The products come direct/ straight to your house.*
Die Preise sind **reduziert**. — *The prices are reduced.*

Mein idealer Wohnort (pages 112–113):

Wo **würdest** du **am liebsten** wohnen? — *Where would you prefer to live?*
Wo **würdest** du gern leben? — *Where would you like to live?*
Wie **wäre** deine ideale Umgebung? — *What would be your ideal area be like?*
Was **hätte** dein idealer Wohnort? — *What would your ideal place to live have?*

ziemlich	quite
grün	green
hell	bright, light
modern	modern
sauber	clean
riesig	huge

der Baum	tree
der Wohnort	place to live, place of residence
die *Großstadt	city
die **Hauptstadt**	capital city
die *Kleinstadt	small town
die Möglichkeit	possibility
die Pflanze	plant
die Umgebung	surroundings
die Wohnung	flat
das Dorf	village
das Fitness-Studio	gym
das Geschäft	shop
das Haus	house

Bei mir zu Hause (pages 114–115):

Zimmer zu Hause	Rooms at home

Im Badezimmer … — *In the bathroom …*
- *dusche ich. — *I shower.*
- *wasche ich mir die Haare. — *I wash my hair.*

Im Büro / Im *Arbeitszimmer arbeite ich. — *I work in the office/study.*
Im *Esszimmer / in der *Essecke esse ich (zu Mittag / zu Abend). — *I eat (lunch/dinner) in the dining room / dining area.*

In der *Garage *parken wir das Auto. — *We park the car in the garage.*
Im Garten lese ich. — *I read in the garden.*
In der Küche frühstücke ich. — *I have breakfast in the kitchen.*

Im *Schlafzimmer … — *In the bedroom …*
- höre ich Musik. — *I listen to music.*
- mache ich meine Hausaufgaben. — *I do my homework.*
- schlafe ich. — *I sleep.*

Im Wohnzimmer … — *In the living room …*
- sehe ich fern. — *I watch TV.*
- spiele ich auf dem Computer. — *I play on the computer.*

kochen	to cook
der *Dachboden	loft
der Keller	cellar
die Haustür	front door
die *Waschmaschine	washing machine
das Fenster	window
das Gebäude	building

Kapitel 1–5 Grammatik: Wiederholung

Compound nouns

 1 Form <u>ten</u> compound nouns by combining a word from box A and box B, starting each word with a noun from box A. Write down the compound nouns with the correct article (*der*, *die* or *das*), then translate these into English.

Example: der Lehrer + das Zimmer → das Lehrerzimmer – staff room

A	B
der Lehrer	das Restaurant
die Stadt	das Geschäft
der Rücken	die Flasche
die Schule	das Zimmer
das Wasser	das Tier
das Fastfood	der Kuchen
die Sonne	die Schmerzen
der Liebling	die Mitte
der Sport	die Brille
der Geburtstag	das Buch

Remember that the gender of the compound noun is always determined by the gender of the final noun. Some compound nouns also need a 'combining letter' between the two words, such as *-n-* or *-s-*.

 2 Which three of the compound nouns need to have a combining letter?

Possessive adjectives

 3 Everyone loves their pet! Copy and complete the sentences with the correct possessive adjective, using the words from the box.

1 Ich liebe mein Haustier.
2 Du liebst ___ Haustier.
3 Er liebt ___ Haustier.
4 Sie liebt ___ Haustier.
5 Wir lieben ___ Haustier.
6 Ihr liebt ___ Haustier.
7 Frau Maier, Sie lieben ___ Haustier.
8 Die Kinder lieben ___ Haustier.

sein Ihr euer dein ihr ihr unser ~~mein~~

Pronouns, possessive adjectives and plural nouns

 4 Rewrite the German sentences to match the English translations by changing the <u>underlined</u> words to plural forms.

Example: 1 *Wir wohnen mit unseren Katzen in Berlin.*

1 <u>Ich wohne</u> mit <u>meiner</u> Katze in Berlin. We live with our cats in Berlin.
2 <u>Ich schwimme</u> gern, aber <u>meine</u> Lieblingssportart ist Basketball. We like swimming but our favourite sport is basketball.
3 <u>Er findet seinen</u> Bruder süß. They find their brothers sweet.
4 <u>Sie geht</u> mit <u>ihrer</u> Familie ins Museum. They go with their families to the museum.
5 <u>Ich gehe</u> mit <u>meinem</u> Hund laufen. We go running with our dogs.
6 <u>Er benutzt sein</u> Handy viel zu oft. They use their mobiles much too often.
7 <u>Ich finde meinen</u> Freund lustig. We find our friends funny.
8 <u>Du hast deinen</u> Geburtstag im Mai gefeiert. You (pl) celebrated your birthdays in May.

Grammatik: Wiederholung — Kapitel 1–5

Comparatives and superlatives

 Copy and complete the texts with the correct standard, comparative and superlative adjectives and adverbs to match the English translations.

Go back to page 92 to refresh your memory on how to form the comparative and superlative. Then test a partner.

1

My grandfather has a small house. He has a smaller house than my aunt, but my uncle has the smallest house in our family.

Mein Großvater hat ein kleines Haus. Er hat ein ___ Haus als meine Tante, aber mein Onkel hat das ___ Haus in unserer Familie.

2

My brother cooks well. He cooks better than my mother, but our grandma cooks the best.

Mein Bruder kocht ___. Er kocht ___ als meine Mutter, aber unsere Großmutter kocht ___ ___.

3

My friend Noah is intelligent, but my friend Toni is more intelligent. Our friend Oskar is the most intelligent student in our class.

Mein Freund Noah ist ___, aber meine Freundin Toni ist ___. Unser Freund Oskar ist der ___ Schüler in unserer Klasse.

4

His grandfather is 85 years old. He is old, but *her* grandfather is older because he is 87. Mia, your grandfather is the oldest because he will soon be 90.

Sein Großvater ist 85 Jahre alt. Er ist ___, aber ihr Großvater ist ___, weil er 87 ist. Mia, dein Großvater ist der ___, weil er bald 90 wird.

Relative pronouns

 Read the English sentences and decide if the word in bold is:
a the subject   b the object   c something non-specific.
Then copy and complete the German translations with the correct relative pronoun.

| der | den | das | die |
| was | wo | die | das |

1 English is a subject **which** is very useful.   Englisch ist ein Fach, ___ sehr nützlich ist.
2 Volleyball is a sport **which** I play often.   Volleyball ist eine Sportart, ___ ich oft spiele.
3 In the town centre there are shops **which** sell everything.   Im Stadtzentrum gibt es Geschäfte, ___ alles verkaufen.
4 We have a teacher **who** is quite strict.   Wir haben einen Lehrer, ___ ziemlich streng ist.
5 Karneval is a festival **which** takes place annually.   Karneval ist ein Fest, ___ jährlich stattfindet.
6 Peter Fox is a German musician **who** I like.   Peter Fox ist ein deutscher Musiker, ___ ich mag.
7 Listening to music is something **which** I love.   Musik hören ist etwas, ___ ich liebe.
8 The place **where** I live is always quiet.   Der Ort, ___ ich wohne, ist immer ruhig.

hundertneunundzwanzig

Kapitel 1–5 Grammatik: Wiederholung

Cases following prepositions

 Copy and complete the sentences with the correct definite article.

1. Ich gehe in das Modegeschäft (n) neben ___ Kirche (f).
2. Er arbeitet in ___ Museum (n) gegenüber von ___ Bahnhof (m).
3. Wir werden uns vor ___ Café (n) treffen, das um ___ Ecke (f) ist.
4. Sie warten in ___ Bus (m) vor ___ Schule (f).
5. Sie fahrt mit ___ Auto (n) in ___ Stadt (f).
6. Wir sind mit ___ Bahn (f) in ___ Schweiz (f) gefahren.

> Remember that some prepositions take the accusative case (*für, um, durch, gegen, entlang, bis, ohne*), some take the dative case (*aus, außer, bei, gegenüber, mit, nach, seit, von, zu*), and some can take either (*an, auf, in, hinter, neben, über, unter, vor, zwischen*), depending on whether or not there is movement:
>
> movement = accusative: *Ich fahre in **die** Stadt.*
> no movement = dative: *Ich bin in **der** Stadt.*

Question words

 Match up the questions and answers.

1. Um wie viel Uhr ist das Frühstück?
2. Mit wem fährst du?
3. Wer isst Pommes?
4. Wohin kommt dieser neue Tisch?
5. Wann beginnt das Spiel?
6. Wo ist der Computer?
7. Wie viele Zimmer hat das Ferienhaus?
8. Wie fühlst du dich?

a Mein Freund.
b Zehn.
c Nach dem Abendessen.
d Von 8:00 bis 10:00 Uhr.
e Mit meinem Bruder.
f In der Ecke.
g Ziemlich müde.
h In die Ecke.

Translating the preposition *seit*

 Translate the text into English.

> Meine Mutter kommt aus Italien, aber sie lebt seit 1990 in Österreich. Als sie jünger war, hat sie in Südtirol gelebt und spricht seit ihrer Kindheit Deutsch. Wir wohnen seit vier Jahren in einer kleinen Stadt in der Nähe von den Bergen. Seit vielen Jahren gibt es im Dezember einen Weihnachtsmarkt in der Altstadt. Ich finde das eine sehr schöne Tradition. Seit letztem Jahr darf ich den Markt ohne meine Eltern besuchen.

> The preposition *seit* is used with the present tense to say how long something has been happening.
> Use 'since' to translate *seit* when you are giving a specific time reference, such as a date. Use 'for' when you want to indicate a duration of time.

Infinitive constructions with *zu*

 Write the correct letter (a–e) to match up the sentence halves. Then translate the sentences into English.

1. Wir möchten gute Noten bekommen,
2. Ich habe heute Abend vor,
3. Nächste Woche will ich aktiver sein,
4. Sara hat beschlossen,
5. Es ist oft schwierig,

a ihr Handy weniger zu benutzen.
b ein guter Freund zu sein.
c früher ins Bett zu gehen.
d um in der Oberstufe studieren zu können.
e um fit zu werden.

Grammatik: Wiederholung — Kapitel 1–5

Forming the imperfect tense

 Copy and complete the sentences with the correct imperfect tense form of the verb in brackets.

> Remember that some verbs are irregular and have a change of stem in the imperfect tense.
> Go back to page 112 to refresh your memory on how to form the imperfect tense. Then test a partner.

1 Er *spielte* gern Tennis. (*spielen*)
2 Ich ___ meine Hausaufgaben. (*machen*)
3 Wir ___ in der Schweiz. (*wohnen*)
4 Meine Schwester ___ an der Uni. (*studieren*)
5 Ich ___ mir neue Kleidung. (*kaufen*)
6 Die Schüler ___ Briefe. (*schreiben*)
7 Es ___ viele Geschäfte im Stadtzentrum. (*geben*)
8 Er ___ gestern einen Unfall. (*haben*)
9 Wir ___ zu Fuß zum Park. (*gehen*)
10 Das Wetter ___ letzte Woche sehr schlecht. (*sein*)

The conditional

 Copy and complete the sentences with the correct conditional form of *werden*. Then translate the sentences into English.

Example: 1 *If I had time, I would go swimming.*

1 Wenn ich Zeit hätte, *würde* ich schwimmen gehen.
2 Wenn ihr Geld hättet, ___ ihr nach Österreich fahren.
3 Wenn mein Bruder nicht so laut wäre, ___ wir uns besser verstehen.
4 Wenn das Wetter besser wäre, ___ meine Schwester in der Sonne liegen.
5 Wenn ich älter wäre, ___ ich mir ein Auto kaufen.
6 Wenn du ein besseres Zeugnis hättest, ___ deine Eltern sehr zufrieden sein.

> Be careful when using the conditional, as it looks and sounds similar to the future tense in German.
> Ich **werde** Fahrrad fahren. I **will** go cycling.
> Ich **würde** Fahrrad fahren. I **would** go cycling.
>
> These three verbs sound very similar, but they have very different meanings.
> Ich **werde** … I will … (future tense)
> Ich **würde** … I would … (conditional)
> Ich **wurde** … I became … (imperfect tense)
>
> Practise reading out the verbs.

Recognising different tenses

 Decide if the sentences are in the past, future or conditional.

1 Wir konnten nichts essen.
2 Sie hatte keine Ahnung.
3 Mein Mathelehrer wird heiraten.
4 Möchtest du in der Schweiz leben?
5 Julia hat einen guten Bericht geschrieben.
6 Meine Tante würde gern ins Kino gehen.
7 Nach dem Abendessen werden wir fernsehen.
8 Zum Nachtisch gab es Eis.
9 Das Kind hätte gern eine Katze.
10 Das Wetter war sehr schlecht.

Using different tenses

 Copy and complete the sentences with the correct verb form. Then translate the sentences into English.

Example: 1 *Sometimes we cycle in the park.*

1 Manchmal *fahren* wir im Park Fahrrad.
2 Wir ___ mit dem Zug nach Wien gefahren.
3 Gestern ___ das Wetter sehr schön.
4 Wenn sie mehr Zeit hätte, ___ sie ins Kino gehen.
5 In der Zukunft ___ er im Ausland arbeiten.
6 Wenn ich älter bin, ___ ich eine Weltreise machen.

| ~~fahren~~ | werde | war |
| sind | möchte | würde |

> Use the time phrases and other language in each sentence to help you work out which tense is needed.

Kapitel 6 Schöne Ferien!

Im Urlaub und unterwegs
- Learning about German-speaking travel destinations
- Forming the imperative

Herzlich Willkommen!

Wir bieten Ihnen einen spannenden Aufenthalt in drei deutschsprachigen Ländern an: Man hat die Chance, viele tolle Orte zu entdecken. Wir zeigen Ihnen die höchsten Berge, die schönsten Seen, die längsten Flüsse, die beliebtesten Städte und die interessantesten Touristenattraktionen. Drei Länder, tausende schöne Reiseziele. Sind Sie bereit? Los geht's!

Phantasialand ist ein riesiger Freizeitpark in Deutschland. Hier sind die spannendsten Achterbahnen und die beliebtesten Shows – wunderbare Attraktionen für alle. Erleben Sie eine Welt voller Action und Spaß und genießen Sie aufregende Momente mit Ihrer Familie!

Kommen Sie nach Berlin und besuchen Sie das **Brandenburger Tor**, das bekannteste und schönste Tor in Deutschland. Als Symbol des Falles der Mauer und der deutschen Wiedervereinigung zieht es jedes Jahr viele Touristen an.

Der **Schwarzwald** ist ein sehr alter Wald und ist ideal zum Wandern und Klettern. Entdecken Sie die eindrucksvollen Berge und probieren Sie die leckere Schwarzwälder Kirschtorte! Gehen Sie nach draußen in die Natur und machen Sie wunderbare Fotos von der schönsten Landschaft Deutschlands.

Die **Krimmler Wasserfälle** im Nationalpark Hohe Tauern sind die höchsten Wasserfälle in Österreich. Mit einer Höhe von 380 Metern bieten sie einen unglaublichen Blick an. Das Wasser ist klar und sauber, und die Luft ist frisch! Erleben Sie die wunderbare Kraft des Wassers in der Natur. Tauchen empfehlen wir nicht, aber bringen Sie Ihre Jacke mit – es kann manchmal nass sein!

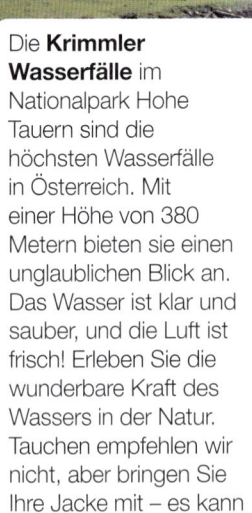

Churwalden Pradaschier ist die berühmteste, traditionellste Rodelbahn in der Schweiz. Sie ist genau 3 060m lang und ist auch die längste Rodelbahn in der Schweiz. Genießen Sie die Spannung der Abfahrt – mit garantiert viel Adrenalin!

die Wiedervereinigung	reunification
der Freizeitpark	theme park
die Achterbahn	roller coaster
eindrucksvoll	impressive
die Schwarzwälder Kirschtorte	Black Forest gateau
die Rodelbahn	toboggan run

Kulturzone

Kapitel 6

 Lesen 1 Read the brochure, then copy and complete the sentences with words from the box below. There are more words than gaps.
1. The Brandenburg Gate attracts … visitors every year.
2. *Phantasialand* is a … theme park in Germany.
3. The Black Forest is an … forest.
4. The … from the Krimml Waterfalls is unbelievable.
5. The Churwalden Pradaschier is the … toboggan run in Switzerland.

oldest	view
longest	impressive
old	descent
numerous	highest
warm	huge

 Lesen 2 Read the brochure again and answer the questions in English.
1. What does the Brandenburg Gate symbolise?
2. How are the rollercoasters described at *Phantasialand*?
3. Which <u>two</u> outdoor activities are suggested for the Black Forest?
4. In which <u>two</u> ways is the water at the Krimml Waterfalls described?
5. How long is the toboggan run at Churwalden Pradaschier?

 Lesen 3 Find <u>nine</u> imperative verbs in the brochure and translate them into English.

 Hören 4 Listen and write down the words you hear to complete the sentences.
1. ▒▒▒ das Miniatur Wunderland in Hamburg, ▒▒▒ Modelleisenbahn Europas.
2. ▒▒▒ das Mercedes-Benz Museum in Stuttgart und ▒▒▒ nicht, sich die ▒▒▒ Autos der Welt ▒▒▒.
3. ▒▒▒ die Großglockner Hochalpenstraße, die ▒▒▒ in ▒▒▒.

> **G**
> To give instructions or recommendations, use the **imperative** form.
>
> In a formal situation, such as a brochure, use the *Sie* form of the **verb**, followed by the word **Sie**.
>
> ***Besuchen Sie*** die Alpen in der Schweiz!
> **Visit** the Alps in Switzerland!
> ***Kommen Sie*** nach Österreich!
> **Come** to Austria!
>
> *Sein* has an irregular imperative form:
> ***Seien Sie*** glücklich in Norddeutschland!
> **Be** happy in northern Germany!
>
> Page 144

 Sprechen 5 In pairs, take turns to read out the text. Pay attention to the *a/ä* and *o/ö* sounds. Then listen and check.

Schloss Neuschwanstein ist ein schönes, historisches Schloss in Deutschland. Man hat das Schloss im neunzehnten Jahrhundert gebaut. Es liegt 940 Meter hoch in den Bergen, aber es ist nicht das größte oder das älteste Schloss in der Bundesrepublik Deutschland. Burg Burghausen ist die größte und längste Burg in Deutschland und die Reichsburg in Cochem ist wahrscheinlich die älteste Burg.

die Burg fortress

> Remember that an umlaut changes the pronunciation of a vowel.
>
> **a** can be either short (as in bek**a**nnt) or long (as in **A**benteuer).
>
> **ä** sounds like 'e' in 'g**e**t'.
> **a**lt → **ä**lteste
>
> **o** can be either short (as in t**o**ll) or long (as in F**o**t**o**s).
>
> **ö** sounds like 'ur' in 'ch**ur**n'.
> gr**o**ß → gr**ö**ßte
>
> Listen and repeat the words.

 Lesen 6 Translate the text in exercise 5 into English.

Schreiben 7 Research and write 90 words advertising an attraction in a German-speaking country. Include superlatives and imperatives.

> Remember that we use **superlatives** to say something is 'the most'. In German, add **-(e)st** to the end of the adjective and make sure it agrees with the noun.
> *Hier sind die* **spannendsten** *Achterbahnen.*

hundertdreiunddreißig **133**

1 Wo fahren wir hin?

- Describing different holiday destinations
- Forming questions
- Discussing advantages and disadvantages

Lesen 1 Read the advert for *Ferienpark Müller*. Is each statement below true or false?

Willkommen im Ferienpark Müller!

Sind Sie sehr aktiv? Hier gibt es richtig viel zu tun. Für Fahrradfahrer gibt es im Frühling, im Sommer und im Herbst schöne Ausflüge in die Natur und man kann auch in den Wäldern oder am Strand wandern gehen. Für Tennisspieler gibt es riesige Tennisplätze. Wenn Sie gern schwimmen gehen, können Sie im See – oder auch im Meer – schwimmen gehen!

Oder vielleicht wollen Sie einfach ein bisschen Ruhe haben? Man kann am Strand liegen und ein gutes Buch lesen, oder in unserer hübschen Landschaft spazieren gehen, um schöne Fotos zu machen. Natürlich gibt es auch leckeres Essen im Restaurant!

Im Ferienpark gibt es eine Touristeninformation, wo man Ihnen gerne weiterhilft. Worauf warten Sie? Denken Sie schon dieses Jahr über einen Urlaub bei uns nach!

In der unglaublichen Kulturlandschaft der Rostocker Küste finden Sie den idealen Ferienpark Müller. Es gibt zahlreiche Aktivitäten für Besucher. Erleben Sie hier einen wunderbaren Urlaub!

Möchten Sie die Kultur kennenlernen? Man kann in der Nähe Museen und kulturelle Veranstaltungen besuchen. Der Schlossbesuch ist sehr beliebt und man kann auch Geschenke in den lokalen Geschäften, und donnerstags und samstags auf dem Markt, kaufen.

1. *Ferienpark Müller* is situated on the coast.
2. You can visit a castle.
3. You can buy presents from the market on Sundays.
4. There are bike excursions in winter.
5. You can take photos on walks in the country.
6. There isn't anywhere to eat.

G Remember the simple way to **form questions** in German: simply swap around the **subject** and **verb**.

Sie <u>sind</u> sehr aktiv. → <u>Sind</u> **Sie** sehr aktiv?
Er <u>geht</u> gern wandern. → <u>Geht</u> **er** gern wandern?
Man <u>kann</u> hier schwimmen gehen. →
<u>Kann</u> **man** hier schwimmen gehen?

Page 144

Lesen 2 Read the advert again. Copy and complete the sentences.

1. To get to know the culture, you can visit … and go to cultural events.
2. The castle tour is very …
3. You can go hiking in the forests and …
4. You can swim in the sea or …
5. You can relax on the beach by …
6. You can get help from … at the holiday park.

e is usually short (j**e**tzt) if it's followed by a double consonant (e.g. *tt*, *ck*, *ch* or *tz*), or if it's at the end of a word.
e is usually long (s**e**hr) if it's followed by any other consonant. However, **e** is short (mach**e**n) if it is the final syllable of a word.

Listen and repeat the tongue twister. Then practise reading it out.

*Im H**e**rbst mach**e**n wir gern F**e**ri**e**n an der Küst**e**. J**e**tzt hat man Zeit, Büch**e**r über Kultur zu l**e**s**e**n und die Ruh**e** zu g**e**nieß**e**n. Spazi**e**r**e**n g**e**hen währ**e**nd d**e**s Auf**e**nthalts, das tut gut!*

134 hundertvierunddreißig

Kapitel 6

Sprechen 3 In pairs, take turns to ask and answer questions about what people can or can't do at *Ferienpark Müller*.

- *Kann man im Ferienpark Müller <u>Basketball spielen</u>?*
- *Nein. Man kann im Ferienpark Müller nicht <u>Basketball spielen</u>.*
- *Kann man <u>ein gutes Buch lesen</u>?*

Hören 4 Listen to a family discussing holiday ideas. Copy and complete the table. (1–3)

	suggestion	advantage	disadvantage
1	the Baltic Sea		

die Ostsee — the Baltic Sea

Hören 5 Listen again and select the correct option to complete each sentence.

1. The Baltic Sea is in the **north / east / south** of Germany.
2. Mia's dad suggests staying in a **tent / hotel / holiday home** in Vienna.
3. They will travel to the Black Forest by **train / car / coach**.

> Use these phrases to give your opinion in a discussion:
>
> ***Du hast gesagt**, (dass es dort sehr kalt ist),*
> ***aber ich denke**, (dass es im Sommer sehr heiß ist).*
> ***Auf der einen Seite** (ist es sehr beliebt),*
> ***aber auf der anderen Seite** (ist es zu laut).*
>
> It's also good to add some interjections into your conversations:
>
> ***Du hast Recht!*** You're right!
> ***Das stimmt!*** That's right!
> ***Genau!*** Exactly!
> ***Richtig!*** Correct!

Sprechen 6 In pairs, discuss the advantages and disadvantages of different types of holidays using the key language box and the tip box.

- *Was denkst du über einen Urlaub im Ferienpark?*
- *Meiner Meinung nach ist das eine gute Idee, weil man wandern gehen kann.*
- *Du hast Recht! Ein Vorteil davon ist, dass es extrem schön ist.*
- *Auf der anderen Seite ist es im Winter besonders kalt …*

Was denkst du?						
Ein Vorteil/Nachteil davon ist, dass es				extrem besonders ein bisschen echt ganz (gar) nicht wirklich	günstig interessant kalt langweilig schön spannend wunderbar	ist.
Ich finde das	eine gute Idee, eine schlechte Idee,		es weil da			
Meiner Meinung nach ist das	ein guter Vorschlag, ein schlechter Vorschlag,			man	leckeres Essen probieren (nicht) (Tennis) spielen in den Seen schwimmen in den Bergen wandern am Strand liegen	kann.

Schreiben 7 Translate the text into German.

> Use a form of *mögen* + noun.
>
> Think about adjective endings.

> Are you extremely active? **Do you like** lakes and mountains? Visit Bregenz in Austria, because it is <u>so beautiful</u>. There are many shops and museums, <u>interesting markets</u> and <u>delicious food</u>. You can go swimming, buy presents and play tennis. In my opinion, the town is perfect, because it is really exciting.

hundertfünfunddreißig **135**

2 Wo werden wir wohnen?

- Describing types of holiday accommodation
- Using *wer*, *wen* and *wem*
- Recognising negatives

Lesen 1

Write the correct letters to match the photos (a–f) to the types of accommodation (1–6).

1 das Ferienhaus
2 das Zelt
3 das Hotel
4 der Ferienpark
5 die Ferienwohnung
6 das Hostel

Hören 2

Listen to the adverts for different types of holiday accommodation. Write the correct letter to match the pictures (a–f) to each advert. (1–6)

Hören 3

Listen to and read the conversation. Translate the questions below into English, then answer the questions.

1 Alina
Hallo liebe Leute, jetzt müssen wir uns entscheiden. Was machen wir im Sommer? Ich möchte gerne irgendwo hinfahren, wo es warm und sonnig ist, am besten ins Hotel. <u>Ich will einfach nicht kochen</u>. Ich möchte nur ruhig sitzen, mein Buch lesen und etwas Kaltes trinken.

2 Halim
Also, ich möchte so gerne draußen sein! Ich will Fahrrad fahren und klettern. Am liebsten möchte ich mit euch im Zelt wohnen, am Feuer kochen und mit der Sonne aufstehen – und das kostet nicht viel! Wir können jeden Tag mindestens 10 Kilometer wandern und <u>wir werden keine Technologie benutzen</u>. Wir werden so gesund sein!

3 Ben
<u>Nie im Leben! Ich will weder im Zelt wohnen noch Sport treiben</u>. Ich brauche WLAN und muss meinen Computer mitbringen. Ich will mit meinen Freunden online sprechen und Fastfood essen. Aber ich möchte auch am Strand liegen und <u>nichts machen</u>.

4 Maryam
Ich will mit meinen Freunden wegfahren. Ich möchte mit der Bahn reisen und viele neue Städte und Länder sehen. <u>Wir wollen ohne unsere Familien tanzen und feiern</u> und wir wollen günstig essen und schlafen. <u>Aber das muss nicht dieses Jahr sein</u>, ich kann im Sommer mit euch kommen! Aber <u>niemand will dasselbe machen</u>, also wie können wir uns entscheiden?

1 Für wen ist Technologie wichtig?
2 Wer will keine Technologie benutzen?
3 Mit wem will Maryam Urlaub machen?
4 Für wen ist viel Bewegung wichtig?
5 Wer will ohne die Familie fahren?
6 Wer will billig essen und schlafen?
7 Für wen ist das Wetter wichtig?
8 Mit wem will Ben sprechen?

> **G**
> Most interrogatives (question words) don't change their form depending on the case. However, **wer** changes its endings in the accusative and dative.
>
> Nominative: *Wer will zu Hause bleiben?*
> **Who** wants to stay at home?
> Accusative: *Für wen ist eine Ferienwohnung am besten?*
> For **whom** is a holiday apartment the best?
> Dative: *Mit wem wollen sie fahren?*
> With **whom** do they want to travel?
>
> Page 144

Sprechen 4

Read out Halim's speech bubble. Pay attention to the **ch** sounds.

ch is pronounced like the 'ch' in 'Lo**ch** Ness' when it follows *a, o, u* or *au* (e.g. m**a**ch**en**). When **ch** follows any other letter, it is a softer sound, like the 'h' in '**H**ugh' (e.g. ni**ch**t).

Listen and repeat the sentence. Then practise saying it quickly.
*I**ch** mö**ch**te ni**ch**t se**ch**s Nä**ch**te oder eine Wo**ch**e bleiben; i**ch** brau**ch**e do**ch** a**ch**t Nä**ch**te!*

136 *hundertsechsunddreißig*

5 Translate the underlined phrases in exercise 3 into English.

6 Translate the sentences into German.
1. For whom is the hostel the best?
2. Who wants to sleep in a tent?
3. For whom is the food important?
4. Who doesn't want to go hiking?
5. With whom does Halim want to go on holiday?
6. For whom is the hotel the best?

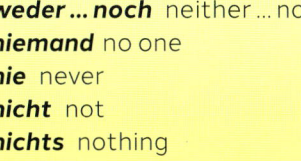

Watch out for words with a negative meaning:
ohne without
kein no, not a
weder … noch neither … nor
niemand no one
nie never
nicht not
nichts nothing

7 Look at the photos. Prepare a description of them and practise with your partner.

Auf dem ersten/zweiten Foto Auf der linken/rechten Seite Vorne Im Hintergrund	gibt es sehe ich sieht man	einen Ferienpark eine Ferienwohnung ein Ferienhaus ein Hotel ein Hostel ein Zelt	in einer Stadt. auf dem Land. am Meer. in den Bergen. am See.
Es gibt Ich sehe Man sieht		einen Mann/Jungen. eine Frau / eine Familie. ein Mädchen.	
Er/Sie trägt Sie tragen		eine Jacke. ein T-Shirt.	
Das Wetter ist		gut/schlecht/sonnig/warm/kalt.	
Die Leute sehen		glücklich/traurig müde/ernst	aus.
Sie lachen/lächeln.			

8 Choose an accommodation type from exercise 1. Describe why you would like to stay there and not at the other places.

Am liebsten möchte ich	in einem Ferienpark in einem Zelt in einem Hotel in einem Hostel in einem Ferienhaus in einer Ferienwohnung	wohnen,	weil es	bequem günstig aufregend praktisch (viel zu) teuer schrecklich unpraktisch kalt	ist.
Ich möchte nie				
Ich brauche	WLAN. eine Küche. ein Frühstücksbuffet. ein Restaurant.			
Ich möchte	im Stadtzentrum sein. draußen sein. nicht viel Geld ausgeben.			

3 Mein schrecklicher Urlaub

- Describing problems on holiday
- Revising possessive adjectives
- Practising a holiday role-play

Lesen 1 Read the holiday reviews about recent holidays. Copy and complete the sentences with words from the box. There are more words than gaps.

Reiserin82
★★☆☆☆

Schreckliches Hotel!
Wir waren neulich im Hotel Schneeglanz und wir werden nie wieder dorthin gehen. Wir haben um ein großes Zimmer gebeten, aber es war sehr klein und das war schon schlimm genug. Das größte Problem war aber, dass sie am ersten Tag unsere Taschen verloren haben, und wir haben sie nicht wiedergefunden! Im Zimmer gab es keinen Tisch und das Fenster war kaputt. Ich war mit diesem Hotel völlig unzufrieden und ich kann es überhaupt nicht empfehlen. Ich habe etwas Besseres erwartet!

UrlaubLiebhaberin
★★☆☆☆

Aua, Kopfschmerzen!
Zuerst war alles in Ordnung, aber am zweiten Tag gab es eine Disko im Hotel. Ich habe versucht, etwas fernzusehen, aber die Musik war unglaublich laut und der Lärm war sehr unangenehm. Mein Bett war auch sehr unbequem. Das Hotel hat ein anderes Zimmer für mich gefunden, und das war viel besser. Dann habe ich meine Kreditkarte verloren! Im Großen und Ganzen war das Hotel für mich nicht ideal und das hat mich enttäuscht.

Sonne-Fan-Nr1
★☆☆☆☆

Vermeiden Sie dieses Hotel!
Dieses Hotel ist das schlechteste Hotel überhaupt – alles war schmutzig und in einem sehr schlechten Zustand. Mein Zimmer im Hotel war klein und kalt, und es gab kein Fitness-Studio. In meinem Zimmer konnte ich nicht fernsehen, das WLAN funktionierte nicht, und der große Stuhl in meinem Zimmer war schon kaputt. Es gab so viele Schäden, dass ich mit dem Manager gesprochen habe, aber er war unhöflich und hat nichts gemacht. Es war auch sehr teuer: €180 pro Nacht! Leider habe ich nur schlechte Erinnerungen von diesem Urlaub!

1. Reiserin82 stayed at Hotel Schneeglanz …
2. Hotel Schneeglanz lost Reiserin82's …
3. UrlaubLiebhaberin's bed was …
4. UrlaubLiebhaberin's second room was …
5. Sonne-Fan-Nr1 found their room small and …
6. Sonne-Fan-Nr1 thought the manager was …

rude	bags	worse
recently	uncomfortable	yesterday
cold	credit card	too hard
better	too small	too hot

Sprechen 2 Read out Sonne-Fan-Nr1's review. Then listen and check.

Lesen 3 Translate UrlaubLiebhaberin's review into English.

Hören 4 Listen to some people talking about problems on holiday and write down what went wrong. (1–4)

Was ist das Problem?

Ich habe	meinen	Schlüssel	verloren. vergessen.
	meine	Tasche Kreditkarte	
	mein	Ticket Handy Tablet	
	meine	Taschen	

Ich möchte mich beschweren!

Mein	Schlüssel Stuhl	war	kaputt.
Meine	Tür		
Mein	Bett		unbequem.
	Zimmer		schmutzig.
Die	Mitarbeiter	waren	unhöflich. unangenehm.

5 Translate the sentences into German.
1 I lost my jacket, and the employees were impolite.
2 He lost his phone, and the door was broken.
3 We lost our key, and our Wi-Fi was broken.
4 They lost their bags, and their room was dirty.

Remember that **possessive adjectives** (my, his, her, etc.) change in German depending on the case and the gender.

	nominative	accusative
masc	mein	mein**en**
fem	mein**e**	mein**e**
neut	mein	mein
pl	mein**e**	mein**e**

All possessive adjective endings follow the same pattern as the indefinite article.

subject	possessive adjective stem
ich	mein-
du	dein-
er/sie/es	sein-/ihr-/sein-
wir	unser-
ihr	euer-
Sie	Ihr-
sie	ihr-

Page 145

6 Listen to the conversation and write down the words you hear.
- Anna-Lena, was machst du am liebsten in den 1 ?
- Normalerweise fahre ich jährlich an die 2 und ich wohne in einem schönen 3 .
- Und was machst du gern auf 4 ?
- Ich liege gern am 5 und ich schwimme jeden Tag im 6 .
- Beschreib mir deine letzten Ferien!
- Also, letztes Jahr habe ich in einer 7 in den 8 in der Schweiz gewohnt, aber das hat keinen Spaß gemacht!
- Ach, nein! Warum nicht?
- Die Wohnung war 9 , das WLAN war 10 und es hat jeden Tag geregnet. Das Essen war aber lecker und ich habe jeden Tag Musik gehört. Der Flug nach Hause war aber so 11 ! Wie waren deine letzten Ferien?
- Wirklich toll, danke! Ich habe mit meiner Familie in einem 12 gewohnt und das hat viel Spaß gemacht!

7 Read the conversation in exercise 6 again and write the letters of the **four** aspects that were disappointing for Anna-Lena.
a holiday accommodation
b music
c food
d the weather
e the flight
f the internet

8 In pairs, prepare and practise the role-play about holidays.

You are talking to your German friend.
You should address your friend as *du*.
- Was ist dein Lieblingsurlaub und warum?
- Say what your favourite kind of holiday is and why.
- Was machst du normalerweise in den Ferien?
- Give **two** details about what you normally do.
- Beschreib die letzten Schulferien. Was für Probleme gab es?
- Give **one** detail about your last school holiday and **one** detail about a problem you had.
- Mit wem verbringst du gern Zeit in den Ferien?
- Say who you like to spend time with in the holidays.
- Ask a question about a holiday.
- Give an appropriate answer.

hundertneununddreißig

4 Wie waren die Schulferien?

- Describing a past holiday
- Using prepositions with the genitive
- Talking about the weather in the past

Lesen 1 Read the messages and select the correct pictures (a–s) from each box below for each person.

> Grüß Gott! Ich bin letzte Woche nach Kitzbühel in Österreich geflogen und es hat viel Spaß in den Bergen gemacht! Ich habe in einem Ferienhaus gewohnt. Es hat viel geschneit und es war sehr kalt – nur 3 Grad – ideal zum Skifahren! Letztes Jahr bin ich in einer Ferienwohnung geblieben, aber dieses Jahr war es besser! ❤❤
> **Yusef**

> Moin moin! Neulich waren meine Freunde und ich an der Küste in der Nähe von Lübeck in Norddeutschland. Wir haben in einem Zelt am Strand geschlafen und das war ganz spannend. 🙂 Glücklicherweise war das Wetter nicht zu kalt, aber auch gar nicht heiß. Es war aber am Strand sonnig und es gab ein bisschen Wind. Die frische Luft hat mir wirklich gut gefallen.
> **Yannie**

Land

Region

Wo gewohnt?

Wetter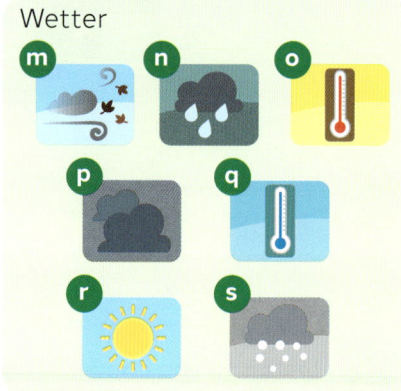

Hören 2 Listen to some more people describing their past holidays and select the correct pictures in exercise 1 for each person. (1–2)

> **G** You can describe the weather in the past by:
> - using an adjective: *Das Wetter war **schön**. Es war **sonnig**.*
> - using a verb: *Es **hat geregnet**. Es **hat geschneit**.*
> - using a noun: *Es gab **Wind**. Es gab **Schnee**.*
>
> Page 145

Schreiben 3 Write your own description of a past holiday.

Wo hast du gewohnt?			
Ich habe Er/Sie hat Wir haben	mit der Familie in einem Ferienhaus/Hotel/Zelt in einer Ferienwohnung	auf einer Insel an der Küste am Meer an einem See	gewohnt.
Ich bin Er/Sie ist Wir sind	zu Hause		geblieben.
Was hast du gemacht?			
Ich habe Er/Sie hat Wir haben	einen Ausflug		gemacht.
	Fußball		gespielt.
	die Museen		besucht.
	leckeres Essen		gegessen.
	Bücher		gelesen.
Ich bin Er/Sie ist Wir sind	einkaufen/spazieren/wandern		gegangen.
	im Meer / im See		geschwommen.

> There are different ways to say hello and goodbye in different parts of the German-speaking world. *Grüß Gott! Moin moin! Grüß dich! Grüezi! Tschüss!*

4 Select an option from each highlighted box and write down your choices in secret. Ask your partner the questions. Your partner has to answer, guessing which options you selected. If your partner goes wrong, start again!

- Wohin bist du gefahren?
- Ich bin nach **Berlin / Wien / Bern** gefahren.
- Wo hast du gewohnt?
- Ich habe **in einem Zelt / mit meiner Familie / in einem Ferienhaus** gewohnt. Das war **an der Küste / in den Bergen / in einer großen Stadt**.
- Was hast du gemacht?
- Wir haben **leckeres Essen gegessen / Geschenke gekauft / die Museen besucht** und wir sind **wandern / einkaufen / schwimmen** gegangen.
- Wie war das?
- Ich habe das gut gefunden, weil es ziemlich **interessant / lustig / schön** war, aber es war auch ein bisschen **langweilig / kalt / heiß**.

ß (Eszett or scharfes S) and **ss** are both pronounced like 'ss' in 'le**ss**'.

s on its own sounds more like the English 'z' in '**z**oo'.

Listen and repeat the words.

sehr	**s**uper
Sonne	**S**ee
gro**ß**	Spa**ß**
hei**ß**	Fu**ß**ball
intere**ss**ant	ein bi**ss**chen
E**ss**en	Wa**s**ser

5 Listen to and read a description of Emilia's holiday. Put the pictures (a–i) in order by writing the correct letters.

Meine Sommerferien waren echt toll! Ich bin mit meiner Familie nach Stuttgart in Süddeutschland gefahren und wir haben drei Tage in einer Ferienwohnung in der Stadtmitte gewohnt.

Am ersten Tag gab es viel Wind und das Wetter war leider sehr kalt, aber **trotz des Wetters** hat es Spaß gemacht. Zunächst haben wir die Museen besucht und danach sind wir einkaufen gegangen, um Geschenke zu kaufen. Wir haben dann **wegen des Windes** in einem schönen Restaurant gegessen und ein leckeres Essen genossen. Nach dem Essen haben wir im Ferienhaus Musik gehört, aber mein Bruder hat Bücher gelesen.

Das Wetter war am zweiten Tag sehr heiß und es gab viel Sonne. Zuerst haben wir den Fluss entdeckt und danach sind mein Vater und ich spazieren gegangen, aber meine Mutter hat ein Schloss besucht. Schließlich haben wir dann Eis gegessen, aber **statt eines Eises** habe ich ein Stück Kuchen gegessen.

Während meines Urlaubs habe ich viele schöne Orte gesehen und viel Spaß gehabt. Was für ein wunderbarer Urlaub!

Emilia 🙂 ❤️

6 Translate the phrases in **bold** in exercise 5 into English.

7 Imagine you have won a holiday to a destination on page 132. Write a description of your holiday. Include the following points:

- where you went (including the type of area)
- which type of accommodation you stayed in and your opinion of it
- what the weather was like
- which activities you did.

G Some **prepositions** always take the **genitive** case in German:

während	during, whereas	während **meines** Urlaub**s**	
statt	instead of	statt **einer** Wohnung	
trotz	despite	trotz **des** Wetter**s**	
wegen	because of	wegen **der** Touristen	

Note that for masculine and neuter nouns, you add **-s** to the end of the noun (or **-es** if the noun has one syllable):
während **des** Jahr**es**   during the year

Page 146

Add complexity to your writing by giving opinions in the past tense.
Imperfect tense: Das **war** wirklich gut.
Perfect tense: Ich **habe** das ziemlich schlecht **gefunden**.

Remember to justify your opinions and add variety by using a range of conjunctions.
Das war wunderbar, **weil** es sehr spannend war.
Ich habe das ziemlich schlecht gefunden, **da** es extrem anstrengend war.
Das hat Spaß gemacht, **obwohl** es geregnet hat.

hunderteinundvierzig

5 Ich möchte um die Welt reisen!

- Describing future and ideal holidays
- Using interrogative and demonstrative adjectives
- Practising the **w** and **v** sounds in German

Lesen 1
Read Lukas's message to his exchange partner, Jack. Copy and complete the table for Tuesday, Wednesday and Thursday.

Hallo, Jack!

Ich freue mich auf deinen Besuch im Juli bei uns hier in Heidelberg! Ich habe schon fast alles geplant.

Du wirst am Montag um 20:00 Uhr ankommen – wir werden also zuerst essen und danach werde ich dir dein Zimmer zeigen. Du wirst im Zimmer von meinem Bruder schlafen, denn er wird an der Universität in Berlin sein. Nach der langen Reise wirst du bestimmt müde sein!

<u>Welche Aktivitäten würdest du gern machen?</u> <u>Welche Gebäude in Heidelberg würdest du gern sehen?</u>

Am Dienstag geht es dann los! Wir werden mit meiner Familie in den Bergen wandern gehen. <u>Der Blick von diesen Bergen ist ganz wunderbar.</u> Zuerst werden wir mit der Bergbahn zum Heidelberger Schloss fahren und dann werden wir spazieren gehen. <u>Dieses Schloss ist über 800 Jahre alt.</u>

Wir werden am Mittwoch mit meinen Freunden die Geschäfte in der Stadtmitte besuchen, um einzukaufen. Ich liebe das Stadtzentrum, weil es wirklich traditionell ist, aber es gibt auch viele moderne Läden und Cafés dort. Wir werden vielleicht mit dem Fahrrad fahren.

Und dann am Donnerstag, an deinem letzten Tag bei uns in Heidelberg, werden wir das *Deutsche Apotheken-Museum* besuchen! 2 000 Jahre Medizingeschichte in einem Gebäude! <u>Wir wohnen in der Nähe von diesem Museum</u> – wir werden also zu Fuß gehen.

Noch eine wichtige Frage: <u>Welches Essen magst du am liebsten?</u>

Bis bald,
Lukas

| **die Apotheke** | chemist's, pharmacy |

das Heidelberger Schloss

	activity	transport
Tuesday		

> **G** To say 'which …?', use the **interrogative adjective welch-** with the correct ending to agree with the noun that follows.
>
> masc **Welcher** Ausflug ist am interessantesten?
> fem **Welche** Straßenbahn fährt in die Stadt?
> neut **Welches** Zimmer ist am billigsten?
> pl **Welche** Gebäude sind schöner?
>
> To say 'this …' or 'these …', use the **demonstrative adjective dies-**, which follows the same pattern.
>
> masc **Dieser** Ausflug ist interessant.
> fem **Diese** Straßenbahn, Linie 5.
> neut **Dieses** Zimmer im ersten Stock.
> pl **Diese** Gebäude in der Stadtmitte.
>
> Page 147

Lesen 2
Read Lukas's message again and answer the questions in English.

1. What will they do first when Jack arrives?
2. Where is Lukas's brother?
3. What will Jack want to do at the end of Monday?
4. How does Lukas describe Heidelberg Castle?
5. Which <u>two</u> things does Lukas describe as 'modern' in the town centre?
6. What will they see in the museum?

Lesen 3
Translate the <u>six underlined</u> sentences in exercise 1 into English.

Sprechen 4
Read out the paragraph in **bold** in exercise 1. Pay attention to the **w** and **v** sounds. Then listen and check.

> The German **w** sound is pronounced like the English 'v'.
> The German **v** sound is pronounced like the English 'f', except in loanwords such as *Souvenir*.
> Listen and repeat the words.
>
> **w**erden **v**ier **w**ürden **V**ater
> **w**andern **v**erbringen **W**ien **w**ie **v**iel

5 Listen to Anna and Felix discussing holidays. Copy and complete the table. (1–2)

last holiday	next holiday	ideal holiday

6 In pairs, take turns to ask and answer the questions.
- Was wirst du in den Sommerferien machen?
- Ich werde zu Hause bleiben.
- Welche Aktivitäten wirst du machen?
- Ich werde mit meinem Freund Handball spielen ...
- Wie wäre dein Traumurlaub?
- Ich würde mit dem Flugzeug nach Amerika reisen ...
- Was würdest du dort machen?
- Ich würde die Kultur entdecken und ...

> **G** Remember that in the **future** and **conditional** tenses, the second verb in a sentence is in the infinitive form at the end of the clause.
>
> Future tense: Ich **werde** mit dem Zug fahren.
> I **will** travel by train.
>
> Conditional: Ich **würde** mit dem Zug fahren.
> I **would** travel by train.
>
> Imperfect subjunctive:
> Wie **wäre** dein Traumurlaub?
> What **would** your dream holiday **be** like?
>
> Remember also that umlauts change the sound of vowels in German.
>
> Page 146

7 Write about your past and ideal holidays. Include the following points:
- what you did last year and your opinion of it
- where you would go on your ideal holiday
- how you would get there
- what you would do.

> The German consonants -**b**, -**d** and -**g** are sometimes unvoiced. This means they have a slightly different sound often when they are at the end of a word.
> -**b** sounds like a -p: Urlau**b**, Hal**b**bruder
> -**d** sounds like a -t: Stran**d**, Freun**d**, Han**d**ball, Deutschlan**d**
> -**g** sounds less hard: Zu**g**, we**g**
>
> Listen and repeat the words.

Was wirst du in den Ferien machen?
Wie wäre dein Traumurlaub?

Ich werde Wir werden	in den (Sommer)ferien in der Zukunft	zu Hause bleiben.		
Ich würde Wir würden	nach den Prüfungen nächstes Jahr	mit dem Boot mit dem Flugzeug mit dem Zug	nach	Amerika Deutschland Berlin	fahren. reisen.

Welche Aktivitäten wirst/würdest du dort machen?
Was wirst/würdest du dort machen?

Ich werde Ich würde		(zehn) Tage in (Köln)	bleiben. verbringen.
		durch (Amerika)	fahren. reisen. wandern.
	mit meinem Partner mit meiner Partnerin mit meinem Freund mit meiner Freundin mit meiner Familie mit meinen Eltern mit meinen Freunden mit meinen Freundinnen	diese Museen	besuchen.
		die Kultur	entdecken. erleben.
		im Meer/See	schwimmen.
		einkaufen/spazieren	gehen.
		Ausflüge / Fotos / einen Kurs	machen.
		Tennis/Basketball	spielen.
		in der Sonne mich	liegen. entspannen.

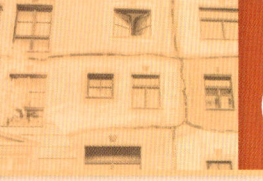

Grammatik 1

Forming the imperative (Culture, page 133)

1 Copy and complete the sentences with the *Sie* form of the imperative.

Example: 1 *Besuchen Sie den größten Freizeitpark in Deutschland!*

1 ▭ ▭ den größten Freizeitpark in Deutschland! (*besuchen*)
2 ▭ ▭ nach Österreich! (*kommen*)
3 ▭ ▭ am besten mit dem Bus! (*fahren*)
4 ▭ ▭ die leckere Schwarzwälder Kirschtorte! (*genießen*)
5 ▭ ▭ ihre warme Kleidung nicht! (*vergessen*)
6 ▭ ▭ die schönsten Berge der Welt! (*sehen*)

2 Rewrite each sentence from exercise 1 in both the *du* and the *ihr* form.

Example: 1 *Besuch / Besucht den größten Freizeitpark in Deutschland!*

 In formal situations, the **imperative** is formed using the *Sie* form of the **verb** followed by the pronoun *Sie*.
***Besuchen Sie** die Alpen in der Schweiz!*

In informal situations, use the *du* and *ihr* forms of the imperative.

- For one person: use the *du* form of the verb without the **-st** ending and omit *du*. **-e** is sometimes added to the end if it makes pronunciation easier.
***Besuch** die Alpen in der Schweiz!*
***Entdecke** den Schwarzwald!*

- For more than one person: use the *ihr* form of the verb and omit *ihr*.
***Besucht** die Alpen in der Schweiz!*

sein is irregular in the *du*, *ihr* and *Sie* forms.
du: ***Sei** aktiv in den Bergen!*
ihr: ***Seid** aktiv in den Bergen!*
Sie: ***Seien Sie** aktiv in den Bergen!*

Forming questions (Unit 1, page 134)

3 Rewrite the statements as questions.

Example: 1 *Bist du in der Schweiz?*

1 Du bist in der Schweiz.
2 Man kann dort einkaufen gehen.
3 Wir gehen am Samstag in die Stadt.
4 Sie brauchen ein großes Zimmer.
5 In Österreich war es besonders sonnig.
6 Du wirst nächstes Jahr in einem Zelt schlafen.

4 In pairs, take turns to ask and answer the questions from exercise 3. Invent your own answers.

Using *wer*, *wen* and *wem* (Unit 2, page 136)

5 Select the correct interrogative pronoun to complete each sentence.

Example: 1 *Wer*

1 **Wer / Wen / Wem** will nach Österreich fahren?
2 Mit **wer / wen / wem** fährst du nach München?
3 **Wer / Wen / Wem** möchte Frühstück?
4 Für **wer / wen / wem** soll ich die Tickets kaufen?
5 Bei **wer / wen / wem** wirst du in Berlin wohnen?
6 Für **wer / wen / wem** ist das Wetter wichtig?

 Look carefully at the meaning of the sentence to help you decide which case you need. Knowing which prepositions take which case will help you.

6 Write <u>six</u> more questions of your own, two each for *wer*, *wen* and *wem*.

Possessive adjectives (Unit 3, page 139)

7 Write the correct possessive adjectives in the nominative case to fill the gaps.

nominative	my	your (sg, informal)	his	her	its	our	your (pl, informal)	your (sg and pl, formal)	their
masc	mein	dein	1 sein	ihr	sein	unser	2	Ihr	3
fem	meine	deine	seine	4	seine	unsere	5	Ihre	ihre
neut	mein	dein	sein	ihr	6	unser	euer	7	ihr
pl	meine	deine	seine	ihre	seine	8	eure	9	10

8 Translate the sentences into German using the correct possessive adjectives.

1. Our father lives in Austria.
2. Their hotel is very dirty.
3. His photos were very beautiful.
4. Your (sg, informal) jacket is in the hotel.
5. I love your (pl, informal) music!
6. She forgot her laptop.
7. We need our bags.
8. I can't find your (sg/pl, formal) holiday house.

Think carefully about the subject and object of each sentence and remember that only the masculine form changes in the accusative.

Nominative: *Das ist* **mein** *Laptop*.
Accusative: *Ich habe* **meinen** *Laptop verloren*.

Weather in the past tense (Unit 4, page 140)

9 Listen and write the words you hear to complete each sentence.

Example: 1 war ...

1. In der ersten Woche ____ ____ so ____, und ____ ____ ____! Aber ____ ____ in der zweiten Woche, denn ____ ____ ____.
2. In der ersten Woche in Frankreich ____ ____ besonders ____, aber ____ ____ ein bisschen ____. In der zweiten Woche ____ ____ leider ____ ____.
3. In der ersten Woche ____ ____ in der Schweiz ____ ____. In der zweiten Woche ____ ____ ____, aber ____ ____ noch ____.

To talk about the weather in the past:
- use the imperfect form **es war** + <u>adjective</u>:
  Es war <u>kalt</u>, aber ganz <u>sonnig</u>.
  In der ersten Woche **war das Wetter** sehr <u>heiß</u>.
- use verbs in the perfect tense:
  Es hat jeden Tag **geschneit**.
  In der zweiten Woche **hat es geregnet**.
- use the imperfect form **es gab** + <u>noun</u>:
  Es gab leider ein bisschen <u>Wind</u>.
  In der ersten Woche **gab es** viel <u>Sonne</u>.

10 In pairs, take turns to ask and answer questions about what the weather was like in the past tense. Use the pictures to help you.

- *Wie war das Wetter?*
- *Es war ... / Es hat ... / Es gab ...*

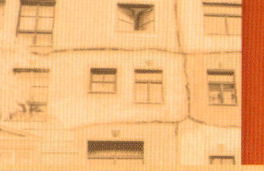

Grammatik 2

Prepositions followed by the genitive (Unit 4, page 141)

 1 Select the correct word for 'the', 'a' or 'my' to complete each sentence.

Example: 1 Trotz **des** Wetters bin ich in der Stadt einkaufen gegangen.

1. Trotz **des / der / das** Wetters (*n*) bin ich in der Stadt einkaufen gegangen.
2. Während **meinen / meiner / meines** Urlaubs (*m*) bin ich wandern gegangen.
3. Sie hat wegen **einer / ein / eines** Problems (*n*) mit ihrer Tasche eine neue Jacke gekauft.
4. Ich habe während **der / des / die** Aktivitäten (*pl*) viel Spaß gehabt.
5. Er isst Obst statt **eines / einer / einem** Eises (*n*).
6. Wir haben während **des / die / der** Woche (*f*) viel leckeres Essen gegessen.

 2 Translate the sentences from exercise 1 into English.

masc	fem	neut	pl
definite article: the			
des + -(e)s	der	des + -(e)s	der
indefinite article: a, an, negatives and possessive adjectives			
eines + -(e)s	einer	eines + -(e)s	keiner / meiner

The future tense (Unit 5, page 143)

 3 Listen and write down the words you hear to complete each sentence.

Example: 1 *wirst, …*

1. Arda, wo ___ du in den Sommerferien ___?
2. Wir ___ den Freizeitpark Phantasialand ___.
3. Wann ___ sie die Reise ___?
4. Mein Vater ___ das ganz langweilig ___.
5. Warum ___ Sie in Deutschland ___, Frau Wagner?
6. Es ___ Spaß ___, ___ zu ___.

Remember to form the future tense with the correct form of *werden* and the infinitive.

ich	werde
du	wirst
er/sie/es/man	wird
wir	werden
ihr	werdet
Sie	werden
sie	werden

 4 Read out the sentences from exercise 3. Pay attention to the **w** sound.

The conditional (Unit 5, page 143)

 5 Complete the conjugation of *würden* (would) with the words given.

Example: 1 *würde*

würden   würde   würde   würden   würdest   würdet   würden

ich	1	wir	4
du	2	ihr	5
er/sie/es/man	3	Sie	6
		sie	7

Remember: to form the conditional, use the correct form of **würden** and put the infinitive at the end of the clause.

Mein Vater und ich **würden** zu Fuß gehen.
My dad and I **would** go by foot.
Ich **würde** nach Amerika reisen. I **would** travel to America.

6 Translate the sentences into German.

1. I would travel to Munich.
2. We would spend 10 days in Germany.
3. My sister would visit the museums.
4. Would you organise a holiday?

146 *hundertsechsundvierzig*

Using interrogative and demonstrative adjectives (Unit 5, page 142)

Remember that **welcher** and **dieser** need to agree with the noun that follows, both in gender and in case.

	nominative	accusative	dative
masc	**Welcher** Urlaub ist am billigsten? **Dieser** Urlaub in der Schweiz.	**Welchen** Urlaub hast du gewählt? **Diesen** Urlaub in der Schweiz.	In **welchem** Urlaub kannst du dich entspannen? In **diesem** Urlaub!
fem	**Welche** Schule ist größer? **Diese** Schule in Bern.	**Welche** Schule hast du besucht? **Diese** Schule in Bern.	Mit **welcher** Freundin gehst du in die Schule? Mit **dieser** Freundin.
neut	**Welches** Foto ist schöner? **Dieses** Foto mit den Tieren.	**Welches** Foto hast du am schönsten gefunden? **Dieses** Foto mit den Tieren.	Auf **welchem** Foto sind Tiere? Auf **diesem** Foto.
pl	**Welche** Geschäfte sind heute geöffnet? **Diese** Geschäfte in der Stadtmitte.	**Welche** Geschäfte hast du besucht? **Diese** Geschäfte in der Stadtmitte.	In **welchen** Geschäften hast du eingekauft? In d**iesen** Geschäfte**n**.

 7 Listen and write the words for 'which' or 'this'/'these' to complete each sentence.

Example: 1 *Welche*

1 ____ Tage (*pl*) sind im Moment frei?
2 ____ Kirche (*f*) ist sehr hübsch.
3 ____ Berg (*m*) ist der schönste Berg in Europa.
4 ____ Stadt (*f*) werden wir nächstes Wochenende besuchen?
5 Ich finde ____ Museen (*pl*) besonders interessant.
6 Entschuldigung! Gehört Ihnen ____ Tasche (*f*)?
7 Tom? Erika? ____ Schlüssel (*m*) habt ihr?
8 Ich glaube, dass ____ Schloss (*n*) in ____ Land (*n*) sehr berühmt ist.

 8 Translate the sentences from exercise 7 into English.

Consolidating key grammar points

 9 Put the words in the correct order to make questions. Then translate them into English.

1 möchtest / Land / du / besuchen / Welches / nächstes Jahr / ?
2 fahren / möchtest / Mit / du / in Urlaub / fahren / wem / ?
3 würdest / du / während / Besuchs / machen / deines / Was / ?
4 das Wetter / deines / während / Wie / Urlaubs / wäre / ?
5 mir / würdest / du / Welche / geben / Ferientipps / ?

Los geht's!

 10 In pairs, take turns to ask and answer the questions in exercise 9, using the pictures to help you.

Kapitel 6 Lese- und Hörtest

Reading

A *relaxing break*. You read this advert for a holiday resort.

Hier finden Sie über zwanzig Ferienwohnungen in einer wunderbaren Berglandschaft. Von jeder Wohnung kann man den See und die höchsten Wasserfälle des Landes sehen. Entdecken Sie tolle Orte, die beliebtesten Dörfer, die berühmtesten Märkte der Gegend und die schönste Natur der Welt.

Jede Wohnung hat fünf Betten, eine Küche, ein Badezimmer und ein Wohnzimmer, das eine ganze Familie genießen kann. Im Dorf gibt es traditionelle Läden und Cafés, wenn Sie nicht kochen oder Frühstück machen möchten. Man kann auch das alte Schloss oder die berühmte Kirche besuchen. Wandern Sie durch die Wälder und suchen Sie Forellen im Fluss. Frische **Forelle** steht auf jeder Speisekarte in dieser Region.

Im Ferienort gibt es mehrere Aktivitäten für alle Besucher. Bleiben Sie länger als drei Nächte und bekommen Sie einen günstigen Preis. Verbringen Sie Ihren nächsten Urlaub bei uns!

> Use the context given in the rubric to help you work out words you don't know in the text. In this case it is clearly about a holiday in the mountains.

> Elements of many of the incorrect answer options will be somewhere in the text, so you need to read carefully to work out which answer is correct.

Complete these sentences. Write the correct letter, **A**, **B** or **C**, for each question.

1. From every holiday apartment you can see waterfalls and …
   A the sea. **B** mountains. **C** the lake.
2. Each flat …
   A can accommodate two families.
   B is self-catering. **C** is close to shops.
3. You can …
   A have breakfast in the woods.
   B swim in the river. **C** visit the castle.
4. If you book for longer than three nights you …
   A pay less. **B** can take part in many activities.
   C might win a prize.
5. Read the last two sentences of the second paragraph again. What might you do with a **Forelle**? Write the correct letter, **A**, **B** or **C**.
   A play with it **B** walk on it **C** eat it

> You are not expected to have learned this word. Work it out from the context of the rest of the sentence.

Translate these sentences into English.

1. In den Sommerferien verbringen wir zehn Tage auf einer Insel.
2. Meine Eltern **finden** es besonders spannend, in einem Zelt zu bleiben.
3. Wir gehen schwimmen und liegen in der Sonne auf dem Strand.
4. **Während des Urlaubs** sind wir an der Küste wandern **gegangen**.
5. Nächstes Jahr **werde** ich Ausflüge mit meinen Eltern **machen**.

> Will you phrase this using the same word in English or find another way to express the opinion?

> Think carefully about how to translate this construction.

> Which two tenses are these verbs and how will you translate them?

> Take care to use the correct tense in your English translation.

148 *hundertachtundvierzig*

Listening

Weather. Arda and his sister Elif are talking about the weather during the holidays.

Which **two** types of weather does each sibling describe? Write the **two** correct letters (A–F) for each person.

A	cold
B	hot
C	rainy
D	sunny
E	snowy
F	windy

My holiday. Charlotte is talking about her holidays this year. What does she say? Listen to the recording and write **A, B** or **C** for each question.

1

(i) When on holiday, Charlotte prefers …
  A being active. **B** learning about things. **C** relaxing.

(ii) They stayed …
  A in a peaceful location. **B** by the sea. **C** near a shop.

(iii) Unfortunately, they …
  A forgot the Wi-Fi code. **B** lost their bags. **C** broke the bath.

2

(i) At first, the weather was …
  A windy. **B** sunny. **C** rainy.

(ii) To get to Austria, Charlotte is going by …
  A car. **B** plane. **C** train.

(iii) Charlotte and her family are going to go …
  A skiing. **B** camping. **C** swimming.

> This listening task is in two parts, with a pause in between the two sections. Read the different answer options for each part before you listen to the recording and think about which German words you might hear.

Dictation

You will hear five short sentences. Write down exactly what you hear in German.

> Think about how these sounds are pronounced, when you write down what you hear:
> long *a*, short *a* and *ä*
> long *e* and short *e*
> long *o*, short *o* and *ö*
> *w* and *v*
> *s*, *ss* and *ß*

hundertneunundvierzig **149**

Kapitel 6 — Mündlicher Test

Role-play

1 Look at the role-play card and prepare what you are going to say.

> You are talking to your Swiss friend.
> 1 Say what you like doing in the summer holidays. (Give **two** details.)
> 2 Say what sort of holiday accommodation you like and why. (Give **one** opinion and **one** reason.)
> 3 Say how important the weather is to you on holiday. (Give **one** detail.)
> 4 Say where you would like to go on holiday and how you would like to travel there.
> 5 ? Ask your friend a question about holidays.

This could include activities you do when you stay at home.

You could use *Ich mag ...* Remember to put the verb at the end if you use *weil*.

You must use the conditional.

You could use a question word like *Wo* or *Was*, or just invert the verb to ask an opinion e.g. *Magst du ...?*

2 Practise what you have prepared. Then, using your notes, listen and respond to the teacher.

3 Listen to Kim's answers. Make notes in English of how she answers the first four questions. Write out in German the question she asks at the end and translate it into English.

Reading aloud

4 Look at this task. With a partner, read the sentences aloud, paying attention to the underlined letters.

> Während der Ferien habe ich zwei Wochen in einem großen Hotel verbracht.
>
> Am Sonntag waren die Geschäfte geöffnet.
>
> Wir konnten nichts zu essen kaufen.
>
> Am Montag bin ich in einen Geschenkeladen gegangen.
>
> Wenn es wirklich schön ist, gehen wir ins Wasser.
>
> Trotz des schlechten Wetters sind wir jeden Tag am Strand spazieren gegangen.

Think carefully about how to pronounce these sounds:
long *a*, short *a* and *ä*
long *e* and short *e*
long *o*, short *o* and *ö*
w and *v*
s, *ss* and *ß*
ch
-b, *-d* and *-g*

5 Listen and check your pronunciation.

6 Listen to the teacher asking four follow-up questions. Translate each question into English and prepare your own answer in German to each one. Then listen again and respond to the teacher.

Keep your answers to the follow-up questions short and accurate. Avoid giving too much detail that might lead you to make grammatical or pronunciation errors.

Photo card

7 Look at the photos and listen to Kim describing them. Answer the questions.
1. Which word does Kim use to describe how the six young people in the first photo look? What does this word mean in English?
2. Which reason does Kim give to explain why they look happy?
3. What does Kim say three of them are wearing?
4. How long does Kim think they will stay?
5. What does Kim say she can see in the background of the second photo?
6. What reason does Kim give for the second group to look happy?

You will be asked to talk about the content of these photos. You must say at least one thing about each photo.

After you have spoken about the content of the photos, you will be asked questions related to any of the topics within the theme of **Communication and the world around us**.

Your responses should be as **full and detailed** as possible.

8 Prepare your own description of the photos. Then, with a partner, take turns describing them.

> Auf dem ersten Foto gibt es ...

9 The teacher says to Kim, *Beschreib, wo du wohnst*. Listen and write down the eight missing words to complete Kim's response.

> Mein Haus ist ziemlich groß und **1**. Meine Geschwister, meine Eltern und ich schlafen **2** und dort gibt es auch zwei **3**. Unten ist ein **4** Wohnzimmer, und da sitzt die ganze Familie abends **5**, wenn wir fernsehen wollen. **6** dem Wohnzimmer ist die große Küche, wo wir nicht nur kochen, sondern auch essen. Im **7** gibt es ein Büro, denn meine Eltern arbeiten von zu Hause aus. **8** dem Büro ist ein Spielzimmer, wo wir Tischtennis spielen.

10 The teacher then asks, *Was gibt es für Touristen in deiner Region?* Listen to Kim's response and answer the questions.
1. What does Kim say is very beautiful?
2. Which activity does Kim suggest tourists can do before going to eat in a restaurant?
3. Which **three** accommodation options does she mention?
4. Which negative aspect does Kim mention?
5. What does Kim say is an advantage for tourists?

11 Listen to two more follow-up questions and prepare your answers. Then respond to the recording. Make your answers as full as possible, including opinions and reasons.

12 Prepare your own answers to as many of the Module 6 questions on page 227 as you can. Then practise with your partner.

Kapitel 6 Schreibtest

Translation

 Read the English sentences and Callum's translation of them. Fill in the gaps, using verbs and past participles from the box. There are more words than gaps.

genießen soll spazieren
vergessen besuchen reisen
verloren kann entdecken
aussieht gefunden wandern

1 You can discover many plants and animals in the mountains.
2 We like most of all to go hiking in the forest and swimming in the lakes.
3 We enjoy nature and the fresh air.
4 During the holidays we lost our bags and never found them.
5 I intend to go walking by the river since it looks particularly beautiful.

1 Man ____ viele Pflanzen und Tiere in den Bergen ____.
2 Wir gehen am liebsten im Wald ____ und in den Seen schwimmen.
3 Wir ____ die Natur und die frische Luft.
4 Während des Urlaubs haben wir unsere Taschen ____ und haben sie nie ____.
5 Ich habe vor, am Fluss ____ zu gehen, da er besonders schön ____.

 Translate the following sentences into German.

1 In autumn we often stay in a hotel on a lake.
2 During the holiday we visit many museums.
3 I love swimming and I always lie on the beach.
4 Last year I lost my bag and there was no wifi in the hotel.
5 We intend to spend a week on the coast with friends.

150-word writing task

 Look at this writing exam task and then, for each bullet point:

1 think about the vocabulary and structures you have learned, which you could use in your answer. For example:
   - **nouns**, **verbs** and **adjectives** to write about holidays
   - **verbs of opinion** and **adjectives** to give reasons
   - language for **narrating a story** about an activity you did
   - connectives and intensifiers you would like to use
2 write down three or four ideas for what you could write about
3 identify which tense(s) you could use in your answer.

You are writing about holidays for an online magazine.

Write approximately **150** words in **German**.

You **must** write something about both bullet points.

Describe:
- what makes a good holiday for you
- which activities you did during the last holidays.

Kapitel 6

 Read Callum's answer to the exam task. Answer the questions in the coloured boxes (1–5).

1 How could Callum **avoid repetition** here?

2 This is an example of **complex language**. What does it mean? Find three more examples of complex language in the text.

3 What **grammatical structure** is this? Find two other examples.

In den Ferien fahre ich am liebsten nach Spanien. Es ist heiß. Für mich ist schönes Wetter sehr wichtig. Ich liege gern in der Sonne. Am liebsten bleiben wir in einem bequemen Hotel an der Küste. Wir können im Meer schwimmen oder abends am Strand spazieren gehen. Wandern gefällt mir nicht, weil es langweilig ist. Meine Eltern machen gern Ausflüge und mein jüngerer Bruder ist immer aktiv, aber ich liebe meine Ruhe.

Im Herbst sind wir mit dem Zug nach München gefahren und wegen der Reise habe ich diesen Urlaub schlecht gefunden, da es extrem langweilig und anstrengend war. Während meines Urlaubs habe ich viele alte Schlösser, Museen und alte Gebäude gesehen und an verschiedenen Veranstaltungen teilgenommen. Ich bin in die Geschäfte und auf die Märkte gegangen, um schöne Sachen zu kaufen. Es hat manchmal geregnet, aber trotz des Wetters sind wir mit dem Fahrrad durch die Stadt gefahren.

4 Which connective could you use here to form an **extended sentence**? Which other connectives does Callum use?

5 Callum uses a **variety of plural nouns**. What do these words mean? Find two more examples.

 Read Callum's answer again and write the letters of the three correct statements.

A	Callum likes sunbathing.
B	Callum went hiking last year.
C	Callum's family are happy doing nothing.
D	Callum's last holiday was in the autumn.
E	Callum did a lot of sightseeing on holiday.
F	The poor weather stopped Callum doing outdoor activities.

 Prepare your own answer to the task.
- Think about how you can develop your answer for each bullet point.
- Look back at your notes from exercises 3 and 4.
- Look at the 'Challenge checklist' and consider how you can show off your German!
- Write a **brief** plan and organise your answer into paragraphs.
- Write your answer and then carefully check for accuracy.

Challenge checklist

- ✓ Past and present time frames
- ✓ Connectives and time phrases
- ✓ Some extended sentences (*Die Reise ist schnell, aber macht keinen Spaß.*)
- ✓ An opinion (*Ich finde die Reise lang.*)

- ✓ Different persons of the verb (*die Reise, meine Eltern*)
- ✓ Intensifiers and qualifiers (*völlig, ganz*)
- ✓ A wider range of interesting vocabulary (*unglaublich, unzufrieden, entdecken*)
- ✓ Use of plurals (*die Wälder, die Museen*)

- ✓ Complex language: infinitive constructions, genitive prepositions
- ✓ Past participles using *sein*
- ✓ Expressing opinions (*ich habe es … gefunden, wir haben … genossen*)
- ✓ Use of synonyms (*die Ferien/der Urlaub, fahren/reisen, weil/da*)
- ✓ Varied time phrases
- ✓ Varied conjunctions (*da, wenn, sondern*)

hundertdreiundfünfzig

Kapitel 6 Wörter

Key:
bold = this word will appear in higher exams only
* = this word is not on the vocabulary list, but you may use it in your own sentences

Im Urlaub und unterwegs (pages 132–133):

Reiseziele	Travel destinations
alt	old
bekannt	well-known, famous
beliebt	popular
berühmt	famous
*eindrucksvoll	impressive
historisch	historic
hoch	high, tall
lang	long
riesig	huge, great
schön	lovely, beautiful
spannend	exciting, thrilling, tense
traditionell	traditional
unglaublich	incredible
wunderbar	wonderful
bauen	to build
wandern	to hike
klettern	to climb
tauchen	to dive
der Berg	mountain
der *Freizeitpark	theme park
der Wald	forest, wood
die *Burg	castle
das Schloss	castle

Wo fahren wir hin? (pages 134–135):

Vorteile und Nachteile	Advantages and disadvantages
Was denkst du?	What do you think?
Ich denke, dass …	I think that …
Du hast gesagt, dass …	You said that …
Auf der einen Seite …	On the one hand …
Auf der anderen Seite …	On the other hand …
Du hast Recht!	You're right!
Das stimmt!	That's right!
Genau!	Exactly!
Richtig!	Correct!
Ein Vorteil / Ein Nachteil davon ist, dass es … ist.	An advantage / A disadvantage of it/this is, that it is …
Meiner Meinung nach ist das …	In my opinion that is …
Ich finde das …	I think that is …
… eine gute/schlechte Idee, …	… a good/bad idea, …
… ein guter/schlechter **Vorschlag**, …	… a good/bad suggestion, …
weil/da es … ist.	because/since it is …

besonders	particularly
ein bisschen	a little
echt	really
extrem	extremely
ganz	quite
(gar) nicht	not (at all)
wirklich	really
günstig	cheap, good
hübsch	pretty
interessant	interesting
langweilig	boring
schön	lovely, beautiful
spannend	exciting, thrilling, tense
wunderbar	wonderful
weil/da man … kann.	because/since you can …
leckeres Essen **probieren**	try delicious food.
(nicht) (Tennis) spielen	(not) play (tennis).
in den Seen schwimmen	swim in the lakes.
in den Bergen wandern	hike in the mountains.
am Strand liegen	lie on the beach.

Wo werden wir wohnen? (pages 136–137):

Die *Ferienunterkunft	Holiday accommodation
Auf dem ersten/zweiten Foto gibt es …	In the first/second photo, there is …
Auf der linken/rechten Seite sehe ich …	On the left-hand/right-hand side I see …
Vorne / Im Hintergrund sieht man …	At the front / In the background we/you can see …
einen Ferienpark	a holiday park
eine Ferienwohnung	a holiday apartment
ein Ferienhaus	a holiday house
ein Hotel	a hotel
ein *Hostel	a hostel
ein **Zelt**	a tent
in einer Stadt.	in a town.
auf dem Land.	in the countryside.
am Meer.	at the seaside / by the sea.
in den Bergen.	in the mountains.
am See.	at/on a lake.
Es gibt …	There is …
Ich sehe …	I (can) see …
Man sieht …	We/You (can) see …
einen Mann / einen Jungen.	a man / a boy.
eine Frau / eine Familie.	a woman / a family.
ein Mädchen.	a girl.

Er/Sie trägt …	He/She is wearing …
Sie tragen …	They are wearing …
eine Jacke.	a jacket.
ein T-Shirt.	a T-shirt.
Das Wetter ist …	The weather is …
gut/sonnig/warm.	good/sunny/warm.
schlecht/kalt.	bad/cold.
Die Leute sehen … aus.	The people look …
glücklich/traurig	happy/sad.
müde/ernst	tired/serious.
Am **liebsten** möchte ich in … wohnen, …	Most of all I would like to stay in …, …
Ich möchte nie in … wohnen, …	I would never like to stay in … , …
einem Ferienpark	a holiday park
einer Ferienwohnung	a holiday apartment
einem Ferienhaus	a holiday house
einer Ferienwohnung	a holiday apartment
weil es … ist.	because it is …
aufregend	exciting
bequem	comfortable
günstig	cheap
praktisch	practical
schrecklich	terrible

(viel zu) teuer	(much too) expensive	eine Küche.	a kitchen.
unpraktisch	impractical	ein *Frühstücksbuffet.	a buffet breakfast.
		ein Restaurant.	a restaurant.
Ich brauche …	I need …	im Stadtzentrum sein.	to be in the town/city centre.
Ich möchte …	I would like …	draußen sein.	to be outside.
WLAN.	WiFi.	nicht viel Geld ausgeben.	to not spend much money.

Mein schrecklicher Urlaub (pages 138–139):

Probleme im Urlaub	*Problems on holiday*	Mein Stuhl war …	My chair was …
Was ist das Problem?	What is the problem?	Meine Tür war …	My door was …
Ich habe … vergessen/verloren.	I have forgotten/lost …	Mein Bett/Fenster/Zimmer war …	My bed/window/room was …
meinen **Schlüssel**	my key.	kaputt.	broken.
meine *Kreditkarte/Tasche	my credit card/bag.	unbequem.	uncomfortable.
mein Handy/*Tablet/Ticket	my mobile phone/tablet/ticket.	schmutzig.	dirty.
		Die Mitarbeiter waren …	The employees were …
meine Taschen	my bags.	unhöflich.	impolite.
		unangenehm.	unpleasant.

Wie waren die Schulferien? (pages 140–141):

Schulferien	*School holidays*	Ich habe / Er hat / Sie hat / Wir haben …	I/He/She/We …
Wo hast du gewohnt?	Where did you stay?	einen **Ausflug** gemacht.	went on an excursion.
Ich habe / Er hat / Sie hat / Wir haben … gewohnt.	I/He/She/We stayed …	Fußball gespielt.	played football.
mit der Familie …	with the family …	die **Museen** besucht.	visited the museums.
in einem Ferienhaus …	in a holiday home …	leckeres Essen gegessen.	ate some delicious food.
in einem Hotel …	in a hotel …	Bücher gelesen.	read some books.
in einem **Zelt** …	in a tent …		
in einer Ferienwohnung …	in a holiday apartment …	das Wetter	weather
auf einer Insel	on an island.	heiß	hot
an der Küste	at the coast.	kalt	cold
am Meer	at the seaside.	Es gab *Regen.	There was rain.
an einem See	at/by a lake.	Es gab Schnee.	There was snow.
Ich bin zu Hause geblieben.	I stayed at home.	Es gab Wind.	There was wind.
Was hast du gemacht?	What did you do?	Es gab viel Sonne.	There was a lot of sun.
		Es hat geregnet.	It rained.
		Es hat geschneit.	It snowed.

Ich möchte um die Welt reisen! (pages 142–143):

Urlaube	*Holidays*	Welche Aktivitäten wirst/**würdest** du dort machen?	What activities will/would you do there?
Was wirst du in den Ferien machen?	What will you do in the holidays?	Was wirst/**würdest** du dort machen?	What will/would you do there?
Wie **wäre** dein Traumurlaub?	What would your dream holiday be like?	Ich werde/**würde** …	I will/would …
Ich werde …	I will …	mit meinem Partner / mit meiner Partnerin	with my partner
Wir werden …	We will …		
Ich **würde** …	I would …	mit meinem Freund / mit meiner Freundin	with my friend
Wir **würden** …	We would …		
in den (Sommer)ferien	in the (summer) holidays	mit meiner Familie	with my family
in der Zukunft	in future	mit meinen Eltern	with my parents
nach den Prüfungen	after the exams	mit meinen Freunden / mit meinen Freundinnen	with my friends
nächstes Jahr	next year		
zu Hause bleiben.	stay at home.	(zehn) Tage in (Köln) bleiben.	stay in (Cologne) for (ten) days.
		(zehn) Tage in (Köln) verbringen.	spend (ten) days in (Cologne).
mit dem **Boot**	by boat	durch (Amerika) fahren/reisen/wandern.	go/travel/hike through (America).
mit dem Flugzeug	by aeroplane		
mit dem Zug	by train	diese **Museen** besuchen.	visit these museums.
		die Kultur **entdecken**/erleben.	discover/experience the culture.
nach … fahren/reisen.	go/travel to …	im Meer / im See schwimmen.	swim in the sea/lake.
*Afrika	Africa.	einkaufen gehen.	go shopping.
Amerika	America.	spazieren gehen.	go for a walk.
Berlin	Berlin.	**Ausflüge** / Fotos / einen Kurs machen.	go on excursions / take photos / do a course.
Deutschland	Germany.	Tennis/Basketball spielen.	play tennis/basketball.
		in der Sonne liegen.	lie in the sun.
		mich entspannen.	relax.

hundertfünfundfünfzig

Kapitel 7 — Unsere Welt

Wir verbessern die Welt!
- Learning more about activism in German-speaking countries
- Using more prepositions with the genitive

Wir sind dabei!

a
Organisation:	FlüWi Österreich
Gründer:	David Zistl, Otto Simon, Michal Sikyta
Gegründet:	2015
Zweck:	Flüchtlingen zu helfen, ein Zimmer und Bett zu finden
Initiative:	Leute, die leere Zimmer in Wohnungen und Häusern haben, mit Flüchtlingen, die kein Zuhause in Österreich haben, in Kontakt zu stellen

b
Organisation:	Keine Macht den Drogen (KMDD)
Gründer:	die deutsche Regierung und berühmte Sportstars
Gegründet:	1990
Zweck:	zu verhindern, dass junge Leute drogenabhängig werden
Initiative:	Freizeitaktivitäten (z. B. Klassenfahrten, Workshops), um junge Leute zu bilden

c
Organisation:	#notjustdown
Gründer:	Geschwister Marian und Tabea Mewes
Gegründet:	2017
Zweck:	über Down-Syndrom zu informieren
Initiative:	ein Blog über ihre Erfahrungen

die Macht — power

d
Mein Vorbild ist Fatih Akin. Er ist 1973 in Hamburg geboren. Seine Eltern waren Gastarbeiter aus der Türkei. Sie sind **während der 60er Jahre** nach Deutschland gekommen, um Arbeit zu finden. Er hat eine große Zahl von erfolgreichen Filmen gemacht und hat viele Preise gewonnen. Fatih kämpft für eine bessere Gesellschaft. **Trotz seines Erfolgs** arbeitet er freiwillig für die Organisation „Soul Kids". Er hat sein Leben lang viele Kinder unterstützt. **Wegen seiner Geschichte** interessiert er sich für die Rechte von Flüchtlingen. **Das Ziel seines Lebens** ist es, die Welt zu verbessern.

e
Mein Vorbild ist Eneas Pauli. Eneas ist Co-Präsident*in des „Transgender-Netzwerks" in der Schweiz und identifiziert sich als nicht-binär. Eneas kämpft gegen Transphobie. Eneas' Ziel ist es, sichere Orte für Transmenschen im öffentlichen Raum zu entwickeln. **Statt des Konflikts** möchte Eneas eine Welt, wo alle die Chance haben, so sein zu können, wie sie wollen. **Trotz des Fortschritts** bei Transrechten findet Eneas, dass die Menschen oft kritisieren, statt die Person einfach zu akzeptieren.

Deutschland brauchte in den 60er Jahren mehr Arbeiter. Es gab nicht genug Leute im Land und man hat sich deshalb entschieden, Arbeiter im Ausland zu suchen. Man hat die sogenannten Gastarbeiter aus verschiedenen Ländern eingeladen, nach Deutschland zu kommen, und sie haben dort gewohnt und gearbeitet, aber es war nicht immer einfach für sie. Nach 1973 gingen elf Millionen Arbeiter aus dem Ausland zurück in ihre eigenen Länder. Andere haben sich dafür entschieden, in Deutschland zu bleiben und dort zu leben. Sie sind danach Staatsbürger geworden. Die größte Gruppe von Migranten in Deutschland kommt aus der Türkei.

der Staatsbürger (–) — citizen

Kulturzone Kapitel 7

 1 Read fact files a–c. Then read the paragraph about the organisation *FlüWi Österreich* and translate the text into English.

> David Zistl, Otto Simon und Michal Sikyta haben 2015 die Organisation FlüWi Österreich gegründet. Der Zweck der Organisation ist es, Flüchtlingen zu helfen, ein Zimmer und ein Bett zu finden. Die Organisation stellt Leute, die leere Zimmer in ihrer Wohnung oder ihrem Haus haben, in Kontakt mit Flüchtlingen.

 2 Now choose **one** of the other two organisations (*KMDD* or *#notjustdown*) and write a similar paragraph to the one above to describe it.

 3 Read texts (**d**) and (**e**) and answer the questions with the correct name: Fatih Akin (**F**) or Eneas Pauli (**E**).

1. Who was born in Germany?
2. Whose main work is in film?
3. Who fights against transphobia?
4. Who works for a children's organisation?
5. Who wants everyone to have the right to be themselves?
6. Who fights for a better society?

 Remember that some prepositions in German always take the **genitive** case:

statt	statt *des* Konflikts	instead of
trotz	trotz *des* Fortschritts	despite
während	während *der* 60er Jahre	during
wegen	wegen *seiner* Geschichte	because of

	masc	fem	neut	pl
definite article	des	der	des	der
indefinite article	eines	einer	eines	–

The genitive case can also be used to show possession:

*der Zweck **der** Aktion* — the purpose **of the** campaign
*das Ziel **seines** Leben**s*** — the goal **of his** life

Page 168

 4 Translate the phrases in **bold** in texts (**d**) and (**e**) into English.

 5 Listen and write down the words you hear. Then read them out, paying attention to the *-tion* sounds. (1–6)

 The t in **-tion** is pronounced as 'ts', as in the English word 'ca**ts**', with the tip of the tongue just behind the top teeth, e.g. Organisa**tion**.

 6 In pairs, discuss who you find inspiring and why.

- Wer ist dein Vorbild?
  - Mein Vorbild ist …
- Wofür/Wogegen kämpft er/sie/xier?
  - Er/Sie/Xier kämpft für/gegen …
- Was hat er/sie/xier gemacht?
  - Er/Sie/Xier hat …

Was sind deine Pronomen? xier is a gender-neutral pronoun that can be used instead of *er* or *sie*:
Xier geht schwimmen.

nominative	accusative	dative
xier	xien	xiem

xies is used instead of *sein* or *ihr*: *Das ist xies Buch.*

	masc	fem	neut
nominative	xiesa	xiese	xies
accusative	xiesan	xiese	xies
dative	xiesam	xieser	xiesam

There are also gender-neutral nouns:
der*die Freund*in	friend
der*die Lehrer*in	teacher
der*die Sänger*in or die singende Person	singer
der*die Student*in	student
der*die Studierende	student

 The **x** in the gender-neutral pronouns is pronounced 'ks'.

hundertsiebenundfünfzig **157**

1 Was ist dir wichtig?

- Discussing issues facing young people today
- Using verbs followed by prepositions
- Asking questions which include prepositions

 Lesen 1 Read the quiz and decide which three things are the most important to you.

Was ist dir wichtig im Leben?

- Meine Freunde sind mir das Wichtigste.
- Der Beruf ist mir das Wichtigste.
- Die Familie ist für mich das Wichtigste.
- Die Jobsicherheit ist mir das Wichtigste.
- Die Ausbildung ist mir das Wichtigste.
- Das Studium ist für mich das Wichtigste.
- Die Interessen sind für mich das Wichtigste.
- Der Lohn ist mir das Wichtigste.
- Die Freiheit ist für mich das Wichtigste.

Hören 2 Listen to some young people explaining what is most important to them. (1–6) Match each person to an issue below (a–f).

- **a** work and job security
- **b** friends and family
- **c** education and studies
- **d** interests
- **e** communication and freedom
- **f** career and pay

 Sprechen 3 In pairs, ask and answer questions about what is most important to you.
- Was ist dir das Wichtigste im Leben?
- Mir ist (die Familie) das Wichtigste.
- Ist dir die Arbeit wichtig?
- Mir ist die Arbeit (nicht / ein bisschen / ziemlich / sehr) wichtig.

G Adjectives can be used to create nouns.
gut: **Das Gute** ist … **The good thing** is …
schlecht: **Das Schlechte** daran ist … **The bad thing** about it is …

Superlative forms can also be used.
wichtig: Mir ist die Gesundheit **das Wichtigste**.
For me, health is **the most important thing**.

The noun has a capital letter, as with all nouns, and the gender is neuter unless you are describing something plural.

Page 168

 There are two ways to say 'for me' or 'for' someone else:
mir / für mich	for me
dir / für dich	for you
ihm / für ihn	for him
ihr / für sie	for her
ihnen / für sie	for them

 Hören 4 Listen to three generations of the same family discussing what is most important to them and why. Copy and complete the table in English. (1–3)

	generation	most important	important
1			

Zu welcher Generation gehörst du?

1946–1964 geboren	Babyboomer	nach 1945 aufgewachsen
1965–1979 geboren	Generation X	mit dem Fernsehen und den ersten Computern aufgewachsen
1980–1995 geboren	Millennials (Generation Y)	mit dem Internet aufgewachsen
1996–2010 geboren	Generation Z	mit YouTube, den sozialen Medien und der modernen Technologie aufgewachsen
nach 2011 geboren	Generation Alpha	

aufwachsen — to grow up

5 Listen to and read the texts. Which statement below relates to which person?

Kapitel 7

Worum machst du dir Sorgen?

Worum machst du dir Sorgen?
Ich mache mir Sorgen um Gewalt. Irgendwann muss man Probleme diskutieren, um Konflikt zu vermeiden. Gewalt ist eine große Gefahr für die ganze Welt.
Worauf hoffst du?
Ich hoffe auf eine bessere Zukunft und auf Sicherheit für alle Menschen. **Amelia, 16**

Wovor hast du Angst?
Ich habe Angst vor dem Klimawandel. Ich hoffe auf eine bessere Zukunft für mich und meine Kinder.
Womit bist du zufrieden?
Ich bin mit dem Schulstreik zufrieden. Wir haben jeden Freitag am Schulstreik teilgenommen und ich glaube, das war sehr erfolgreich. **Arda, 15**

Worüber sprichst du mit deinen Freunden?
Wir sprechen oft über die Schule und die Klassenarbeiten. Wir leiden unter dem hohen Druck und manchmal sind wir nicht mit den Noten zufrieden.
Womit bist du zufrieden?
Ich bin mit meiner Gesundheit zufrieden. Früher war ich überhaupt nicht fit, aber dieses Jahr mache ich mehr Sport und ich esse gesund. **Yasmin, 15**

Worum machst du dir Sorgen?
Ich mache mir Sorgen um den Welthunger. Viele Kinder sind arm und das muss man irgendwie ändern. Ich denke, dass alle Kinder dieselben Chancen haben sollten.
Worauf hoffst du?
Ich hoffe auf mehr Geld für alle. Im Moment ist alles so teuer und meine Eltern machen sich große Sorgen darum. **Joel, 15**

Der Schulstreik für den Klimaschutz hat in Schweden mit Greta Thunberg begonnen. In Deutschland ist Luisa Neubauer an der Spitze der Organisation. Jeden Freitag gehen die Teilnehmer nicht in die Schule, sondern sie stehen vor der Schule oder sie sind in der Stadt mit Postern für den Klimaschutz.

der Schulstreik school strike

1 I am worried about climate change.
2 I hope for more money for everyone.
3 I am happy with my health.
4 I talk about my education with my friends.
5 I am worried about child poverty.
6 I am worried about violence.

To say something is 'the same', combine the article and the word *selb*, which acts as an adjective:

derselbe Mann	the same man
dieselbe Frau	the same woman
dasselbe Mädchen	the same girl
dieselben Chancen	the same opportunities

G

Many verbs in German are followed by **prepositions**. Remember which case each preposition takes and make sure the article that follows agrees with the noun.

hoffen **auf** (+acc)	to hope **for**
kämpfen **für** (+acc)	to fight **for**
sprechen **über** (+acc)	to speak **about**
sich Sorgen machen **um** (+acc)	to worry **about**
arbeiten **an** (+dat)	to work **at/on**
zufrieden sein **mit** (+dat)	to be happy **with**
Angst haben **vor** (+dat)	to be afraid **of**

When asking and answering questions using verbs followed by prepositions, you can add **wo(r)**... or **da(r)**... to the preposition.
Woran arbeitest du? **What** are you working **on**?
Ich arbeite **dar**an. I'm working **on it**.

Pages 168–169

---

6 Read the texts in exercise 5 again and find examples of verbs followed by prepositions.

7 Write about your priorities in life, what you're happy with and what you hope for.
- Was ist dir das Wichtigste im Leben?
- Womit bist du zufrieden?
- Worauf hoffst du?

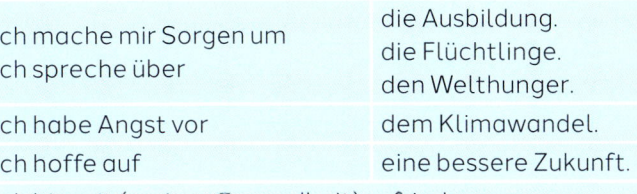

Ich mache mir Sorgen um	die Ausbildung.
Ich spreche über	die Flüchtlinge.
	den Welthunger.
Ich habe Angst vor	dem Klimawandel.
Ich hoffe auf	eine bessere Zukunft.
Ich bin mit (meiner Gesundheit) zufrieden.	

2 Unser armer Planet

- Discussing how environmental issues are being addressed
- Revising compound nouns
- Using phrases of argument and disagreement

 1 Listen to the environmental concerns. (1–6) Write the correct letter to match each issue (a–f) to a speaker. Then listen again and write down any extra details.

Was ist das größte Umweltproblem in deinem Land?

a — das extreme Wetter

b — der Plastikmüll

c — die Luftverschmutzung

d — die steigenden Temperaturen

e — die Zerstörung der Wälder

f — die Wasserverschmutzung

steigend	rising, increasing
zustimmen	to agree

 2 In groups, discuss the environmental problems in exercise 1. Which is the biggest problem, in your opinion?

- *Meiner Meinung nach ist der Plastikmüll das größte Problem.*
- *Ich stimme nicht zu. Das größte Problem ist die Zerstörung der Wälder.*
- *Das stimmt nicht! Laut einer Studie ist das wichtigste Problem die Luftverschmutzung.*

| Meiner Meinung nach | ist … | das größte Problem. / das wichtigste Problem. |
| Laut einer Studie | sind … | die größten Probleme. / die wichtigsten Probleme. |

Du hast Recht.
Das stimmt (nicht).
Ich stimme (nicht) zu.
Im Gegenteil.

 3 Translate the poster into English.

Was soll man dagegen tun?

- Um die Luftverschmutzung zu reduzieren, soll man Elektroautos fahren.
- Um die steigenden Temperaturen zu reduzieren, soll man mehr Bäume pflanzen.
- Um Plastikmüll zu vermeiden, soll man Plastikflaschen verbieten.
- Um unsere Wälder zu retten, soll man recycelte Sachen kaufen.
- Um Müll zu vermeiden, soll man alles Mögliche trennen und recyceln.
- Um Energie zu sparen, soll man grüne Energiequellen entwickeln.

> Remember that **um** … **zu** means '(in order) to'.
> **Um** die Zerstörung der Wälder **zu** verhindern, …
> In order to prevent the destruction of the forests, …

pflanzen	to plant
die Energiequelle (-n)	source of energy

4 Read the texts about the environmental activists. Answer the questions in English.

Wir müssen den Klimawandel stoppen!

Luisa Neubauer hat den Schulstreik für den Klimaschutz in Deutschland organisiert. Ihrer Meinung nach sind die größten Probleme die Lärmverschmutzung und die Luftverschmutzung.

Der Deutsche Felix Finkbeiner hat die Organisation „Plant-for-the-Planet" gegründet. Felix meint, dass Bäume die effektivste und natürlichste Lösung des Problems der steigenden Temperaturen sind.

Tim Noack hat 2018 „Mantahari Oceancare" gegründet. Als Taucher in Asien hat er die Unterwasserwelt wunderbar gefunden. Deswegen ist der Plastikmüll für ihn das schlimmste Problem für die Umwelt. „Mantahari" ist eine Webseite mit einem Online-Geschäft.

Die Schweizerin Lisa Schneider hat Bücher über die Klimakrise geschrieben. Ihrer Meinung nach sind Kinder, Jugendliche und Erwachsene nicht umweltbewusst und sie möchte ihnen helfen, die Umwelt zu respektieren.

1 What did Luisa organise?
2 What does Luisa think are the biggest environmental problems?
3 What organisation did Felix found?
4 Why does Felix think trees are the answer to environmental problems?
5 What did Tim do in 2018?
6 What does Tim consider to be the biggest environmental challenge?
7 How has Lisa helped the environment?
8 What is Lisa's opinion of young people?

> **G** Remember that **compound nouns** can be formed from
> - two nouns:
>   Luft + Verschmutzung → die Luftverschmutzung
> - a verb and a noun:
>   trinken + Wasser → das Trinkwasser
> - an adjective and a noun:
>   klein + Stadt → die Kleinstadt
>
> Sometimes the e at the end of the first noun is omitted:
> Schule + Buch → das Schulbuch
>
> When the first noun ends in a consonant, it is common to add an s to link the words:
> Verkehr + Mittel → das Verkehrsmittel
>
> The gender of a compound noun will always be determined by the gender of the final noun in the word.
>
> Page 170

5 Read the texts in exercise 4 again. How many examples of compound nouns can you find?

6 Listen and write down the sentences you hear. Pay attention to the compound nouns. (1–6)

7 Listen to some young people talking about environmental problems. Write down one thing that each person has done recently to help the environment. (1–4)

> Pay careful attention to the pronunciation of **compound nouns**, making sure you emphasise the first part of the noun and pronounce each individual part clearly.
>
> Listen and repeat the words.
> **Luft**verschmutzung
> **Trink**wasser

8 In pairs, discuss these questions.
- Was ist das wichtigste Umweltproblem?
- Was hast du neulich gemacht, um die Umwelt zu schützen?

Ich habe mich entschieden, Ich habe angefangen, Ich habe versucht,	an einem Schulstreik teilzunehmen. „grüne" Produkte zu kaufen. den Müll zu trennen. öfter zu Fuß zu gehen. Energie zu sparen.
Ich habe	an einem Schulstreik teilgenommen. recycelte Produkte gekauft. den Müll getrennt. Energie gespart.
Ich bin	öfter zu Fuß gegangen.

3 Jeder kann was tun!

- Discussing personal responsibilities and actions
- Using *wollen* (to want to)
- Using three different time frames in speaking

1 Listen to Hanna and Mika completing the survey. Write the letters that each person gives for their answers.

Example: Hanna – 1 B

der Feind	enemy
wiederverwendbar	reusable
die Wegwerftasse	disposable cup

Bist du ein Umweltfreund oder ein Umweltfeind?

1 Wie oft trennst du den Müll?

- A jeden Tag
- B manchmal
- C nie

2 Was recycelst du?

- A Plastikflaschen, Metall und Papier
- B Plastik
- C nichts

3 Wie oft machst du das Licht aus?

- A wenn ich das Zimmer verlasse
- B ab und zu
- C selten

4 Woraus trinkst du deine Getränke?

- A immer aus einer wiederverwendbaren Tasse
- B manchmal aus einer wiederverwendbaren Tasse
- C aus einer Wegwerftasse

5 Was für Kleidung kaufst du?

- A Secondhandkleidung
- B „grüne" Kleidung
- C billige Kleidung

6 Sparst du Energie und Wasser?

- A ja, Energie und Wasser
- B nur Energie
- C nein

Meistens A	Meistens B	Meistens C
Du bist ein Umweltfreund! Du trennst und recycelst, du sparst Wasser und Energie und du kaufst Secondhandkleidung oder „grüne" Kleidung.	Du bist ziemlich umweltfreundlich, aber du sollst mehr tun. Du sollst vielleicht mehr Energie oder Wasser sparen.	Du bist ein Umweltfeind! Du sollst mehr tun. Du sollst Plastik nicht wegwerfen, sondern recyceln, und du sollst Energie und Wasser sparen.

2 In pairs, complete the survey. Then translate the paragraph from the answer key which corresponds to most of your answers into English.

3 Write a paragraph answering this question.

> Wie umweltfreundlich bist du?

Ich kaufe		„grüne" Produkte. umweltfreundliche Produkte. billige Kleidung / Secondhandkleidung.
Ich spare	immer jeden Tag (nicht) oft manchmal ab und zu selten nie	Energie. Wasser.
Ich recycle		Metall. Papier.
Ich werfe		Plastik(flaschen) weg.
Ich trenne		den Müll.
Ich trinke		aus einer wiederverwendbaren Tasse. aus einer Wegwerftasse.
Ich mache		das Licht aus.

162 *hundertzweiundsechzig*

Lesen 4 Read the text about becoming a member of the 'Young Greens'. Translate the sentences in **bold** into English.

Was kann man tun? Wie kann man helfen? Die Jungen Grünen haben die Antwort!

Willst du etwas Gutes tun? Akzeptierst du, dass wir alle für die Umwelt verantwortlich sind? Willst du gegen die Umweltverschmutzung kämpfen? **Willst du die Umwelt schützen?** Ist Recycling dir wichtig?

Willst du in einer gerechten Welt leben? **Willst du allen Menschen helfen, die gleichen Rechte zu haben?** Willst du neue Freunde finden und zusammen aktiv in der Gesellschaft sein?

Als Mitglied der Jungen Grünen kannst du in einer Gruppe arbeiten, um die Welt zu verbessern. **Du kannst Geld sammeln** und an verschiedenen Projekten teilnehmen. Du kannst einen Verein oder eine Veranstaltung in deiner Schule organisieren. **Du sollst die Situation ändern. Du kannst dadurch dem Planeten helfen.**

Bist du bereit? **Dann musst du heute „Ja" sagen!**

Hören 5 Listen to Franziska, Peter and Lotte discussing what they do to help the environment. Copy and complete the table in English.

	regularly	in the past	in future, wants to ...
Franziska			

Hören 6 Listen and write down the words you hear, paying attention to the **-er** sounds. Then translate them into English. (1–6)

Sprechen 7 In pairs, practise describing the photo and answering the questions below.

Describe this photo.

1. Wie umweltfreundlich bist du?
2. Was hast du letzte Woche für die Umwelt gemacht?
3. Willst du Mitglied einer Umweltorganisation sein?
4. Was wirst du in der Zukunft machen, um umweltfreundlicher zu sein?

G **wollen** (to want to) is a modal verb which can be used with a noun on its own:
*Ich **will** eine bessere Welt.*
I **want** a better world.
It can also be used with another verb in its <u>infinitive</u>:
***Willst** du die Umwelt <u>schützen</u>?*
Do you **want** <u>to protect</u> the environment?

ich will   wir wollen
du willst   ihr wollt
er/sie/es/man will   Sie/sie wollen

Remember, *wollen* should not be confused with *werden*:
ich **will**   I want (to)
ich **werde**   I will

Page 170

-er at the end of a word is 'unstressed':
*Um die Welt bess**er** zu schützen, soll man wenig**er** Energie benutzen.*

-er can also be 'stressed':
*Die **Er**nährung soll grün**er** w**er**den.*

Listen and repeat the sentences.

Remember that in the exam, you will be given two photos and will need to say something about both of them. You will then be asked a series of questions relating to the theme to which the topic belongs (in this case, Communication and the world around us). Be prepared to use a variety of tenses and to develop your responses, giving opinions and reasons.
Remember to use the key language on page 232 when describing photos.
Auf dem Foto sieht man ...
Im Hintergrund sieht man ...

4 Wir wollen eine bessere Welt!

- Discussing international responsibilities and actions
- Using the conditional of *sollen*
- Using *man* to avoid the passive

Lesen 1 Match the sentences to the international organisations (a–f).

Was macht diese internationale Organisation?

Diese Organisation …

1 … reguliert Fußball und internationale Fußballwettbewerbe.

2 … arbeitet für bessere Gesundheitssysteme in allen Ländern.

3 … hilft Menschen in Krisensituationen.

4 … kämpft für den Naturschutz.

5 … hilft kranken Menschen.

6 … verbessert das Leben von Kindern weltweit.

> **G** **helfen** is a stem-changing verb:
> ich **helfe**
> du **hilfst**
> er/sie/es/man **hilft**
>
> The object of the verb **helfen** is in the dative case:
> Ich **helfe** den Nachbarn in meiner Gegend.
> I **help** the neighbours in my area.
>
> Kann ich Ihnen **helfen**?
> Can I **help** you?

a ICRC

Internationales Rotes Kreuz

b WWF

Organisation für Natur- und Artenschutz

c FIFA

Weltfußballverband

d WHO

Weltgesundheitsorganisation

e MSF

Ärzte ohne Grenzen

f STC

Save the Children

Save the Children

der Naturschutz *nature conservation*

Sprechen 2 In pairs, check your answers. Take turns to read out a sentence from exercise 1 and say which organisation it describes.

Practise reading out the names and abbreviations of the organisations. Think carefully about how to pronounce the letters of the alphabet.

Hören 3 Listen. Copy and complete the table in English. (1–6)

	organisation	when founded	key work
1			

Kapitel 7

 4 Listen and write down the missing words you hear.

1 Ich ____ mehr für die ____ machen.
2 Sollten wir in ____ Energien ____?
3 Du ____ gegen Welthunger ____.
4 Man sollte die ____ aller ____ fordern.
5 Ihr ____ zusammen ____.
6 Die ____ sollte ____ helfen.

> **G** *Sollten* is the conditional form of *sollen* and means 'should'. Just as in the present tense, the conditional form of modal verbs also sends the second verb (the underlined infinitive) to the end of the clause.
> Man **sollte** Menschenrechte <u>respektieren</u>.
> You/They/One **should** respect human rights.
> ich sollte   wir sollten
> du solltest   ihr solltet
> er/sie/es/man sollte   Sie/sie sollten
> Page 171

 5 Read the texts and decide which statements below apply to which organisation (the **EU** or the **UN**).

Man hat die EU (die Europäische Union) erst 1993 gegründet. Die Fahne der EU ist blau mit gelben Sternen. Die EU hat siebenundzwanzig Mitgliedsländer und 448 Millionen Einwohner. In der EU spricht man viele Sprachen – es gibt vierundzwanzig offizielle Sprachen! Die Organisation kontrolliert viele Grenzen in Europa. Wenn jemand in einem Mitgliedsland der EU lebt, kann man oft ohne Reisepass zwischen den Mitgliedsländern reisen. Die EU hat ihr eigenes Geld – den Euro.

Man hat die UN (die Vereinigten Nationen) 1945 gegründet. Die Fahne der UN ist hellblau mit einem weißen Bild der Erde darauf. Es gibt hundertdreiundneunzig Mitgliedsländer. Es gibt sechs offizielle Sprachen. Die Organisation arbeitet mit fast allen Ländern der Welt. Es ist notwendig, dass die Länder der UN Menschenrechte respektieren. Wenn es Streit gibt, muss man zusammenkommen und langfristige Lösungen finden, um Krieg zu verhindern. Die UN organisiert Essen für hundertachtundzwanzig Millionen Menschen. Niemand sollte heute Hunger leiden.

die Fahne	flag
die Grenze	border/frontier
der Reisepass	passport

1 You often don't need a passport when travelling between member countries.
2 It has 193 member countries.
3 There are 24 official languages.
4 It has its own currency.
5 The member countries must respect human rights.

> **G** *Man* + verb is used when we don't want to specify a person or organisation. In English we often say 'you' or 'they', and occasionally 'one'.
> **Man sollte** den Welthunger **verhindern**.
> **You/They/One should prevent** world hunger.
> *Man* + verb can also be used to avoid the passive voice in German.
> **Man sollte** den Welthunger **verhindern**.
> World hunger **should be prevented**.
> Page 171

 6 Translate the sentences into German.

Remember that there are two different ways to say this.

1 It is important to me to be part of an organisation.
2 I am a member of the Young Greens.
3 It was founded in 2004 and it fights for the protection of nature.
4 International organisations are necessary.
5 They should support people to improve our world.

You can use man *here to avoid the passive.*

Remember to use the conditional form of the verb here.

Which case do we use to show possession?

How do we say '(in order) to'?

hundertfünfundsechzig **165**

5 Dialog ist wichtig!

- Expressing and justifying complex opinions and points of view
- Using phrases of debating in speaking
- Pronouncing *r* sounds correctly

1 Listen to and read the statements. Is each person for or against eating meat?

Vegan essen: bist du dafür oder dagegen?

Layla
Ich esse sehr gern Fleisch und das schmeckt mir so gut! Das kann ich nicht aufgeben.

Arda
So wenige vegane Gerichte auf der Speisekarte? Nein, danke.

Mika
Nur Gemüse essen? Das wäre so langweilig!

Kim
Ich will nicht, dass Tiere für mich leiden und Gemüse ist auch lecker und gesünder als Fleisch.

Yannie
Man soll Tiere unbedingt schützen.

Julian
Die Fleischindustrie verursacht auch Umweltverschmutzung.

2 Listen to and read the conversation. Find the German expressions in **bold** for the opinion phrases below.

Anna: Warum bist du Veganer, Bruno?
Bruno: **Ich bin der Meinung**, **dass** die Umwelt sehr wichtig ist. Die Fleischindustrie verursacht Umweltverschmutzung und das finde ich ganz schlimm.
Anna: **Das stimmt**, aber Fleisch schmeckt mir so gut und **außerdem** gibt es nur wenige vegane Gerichte in Restaurants. **Ich glaube**, das wäre ein Problem für mich.
Bruno: Naja, **auf der einen Seite** gibt es nicht immer eine große Auswahl, aber **auf der anderen Seite** ist das Essen oft lecker und gesünder. **Ich meine** trotzdem, dass man Tiere unbedingt schützen soll.
Anna: Haben Pflanzen **jedoch** nicht auch Gefühle?
Bruno: Vielleicht, aber ich will sowieso nicht, dass Tiere für mich leiden. **Im Gegenteil**! Ich finde es total wichtig, dass wir alle Tierarten schützen. **Übrigens** ist es heute ganz einfach, Alternativen zu finden.
Anna: **Du hast Recht**. Vielleicht werde ich versuchen, Vegetarierin zu werden. Ich bin mir nicht sicher, ob ich auch ohne Milchprodukte leben kann!

> *die Auswahl*   selection

1 on the one hand
2 on the other hand
3 I am of the opinion that
4 I think
5 however
6 moreover, besides
7 by the way, what's more
8 you're right
9 that's true
10 I believe
11 on the contrary

3 Read the conversation again and categorise the German expressions in exercise 2 as follows: presenting opinions, agreeing, disagreeing, adding arguments, presenting two sides of an argument.

hundertsechsundsechzig

4 Listen to some young people giving their opinions on the meat industry and write down the opinions mentioned in English. (1–4)

5 In a group, discuss your opinion of veganism. Are you for or against it? Use as many of the phrases from exercise 2 as possible.

- *Sollte man Veganer*in sein? Was denkst du?*
- *Ja, vielleicht. Auf der einen Seite ist das gesünder, auf der anderen Seite esse ich aber gern Fleisch. Was ist deine Meinung zum Veganismus?*
- *Ich meine, dass …*

 6 Listen to and read the statements for and against 'green' energy. Copy and complete the table with the numbers of the statements.

1. Sie sind eine saubere Alternative.
2. Sie werden in der Zukunft Geld sparen.
3. Wenn die Sonne nicht scheint, funktioniert das nicht.
4. Die Gebäude sind überhaupt nicht schön.
5. Es gibt keine Risiken.
6. Wenn es keinen Wind gibt, funktioniert das nicht.
7. Sie helfen, den Klimawandel zu verhindern.
8. Sie kosten viel Geld.

für „grüne" Energien	gegen „grüne" Energien

7 In pairs, take turns to read out the sentences in exercise 6. Pay attention to the *r* sounds. Then, using the expressions from exercise 2, discuss the pros and cons of 'green' energy.

8 Write approximately 150 words about ways to improve the world. Include the following points:
- what you and others do to make the world better
  Um die Welt zu verbessern, … ich …
- what people, including international organisations, should do in the future.
  Internationale Organisationen sollten …

> The consonantal **r** is a rolled sound at the back of the throat:
> b**r**auchen, **R**isiken, funktionie**r**en, **Pr**oblem
>
> The vocalic **r** sounds more like a vowel sound:
> ve**r**hindern, einfache**r**, Kinde**r**, fü**r**
>
> Some words contain both **r** sounds:
> ande**rer**, besse**rer**, Vegeta**r**ie**r**in
>
> Listen and repeat the words.

Grammatik 1

The genitive case (Culture, page 157)

1 Copy and complete the sentences with the correct genitive form of the definite article.

1. Er ist wegen ___ Arbeit (*f*) nach Deutschland gekommen.
2. Trotz ___ Erfolgs (*m*) habe ich nicht viel Geld.
3. Was hat sie während ___ Lebens (*nt*) gemacht?
4. Wir sollen Windenergie statt ___ alten Energien (*pl*) benutzen.

2 Translate the phrases into German.

Example: 1 das Haus **meines Bruders**

1. *my brother's house* – das Haus ___
2. *my sister's town* – die Stadt ___
3. *my mother's shop* – das Geschäft ___
4. *my father's job* – der Beruf ___
5. *my uncle's family* – die Familie ___
6. *my parents' friends* – die Freunde ___

 When using the genitive to say that something belongs to a particular person, the part showing possession usually comes after the noun. Remember to add *-(e)s* to the end of a masculine or neuter noun.

	genitive
masc	das Zimmer **meines Bruders**
fem	das Zimmer **meiner Schwester**
neut	das Zimmer **meines Kindes**
pl	das Zimmer **meiner Eltern**

Using adjectives to make nouns (Unit 1, page 158)

3 Change these adjectives into nouns.

Example: 1 das Schwierige

1. schwierig
2. einfach
3. schlimm
4. wichtigste
5. gut
6. größte

 Remember that nouns can also be created from a standard or a superlative adjective.
das Schön**e** the beautiful thing
das Schön**ste** the **most** beautiful thing

4 Translate the sentences into German. Change each adjective into a noun.

Example: 1 Das Schwierigste ist das Studium.

1. The most difficult thing is studying.
2. The easy thing is recycling.
3. The worst thing is violence.
4. The important thing is health.
5. The good thing for me is freedom.
6. The biggest thing for him is a good job.

Verbs followed by prepositions (Unit 1, page 159)

5 Write the correct letter to match each preposition to the correct verb.

Example: 1 d

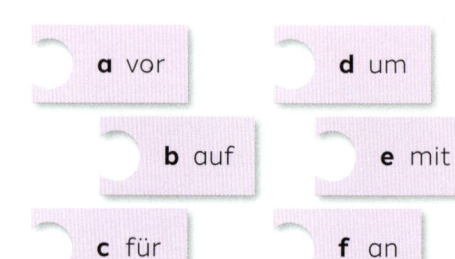

Verbs followed by prepositions (Unit 1, page 159)

 6 Copy and complete the sentences with the correct preposition. Then write questions for each sentence.

Example: 1 *Ich kämpfe für Menschenrechte. Wofür kämpfst du?*

1 Ich kämpfe ___ Menschenrechte.
2 Ich arbeite ___ einem Schulprojekt.
3 Ich mache mir Sorgen ___ Welthunger.
4 Ich habe Angst ___ Gewalt.
5 Ich hoffe ___ eine bessere Welt.
6 Ich bin ___ meiner Gesundheit nicht zufrieden.

Asking questions which include prepositions (Unit 1, page 159)

 7 Match up the *wo* pronouns to their English translations.

1 wodurch
2 woneben
3 woraus
4 worin
5 worunter
6 wozwischen

a under which
b through which
c between which
d next to what
e in what/into which
f from what/which

 8 In pairs, play noughts and crosses. Answer each question using *da(r)...* to win the square.

- *Worum machst du dir im Moment Sorgen?*
- *Um die Umwelt. **Darum** mache ich mir Sorgen.*

Worum machst du dir im Moment Sorgen?	Woran arbeitest du im Moment?	Worüber sprichst du im Moment in der Schule?
Um die Umwelt	An meiner Ausbildung	Über (die) Flüchtlinge
Womit bist du im Moment zufrieden?	Worauf hoffst du?	Wovor hast du Angst?
Mit der Gesundheit	Auf eine bessere Zukunft	Vor (der) Gewalt
Wofür kämpfst du?	Worüber sprichst du mit deinen Freunden?	Womit bist du im Moment nicht zufrieden?
Für (die) Menschenrechte	Über das Geld	Mit dem Einkommen

Grammatik 2

Compound nouns (Unit 2, page 161)

Lesen 1 Create **eight** compound nouns by combining nouns from the word cloud. Then translate them into English.

Example: die Tierart – species

die Welt das Mittel die Art
der Wandel der Verkehr
das Klima das Unterwasser
die Umwelt
(das) Plastik die Flasche
das Wasser
die Katastrophe die Verschmutzung
die Schule
der Streik das Tier

> Remember that some compound nouns lose or add an extra letter in the middle and the second noun changes to lower case when combined into the compound nouns. The compound noun takes the same gender as the final noun in the word.
>
> Schule + Buch → das Schulbuch

Modal verbs (Unit 3, page 163)

Hören 2 Listen and write down the answers to the questions.

Example: 1 Ich kann mit dem Fahrrad zur Schule fahren.

Umweltfreundlich in der Schule

1. Was kannst du machen, Lea?
2. Was musst du machen, Tim?
3. Was sollst du machen, Mia?
4. Was sollen die Lehrer machen?
5. Was können die Kinder machen?
6. Was müssen die Eltern machen?

Schreiben 3 Translate the sentences into German.

1. I should recycle paper.
2. We can buy 'green' school things.
3. They should never use plastic bottles.
4. We want to protect the environment.
5. I want to save more energy.
6. We must go into town by bike.
7. You can go to school on foot.
8. I must not buy paper.

Kapitel 7

The conditional of *sollen* (Unit 4, page 165)

 Copy and complete the sentences with the correct conditional form of *sollen* (should). Then read the sentences out to a partner.

Example: 1 Wir **sollten** Umweltverschmutzung vermeiden.

1 Wir ___ Umweltverschmutzung vermeiden.
2 Die Regierung ___ in grüne Energien investieren.
3 Man ___ Lösungen finden.
4 Wir ___ etwas dagegen machen.
5 Er ___ gegen Welthunger kämpfen.
6 Ich ___ helfen.

 Modal verbs in the conditional take these verb endings:

ich	soll**te**
du	soll**test**
er/sie/es/man	soll**te**
wir	soll**ten**
ihr	soll**tet**
Sie	soll**ten**
sie	soll**ten**

 Translate the sentences into German using the conditional.

1 We should find solutions.
2 They should all help.
3 We should avoid environmental pollution.
4 I should live in a clean city.
5 She should fight against world hunger.
6 We should invest in green energies.

Using *man* (Unit 4, page 165)

 Translate the sentences into English using the passive voice.

Example: 1 Water pollution should be prevented.

Was kann man tun?
1 Man soll die Wasserverschmutzung verhindern.
2 Man muss Menschenrechte respektieren.
3 Man hat die EU 1993 gegründet.
4 Man muss Lösungen finden.
5 Man kann grüne Energie benutzen.
6 Man soll alle Probleme lösen.

 Remember that the passive voice puts the emphasis on the thing that can be done, rather than on the person or organisation doing it.
Man sollte den Welthunger **verhindern**.
World hunger **should be prevented**.

Los geht's!

 Listen and write down the words you hear to complete each sentence.

Example: 1 Das **Schlimmste** ist die …

1 Das ___ ist die ___.
2 ___ hoffst du?
3 Ich ___ eine ___.
4 ___ gehe ich immer zu Fuß.
5 Das sind die ___ ___ ___.
6 Ich ___ ___.
7 Die ___ den ___.
8 ___ Elektroautos ___.

Kapitel 7 Lese- und Hörtest

Reading

 Being vegetarian. You read Tim's blog about his lifestyle. Complete the sentences below. Write the correct letter, **A**, **B** or **C**, for each question.

Seit Jahren bin ich Vegetarier, weil das umweltfreundlicher und besser für die Natur ist. Meiner Meinung nach kann man auch Tiere schützen, wenn man Fleisch und Fisch aufgibt.

Das Gute ist auch, dass man mehr Platz für Gemüse und Obst in der Welt hat, und damit kann man gegen Hunger kämpfen. Vegetarier zu sein ist gesünder und kann viele Krankheiten verhindern.

Veganer zu sein ist mir zu extrem. Viele vegane Produkte sehen wie Fleischprodukte aus und das finde ich ein bisschen unnatürlich. Ich kann ohne Käse und Milch nicht leben, aber ich bin davon überzeugt, dass man weder Fleisch noch Fisch braucht, um gesund zu sein. Laut der Wissenschaft gibt es viele Vorteile und keine Nachteile und ich denke, dass es einfach ist, Fleisch aufzugeben.

1. Tim turned vegetarian ...
   A years ago.   B to have more pets.
   C to be more natural.
2. Tim wants to ...
   A grow his own fruit and vegetables.
   B fight disease.   C feed the world.
3. In Tim's opinion, being vegetarian makes you ...
   A more hungry.   B healthier.
   C more likely to become ill.
4. Tim is not a vegan because ...
   A he likes dairy products.
   B vegan food has unnatural ingredients.
   C he doesn't want to give up fish.
5. Tim thinks that meat and fish ...
   A are hard to give up.
   B have scientifically-proven benefits.
   C are not essential.

 Issues facing young people. Read the article expressing young people's concerns. Answer the following questions in English. You do not need to write in full sentences.

Für mich ist das Wichtigste der Klimawandel, weil wir unsere Erde verschmutzen. Wir müssen die Situation verändern, um unsere Umwelt zu schützen, weil wir alle dafür verantwortlich sind. Wir müssen den Plastikmüll in den Meeren reduzieren, um die **Schildkröten** zu retten. Wie Fische sind sie ein wichtiger Teil der Unterwasserwelt. **Paula**

Ich mache mir Sorgen um meine Ausbildung und den Druck in der Schule. Ich bin immer traurig, weil ich mit meinen Noten unzufrieden bin. Es macht mich krank, aber ich kann mit meinen Eltern darüber nicht sprechen. Trotz meiner Probleme bin ich positiv und ich freue mich schon auf mein Studium an der Uni. **Elias**

Meiner Meinung nach ist die Gewalt das Schlimmste. Ich mache mir Sorgen um die Flüchtlinge, die wegen der Gefahren in ihrem eigenen Land nach Europa kommen, um eine bessere Zukunft zu finden. Wir müssen allen Menschen helfen, die gleichen Rechte zu haben. Ich hoffe auf die Sicherheit für alle Leute. **Leonie**

1. Why does Paula feel we all need to act?
2. Name **one** action Paula feels should be taken to help the environment.
3. What upsets Elias?
4. What makes him feel more positive?
5. Name **one** positive outcome Leonie hopes for.
6. Read the first paragraph again. What are **Schildkröten**?
   A plants   B animals
   C natural resources

> When answering open questions, you may need to follow a sequence of information over several clauses or sentences to find the answer. Focus carefully on the meaning and don't be misled by distractors (words in the passage that might lead you to an incorrect answer).
>
> Sometimes there is more than one possible answer to a question, often indicated by 'Give one detail'. Choose an answer you know is definitely correct. Don't give more than one answer.

3 Translate these sentences into English.

1. In Zukunft werde ich regelmäßig zu Fuß gehen.
2. Die Schüler möchten eine saubere Umwelt schaffen.
3. In den Sommerferien hat mein Bruder kranken Tieren geholfen.
4. Ich glaube, dass man Kleidung recyceln soll, um Müll zu vermeiden.
5. Meine Freunde sind wegen des schlechten Wetters mit dem Auto in die Schule gefahren.

> Pay attention to verb tenses in translations. In these sentences, there are two sentences in the perfect tense, one sentence in the present tense containing a modal verb, one sentence in the future tense and one containing a conditional verb, so make sure you can distinguish them correctly. There is a lot of topic-specific vocabulary here, so think carefully about what you have learned.

Listening

4 *Protecting the environment.* Milan, Hanna, Robin and Annika are talking about what their families do for the environment. What opinions do they have of their families' actions?

Listen to the recording and write down **P for a positive opinion, N for a negative** opinion and **P+N for a positive and negative** opinion.

1. Milan
2. Hanna
3. Robin
4. Annika

> Use the context summary to help you anticipate vocabulary and structures you might hear. Try to recall some of the more technical vocabulary on this topic that you have learned.

> Listen until the end of each extract, to make sure you have heard everything each person says. You will hear each extract twice, so write down P, N or P+N after the first listening and use the repeat to check whether your assumptions were correct.

> You need to identify opinions, so listen out for negatives (*kein, nicht*), words such as *Vorteil* (advantage) and *Nachteil* (disadvantage), and for words or phrases that indicate a change of opinion, such as *aber, leider, auf der anderen Seite*.

Dictation

5 You will hear five short sentences. Write down exactly what you hear in German.

> Think carefully about how these sounds, letters and words are pronounced, when writing down what you hear:
> -tion
> -er
> r

Kapitel 7 Mündlicher Test

Role-play

 1 Look at the role-play card and prepare what you are going to say.

> Keep to something you know how to say in German. Don't make your response too complicated.

> You are talking to your Swiss friend about what is important in your life.
> 1 Say **what is important** for you in life. (Give **two** details.)
> 2 Describe **one** thing about the environment which **you think** is bad.
> 3 Give your **opinion** of being vegetarian or vegan and say why. (Give **one** detail and **one** reason.)
> 4 Say **two** things **you have done recently** to help protect the environment.
> 5 ? Ask your friend **a question** about the environment.

> If you start with *Ich finde es schlecht, dass…* remember that the verb goes to the end.

> If you begin with *Meiner Meinung nach*, the verb comes next.

> Remember to use the perfect tense.

> To form a question, you can use a question word, or use subject–verb inversion.

 2 Practise what you have prepared. Then, using your notes, listen and respond to the teacher.

 3 Listen to Taylor's response and answer the questions.
1 Which **two** things does he say are important for him?
2 Which problem does he mention?
3 Which reason does he give for being vegetarian?
4 Which **two** things has he done recently?
5 Write down, in **English**, the question he asks at the end.

Reading aloud

 4 Look at this task. With a partner, read the sentences aloud, paying attention to the underlined letters.

> Die Leh<u>r</u>e<u>r</u> und Schü<u>ler</u> machen ge<u>r</u>ade eine Umwelt<u>tion</u> in mein<u>er</u> Schule.
>
> Wir <u>v</u>ersuchen, kein Papi<u>er</u> wegzuw<u>er</u>fen, und wollen meh<u>r</u> Kleidung <u>r</u>ecyceln.
>
> Diese Gene<u>ration</u> <u>v</u>ersteht die <u>P</u>robleme d<u>er</u> Welt bess<u>er</u> als uns<u>ere</u> El<u>ter</u>n.
>
> Ich <u>w</u>erde fü<u>r</u> eine int<u>er</u>na<u>tion</u>ale O<u>r</u>ganisa<u>tion</u> a<u>r</u>beiten.
>
> Kind<u>er</u> und <u>Er</u>wachsene in allen Länd<u>ern</u> sollten die gleichen <u>R</u>echte haben.

> Think carefully about how to pronounce these sounds, letters and words:
> *-tion*
> *er*
> *r*
> Remember where the stress falls in a compound noun.

 5 Listen and check your pronunciation.

 6 Listen to the teacher asking four follow-up questions. Translate each question into English and prepare your own answer to each one. Then listen again and respond to the teacher.

> Think about some of the topic-specific vocabulary you have learned. For the first follow-up question, you could mention issues such as *Flüchtlinge, Klimawandel, Gewalt gegen arme/junge Menschen, Jobsicherheit, Ausbildung*.

Photo card

Look at the photos and listen to Taylor describing the photos. Answer the questions.

1. Who are the adults in the first photo, according to Taylor?
2. What does Taylor say about the younger boy?
3. Why does Taylor think it is a cold day?
4. Why are the teenagers happy?
5. In the second photo, what does Taylor say the three women have been doing?

You will be asked to talk about the content of these photos. You must say at least one thing about each photo.

After you have spoken about the content of the photos, you will be asked questions related to any of the topics within the theme of **Communication and the world around us**.

Your responses should be as **full and detailed** as possible.

Prepare your own description of the photos. Then, with a partner, take turns describing them.

> Auf dem ersten Foto gibt es ...

Listen to the teacher's first follow-up question, *Was hast du neulich gemacht, um der Umwelt zu helfen?* Listen to Taylor's response and write down <u>three</u> actions he mentions.

Listen to Taylor answering the question, *Was wirst du in der Zukunft machen, um die Umwelt zu schützen?* Write down <u>five</u> positive actions Taylor plans to take.

Listen to two more follow-up questions and prepare your answers. Then respond to the recording. Make your answers as full as possible, including opinions and reasons.

You may be asked questions in different tenses, such as *Was **hast** du letztes Wochenende **gemacht**?* and *Was **wirst** du nächstes Wochenende **machen**?*

You could just say the same thing and change the tense of the verb: *Ich habe den Müll getrennt* and *Ich werde den Müll trennen*. However, it's better to show off your language and vocabulary by varying what you say, using different persons of the verb and adding subordinate clauses. For example, *Letztes Wochenende habe ich mit meinem Vater den Müll getrennt. Nächstes Wochenende werden meine Familie und ich kein Fleisch essen, weil es besser für die Umwelt und unsere Gesundheit ist.*

Prepare your own answers to as many of the Module 7 questions on page 227 as you can. Then practise with your partner.

Kapitel 7 Schreibtest

Translation

 Look at the translation task and Cara's translation of the sentences. Correct the <u>two</u> mistakes in each German sentence.

1 I worry about the future of the environment.
2 For refugees, security is the most important thing.
3 We should use electric cars to reduce air pollution.
4 Yesterday I recycled bottles and newspapers.
5 Many people are frightened about climate change.

1 Ich habe Angst vor der Zukunft der Erde.
2 Für Einwohner ist die Freiheit das Wichtigste.
3 Wir sollten Busse benutzen, um Luftverschmutzung zu vermeiden.
4 Gestern haben wir Gläser und Zeitungen recycelt.
5 Viele Menschen machen sich Sorgen um die Luftverschmutzung.

 Translate these sentences into German.

1 For me, climate change is the most important thing.
2 I worry about the environment.
3 My brother is frightened of violence in the town centre.
4 I should travel by bike to avoid air pollution.
5 Last week my friend separated the rubbish.

150-word writing task

 Look at this writing exam task and then, for each bullet point:

1 think about the vocabulary and structures you have learned, which you could use in your answers. For example:
   - **nouns**, **verbs** and **adjectives** to write about the environment and other issues of concern
   - **verbs of opinion** and **adjectives/adverbs** to give reasons
   - how to explain what you **will do** and **why**
   - **connectives**, **intensifiers** and **sequencers** you would like to use.
2 write down three or four ideas for what you could write about
3 identify which tense(s) you could use in your answer.

You are writing about issues you are concerned about for an online magazine.

Write approximately **150** words in **German**.

You **must** write something about both bullet points.

Describe:
- your greatest concerns or fears
- your plans for being more environmentally friendly in the future.

Lesen 4 Read Cara's answer to the exam task. Answer the questions in the coloured boxes (1–5).

1 This is an example of **complex language**. What does it mean? Find <u>three</u> more examples of complex language in the text.

2 What **grammatical structure** is this? What other examples can you find?

Ich mache mir Sorgen um die Probleme der Welt. Für mich ist der Klimawandel das wichtigste Problem, weil das heiße Wetter leider sehr schlecht für Menschen und Tiere ist. Man sollte mehr tun, um die Umwelt zu schützen.

Ein großes Problem ist die Wasserverschmutzung. Viele Menschen werfen Müll in die Flüsse oder sogar ins Meer und viele Fische sterben. Es ist schlecht, wenn man dort schwimmen will.

Ich habe Angst vor dem Krieg. Flüchtlinge verlassen oft ihre Länder, da es so viel Gewalt gibt. Ich mache mir Sorgen um die Kinder.

Wegen des Klimawandels wäre ich gern grüner. Es gibt zu viele Autos in den Städten. Das finde ich schlecht. Statt des Autos sollte man den Bus nehmen. Wenn ich in Zukunft ein Auto hätte, wäre es nur ein Elektroauto. Elektroautos produzieren nicht so viel Luftverschmutzung.

Ich werde versuchen, häufiger den Müll zu trennen und Glas und Papier zu recyceln. Ich hoffe, dass die Welt schöner wird.

3 How could Cara **avoid repetition** in these pairs?

4 Cara uses a **variety of adverbs**. What do these words mean? Find <u>two</u> more examples.

5 Which connective could you use here to form an **extended sentence**? What other connectives does Cara use?

Lesen 5 Read Cara's answer again and answer the questions in English.

1 What does Cara think is the most important problem?
2 What does Cara say is a consequence of water pollution?
3 What frightens Cara?
4 What is Cara's opinion about owning a car in future?
5 What is Cara's hope for the future?

Schreiben 6 Prepare your own answer to the task.

- Think about how you can develop your answer for each bullet point.
- Look back at your notes from exercises 3 and 4.
- Look at the 'Challenge checklist' and consider how you can show off your German!
- Write a **brief** plan and organise your answer into paragraphs.
- Write your answer and then carefully check for accuracy.

Challenge checklist

- ✓ Present and future time frames of simple verbs
- ✓ Connectives and time phrases
- ✓ Some extended sentences
- ✓ An opinion (*Die Umwelt ist wichtig.*)

- ✓ A wider range of tenses
- ✓ Different persons of the verb (*man, die Umwelt*)
- ✓ Adverbs (*übrigens, überhaupt, vor allem*)
- ✓ Interesting vocabulary (*der Zweck, die Chance, die Sicherheit, die Flüchtlinge, schützen, retten*)
- ✓ Subordinating conjunctions (*weil, dass*)

- ✓ Use of modal verbs in different tenses
- ✓ Complex language: infinitive constructions, use of the genitive, compound nouns
- ✓ The conditional and imperfect subjunctive
- ✓ Adjectival nouns (*das Größte, das Wichtigste*)
- ✓ More varied conjunctions (*wo, da, wenn, weder … noch …, sowohl … als auch …*)
- ✓ Verb + preposition (*sprechen über, kämpfen für/gegen, sich Sorgen machen um*)

Kapitel 7 Wörter

Key:
bold = this word will appear in higher exams only
* = this word is not on the vocabulary list, but you may use it in your own sentences

Wir verbessern die Welt! (pages 156–157):

Wir verbessern die Welt!	We're improving the world!
der Blog	blog
der Erfolg	success
der **Flüchtling**	refugee
der **Fortschritt**	progress
der **Konflikt**	conflict
der Mensch	person
der **Zweck**	purpose
die Aktion	action, campaign
die **Bevölkerung**	population
die Erfahrung	experience
die Geschichte	story
die Geschwister	brothers and sisters, siblings
die **Organisation**	organisation
die **Regierung**	government
die Zahl	number
das Ausland	abroad
das Leben	life
das Ziel	goal
das *Zuhause	home
aufbauen	to build up
bilden	to educate
entwickeln	to develop
gründen	to start, found, establish
informieren	to inform
kämpfen	to fight, struggle
(in Kontakt) stellen	to put (in contact)
verhindern	to prevent
abhängig	dependent
erfolgreich	successful
leer	empty
süchtig	addicted
dabei	with it
deshalb	therefore
gegen	against
statt	instead of
trotz	despite, in spite of
über	over, about
während	during
wegen	because of
wofür	for what
wogegen	against what
*xier	they

Was ist dir wichtig? (pages 158–159):

Wichtige Themen in der Welt	Important topics in the world
Ich habe Angst vor dem **Klimawandel**.	I'm afraid of climate change.
Ich bin mit (meiner Gesundheit) **zufrieden**.	I am happy/satisfied with (my health).
Ich hoffe auf eine bessere Zukunft.	I hope for a better future.
Ich mache mir Sorgen um …	I worry about …
Ich spreche über …	I talk about …
Ich kümmere mich um …	I care / am concerned about …
die Ausbildung	education
die **Flüchtlinge**	refugees
den Welthunger	world hunger

… ist mir wichtig	… is important to me
der Beruf	job
der Lohn	pay, wage
die Arbeit	work
die Familie	family
die Sicherheit	security
die Sorge	worry
das **Gute**	the good thing
das **Schlechte**	the bad thing
das **Wichtigste**	the most important thing

Unser armer *Planet (pages 160–161):

Umweltprobleme	Environmental problems
Meiner Meinung nach ist … das **größte/wichtigste** Problem.	In my opinion … is the biggest / most important problem.
Laut einer **Studie** sind … die **größten/wichtigsten** Probleme.	According to a study … are the biggest / most important problems.
der *Plastikmüll	plastic rubbish
die Luftverschmutzung	air pollution
die Wasserverschmutzung	water pollution
die steigenden Temperaturen	the rising temperatures
die Zerstörung der Wälder	the destruction of forests
das extreme Wetter	the extreme weather
Du hast Recht.	You're right.
Das stimmt (nicht).	That's (not) right.
Ich *stimme (nicht) zu.	I (don't) agree.
*Im **Gegenteil**.	On the contrary.
Ich habe mich entschieden, …	I (have) decided, …

Ich habe angefangen, …	I (have) started, …
Ich habe versucht, …	I (have) tried, …
an einem *Schulstreik teilzunehmen.	to take part in a school strike.
grüne **Produkte** zu kaufen.	to buy green products.
den Müll zu **trennen**.	to separate the rubbbish.
öfter zu Fuß zu gehen.	to go on foot / walk more often.
Energie zu sparen.	to save energy.
Ich habe …	I …
an einem *Schulstreik teilgenommen.	took part in a school strike.
*recycelte **Produkte** gekauft.	bought recycled products.
den Müll **getrennt**.	separated the rubbish.
Energie gespart.	saved energy.
Ich bin öfter zu Fuß gegangen.	I went on foot / walked more often.

Jeder kann was tun! (pages 162–163):

Persönliche Verantwortung für die Umwelt — *Personal responsibility for the environment*

Ich kaufe …	I buy …
„grüne" **Produkte**.	'green' products.
*umweltfreundliche **Produkte**.	eco-friendly products.
billige Kleidung.	cheap clothing.
Secondhandkleidung	second-hand clothing.
Ich spare …	I save …
jeden Tag …	every day.
(nicht) oft …	(not) often.
manchmal …	sometimes.
ab und zu …	now and again.
selten …	rarely.
nie …	never.
Energie.	energy, power
Wasser.	water
Ich recycle …	I recycle …
Ich werfe … weg.	I throw … away.
*Metall	metal
Papier	paper
(*Plastik)flaschen	(plastic) bottles
Ich **trenne** den Müll.	I separate the rubbish.
Ich trinke …	I drink …
aus einer *wiederverwendbaren *Tasse.	from a reusable cup.
aus einer *Wegwerftasse.	from a disposable cup.
Ich *mache das Licht *aus.	I turn the light off.
schützen	to protect
sammeln	to collect
ändern	to change
verantwortlich	responsible
gerecht	fair, just
gleich	equal
verschieden	different
der Verein	association, club
die **Ernährung**	food
die **Gesellschaft**	society
die Rechte	rights
die Situation	situation
die **Veranstaltung**	event
das Geld	money
das Mitglied	member

Wir wollen eine bessere Welt! (pages 164–165):

Internationale Verantwortungen — *International responsibilities*

Was … man machen, um eine bessere Welt zu **schaffen**?	What … be done to create a better world?
kann	can
muss	must
sollte	should
der Mensch	person
der Naturschutz	protection of nature
der Welthunger	world hunger
die **Lösung**	solution
die **Organisation**	organisation
die Umweltverschmutzung	environmental pollution
das Kind	child
das Leben	life
das Problem	problem, difficulty
die Menschenrechte	human rights
anfangen	to begin, start
benutzen	to use
sich entscheiden	to decide
fordern	to demand
helfen	to help
kämpfen (für/gegen)	to fight (for/against)
organisieren	to organise
unterstützen	to support
verbessern	to improve
verhindern	to prevent
arm	poor
international	international
*weltweit	worldwide

Dialog ist wichtig! (pages 166–167):

*Meinungsäußerung — *Expressing opinions*

Du hast gesagt, (dass) …	You said that …
… aber ich denke, dass …	… but I think that …
Das glaube ich nicht.	I do not think so.
Du hast Recht.	You are right.
Ich bin der Meinung, dass …	I am of the opinion that …
Das **Gute** ist, (dass) …	The good thing is that …
Es geht **darum**, …	It is about …
Ich meine trotzdem, dass …	Nevertheless, I think that …
(Aber) viele Leute sagen, (dass) …	(But) a lot of people say (that) …
Auf der einen Seite …, (aber) auf der anderen Seite …	On the one hand … (but) on the other hand …
funktionieren	to work, function
leiden	to suffer
schmecken	to taste
verursachen	to cause
die Pflanze	plant
die Tierart	species
das Fleisch	meat
das **Gericht**	dish, meal
außerdem	in addition, besides
*im **Gegenteil**	on the contrary
jedoch	however
übrigens	by the way, what's more
unbedingt	absolutely

Kapitel 8: Wie sieht die Zukunft aus?

Ich will helfen
- Learning about military and civilian service
- Revising verbs and constructions with *zu*

a) Immer beliebter: ein Freiwilliges Soziales Jahr

In Deutschland, Österreich und der Schweiz gibt es das sogenannte **F**reiwillige **S**oziale **J**ahr (**FSJ**). Wenn die Schule zu Ende ist, haben junge Menschen die Gelegenheit, dadurch persönliche und Arbeitserfahrungen zu sammeln. Zur gleichen Zeit können sie etwas Positives für die Gesellschaft leisten. Rund 47 000 Jugendliche machen jedes Jahr ein FSJ in Deutschland.

Man macht ein Freiwilliges Soziales Jahr,

1. um praktische Erfahrung zu sammeln.
2. um einen Arbeitsalltag zu erleben.
3. um anderen Menschen zu helfen und etwas Gutes zu tun.
4. um sich über die Arbeitswelt zu informieren.
5. um neue Leute kennenzulernen.
6. um ungefähr 500 Euro pro Monat Taschengeld zu bekommen.

Beispiele von Arbeitsbereichen im FSJ

Man kann …

A älteren Menschen helfen.

B mit Kindern arbeiten.

C der Gesellschaft helfen.

D mit Flüchtlingen arbeiten.

E im Krankenhaus arbeiten und Patienten pflegen.
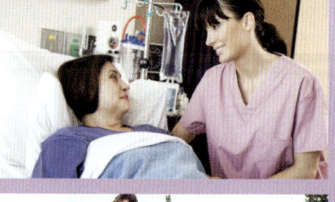

F Tieren und der Umwelt helfen.

freiwillig — voluntary

b) Was junge Leute sagen, die das FSJ machen wollen

Silvia: Ich habe vor, ein FSJ zu machen, um neue Leute zu treffen und sinnvolle Erfahrungen zu sammeln. Ich bin bereit, hart zu arbeiten. Außerdem hoffe ich, mich selbst besser kennenzulernen.

Katharina: Nach der Schule möchte ich beginnen, mit Kindern zu arbeiten. Das FSJ wird mir helfen herauszufinden, welcher Beruf zu mir passt. Vielleicht wird es meine Ideen zum Leben ändern, wer weiß!

Malik: Ich habe mich entschieden, ein FSJ zu machen, um mich über mögliche Berufe zu informieren. Es war keine leichte Entscheidung, aber ich hoffe, danach eine bessere Vorstellung davon zu haben, was ich studieren möchte.

Robin: Ich habe vor, ein FSJ zu machen, um den Arbeitsalltag zu erleben. Ich interessiere mich für viele Dinge und hoffe, später auf jeden Fall verschiedene Ausbildungen zu machen.

der Arbeitsalltag — everyday working life

Kulturzone — Kapitel 8

 Lesen 1 Read the first part of the article (**a**). Find the German for the phrases below.
1 a voluntary social year
2 to gain personal and professional experience
3 to do something positive for society
4 to help other people
5 to get to know new people
6 fields of work
7 to work with refugees
8 to care for sick people

 In Germany, compulsory military service (*Wehrpflicht*) was abolished in 2011. However, Austria and Switzerland still require most adult male citizens to do the equivalent of a few months of military service.

Conscientious objectors (i.e. people who don't want to be trained for war) can choose civilian service (*Zivildienst*) instead of military service. Women in all three countries are allowed to join the armed forces (or the civilian service), but they are not obliged to do so.

In Germany, Austria and Switzerland a *Freiwilliges Soziales Jahr* is also a possibility for school leavers.

 Lesen 2 Read about why Silvia, Malik, Katharina and Robin want to do an *FSJ* (**b**) and answer the questions with **S, M, K** or **R**.

Who …?
1 wants to start work straight after school
2 wants to find out what everyday working life is like
3 found the decision to give up a year difficult
4 hopes to get to know themselves better
5 hopes to do different training and qualifications later on
6 thinks doing an *FSJ* could change their attitude to life

G Remember that you need to use **zu** with an infinitive after some verbs:

hoffen to hope   *Lust haben* to be keen
planen to plan   **an**fangen to start
(sich) entscheiden to decide   **vor**haben to intend

Ich **hoffe**, in der Zukunft auf die Universität **zu** gehen.
Ich **habe vor**, den Zivildienst **zu** machen.

Some other constructions also follow the same pattern:

es ist (nicht) leicht, … zu …   it is (not) easy to …
Es ist nicht leicht, jeden Tag acht Stunden **zu** arbeiten.

bereit sein, … zu …   be ready / prepared to …
Ich bin bereit, hart **zu** arbeiten.

Gelegenheit haben, … zu …   have the opportunity to …
Man hat die Gelegenheit, einen Arbeitsalltag **zu** erleben.

Page 192

 Lesen 3 Translate the sentences in **bold** in Silvia, Malik, Katharina and Robin's texts into English.

 Hören 4 Listen and write the letter of the correct area of work from the article (**a**) for each person. (1–6)

 j is pronounced like the English 'y' in 'yes'.
Listen and repeat the words.
*j*edes *J*ahr, *j*etzt
However, how is the letter *J* in *FSJ* pronounced?

 Hören 5 Listen and write down the sentence you hear. Be careful with the *j* sound.

 Sprechen 6 In pairs, write down a sentence in secret, with one phrase from each column below. Take turns to guess the sentence. You can only say how many parts your partner got right, not *which* parts! Keep trying until all three parts are guessed correctly.

- *Ich habe vor, im Sommer eine interessante Arbeit zu finden.*
- *Du hast zwei richtig.*
- *Ich habe vor, nach der Schule eine interessante Arbeit zu finden.*
- *Ja, richtig!*

 Remember that in German you can use the present tense with a future time phrase instead of *Ich werde* (I will) or *Ich will* (I want to).

Ich habe vor,	im Sommer	an der Uni zu studieren.
Ich plane,	nächstes Jahr	mit Kindern zu arbeiten.
Ich hoffe,	später	(eine) interessante Arbeit zu finden.
Ich habe mich entschieden,	nach den Prüfungen	anderen Menschen zu helfen.
Ich habe Lust,	in der Zukunft	neue Leute kennenzulernen.
	nach der Schule	eine Ausbildung zu machen.

hunderteinundachtzig

1 Was wirst du nach deinen Prüfungen machen?

- Discussing plans for after exams
- Using reflexive verbs
- Revising ways to refer to the future

1 Listen to and read the forum posts. Find the German for the phrases below.

Was wirst du nach deinen Prüfungen machen?

Chris: Nach meinen Prüfungen werde ich mich zuerst einmal entspannen: viel schlafen, nichts tun und nur das machen, worauf ich Lust habe. Und im Herbst werde ich in die Oberstufe gehen. Ich werde an meiner Schule bleiben, weil ich mit meinen Freunden in Kontakt bleiben will.

Alina: **Nach meinen Prüfungen werden wir längere Ferien haben** als sonst und ich freue mich darauf. **Ich werde mich mit meinen Freunden treffen und wir werden uns so lange unterhalten**. Ich interessiere mich für Kunst und im September werde ich eine Ausbildung oder eine Lehre machen.

Layla: Nach meinen Prüfungen werde ich mir wahrscheinlich eine **Arbeit suchen**. Ich muss Geld verdienen, weil wir nächstes Jahr keine Schuluniform mehr haben werden und ich mir neue Kleidung kaufen möchte. **Ich habe mich noch nicht entschieden, ob ich an meiner Schule bleiben werde** oder ob ich auf eine andere Schule gehen werde.

1 after my exams
2 I am looking forward to it
3 probably
4 earn money
5 have longer holidays than normal
6 only do what I feel like doing

2 Read the forum posts again and write down <u>two</u> things each person is planning to do. Then translate the sentences in **bold** in the forum posts into English.

> In German you form the future tense with the correct form of **werden** and the <u>infinitive</u>, which goes at the end of the sentence.
> Ich **werde** an meiner Schule <u>bleiben</u>.
> I **will** <u>stay</u> at my school.
> Remember, you can also use **ich will** and **ich möchte** to express future plans.

3 Read the forum posts in exercise 1 again and find examples of reflexive verbs.

4 Rewrite the sentences, replacing the words in **bold** with your own ideas.

1 Ich interessiere mich sehr für **Musik**.
2 Ich kann mich nicht gut konzentrieren, wenn **es laut ist**.
3 Ich freue mich auf **nächstes Wochenende, weil meine Tante zu Besuch kommt**.
4 Ich habe mich entschieden, **eine Arbeit zu suchen**.
5 Ich mache mir Sorgen um **meine Noten**.
6 Ich wünsche mir **schönes Wetter für meinen Geburtstag**.

> **G**
> **Reflexive verbs** always have a pronoun which can be in the accusative or the dative. Common verbs which take the **accusative reflexive pronoun** are:
> sich interessieren (für)   to be interested (in)   sich entspannen   to relax
> sich treffen (mit)   to meet   sich entscheiden   to decide
> sich konzentrieren (auf)   to concentrate (on)
> Am Wochenende werde ich **mich** entspannen.
> At the weekend I will relax.
>
> Common verbs which take the **dative reflexive pronoun** are:
> sich wünschen   to wish   sich Sorgen machen (um)   to worry (about)
> Ich wünsche **mir**, dass alles gut geht.
> I wish for it all to go well.
>
> After **subordinating conjunctions** (dass, weil) and **relative pronouns**, the **reflexive pronoun** comes immediately after the <u>subject</u>.
> Ich habe später keine Zeit, **weil** <u>ich</u> **mich** mit Freunden treffe.
> I have no time later, because I am meeting friends.

Page 193

5 Listen to the plans for next year. Write down at least one detail in English for each person. (1–8)

	viel schlafen, nichts tun,	weil ich mich entspannen möchte.
Ich werde	in die Oberstufe / auf die Berufsschule gehen, mein Abitur machen, nur drei Fächer studieren,	weil ich mich für (Kunst) interessiere. weil ich später (Englisch) studieren will. weil ich eine Ausbildung/Lehre machen möchte.
	an meiner Schule bleiben,	weil ich meine Lehrer mag. weil ich mit meinen Freunden in Kontakt bleiben will.
	(mir) eine Arbeit suchen,	weil ich Geld verdienen möchte.
	nach (Deutschland) fahren, auf eine neue Schule gehen,	weil ich etwas Praktisches machen möchte. weil ich neue Leute kennenlernen möchte.

6 Write a short paragraph about what you are going to do next year and give reasons.

7 Listen to and read the interview. Answer the questions below.

Gespräch mit einem Berufscoach

Coach: Hallo, Finn! Weißt du schon, was du nach deinen Prüfungen machen wirst?

Finn: Nein, ich weiß noch nicht so genau. Auf der einen Seite interessiere ich mich für einen gut bezahlten Job, aber auf der anderen Seite mache ich mir Sorgen, dass ich ohne weitere Ausbildung später nur Jobs bekommen werde, wo ich nicht sehr viel Geld verdiene.

Coach: Für welche Art von Arbeit interessierst du dich denn?

Finn: Hm, ich bin mir nicht so sicher, aber ich denke, dass ich lieber mit Menschen als mit Computern arbeiten möchte. Es gefällt mir einfach nicht, den ganzen Tag vor einem Computer zu sitzen. Ich möchte auch auf jeden Fall eine Arbeit machen, wo ich mich weiterbilden kann.

1 What does Finn say interests him?
2 What is Finn's worry about starting a job straightaway?
3 Why would he prefer to work with people?
4 What does he definitely want from a job?

8 Translate the sentences into German.

1 I am planning to go to university.
2 Are you interested in art?
3 We would like to earn money.
4 He doesn't yet know what he will do in the future.

Use an infinitive phrase with zu.

Remember that this is a reflexive verb in German, and think about the preposition.

Remember that the verb goes to the end in relative clauses.

9 In pairs, ask each other about your plans for the future. Try to answer using longer sentences and give reasons using *weil*.

- *Was wirst du nach deinem Schulabschluss machen?*
- *Nach meinem Schulabschluss werde ich Arbeit finden, weil ich Geld verdienen möchte.*

Was wirst du nach deinen Prüfungen machen?

In der Zukunft Nach meinem Abitur Nächstes Jahr Nach der Schule	möchte ich werde ich will ich	auf die Universität gehen. eine Ausbildung/Lehre machen. einen Job finden.
Nach meinem Schulabschluss	habe ich vor, plane ich,	(Lehrer) zu werden. Geld zu verdienen.
Ich weiß noch nicht, Ich bin mir noch nicht sicher,		was ich später machen möchte. was ich studieren werde.

2 Was ist dein Traumberuf?

- Discussing what jobs you would like to do in the future
- Revising the conditional and imperfect subjunctive
- Using *werden* in different tenses

Lesen 1 Read the survey results. Write the correct letter to match each picture (a–h) to the types of work.

Was für einen Job möchtest du später machen?

1. Ich möchte Kinder oder Erwachsene unterrichten.
2. Ich möchte gegen Onlinemobbing kämpfen.
3. Ich möchte Dinge verkaufen.
4. Ich möchte Menschen helfen, die krank sind.
5. Ich möchte mit Computern arbeiten.
6. Ich möchte mit Tieren arbeiten.
7. Ich möchte Gästen oder Kunden helfen.
8. Ich möchte im Naturschutz arbeiten.

Hören 2 Listen. Copy and complete the sentences in English.

1. Lukas thinks it would be fun to work …
2. Lara would rather not …
3. … would be a possibility for Hanna.
4. Arda would perhaps work with computers in the future because … and …
5. Elif's ideal job would …
6. Max says that his dream job would be to do something for the …

> **G** Remember that the **conditional** is formed using *würde* + <u>infinitive</u>. *Würde* means 'would'.
> *Das **würde** ich nicht <u>machen</u>.* I **would** not <u>do</u> that.
>
> The **imperfect subjunctive** is also used with some verbs, for example *sein*. *Wäre* means 'would be'.
> *Das **wäre** eine Möglichkeit.* That **would be** a possibility.
> *Haben*, *mögen* and *sollen* are also used in the imperfect subjunctive.
>
> *Wenn ich mehr Zeit **hätte**, …* If I **had** more time, …
> *Er **möchte** später Polizist werden.* He **would like** to become a police officer.
> *Das **sollte** man tun.* People **should** do that.
>
> Page 194

Sprechen 3 In pairs, ask and answer questions about what you would like to do in the future.

- *Möchtest du später mit Computern arbeiten?*
- *Ja! Das wäre eine Möglichkeit.*

Möchtest du später (vielleicht) mit … arbeiten?	Das würde mir viel Spaß machen. Das wäre eine Möglichkeit.
Möchtest du in (der) Zukunft (Kinder unterrichten)?	Das würde ich lieber nicht machen. Das würde ich auf keinen Fall machen.
Was möchtest du später werden?	Ich möchte später vielleicht (Lehrer/in) werden.
Was wäre dein Traumberuf?	Mein Traumberuf wäre, etwas für die Umwelt zu tun.

Remember that **ä, ö, ü** are pronounced differently from **a, o, u**.

Listen and repeat the words.

hatte	hätte
war	wäre
mochte	möchte
wurde	würde

184 *hundertvierundachtzig*

4 Listen to and read the texts. Answer the questions below in English.

Generation Z: Deutschlands jüngste Gründerinnen und Gründer von Start-ups

Nour Idelbi: *Safespace*

Nour ist aus Münster und ist 17 Jahre alt. Im Start-up Teens-Finale hat sie in der Kategorie „Services & Plattforms" 10 000 Euro für ihr Konzept *Safespace* gewonnen. **Safespace ist eine Sicherheits-App für Frauen, die alleine nach Hause gehen müssen, wenn es dunkel wird.** Mit der App kann man direkt die Polizei alarmieren oder auch erstmal einfach mit Freunden, der Familie oder anderen Frauen sprechen, die gerade auf *Safespace* sind. Nours Vorbilder sind andere Geschäftsfrauen.

Leonardt Mücke und Liam Metzen: *Coffeecycle*

Die beiden 18-Jährigen haben gemeinsam ein Start-up gegründet, das Kosmetik aus Kaffeesatz produziert – vor allem Seife. *Coffeecycle* reduziert dadurch nicht nur Müll, sondern produziert auch Kosmetik, die besser für unseren Planeten ist. Sie haben keine Vorbilder, aber ihr Ziel ist es, aus den Fehlern anderer Geschäftsleute zu lernen. **Nächstes Jahr will Leonardt neben dem Start-up auch sein Studium beginnen, aber er ist sich noch nicht sicher, was er werden will.**

Bersa Shazimani: *Juniorjob*

Die 19-Jährige hat eine Plattform für Schülerinnen und Schüler geschaffen, die einen Nebenjob oder ein Praktikum suchen. **Sie ist Start-up-Gründerin geworden, weil sie mit 16 einen Nebenjob finden wollte, um Arbeitserfahrungen zu sammeln.** Es war aber sehr schwierig, einen Nebenjob zu finden. Sie glaubt, dass es hilft, wenn man selbst zur jungen Zielgruppe gehört, weil man dann die Probleme dieser Gruppe viel besser versteht und weiß, was diesen jungen Menschen wichtig ist.

der Kaffeesatz	coffee grounds (dregs)
die Seife	soap
der Nebenjob	part-time/extra job
das Praktikum	work experience

1. When can the *Safespace* app be useful for women?
2. Who are Nour's role models?
3. What are the two positive effects of *Coffeecycle*?
4. What is the goal of the founders of *Coffeecycle*?
5. How did Bersa get the idea to create the *Juniorjob* app?
6. Why does she think it's useful to be a member of the target group?

5 Translate the sentences in **bold** in exercise 4 into English.

6 Write six sentences about your future career.
- Was möchtest du später machen?
- Was wäre dein Traumberuf?

> **G** The verb **werden** can be used in different ways in German:
> - to form the future tense:
> *Ich **werde** morgen ins Kino gehen.*
> I **will** go to the cinema tomorrow.
> - to mean 'to become' (or 'get' / 'turn into something'):
> *Ich möchte Arzt **werden**.*
> I would like **to become** a doctor.
> *Das Essen **wird** kalt.*
> The food **is getting** cold.
> *Die Kinder **werden** ungeduldig.*
> The children **are getting/becoming** impatient.
>
> *Werden* can also be used in the past tense.
> Imperfect tense:
> *Das Essen **wurde** kalt.*   The food **got** cold.
> Perfect tense:
> *Das Essen **ist** kalt **geworden**.*   The food **has got** cold.
>
> Page 194

3 Was kannst du gut?

- Discussing strengths and skills
- Revising subordinating conjunctions
- Extending your written work

1 Listen to six young people. Write down the letters of the strengths and skills (a–n) each person mentions. Then try to guess which job (1–6) best suits each person.

die Bühne — stage

Was sind deine Eigenschaften und Fähigkeiten?

a	Ich kann gut zuhören und erklären.	h	Ich arbeite gut in einem Team.
b	Ich kann gut organisieren.	i	Ich zeige Initiative und bin hilfsbereit.
c	Ich kann andere Menschen gut überzeugen.	j	Ich bin stark und kann körperlich viel leisten.
d	Ich kann unabhängig arbeiten.	k	Ich habe gute Sprachkenntnisse.
e	Ich kann andere interessieren.	l	Ich schreibe sehr gern und bin kreativ.
f	Ich kann mich sehr gut konzentrieren.	m	Ich habe viel Verständnis und bin höflich.
g	Ich mag Verantwortung.	n	Ich habe gute Qualifikationen.

1 Lehrer*in

3 Verkäufer*in

5 Autor*in

2 Schauspieler*in

4 Arzt/Ärztin

6 Betreuer*in

2 Listen and check you guessed each job in exercise 1 correctly. Write down <u>one</u> more detail for each person. (1–6)

3 Write sentences about your own strengths and skills. Use the tip box to help you extend your writing.

Try to extend your written work by using **conjunctions**, **expanding** your information and including **opposites**.

- **Conjunction**: *Ich zeige Initiative.* → *Ich bin der Meinung, <u>dass</u> ich Initiative zeige.*
- **Expand**: *<u>Außerdem</u> denke ich, dass … Meine Eltern/Lehrer behaupten <u>auch</u>, dass …*
- **Opposite**: *Ich kann nicht immer unabhängig arbeiten. Ich arbeite <u>jedoch</u> sehr gut in einem Team. Außerdem kann ich mich nicht immer sehr gut konzentrieren, <u>aber</u> ich versuche, mich zu verbessern.*

4 In pairs, read out your sentences from exercise 3 and suggest a job for each other.

qu is pronounced like 'kv' in English.
Listen and repeat the words.
Quiz, be**qu**em, **Qu**alität, **Qu**antität, **Qu**alifikation, Fre**qu**enz, Konse**qu**enz

 5 Listen to and read the text. Answer the questions below in English.

Mein Berufsweg

Lea

Schon seit ich klein war, wollte ich immer mit Tieren arbeiten. **Sobald ich alt genug war**, habe ich einen Job als Hundeausführerin und Katzensitterin gefunden, um Geld zu verdienen. **Ich konnte mich nicht entscheiden, ob ich Katzen oder Hunde lieber hatte**. Nach meinem Schulabschluss habe ich eine Ausbildung zur Tierpflegerin begonnen. **Während ich meine Ausbildung gemacht habe**, habe ich bereits an Wochenenden im Tierpark Berlin geholfen und **während ich studiert habe**, habe ich dort weitergearbeitet. Noch **bevor ich meinen Abschluss hatte**, haben sie mir dort einen Job angeboten. Jetzt arbeite ich schon seit acht Jahren dort. **Seitdem ich im Tierpark angefangen habe**, habe ich schon mit Elefanten gearbeitet. **Nachdem ich zehn Jahre dort gearbeitet habe**, möchte ich dann einen anderen Job suchen.

der Hundeausführer dog walker

1 When did Lea earn money as a dog walker and cat sitter?
2 What could she not decide?
3 When did she start her training in animal care?
4 When was she offered a job?

G All **subordinating conjunctions** link sentences together and send the <u>verb</u> to the end of the clause.

seitdem	since then, since
nachdem	after
bevor	before
während	during, while
sobald	as soon as
solange	as long as
ob	whether, if

Sobald ich alt genug <u>war</u>, …
As soon as I <u>was</u> old enough, …

Während ich studiert <u>habe</u>, …
While I <u>was</u> studying, …

When you start with the subordinating conjunction, the verbs of both parts meet in the middle, separated by a comma. This is called a '**verb-comma-verb**-structure'.
*Sobald ich alt genug **war**, **habe** ich einen Job gesucht.*

Page 195

 6 Translate the phrases in **bold** in exercise 5 into English.

 7 Listen and write down the verbs you hear to complete the sentences.

1 Während ich in der Schule ___, ___ ich nicht viel an meine Zukunft ___.
2 Bevor ich auf die Uni ___, ___ ich ein Praktikum ___.
3 Sobald ich mein Abitur ___, ___ ich eine Stelle ___.
4 Seitdem ich Direktor ___ ___, habe ich mehr Verantwortung.

 8 Imagine you are 25 and rewrite the sentences in exercise 7, changing the second half of each sentence so it's true for you.

- Use the **present tense** for something you have been and are still doing:
  Ich **arbeite** seit acht Jahren als Lehrer.
- Use the **perfect tense** for specific past events:
  Ich **habe** einen Job **gefunden**.
- Use the **imperfect tense** for how things used to be:
  Während ich in der Schule **war**, …
  Ich **konnte** mich nicht entscheiden.
  Ich **wollte** mit Tieren arbeiten.

4 Ein Zwischenjahr? Warum nicht?

- Discussing gap years
- Using adjectives as nouns
- Formulating an argument

1 Listen and write down the percentages you hear.

Was machen die deutschen Jugendlichen in ihrem Zwischenjahr?

- **a** Arbeiten und Reisen: ___ %
- **b** Freiwilligenarbeit: ___ %
- **c** Auslandspraktikum: ___ %
- **d** Urlaub: ___ %
- **e** als Au-pair arbeiten: ___ %
- **f** Sprachreise: ___ %

> Gap years originated in the 1960s, but some say that they are a longstanding tradition that dates back to the 13th century, when craftspeople travelled around the world to perfect their skills (*Wanderjahre*). The modern gap year is a recent phenomenon in Germany and there is no direct translation. Some people say: *ein Jahr aussetzen*. Others call it *ein Sabbatjahr* or *ein Zwischenjahr*. An *FSJ* (*Freiwilliges Soziales Jahr*) is something that some young people undertake during their gap year.

2 Listen to and read the texts. Write down <u>two</u> reasons why each person chose a gap year.

Möchtest du ein Zwischenjahr machen?

Mila: Warum ich ein Zwischenjahr machen möchte? Erstens kann ich mich noch nicht entscheiden, was ich später machen möchte. Ein Zwischenjahr gibt mir Zeit, mich zu entscheiden. **Außerdem möchte ich für ein paar Monate etwas Anderes machen**. Ich brauche eine Pause nach dem Studium.

Paul: Also, ich möchte höchstwahrscheinlich ein Zwischenjahr machen, weil ich gerne reisen möchte. **Ich kann mir im Moment nichts Besseres vorstellen, als fremde Länder zu sehen**. Ich möchte neue Menschen und Landschaften kennenlernen.

Hanna: Ich möchte in meinem Zwischenjahr Arbeitserfahrung gewinnen und Geld verdienen. **Ich muss etwas Neues machen und nicht immer nur lernen**. Außerdem habe ich gehört, dass sowohl Unis als auch Firmen viel Wert darauf legen, dass man schon Arbeitserfahrung hat.

Matteo: Ich denke, dass ich ein Zwischenjahr brauche. Ich muss einmal auf eigenen Beinen stehen und für mich selbst verantwortlich sein. **Ich tue mir selbst wenig Gutes, wenn ich immer nur in meiner Komfortzone bleibe**.

Charlotte: **Es gibt so viel Interessantes in der Welt**. Ich möchte in meinem Zwischenjahr all das machen, was ich bis jetzt nicht machen konnte. Ich mag Herausforderungen!

Tim: Ich möchte in meinem Zwischenjahr Freiwilligenarbeit leisten. Es gibt so viele Probleme in der Gesellschaft und **ich möchte diese Zeit verwenden, um etwas Gutes zu tun**.

3 Translate the sentences in **bold** in exercise 2 into English.

4 Translate the phrases into German.
1 something special
2 nothing bad
3 a lot of good
4 little new
5 everything else (use *ander-*)

> **G** Adjectives can be used as a **noun** after *etwas* (something), *nichts* (nothing), *viel* (a lot), *wenig* (little), *alles* (everything). Just add a capital letter to the adjective and an ending.
> - After *etwas, nichts, viel, wenig*, the ending is *-es*:
>   **Etwas Interessantes** *ist passiert!* Something interesting happened!
>   **Nichts Neues**. Nothing new.
>   *Er hat* **viel Gutes** *getan.* He did a lot of good.
> - After *alles*, the ending is *-e*:
>   **Alles Gute** *zum Geburtstag!* All the best on your birthday!
>
> Page 195

5 Listen to Elena, Jonas and Mia discussing gap years. Answer the questions.
Who …?
1 has a family member who has done a gap year
2 would like to learn something new
3 would like to do something meaningful
4 would like to travel
5 is going to discuss it with someone else
6 would like to get some work experience

> Remember:
> *wäre* = would be
> *würde* + infinitive = would
> *würde gern* + infinitive = would like to

6 In groups, discuss the arguments for and against taking a gap year. Each person says an introductory sentence, then evaluates one side of the argument, then the other side, and then comes to a conclusion.

question	Würdest du gern ein Zwischenjahr machen?	
introduction	Ich weiß noch nicht. Ich bin mir noch nicht sicher. Ich habe noch nicht darüber nachgedacht.	
one side	Auf der einen Seite denke ich,	dass es gut wäre, gleich mit dem Studium zu beginnen. dass es gut wäre, gleich auf die Uni zu gehen. dass ich keine Zeit verlieren möchte. dass ich lieber nach dem Studium ein Zwischenjahr machen würde als vor dem Studium.
other side	Auf der anderen Seite denke ich (aber),	dass ich gern reisen würde. dass ich gern einmal nichts tun würde. dass ich gern ein bisschen Geld verdienen würde. dass ich gern Freiwilligenarbeit machen würde. dass ich gern ein bisschen Berufserfahrung sammeln würde. dass ich etwas Neues lernen möchte. dass ich eine Arbeit finden möchte.
conclusion	Also, ich weiß noch nicht,	aber ich denke, dass ich wahrscheinlich …

7 Write a paragraph describing your opinions about taking a gap year and what you might like or not like to do.

5 Meine Träume für die Zukunft

- Discussing hopes for the future
- Dealing with unfamiliar vocabulary
- Consolidating key language and grammar points

Lesen 1 Read the texts and match the sentences below to the correct person: Lara (**L**), Martin (**M**) or Toni (**T**).

Worauf hoffst du? Wie stellst du dir die Zukunft vor?

Ich hoffe auf eine interessante Arbeit in einem großen Unternehmen und ein gutes Gehalt. Ich möchte mein Potential entwickeln, erfolgreich sein und zeigen, was ich kann. Ich möchte auch viel reisen und die Gelegenheit haben, im Ausland zu arbeiten und neue Kulturen zu entdecken. Heiraten will ich vielleicht nicht, aber eine zivile Partnerschaft wäre eine Möglichkeit.
Lara

Ich hoffe, dass ich später eine gute Partnerin finden werde und dass wir zusammen glücklich sein werden. Ich muss nicht unbedingt heiraten. Einfach zusammenleben ist auch schön, aber ich will bestimmt Kinder haben. Das ist mein größter Wunsch! Anders kann ich mir meine Zukunft gar nicht vorstellen.
Martin

Ich hoffe auf eine wunderbare Gruppe von Freunden. Für mich ist die Unterstützung von Freunden unglaublich wichtig, und es ist toll, wenn man eine gute Work-Life-Balance hat, um die Zeit mit ihnen richtig zu genießen. Heiraten ist mir wichtig, aber nicht sofort. Ich bin im Moment ledig, aber wer weiß, was die Zukunft bringt!
Toni

1. I want to have children.
2. I would like to travel.
3. I would like to get married in the future.
4. I want time for a social life.
5. I would like to be successful.
6. I am not certain about getting married.

> - *Ich hoffe auf* + noun = I'm hoping for ...
>   *Ich hoffe auf eine gute Arbeit.*
> - *Ich hoffe, dass ...* = I'm hoping that ...
>   *Ich hoffe, dass ich heiraten werde.*

Hören 2 Listen to Mila, Felix, Robin and Jana talking about their hopes for the future. Make notes in English.

Sprechen 3 In pairs, take turns to ask and answer these questions.

- *Worauf hoffst du?*
  - *Ich hoffe auf ... / Ich hoffe, dass ich ... werde.*
- *Möchtest du heiraten / Kinder haben / reisen?*
  - *Ja, ... / Nein, ...*
- *Wie wichtig ist dir ein gutes Gehalt?*
  - *Mir ist ... (sehr/nicht) wichtig, weil ...*
- *Wie wichtig sind dir deine Freunde / Freundinnen?*
  - *Mir sind ... (sehr/nicht) wichtig, weil ...*

4 Listen to and read the opinions below and write down two ideas from each text about what the world could be like in 20 years' time. Then translate the words in bold into English and decide whether they are cognates, compound nouns or words that can be worked out from the context.

Wie wird die Welt in 20 Jahren aussehen?

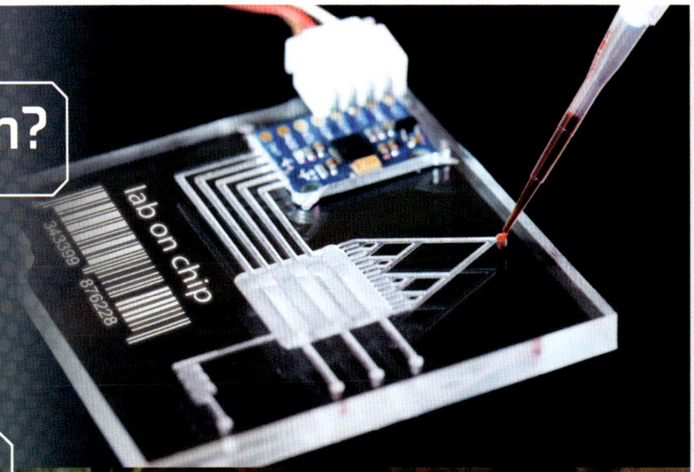

1 Es ist schwer zu sagen, wie die Welt in 20 Jahren aussehen wird, aber ich denke, dass es noch mehr technologischen Fortschritt geben wird. **Künstliche Intelligenz** wird eine größere Rolle im Unterricht und am Arbeitsplatz spielen.

2 Ich habe Angst vor der Zukunft, weil ich denke, dass es mehr **Naturkatastrophen** geben wird. Ich habe auch Angst, dass es viele Tier- und **Pflanzenarten** in der Zukunft nicht mehr geben wird.

3 Ich bin der Meinung, dass mehr **Roboter** für uns arbeiten werden. Sie werden vielleicht die **Einkäufe** vom Geschäft zu uns bringen, große Gebäude sauber machen und vielleicht auch Ärzten öfter im Krankenhaus helfen. Es wird hoffentlich besser als die **Gegenwart** sein.

5 In pairs, discuss what you think will happen in the future.

- Wie sieht die Zukunft deiner Meinung nach aus?
- Ich glaube, dass es mehr Roboter geben wird, und du?
- Ja, ich stimme zu. Ich denke, dass … / Nein, ich stimme nicht zu. Meiner Meinung nach …

Reading texts sometimes contain words you may not have seen before, but there are a number of ways to work out their meaning:
- Does the word look very similar to a word in English? There are a lot of **cognates** in German.
- Is the word made up of two or more words? **Compound nouns** are very common, and breaking them down into words you know helps.
- What is the sentence containing the word about? Use the **context** to work out the meaning.

6 Listen to Jan and Maria and copy and complete the table in English. (1–2)

	what is important to them	what they wanted to do when younger	current future plans
Jan			

7 Write approximately 150 words about career options and the future. Include the following points:
- the issues that are important to you
- your personal and career plans for the future.

Schon seit ich klein war, wollte ich (mit Kindern arbeiten).
Der Vorteil davon ist, dass … / Der Nachteil ist …
Ich hoffe, dass ich in der Zukunft (heiraten werde).
Ich glaube, dass (die Technologie) in der Zukunft (sehr wichtig sein wird).

hunderteinundneunzig **191**

Grammatik 1

Verbs and constructions with *zu* (Culture, page 181)

1 Translate the sentences into English.

1 Ich hoffe, eine Ausbildung zu machen.
2 Ich habe vor, nach den Prüfungen nach Deutschland zu fahren.
3 Ich habe begonnen, praktische Erfahrung zu sammeln.
4 Ich habe mich entschieden, meine Zukunft zu planen.

2 Rewrite the sentences using the verb phrases in brackets and *zu*.

Example: 1 *Ich bin bereit, ein Zwischenjahr zu machen.*

1 Ich mache ein Zwischenjahr. (*Ich bin bereit*)
2 Ich studiere Mathe an der Uni. (*Ich habe mich entschieden*)
3 Ich mache ein FSJ. (*Ich habe vor*)
4 Ich arbeite mit Tieren. (*Ich hoffe*)
5 Ich verdiene viel Geld. (*Ich habe begonnen*)
6 Ich arbeite ein halbes Jahr und reise ein halbes Jahr. (*Ich habe vor*)

3 Rewrite the sentences as questions, using the pronoun in brackets.

Example: 1 *Bist du bereit, hart zu arbeiten?*

1 Ich bin bereit, hart zu arbeiten. (*du*)
2 Wir fahren nach Deutschland, um neue Menschen kennenzulernen. (*ihr*)
3 In Deutschland gibt es wirklich viel zu sehen und zu tun. (*es*)
4 Ich habe die Gelegenheit, viel Deutsch zu sprechen. (*du*)
5 Wir gehen ins Kino, ohne die Karten zu kaufen. (*ihr*)
6 Ich habe Lust, nach dem Abitur zu reisen. (*du*)

4 Translate the sentences into German.

1 I hope to go to Switzerland after the exams.
2 We would like to have the opportunity to speak German.
3 I have decided to go travelling.
4 We intend to earn a lot of money.
5 Do you plan to take a gap year?
6 Would you like to go to university?

5 In pairs, take turns to read out your answers to exercise 4.

 These constructions also use *zu*:

Lust haben, … zu …
to feel like doing something
Ich **habe Lust**, ins Ausland **zu** reisen.

es gibt … zu … there is
Es gibt viel **zu** tun.

die Gelegenheit haben, … zu …
to have the opportunity to
Ich **habe die Gelegenheit**, ein FSJ **zu** machen.

ohne … zu … without
Ohne etwas **zu** sagen, …

statt … zu … instead of
Statt auf die Uni **zu** gehen, …

um … zu … in order to
Um mehr Geld **zu** verdienen, …

Remember that modal verbs in German do **not** use *zu* before the infinitive.

Ich **möchte** nach Hause gehen. →
I **would like to** go home.

Reflexive verbs (Unit 1, page 182)

Schreiben 6 Put the words in order to make sentences. Then translate the sentences.

Example: 1 *Ich interessiere mich sehr für Musik.*

1 interessiere für sehr Musik Ich mich.
2 auf mich das Ich Wochenende nächste freue.
3 mir Planeten Sorgen um mache Ich unseren.
4 mich werde mit treffen jeden Tag Ich Freunden.
5 nicht kann ist konzentrieren, wenn Ich es laut mich gut.
6 eine Sprachreise wünsche meinem Schulabschluss Ich nach mir.
7 den mich Prüfungen Ich nach entspannen möchte.
8 eine zu habe Ich entschieden, Arbeit mich finden.

personal pronouns	reflexive pronouns	
	accusative	dative
ich	mich	**mir**
du	dich	**dir**
er/sie/es/man	sich	sich
wir	uns	uns
ihr	euch	euch
Sie	sich	sich
sie	sich	sich

Note that only the *ich* and *du* forms are different in the dative case.

Hören 7 Listen and write the pronoun you hear to complete each sentence. Then decide whether the pronoun is in the accusative case (**A**) or dative case (**D**).

Example: 1 *uns* – A

1 Wir haben ___ den ganzen Abend unterhalten.
2 Möchtest du ___ einen Job suchen?
3 Er möchte ___ vorstellen.
4 Ich kann ___ das nicht vorstellen.
5 Sie wird ___ zuerst entspannen.
6 Ich werde ___ schön anziehen.
7 Ich habe ___ eine warme Jacke angezogen.
8 Ich habe ___ entschieden, Lehrer zu werden.

If there is only one object in the sentence, the reflexive pronoun will be in the **accusative case**.
*Ich ziehe **mich** an.* I dress (myself).

If there are two objects in the sentence, the reflexive pronoun will be in the dative case.
Ich ziehe mir ein T-Shirt an.
I put a T-shirt on.

Some verbs have a different meaning depending on whether the reflexive pronoun is in the accusative or the dative case, e.g. *sich vorstellen*.
*Ich stelle **mich** vor.* I introduce myself.
*Ich stelle **mir** vor, dass ...* I imagine that ...

Lesen 8 Translate the sentences from exercise 7 into English.

Example: 1 *We talked the whole evening.*

Schreiben 9 Translate the sentences into German. Use the correct accusative or dative pronoun.

Example: 1 *Ich ziehe mich an.*

1 I get dressed.
2 I put on a jacket. (use *anziehen*)
3 I wash myself.
4 I wash my hair.
5 I introduce myself.
6 I imagine that I will win.

Grammatik 2

The conditional and imperfect subjunctive (Unit 2, page 184)

 1 Rewrite the sentences using the conditional or imperfect subjunctive.

Example: 1 Nach dem Abitur **würde** ich ein Zwischenjahr machen.

1 Nach dem Abitur **werde** ich ein Zwischenjahr machen.
2 Ich **werde** zuerst sechs Monate in England arbeiten.
3 Dadurch **werde** ich Berufserfahrung gewinnen und Geld verdienen.
4 Dann **habe** ich drei Monate Zeit, um zu reisen und verschiedene Länder kennenzulernen.
5 Danach **ist** es eine Möglichkeit, drei Monate Freiwilligenarbeit in Südafrika zu machen.

 Remember that the conditional is formed using **würde** + infinitive.
Ich **würde** nach der Schule ein Zwischenjahr machen.
I **would** take a gap year after school.
It can also be used with **gern** to say what you would like to do.
Ich **würde gern** reisen.   I **would like** to travel.

Sein, haben, sollen and mögen are usually used in the **imperfect subjunctive** to express a conditional idea.
Es **wäre** gut.   It **would be** good.
Ich **hätte** Zeit.   I **would have** time.
Er **möchte** Lehrer werden.   He **would like** to be a teacher.
Das **sollte** man tun.   People **should** do that.

	conditional		imperfect subjunctive	
			haben	sein
ich	würde		hätte	wäre
du	würdest		hättest	wärst
er/sie/es/man	würde	+ infinitive	hätte	wäre
wir	würden		hätten	wären
ihr	würdet		hättet	wärt
Sie	würden		hätten	wären
sie	würden		hätten	wären

 2 In pairs, take turns to read out a sentence from exercise 1 and the rewritten version in the conditional or imperfect subjunctive. Pay attention to the umlauts.

Using werden (Unit 2, page 185)

 3 Translate the sentences into English.

1 Ich weiß noch nicht, was ich werden möchte.
2 Er ist Start-up-Gründer geworden, weil er grüne Mode produzieren wollte.
3 Was wirst du später werden?
4 Die Situation wird besser, weil wir alle zusammenarbeiten.
5 Es ist ziemlich schwierig geworden, einen Nebenjob zu bekommen.

	present	imperfect	perfect
ich	werde	wurde	bin geworden
du	wirst	wurdest	bist geworden
er/sie/es/man	wird	wurde	ist geworden
wir	werden	wurden	sind geworden
ihr	werdet	wurdet	seid geworden
Sie	werden	wurden	sind geworden
sie	werden	wurden	sind geworden

To become: Ich **werde** krank.   I **am becoming/getting** ill.
Future tense: Ich **werde** krank werden.   I **will** become/get ill.
Ich **werde** an der Uni studieren.   I **will** study at university.

 4 Listen and write down the translations you hear.

1 In August I am going to do work experience.
2 The weather is getting better.
3 I will definitely not become a teacher!
4 She has become a successful businesswoman.

Subordinating conjunctions (Unit 3, page 187)

5 Choose a subordinating conjunction from the box for each gap. There is more than one possible answer for some of the sentences.

| als | bevor | da | nachdem |
| ob | seitdem | sobald | während |

1 ▭ ich mein Abitur gemacht habe, werde ich gleich auf die Uni gehen.
2 ▭ sie einen Job hat, geht sie öfter in Restaurants essen.
3 ▭ ich an der Uni war, haben meine Eltern einen Hund gekauft.
4 Sie konnte sich nicht entscheiden, ▭ es besser war zu arbeiten oder zu studieren.
5 Er hat einen Nebenjob und spart Geld, ▭ das Studium sehr viel Geld kosten wird.
6 ▭ er jünger war, hatte er vor, Arzt zu werden.
7 Wir gehen spazieren, ▭ es aufhört zu regnen.
8 ▭ ich mich entscheide, will ich wissen, wie es ist, mit Kindern zu arbeiten.

> Remember that these subordinating conjunctions send the verb to the end of the clause:
> *als, bevor, da, dass, nachdem, ob, obwohl, seitdem, sobald, solange, während, weil, wenn*

6 Rewrite the subordinate clauses in the correct order.

Example: 1 *Ich war 14, als meine Schwester auf die Uni ging.*

1 Ich war 14, als **auf die Uni / ging / meine Schwester**.
2 Ich möchte gern eine eigene Wohnung haben, bevor **bin / ich / 30 Jahre alt**.
3 Meine Eltern würden gern mehr reisen, wenn **hätten / sie / mehr Zeit**.
4 Sobald **studiert / an der Uni / mein Bruder**, werde ich in sein Zimmer einziehen.
5 Seitdem **habe / über Flüchtlinge / ich / gelesen / einen Artikel**, möchte ich mit ihnen arbeiten.

Using adjectives as nouns after indefinite pronouns (Unit 4, page 189)

7 Translate the words in brackets into German to complete the sentences. Then translate the completed sentences into English.

Example: 1 *etwas Nettes*

1 Meine Mutter möchte mir ▭ zum Geburtstag schenken. (*something nice*)
2 Im Zwischenjahr habe ich ▭ gelernt. (*much new*)
3 ▭ für die Prüfungen! (*all the best*)
4 Mein Bruder hat ▭ von seinem neuen Job erwartet. (*little interesting*)
5 Ich kann mir ▭ vorstellen, als keine Prüfungen mehr zu haben. (*nothing better*)
6 ▭ kann mit der Zeit ▭ werden. (*something bad, something good*)

> Remember that you can use an adjective as a noun after an indefinite pronoun by adding a capital letter to the adjective and an ending.
> - After *etwas, nichts, viel, wenig*, add **-es**:
>   *etwas Interessantes*
>   something interesting
> - After *alles*, add **-e**:
>   *alles Gute*
>   all the best

Los geht's!

8 Translate the conversation into German.

– What will you do next year?

– I don't yet know, but I hope to do something interesting. Studying is getting more expensive. Before I go to university, I will probably work in order to earn some money. If I had the choice, I would work abroad. That would be something new for me. However, at the moment, I am concentrating on my exams. I am worried about my grades.

| **die Wahl** | choice |

Kapitel 8 Lese- und Hörtest

Reading

 A gap year. You read Alina and Paul's blog posts about taking a gap year. Answer the following questions in English.

> Ich werde wahrscheinlich ein Zwischenjahr* nehmen, weil ich mich noch nicht entscheiden kann, was ich später im Leben machen möchte. Ein Zwischenjahr würde mir die Zeit geben, die ich brauche, um mich endlich zu entscheiden. Ich möchte auch Berufserfahrung sammeln und Geld verdienen. Ich würde gern etwas Neues machen, fremde Länder sehen und interessante Menschen, Kulturen und Landschaften kennenlernen. Ich habe vor, ein ganzes Jahr um die Welt zu reisen. **Alina**

ein Zwischenjahr   a gap year

> Ich brauche eine Pause, bevor ich an der Uni studiere. Ich habe schon so viel gelernt, dass es keine gute Idee wäre, sofort mit dem Studium weiterzumachen. Es gibt so viel Interessantes in der Welt und deshalb möchte ich in meinem Zwischenjahr* verschiedene Dinge machen, die ich bis jetzt nicht machen konnte. Ich möchte in meinem Zwischenjahr Freiwilligenarbeit in Asien leisten. Es gibt viele Probleme in der Gesellschaft und ich möchte diese Zeit benutzen, um etwas Gutes zu tun und andere Menschen zu unterstützen. **Paul**

1. What is Alina not yet sure about?
2. How would a gap year help with this?
3. Name **one** activity Alina would like to do during her gap year.
4. What does Paul feel would **not** be a good idea?
5. Name **one** thing Paul would like to achieve during his gap year.

> Don't be fazed by words you don't know or can't remember. Concentrate on what you do understand. Then use the context, the surrounding language and your knowledge of German grammar and vocabulary to help you work out the meaning of unfamiliar words.

 The future. You read these online posts about the future.

> Nadia: Ich glaube, dass Computer unsere Arbeit machen werden, und ich mache mir Sorgen, dass ich in der Zukunft arbeitslos sein werde.
>
> Jonas: Ich denke, dass die Technologie eine größere Rolle im Unterricht spielen wird. Vielleicht werden wir nicht in die Schule gehen, sondern zu Hause lernen, wo es wirklich ruhig ist und man sich besser konzentrieren kann.
>
> Lara: Meiner Meinung nach werden wir neue Lösungen zu unseren Umweltproblemen finden. Ich habe jedoch Angst, dass diese Fortschritte zu spät sein werden.
>
> Arthur: Die Landschaft ist mir wichtig, aber man baut so viele Häuser und Wohnungen im Moment und ich denke, dass es in der Zukunft sehr wenige grüne Plätze geben wird.

1. What is the opinion of each teenager about the future? Write **P** for a **positive** opinion, **N** for a **negative** opinion and **P + N** for a **positive** and **negative** opinion.
   - (i) Nadia
   - (ii) Jonas
   - (iii) Lara
   - (iv) Arthur
2. What does Jonas say about learning at home? Give **two** details.

Kapitel 8

 Translate these sentences into English.

> Read through your finished translation to make sure it sounds natural. Remember that German word order is often different from English.

> Focus on verb tenses and think about how they translate best into English.

> Ensure you translate every word and don't overlook any 'little' words.

> Watch out for false friends when translating, but also use your knowledge of cognates and near-cognates to help you.

1 Ich möchte sehr gern mit Sprachen arbeiten.
2 Ich habe mich nicht entschieden, ob ich weiterstudieren soll.
3 Vielleicht wird mein Freund eine Ausbildung in einer Firma machen.
4 Freiwilligenarbeit wäre eine Gelegenheit, um die Welt zu reisen.
5 Ich weiß noch nicht, was ich in der Zukunft machen will.

Listening

 Voluntary work. You hear an advert about volunteering. What does it say? Listen to the recording and write **A**, **B** or **C** for each question.

> Before you listen, try noting down the German for the words in the answer options. Listen out for these, as well as for synonyms and compound nouns. Remember that you will hear words related to all the options, so it's essential to listen to the context in which they appear.

1 What positive effect of volunteering is mentioned?
   A It's fun.
   B It makes you a better person.
   C It benefits society.

2 What will you be able to do if you volunteer?
   A get to know new people
   B escape from everyday life
   C develop time-management skills

Plans for next year. You hear Toni and Julian talking about what they are going to do next year. Which two aspects does each person mention? Write the two correct letters for each person.

A	I would enjoy being a student.
B	I'm not keen on sitting more exams.
C	I would like a job working with people.
D	I can't decide whether to work or study.
E	I want to do manual work.
F	I'm concerned about the cost of a degree.

Dictation

 You will hear five short sentences. Write down exactly what you hear in German.

> Think carefully about how these sounds are pronounced when writing down what you hear.
> j
> qu
> ä, ö, ü

hundertsiebenundneunzig

Kapitel 8 — Mündlicher Test

Role-play

1 Look at the role-play card and prepare what you are going to say.

> You are talking to a Swiss friend about jobs and your future.
> 1 Say **one** thing you want to do when you have some free time after exams.
> 2 Say **what** you hope to do next year and **why**. (Give **one** detail and **one** reason.)
> 3 Describe some recent work experience (Give **two** details.)
> 4 Say what you think is important for you in a job. (Give **two** details.)
> 5 ? Ask your friend a question about work.

- You can use the modal verb *ich will* or *ich möchte* here.
- You need to use a past tense here.
- Don't forget to cover both parts.
- Keep this simple: is it money, working hours, nice people?
- The question could be as simple as 'Do you have a job?'

2 Practise what you have prepared. Then, using your notes, listen and respond to the teacher.

3 Listen to Farah's response and answer the questions.
1 What is Farah going to do after her exams?
2 Which reason does she give for wanting to go into the sixth form?
3 Which **two** things does she think are important in a job?

> There are 10 marks available for the role-play, 2 marks per task. Keep your responses short and accurate. Avoid adding extra details in which you might make mistakes and lose marks. You can show off the quality of your German in the reading aloud follow-up questions and the photo card unprepared conversation, where you can gain extra marks for developing your answers.

Reading aloud

4 Look at this task. With a partner, read aloud the sentences, paying attention to the underlined letters.

> Nach meinen Prüfungen möchte ich mich gern mit meinen Freunden treffen.
>
> Was ich nächstes Jahr mache, hängt natürlich von meinen Noten ab.
>
> Jetzt weiß ich jedoch nicht, was ich später machen will, aber auf eine internationale Universität zu gehen ist überhaupt eine Möglichkeit.
>
> Meine Brüder wollen eine sinnvolle Ausbildung machen.

Think carefully about how to pronounce these sounds:
j
ä, ö, ü

5 Listen and check your pronunciation.

6 Listen to the teacher asking four follow-up questions. Translate each question into English and prepare your own answer to each one. Then listen again and respond to the teacher.

> Remember if you are using modal verbs such as *ich will* or *ich möchte* to answer these questions, the second verb, e.g. *arbeiten* or *studieren*, will go to the end of the clause or sentence.

Photo card

 7 Look at the photos and listen to Farah describing them. What does she say? Select the <u>three</u> correct statements.

1 The man and the woman are chatting.
2 They might be earning money for their studies.
3 They probably like their work.
4 There is a bike in the window.
5 The woman is carrying a box.
6 The woman may be a volunteer.

You will be asked to talk about the content of these photos. You must say at least one thing about each photo.

After you have spoken about the content of the photos, you will be asked questions related to any of the topics within the theme of **People and lifestyle**.

Your responses should be as **full and detailed** as possible

 8 Prepare your own description of the photos. Then, with a partner, take turns describing them.

> Auf dem ersten Foto gibt es ...

 9 Listen to the first follow-up question, *Was für Arbeitserfahrungen hast du schon?* and Farah's response. Answer the questions.

1 Where did Farah work?
2 Name **two** activities she did in her job.
3 What was her childhood wish?
4 How does she say her work experience will help her?

 10 Listen to Farah answering the question, *Wie stellst du dir deine persönliche Zukunft vor?* Copy and complete the sentences.

1 Farah does not know whether she will ___.
2 The most important thing for Farah is good ___.
3 Farah would like a house ___.
4 Farah also wants to be ___ and ___.
5 Farah would like to travel ___.
6 She would also like to work ___.

 11 Listen to two more follow-up questions and prepare your answers. Then respond to the recording. Make your answers as full as possible, including opinions and reasons.

 12 Prepare your own answers to as many of the Module 8 questions on page 227 as you can. Then practise with your partner.

Kapitel 8 Schreibtest

Translation

 Look at the translation task. Copy and complete Liam's translation with words from the box.

> sammeln werden entschieden
> arbeitet hat Stelle
> wohnen Traumberuf
> interessiert verdienen

1 My sister intends to become a doctor.
2 He likes working in a shop because he is interested in clothes.
3 I am hoping to earn a lot of money in my dream profession.
4 I want to live abroad to gain experience.
5 I have decided to find a job in a school.

1 Meine Schwester ___ vor, Ärztin zu ___.
2 Er ___ gern in einem Geschäft, weil er sich für Kleidung ___.
3 Ich hoffe, in meinem ___ viel Geld zu ___.
4 Ich will im Ausland ___, um Erfahrung zu ___.
5 Ich habe mich ___, eine ___ in einer Schule zu finden.

 Translate the following sentences into German.

1 I intend to study at university next year.
2 My girlfriend is hoping to become a lawyer in future.
3 I work in a shop at the weekend.
4 We are interested in a career with animals and children.
5 My brother has decided to marry his boyfriend.

150-word writing task

 Look at this writing exam task and then, for each bullet point:

1 think about the vocabulary and structures you have learned, which you could use in your answer. For example:
   - **nouns**, **verbs** and **adjectives** to write about careers
   - **verbs of opinion** and **adjectives** to give reasons
   - ways of expressing **positive** and **negative** points of view
   - how to explain **what your plans for the future are** and **why**
   - **connectives** and **intensifiers** you would like to use.
2 write down three or four ideas for what you could write about
3 identify which tense(s) you could use in your answer.

> You are writing about your plans for the future, for an online magazine.
>
> Write approximately **150** words in **German**.
>
> You must write something about both bullet points.
>
> Describe:
> - the positive **and** negative aspects of a particular profession or job
> - your own plans for the future.

Kapitel 8

 Lesen 4 Read Liam's answer to the exam task in exercise 3. Answer the questions in the coloured boxes (1–5).

1 Liam uses several **modal verbs** followed by **infinitives**. What do these mean? Find <u>four</u> more examples.

2 This phrase introduces **one side of an argument**. What does it mean? Which other words and phrases are used to show different viewpoints?

Meiner Meinung nach muss eine gute Arbeit interessant und sinnvoll sein. Man sollte etwas Wichtiges für die Gesellschaft machen. Die Arbeit als Arzt ist sehr wichtig. Auf der einen Seite kann man Menschen helfen, aber es ist manchmal schwierig. Man muss manchmal nachts arbeiten und die Arbeitsstunden sind lang. Obwohl die Arbeit hart ist, bekommen Ärzte gutes Geld. Wenn die Noten in der Schule nicht gut sind, darf man nicht Arzt werden. Das finde ich schlimm. Viele Menschen sind nett und hilfsbereit. Sie können jedoch nicht als Ärzte arbeiten, weil sie Physik und Chemie nicht verstehen.

Schon als Kind habe ich mich entschieden, Anwalt zu werden. Ich möchte viel Geld verdienen. Ich interessiere mich sehr für Krimis. Ich muss deshalb an der Universität studieren. Das würde mir Spaß machen, weil ich mich gut konzentrieren kann. Ich weiß noch nicht, ob ich heiraten werde, aber ich kann mir gar nicht vorstellen, Kinder zu haben.

3 How could Liam **avoid repetition** in these pairs?

4 This is an example of **complex language in a subordinate clause**. What does it mean? Find <u>three</u> more examples of subordinate clauses in the text.

5 What **grammatical structure** is this? What other <u>two</u> examples can you find?

 Lesen 5 Read Liam's answer again. Copy and complete the sentences.
1 For Liam, a job needs to be interesting and ...
2 He thinks you should do something important for ...
3 Sometimes doctors have to work ...
4 You can't be a doctor if you don't have ...
5 Liam wants to become a ...
6 Liam cannot imagine ...

 Schreiben 6 Prepare your own answer to the task.
- Think about how you can develop your answers for both bullet points.
- Look back at your notes from exercises 3 and 4.
- Look at the 'Challenge checklist' and consider how you can show off your German!
- Write a **brief** plan and organise your answer into paragraphs.
- Write your answer and then carefully check for accuracy.

Challenge checklist

- ✓ Past, present and future time frames
- ✓ Connectives (*und, aber*) and time phrases (*in der Zukunft, nach der Schule, nach den Prüfungen*)
- ✓ Some extended sentences (*Ich möchte reisen und Geld haben.*)
- ✓ An opinion (*Ich finde die Arbeit langweilig.*)

- ✓ A wider range of tenses
- ✓ Different persons of the verb (*die Arbeit, Ärzte*)
- ✓ Intensifiers and qualifiers (*völlig, mehr, lieber*)
- ✓ A wider range of interesting vocabulary (*das Gehalt, die Entscheidung, vorhaben, wahrscheinlich*)
- ✓ Use of compound nouns

- ✓ Infinitive constructions with *zu*
- ✓ Expressions and verbs taking the dative (*es hilft mir, es ist mir wichtig, das macht mir Spaß*)
- ✓ Reflexive verbs (*sich entscheiden, sich interessieren für, sich freuen auf*)
- ✓ Imperfect subjunctive and the conditional
- ✓ Using adjectives as nouns (*etwas Anderes*)
- ✓ More varied conjunctions (*ob, seitdem, sobald*)

zweihunderteins

Kapitel 8 — Wörter

Key:
bold = this word will appear in higher exams only
* = this word is not on the vocabulary list, but you may use it in your own sentences

Ich will helfen (pages 180–181):

Die Zukunft	The future
Ich **habe vor**, …	I intend …
Ich plane, …	I plan …
Ich hoffe, …	I hope …
Ich habe mich entschieden, …	I have decided …
Ich bin **bereit**, …	I am ready …
Ich habe Lust, …	I feel like …
im Sommer	in (the) summer
nächstes Jahr	next year
später	later (on)
nach den Prüfungen	after the exams
in der Zukunft	in (the) future
nach der Schule	after school
an der Uni zu studieren.	to study at uni(versity).
mit Kindern zu arbeiten.	to work with children.
(eine) interessante Arbeit zu finden.	to find an interesting job / interesting work.
anderen Menschen zu helfen.	to help other people.
neue Leute kennenzulernen.	to get to know new people.
eine Ausbildung zu machen.	to do some training / a course.

Was wirst du nach deinen Prüfungen machen? (pages 182–183):

Pläne für die Zukunft	Plans for the future
Nach meinem **Schulabschluss** …	After my school-leaving qualification …
Nach meinem Abitur …	After my A levels …
Nach der Schule …	After school …
Nächstes Jahr …	Next year …
In der Zukunft …	In the future …
möchte ich	I would like …
werde ich …	I will …
will ich …	I want …
auf die Universität gehen.	to go to university.
eine Ausbildung machen.	to do an apprenticeship / some training / a course.
(eine) Arbeit / einen Job finden.	to find employment / a job.
habe ich vor …	I intend …
plane ich …	I plan …
(Lehrer) zu werden.	to become (a teacher).
Geld zu verdienen.	to earn money.
Ich weiß noch nicht, …	I don't know yet …
Ich bin mir noch nicht sicher, …	I'm not sure yet …
was ich später machen möchte.	what I would like to do later.
was ich studieren werde.	what I will study.
Ich werde …	I will …
viel schlafen, …	sleep a lot …
nichts tun, …	do nothing …
weil ich **mich entspannen** muss/möchte.	because I need to / would like to relax.
Ich werde …	I will …
in die **Oberstufe** gehen, …	go into the Sixth Form …
zur *Berufsschule gehen, …	go to technical college …
mein **Abitur** machen, …	do my school-leaving qualification …
nur drei Fächer studieren, …	only study three subjects …
weil ich mich für … interessiere.	because I am interested in …
weil ich später … studieren will.	because I want to study … later on.
an meiner Schule bleiben, …	stay at my school …
weil ich meine Lehrer mag.	because I like my teachers.
weil ich mit meinen Freunden in Kontakt bleiben will.	because I want to stay in contact with my friends.
eine Arbeit suchen, …	look for work, employment …
weil ich Geld verdienen möchte.	because I would like to earn money.
nach … fahren, …	travel to …
auf eine neue Schule gehen, …	go to a new school …
weil ich **etwas Praktisches** machen möchte.	because I would like to do something practical.
weil ich neue Leute kennenlernen möchte.	because I would like to get to know new people.

Was ist dein Traumberuf? (pages 184–185):

Über Jobs reden	Talking about jobs
Möchtest du später (vielleicht) mit/als … arbeiten?	Later on would you (perhaps, maybe) like to work with/as … ?
Möchtest du in (der) Zukunft (Kinder **unterrichten**)?	In (the) future would you like to (teach children)?
Das **würde** mir viel Spaß machen.	That would be a lot of fun.
Das **wäre** eine Möglichkeit.	That would be a possibility.
Das **würde** ich lieber nicht machen.	I would rather not do that.
Das **würde** ich auf keinen **Fall** machen.	There's no way I would do that.
Was möchtest du später werden?	What would you like to become later on?
Ich möchte später vielleicht (Lehrer/in) … werden.	Later on I would perhaps like to become (a teacher) …
Was **wäre** dein Traumberuf?	What would your dream job be?
Mein Traumberuf **wäre**, etwas für die Umwelt zu tun.	My dream job would be to do something for the environment.
gründen	to found, establish
die Erfahrung	experience
das **Vorbild**	example, role model

Was kannst du gut? (pages 186–187):

Eigenschaften und **Fähigkeiten**	*Qualities and abilities*
die **Eigenschaft**	quality
die **Fähigkeit**	ability
Ich bin der Meinung, dass ich *Initiative zeige.	In my opinion / I think that I show initiative.
Außerdem denke ich, dass …	In addition, I think that …
Meine Eltern/Lehrer meinen auch, dass …	My parents/teachers also think that …
Ich bin aber nicht so gut im Planen und ich bin nicht sehr praktisch.	But I'm not so good at planning and I am not very practical.
Außerdem kann ich mich nicht immer sehr gut **konzentrieren**, aber ich versuche, mich zu verbessern.	In addition, I cannot always concentrate very well but I am trying to improve.
unabhängig	independent
hilfsbereit	helpful
leisten	to do, achieve
überzeugen	to convince
das **Kenntnis**	knowledge
das **Verständnis**	understanding

Ein Zwischenjahr? Warum nicht? (pages 188–189):

Ein Zwischenjahr	A gap year
Würdest du gern ein *Zwischenjahr machen?	Would you like to take a gap year?
Ich weiß noch nicht.	I do not know yet.
Ich bin mir noch nicht sicher.	I am not sure yet.
Ich habe noch nicht **darüber nachgedacht**.	I have not thought about it yet.
Auf der einen Seite denke ich, …	On the one hand, I think …
Auf der anderen Seite denke ich (aber), …	(But) on the other hand, I think …
dass es gut **wäre**, gleich mit dem Studium zu beginnen.	that it would be good to start studying immediately.
dass ich keine Zeit verlieren möchte.	that I would not like to waste (any) time.
dass ich lieber nach dem Studium ein *Zwischenjahr machen **würde** als vor dem Studium.	that I would rather take a gap year after my studies than before my studies.
dass ich gern reisen **würde**.	that I would like to travel.
dass ich gern einmal nichts tun **würde**.	that I would like to do nothing for once.
dass ich gern ein bisschen Geld verdienen **würde**.	that I would like to earn a little money.
dass ich gern Freiwilligenarbeit machen **würde**.	that I would like to do volunteer work.
dass ich gern ein bisschen Berufserfahrung sammeln **würde**.	that I would like to gain a little work experience.
Also, ich weiß noch nicht, aber ich denke, dass ich wahrscheinlich …	So / Therefore / For that reason, I don't know yet but I think that I probably …

Meine Träume für die Zukunft (pages 190–191):

Hoffnungen für die Zukunft	Hopes for the future
die Arbeit	work, employment
die Unterstützung	support
die Welt	world
die Zeit	time
die Zukunft	future
das **Gehalt**	salary
das Geld	money
das Haus	house
das Kind	child
das Leben	life
genug	enough
glücklich	happy
künstlich	artificial
nach	after
schön	nice, beautiful
später	later
wichtig	important
heiraten	get married, marry
hoffen	hope
sich vorstellen	imagine
Worauf hoffst du?	What do you hope for?
Möchtest du …?	Would you like to …?
heiraten	get married
Kinder haben	have children
reisen	travel
Wie wichtig ist dir ein gutes **Gehalt**?	How important is a good salary to you?
Wie wichtig sind dir deine Freunde/Freundinnen?	How important are your friends to you?
Wie sieht die Zukunft aus, deiner Meinung nach?	What does the future look like, in your opinion?
Ich glaube, dass es mehr *Roboter geben wird.	I think that there will be more robots.
Ja, ich *stimme zu.	Yes, I agree.
Ich denke, dass …	I think that …

Kapitel 1–8 Grammatik: Wiederholung

The definite article in different cases

 1 Select the correct forms of the definite article to complete each sentence.

1 **Die / Der / Den** Frau (*f*) hat **die / der / den** Mann (*m*) geheiratet, und **dem / die / der** (*f*) Hochzeit war wunderbar.
2 **Die / Das / Dem** Mädchen (*nt*) findet **der / den / dem** Film (*m*) und **der / die / das** Musik (*f*) toll.
3 **Das / Den / Die** Kinder (*pl*) lieben **der / die / den** Farbe (*f*) **der / dem / des** Kleidung. (*f*)
4 **Der / Den / Die** Lehrer (*m*) gab **den / der / dem** Schüler (*m*) und **den / der / dem** Schülerin (*f*) ein neues Buch.
5 **Der / Die / Den** Tierärztin (*f*) hilft **der / die / dem** Katze (*f*) und **der / die / dem** Pferd (*nt*).
6 **Der / Den / Dem** Preis (*m*) **der / des / dem** Hotelzimmers (*nt*) war günstig.

> Think carefully about the function of each noun in the sentence, to help you work out the case needed. Is it the subject or object? Is there a verb that takes the dative? Is there an expression of possession requiring the genitive?

Using interrogative and demonstrative adjectives

 2 Copy and complete the sentences with the correct form of *dieser* and *welcher*.

1 Ich lese dies**es** Buch (*nt*). Welch___ Buch liest du?
2 Welch___ Rock (*m*) kaufst du? Ich kaufe dies___ Rock.
3 Welch___ Farbe (*f*) hast du lieber? Ich mag dies___ Farbe.
4 Ich werde dies___ Fächer (*pl*) nächstes Jahr lernen. Welch___ Fächer wirst du lernen?
5 Ich habe dies___ Kindern (*pl*) geholfen. Welch___ Kindern hast du geholfen?

> *dieser* and *welcher* follow the same pattern as the definite article. Focus on the meaning of the sentence to help you decide which case is needed each time.

The indefinite article and possessive adjectives in different cases

 3 Write the correct form of the indefinite article (*ein*), the negative article (*kein*) or a possessive adjective to complete the translation of the English text.

My friends all have a dream job, but I have no idea what sort of work I want to do in future. A friend of my sister works with computers. That is a job which her friend likes because he has a good income. His wife works in a school. Our uncle, one of my father's brothers, works as a police officer, but that isn't an easy profession.

1 *Meine* Freunde haben alle **2**___ Traumberuf, aber ich habe keine Ahnung, was für **3**___ Arbeit ich in Zukunft machen will. **4**___ Freund **5**___ Schwester arbeitet mit Computern. Das ist **6**___ Job, der **7**___ Freund gefällt, weil er **8**___ gutes Gehalt hat. **9**___ Frau arbeitet in **10**___ Schule. **11**___ Onkel, **12**___ der Brüder **13**___ Vaters, arbeitet als Polizist, aber das ist **14**___ leichter Beruf.

Time phrases in the accusative case

 4 Translate the time phrases into German, using the accusative case.

Example: 1 *jeden Samstag*

1 every Saturday
2 every week
3 every year
4 last Tuesday
5 last week
6 last year
7 next Monday
8 next week
9 next year

> *jeder*, *letzter* and *nächster* follow the same pattern as *dieser* and *welcher*. Days of the week are masculine in German.

Grammatik: Wiederholung — Kapitel 1–8

Adjective endings

 Copy and complete the text, adding the correct endings (if needed) to the adjectives in brackets.

Die Luftverschmutzung in **1** großen (*groß*) Städten ist heute ein **2** (*ernst*) Problem. Die Wasserverschmutzung ist auch **3** (*schlimm*). **4** (*Gesund*) Fische sterben in **5** (*schmutzig*) Flüssen, weil man **6** (*alt*) Dinge ins Wasser wirft. Wir sind alle für die **7** (*wichtig*) Umweltprobleme verantwortlich. Die **8** (*nächst*) Generation, das heißt die **9** (*jung*) Menschen von heute, muss **10** (*neu*) Lösungen für diese **11** (*schwer*) Probleme finden. Es wird keine **12** (*leicht*) Aufgabe sein.

> When adjectives are in front of a noun you need to consider the case, the gender, whether the noun is singular or plural and which article (e.g. words like *der, die, das* or *ein, eine, ein*) is used. Sometimes an adjective takes the place of an article (e.g. *jeder, dieser*) and the ending reflects this. When used after a noun, there is no need for any ending on the adjective.

Adjectival nouns

 Copy and complete the sentences with an adjectival noun. Use the adjectives in brackets and add the correct ending.

1. Ein *Reicher* kann alles kaufen, was er will. (*reich*)
2. Die Ärzte behandeln die ▭ im Krankenhaus. (*krank*)
3. Die Schüler*innen sammeln Geld, um den ▭ zu helfen. (*arm*)
4. Das Hotel bietet einen Tennisplatz und ein Fitness-Studio: für ▭ gibt es viel zu tun. (*sportlich*)
5. Das Geschäft bietet freiwillige Arbeitserfahrung für ▭. (*arbeitslos*)
6. Nur ▭ dürfen rauchen. (*erwachsen*)
7. Dieser neue Film ist toll: sowohl ▭ als auch ▭ werden ihn genießen. (*jung, alt*)
8. Kennst du meine Nachbarn? Der Mann ist ▭, aber seine Frau ist nicht ▭, sondern Amerikanerin. (*deutsch*)

> Form adjectival nouns by using a capital letter on the adjective. Use the correct adjective ending, depending on the gender, number and case of the new noun, and the article (if any) that precedes it.

Adjectives used with the definite article follow this pattern:

	nominative	accusative	dative	genitive
masc	der gut**e** Freund	den gut**en** Freund	dem gut**en** Freund	des gut**en** Freund**es**
fem	die gut**e** Freundin	die gut**e** Freundin	der gut**en** Freundin	der gut**en** Freundin
neut	das gut**e** Kind	das gut**e** Kind	dem gut**en** Kind	des gut**en** Kind**es**
pl	die gut**en** Kinder	die gut**en** Kinder	den gut**en** Kinder**n**	der gut**en** Kinder

Adjectives used with the indefinite article, *kein* and possessive adjectives follow this pattern:

	nominative	accusative	dative	genitive
masc	ein gut**er** Freund	einen gut**en** Freund	einem gut**en** Freund	eines gut**en** Freund**es**
fem	eine gut**e** Freundin	eine gut**e** Freundin	einer gut**en** Freundin	einer gut**en** Freundin
neut	ein gut**es** Kind	ein gut**es** Kind	einem gut**en** Kind	eines gut**en** Kind**es**
pl	keine gut**en** Kinder	keine gut**en** Kinder	keinen gut**en** Kinder**n**	keiner gut**en** Kinder

Adjectives used with no article follow this pattern:

	nominative	accusative	dative	genitive
masc	heiß**er** Kaffee	heiß**en** Kaffee	heiß**em** Kaffee	heiß**en** Kaffee**s**
fem	kalt**e** Milch	kalt**e** Milch	kalt**er** Milch	kalt**er** Milch
neut	gut**es** Wasser	gut**es** Wasser	gut**em** Wasser	gut**en** Wasser**s**
pl	kein**e** Kinder	kein**e** Kinder	kein**en** Kinder**n**	kein**er** Kinder

Kapitel 1–8 Grammatik: Wiederholung

Word order in main clauses

 Rewrite the sentences using correct word order. Begin with the words in bold.

Example: 1 *Wir fahren im Sommer mit dem Zug in die Schweiz.*

1 mit dem Zug / im Sommer / fahren / **Wir** / in die Schweiz
2 **Mein Bruder** / ein Zwischenjahr / in Deutschland / mit seiner Freundin / jetzt / macht
3 mit Kindern / in Zukunft / will / arbeiten / **Samira** / in einem Krankenhaus
4 ab und zu / spiele / **Ich** / im Wohnzimmer / mit meiner Familie / Karten
5 im Computerraum / in der Pause / **Die Schüler*innen** / arbeiten / leise

 Rewrite the sentences in exercise 1, beginning with the time phrase.

Example: 1 *Im Sommer fahren wir mit dem Zug in die Schweiz.*

> In main clauses, the conjugated verb must be the **second** idea. Remember the 'time – manner – place' rule. Any elements which show time, manner or place must come in this order in the sentence.

Word order in subordinate clauses

 Rewrite the sentences, linking them with the connective in brackets. The second sentence will become the subordinate clause.

Example: 1 *Wir lernen Deutsch, weil die Sprache nützlich ist.*

1 Wir lernen Deutsch. Die Sprache ist nützlich. (*weil*)
2 Ich möchte dieses neue Handy. Es ist ziemlich teuer. (*obwohl*)
3 Meine Familie und ich essen Frühstück zusammen. Wir haben Zeit. (*wenn*)
4 Viele Jugendliche wissen jetzt. Rauchen ist gefährlich. (*dass*)
5 Lukas kann am Abend nicht fernsehen. Er muss sich für ein Vorstellungsgespräch vorbereiten. (*da*)

 Rewrite the sentences in exercise 3, beginning with the subordinate clause.

Example: 1 *Weil die Sprache nützlich ist, lernen wir Deutsch.*

- The verb goes to the end in a subordinate clause.
- If there are two verbs, the conjugated verb goes to the end.
- If the sentence begins with the subordinate clause, the first word in the main clause will be the verb. Remember the 'verb – comma – verb' rule.

Subordinate clauses with *wo* and *was*

5 **Write the correct letter (a–d) to match up the sentence halves.**

1 Die Liebe ist alles,
2 Meine Schwester studiert an der Uni,
3 Hast du etwas,
4 Der Mann sagt etwas,
5 Weißt du,
6 Hier ist ein Stadion,

a wo ich auch später studieren will.
b was ich nicht verstehe.
c was man braucht, um glücklich zu sein.
d wo man Fußball spielen wird.
e was du mir erzählen möchtest?
f wo der Bürgermeister ist?

> The question words *wo* and *was* can also be used to introduce a subordinate clause when referring to something of a general nature.

Grammatik: Wiederholung — Kapitel 1–8

Relative clauses

 Copy and complete the sentences with the correct relative pronoun.

1 Ich besuche meine Oma, **der / den / die / das** in Österreich wohnt.
2 Der Lehrer, **der / den / die / das** Geschichte unterrichtet, ist nett.
3 Der Lehrer, **der / den / die / das** ich gar nicht mag, heißt Herr Braun.
4 Der Klimawandel ist ein Problem, **der / den / die / das** sehr ernst ist.
5 Englisch und Sport sind die Fächer, **der / den / die / das** ich in der Schule mag.
6 Der Beruf, **der / den / die / das** ich in der Zukunft machen will, ist Künstler.

> - Relative pronouns follow the same pattern as the definite article (*der, die, das, die*) and translate as 'who', 'which' or 'that'.
> - The relative pronoun must be the same gender as the noun to which it refers, but its case depends on its function (subject, object, etc.) in the relative clause.
> - Relative clauses are also subordinate clauses, so the conjugated verb goes to the end of the clause.

Word order in questions

 Rewrite the statements as questions by changing the word order.
Example: 1 *Hast du Mathe in der nächsten Stunde?*

1 Du hast Mathe in der nächsten Stunde.
2 Wir gehen am Nachmittag ins Kino.
3 Milan trennt heute den Müll.
4 Es gibt Gesetze gegen Umweltverschmutzung.
5 Sie möchten etwas trinken.
6 Die Kinder wollen schwimmen gehen.

> To form questions without a question word, invert the subject and verb:
> *Er ist …* → *Ist er …?*
> Sentences with a question word follow normal word order, so the verb must be the second idea.

Personal pronouns in the nominative, accusative and dative cases

 Copy and complete the sentences with the correct pronouns from the word box.

1 Hier ist Martin. **Er** ist mein Freund. Du solltest ___ kennenlernen. Du könntest mit ___ Fußball spielen.
2 Alina ist meine Schwester. ___ ist nett. Ich rufe ___ jetzt an, um mit ___ zu sprechen.
3 Felix und ich sind Freunde. ___ gehen jetzt ins Stadtzentrum. Siehst du ___? Willst du mit ___ kommen?
4 Mein Name ist Matteo. ___ bin neu an dieser Schule. Kennst du ___? Kunst gefällt ___. Gefällt es ___ auch?

sie	mir	~~er~~
dir	sie	wir
uns	uns	ihn
ihr	ihm	
ich	mich	

Indefinite pronouns: *jemand* and *niemand*

 Copy and complete the German translations with the correct form of *jemand* or *niemand*.

1 Someone is talking loudly.
2 Can I help anyone?
3 I don't talk to anyone about my worries.
4 Do you know someone who works as an actor?
5 No, I don't know anyone.
6 No-one has the right to kill anyone.

1 **Jemand** spricht laut.
2 Kann ich ___ helfen?
3 Ich spreche mit ___ über meine Sorgen.
4 Kennst du ___, der als Schauspieler arbeitet?
5 Nein, ich kenne ___.
6 ___ hat das Recht, ___ zu töten.

> *Jemand* (someone) and *niemand* (no one) need endings in different cases. Use *jemanden* and *niemanden* in the accusative, and *jemandem* and *niemandem* in the dative.

zweihundertsieben 207

Kapitel 1–8 Grammatik: Wiederholung

The present tense

 Copy and complete the sentences with the correct present tense form of the verbs in brackets.
1 Paul (*haben*) keine Geschwister. Er (*sein*) Einzelkind.
2 Meine Mutter (*fahren*) jeden Tag zur Arbeit und (*kommen*) spät nach Hause.
3 Ich (*haben*) keinen Traumberuf und (*wissen*) noch nicht, was ich studieren will.
4 Frida (*lesen*) gern Krimis und sie (*spielen*) gern Fußball.
5 Wir (*sein*) Vegetarier und (*kaufen*) nie Fleisch.
6 Du (*sein*) lustig und du (*hören*) tolle Musik.

Separable verbs in the present tense

 Copy and complete the sentences with the correct present tense form of the verbs in brackets.
1 Wir kaufen samstags im Supermarkt ein. (*einkaufen*)
2 Ich ___ auf meinem Bruder ___. (*aufpassen*)
3 Die erste Stunde ___ um 8.30 Uhr ___. (*anfangen*)
4 Lea ___ abends zwei Stunden ___. (*fernsehen*)
5 Ich ___ um 7.00 Uhr ___. (*aufstehen*)
6 Der Zug ___ spät ___. (*ankommen*)

> Check the Verb tables on page 234 to refresh your memory on how to form the present tense.

seit

 Translate the sentences into German, using *seit* and the verbs in brackets.
1 I have lived in Stuttgart for five years. (*wohnen*)
2 We have been waiting since yesterday. (*warten*)
3 She has been going to her school for three weeks. (*gehen*)

> The preposition *seit* takes the dative and needs to be used with the present tense.

The imperative

 Translate the commands into English and decide which ones you would use if talking to:
a your friend   b a group of friends   c an adult you don't know.

1 Kommt mit uns!
2 Bleiben Sie da!
3 Helfen Sie mir!
4 Hört sofort auf!
5 Gib nicht auf!
6 Ruf mich an!

The perfect tense

 Copy and complete the table, writing the past participles of the verbs from the box below in the correct column.

besuchen	hören	nehmen	sehen
fahren	kaufen	probieren	spielen
gehen	kommen	reisen	verstehen

Ich habe …	Ich bin …
besucht	gefahren

- The past participle usually begins with *ge-* unless there is an inseparable prefix such as *be-* or *ver-*, or if the infinitive ends in *-ieren*.
- The ending is usually *-t* for regular verbs and *-en* for irregular verbs.
- Some irregular verbs also have a change to the stem.
- Remember that verbs indicating movement or a change of state take *sein*, otherwise the auxiliary verb is *haben*.

Grammatik: Wiederholung Kapitel 1–8

Reflexive verbs

Write sentences in the present tense using the personal pronoun and infinitive provided. Then rewrite them in the perfect tense. Translate both sets of sentences into English.

Example: ich, sich freuen, auf den Urlaub
Ich freue mich auf den Urlaub. – I am looking forward to the holiday.
Ich habe mich auf den Urlaub gefreut. – I looked forward to the holiday.

1. ich, sich bewegen
2. du, sich wohl fühlen
3. er, sich konzentrieren, immer
4. wir, sich verstehen, gut
5. ihr, sich interessieren, für Kunst
6. sie (they), sich treffen, um 12 Uhr

> Remember, the reflexive pronouns are *mich, dich, sich, uns, euch, sich*.

The imperfect tense

Copy and complete the translations using the correct imperfect tense verbs from the box.

| blieben | brachten | dachte | fand | ~~fuhr~~ | gingst | half |
| kamen | las | sahen | schrieb | sprachen | | |

1. Sie *fuhr* mit dem Zug nach Berlin. — She went to Berlin by train.
2. Wir ___ zu Hause, aber du ___ in die Stadt. — We stayed at home but you went into town.
3. Ich ___ einen Brief und ___ über die Zukunft nach. — I wrote a letter and thought about the future.
4. Ich ___ in der Küche und dann ___ ein Buch. — I helped in the kitchen and then read a book.
5. Mein Bruder ___ eine Katze und wir ___ sie in die Schule. — My brother found a cat and we brought it into school.
6. Sie ___ ihre Freunde, ___ mit ihrer Lehrerin und ___ nach Hause. — They saw their friends, spoke to their teacher and came home.

Verbs followed by prepositions

Select the correct prepositions to complete the text. Then translate the text into English.

Ich mache mir Sorgen **1** meinen Freund. Er hat Angst **2** dem Klimawandel und kämpft **3** eine sichere Welt. Er hofft **4** eine bessere Zukunft, aber er hat selten Zeit, mit mir **5** seine Ängste zu diskutieren.

vor   auf   für   über   um

Prepositions and cases

Decide which case should follow each preposition and write the article or possessive adjective with the correct ending to fill each gap.

Während **1** d*er* Sommerferien habe ich zwei Wochen mit **2** mein___ Familie in **3** ein___ Hotel in Österreich verbracht. Das Hotel lag in **4** d___ Bergen, nicht weit von **5** ein___ See. Obwohl das Wasser in **6** d___ See ziemlich kalt war, sind wir jeden Tag in **7** d___ Wasser gegangen und sind trotz **8** d___ niedrigen Temperatur **9** d___ Wassers geschwommen. Bei schönem Wetter sind wir durch **10** d___ Wälder und **11** d___ Fluss entlang bis zu **12** d___ nächsten Dorf gewandert.

> Remember that prepositions can take the accusative, dative or genitive cases. Go back to the following pages to refresh your memory on:
> - verbs + prepositions: page 159
> - prepositions + accusative and dative: pages 67, 107, 109, 110 and 115
> - prepositions + genitive: pages 141 and 157.
>
> Remember that some prepositions and articles join together as one word:
> in das → ins
> zu dem → zum

zweihundertneun **209**

Kapitel 1 Wiederholung

Sprechen 1 *Refresh your memory!* Take it in turns with your partner to name as many words connected with school as possible.
- Deutsch, …
- Lehrer, …

Lesen 2 *Refresh your memory!* Match up the sentence halves.

1 Jeden Tag muss
2 Ich soll für
3 Man darf
4 Man muss Respekt
5 Man soll im Gang
6 Ich darf

a im Klassenzimmer nicht essen.
b nicht laufen.
c mein Handy im Unterricht nicht benutzen.
d ich meine Hausaufgaben machen.
e meinen Mathetest lernen.
f zeigen.

Hören 3 *Refresh your memory!* Listen to what the students say about school uniforms. Make notes in English. (1–6)

Example: 1 very practical

Hören 4 *Special events.* Felix is talking to his friends Lena and Tim about special events at school. Which activities took place this year? Write down the letter (A–E) for each of the <u>three</u> correct options.

A	a school walk
B	an art week
C	a sports day
D	a non-uniform day
E	a movie night

Listen carefully to the context in which each event is mentioned. The tense used, any negatives, and other language will help you decide when each event took place.

Lesen 5 *School life.* Translate the following sentences into English.
1 Ich habe dieses Jahr zehn Fächer.
2 Ich glaube, dass Sprachen sehr interessant sind.
3 Letztes Jahr haben wir einen Austausch mit einer Schule in Österreich gemacht.
4 Das hat viel Spaß gemacht, weil wir viel über die Schultypen gelernt haben.
5 Im Unterricht muss ich gut lernen, weil ich nächstes Jahr die Abschlussprüfung mache.

School rules. Read Yasmin's blog. Write the letter, **A**, **B** or **C**, of the correct word or phrase to complete each sentence.

> In meiner Schule gibt es viele strenge Regeln. Die meisten Regeln finde ich notwendig, aber andere sind ein bisschen blöd. Wir müssen im Unterricht total leise sein und dürfen fast gar nicht sprechen, aber ich denke, dass das richtig ist.
>
> Wir bekommen aber jeden Tag so viele Hausaufgaben. Ich bin der Meinung, dass das nicht richtig ist, weil ich fast keine Freizeit habe. Wir dürfen auch das Handy in der Schule nicht benutzen. Ich finde, dass das ungerecht ist, weil es wirklich nicht praktisch ist.

1 Yasmin agrees with ... of the rules at her school.
   A some   B most   C all
2 Yasmin thinks it is right that the students work ... in lessons.
   A quietly   B quickly   C hard
3 Yasmin feels the amount of homework is ...
   A almost none.   B about right.   C too much.
4 Yasmin thinks the ban on mobile phones is ...
   A unfair.   B unwise.   C practical.

Complete the 90-word writing task.

> You are writing to your Swiss friend about your school.
> Write approximately **90** words in **German**.
> You must write something about each bullet point.
> Describe:
> • what your school is like
> • what you did yesterday at school
> • a special school event next year.

Make sure you give the information requested in the bullet points and use the time frames specified.

Read the text aloud and prepare responses to the follow-up questions.

> Es gibt siebenhundert Schüler in meiner Schule in Köln.
>
> Ich lerne sieben Fächer: ich mag Physik, Englisch, Mathe, Spanisch, Theater und Sport, aber Biologie mag ich nicht.
>
> Wir müssen ein weißes Hemd, eine grüne Jacke und schwarze Schuhe tragen.
>
> Nächste Woche machen wir einen Schulausflug.
>
> Wir gehen an einem Tag zwanzig Kilometer zu Fuß.

Follow-up questions:
1 Was machst du in der Mittagspause?
2 Was ist deine Meinung zu deinen Schulfächern?
3 Beschreib deine Schuluniform.
4 Wie findest du deine Lehrer?

Be careful with cognates as they are not pronounced exactly the same way in German. Think carefully about how to pronounce the cognates and these sounds:
o, ö, u, ü
w

Kapitel 2 Wiederholung

 1 Refresh your memory! Match up the English and German question words.

> what   when   why   how   who
> how many   which   how much   where

> wo   wann   wie viel   wer   wie viele
> was   wie   warum   welch…

 Remember that when you use a **question word**, the verb and the subject swap places.

Was machst du in deiner Freizeit?
What do you do in your free time?

 2 Refresh your memory! In pairs, work out the correct order for the part-sentences and read aloud Sara's weekend plans. Start with e.

a am Strand laufen. Danach werden
b wir Fußball im Park spielen. Schließlich
c gehen. Das wird viel Spaß machen,
d Sport machen! Zuerst werde ich Tennis mit
e Nächstes Wochenende werde ich viel
f werden wir mit meinen Brüdern schwimmen
g aber auch sehr anstrengend sein!
h meiner Freundin spielen. Zweitens werden wir

 3 Refresh your memory! Write down the correct separable prefix to complete each sentence.

> an   aus   fern   auf   herunter   mit

1 Ich lade Musik ___.
2 Wir sehen nicht gern ___.
3 Sie bringt ihr Handy überall ___.
4 Du gibst €20 pro Woche für Technologie ___.
5 Sie rufen jeden Tag ihre Freunde ___.
6 Er nimmt ein neues Musikvideo ___.

 4 Free time. Robin is talking about what she has been doing recently. What does she say? Listen to the recording and write **A**, **B** or **C** for each question.

1 Robin's first activity yesterday was to …
   A visit an exhibition.   B go shopping.   C do some art.
2 This morning, Robin did … activities.
   A one   B two   C three
3 The last thing Robin will do today is …
   A download music.   B read her novel.   C visit her friends.

Listen carefully for the correct sequence of events as they are not necessarily mentioned in the order you might expect. Use time phrases and sequencing words to help you and read the questions carefully.

Lesen 5 — *Life as a famous singer.* Read the interview with Mathilde, a singer. How does she feel about these aspects of her life? Write **P** for a **positive** opinion, **N** for a **negative** opinion, **P+N** for a **positive and negative** opinion.

1 Her music
2 Being a role model
3 Her clothing

4 Read the last paragraph again. What would you do with a **Schlafanzug**? Write the correct letter, **A**, **B** or **C**.
  A watch it   **B** listen to it   **C** wear it

Interviewer:	Wie findest du dein Leben als Sängerin?
Mathilde:	Als ich jünger war, war Musik für mich immer das Wichtigste in meinem Leben und ich bin froh, dass mein Hobby auch zum Beruf geworden ist.
Interviewer:	So viele junge Leute hören deine Musik. Du bist ein echtes Vorbild für sie.
Mathilde:	Ja, ich weiß. Und ich muss sagen, ich finde das schwer. Man muss sich in der Öffentlichkeit immer gut verhalten, und das kann manchmal ganz schwierig sein!
Interviewer:	Wie wichtig ist die Mode für dich?
Mathilde:	Ich kaufe sehr gern neue Kleidung, aber zu Hause finde ich meinen **Schlafanzug** viel bequemer. Aber wenn man berühmt ist, muss man immer gut aussehen. Das kann echt teuer sein!

Sprechen 6 — Complete the role-play task.

You are talking to your Austrian friend.
1 Say what you like doing with friends. (Give **two** details.)
2 Say what you will do this weekend. (Give **two** details.)
3 Say how often you watch TV.
4 Say what kind of programmes you enjoy watching and why. (Give **one** opinion and **one** reason.)
5 **?** Ask your friend a question about music.

> You need to ask a question in the role-play; think carefully about the word order in your question for point 5. For the other points, you may be able to adapt the teacher's questions to help you form your responses.

Schreiben 7 — Translate these sentences into German.

1 Every Saturday I go to the cinema with friends.
2 We like comedies, but we prefer to see action films.
3 The film was about two men and a dog and took place in Austria.
4 The cinema had no atmosphere and the film wasn't convincing.
5 Next weekend we are visiting an art exhibition.

Hören 8 — *Dictation.* You will hear <u>five</u> short sentences. Write down exactly what you hear in German.

> Think carefully about how these sounds are pronounced:
> a, ä
> o, ö
> eu
> ie, ei, i
> sp, st, sch

zweihundertdreizehn **213**

Kapitel 3 Wiederholung

 Lesen 1

Refresh your memory! Match the nouns to their meaning in English.

> Entscheidung   Feier   Feuerwerk
> Geschwister   Gesellschaft   Krankenhaus
> Mädchen   Mobbing   Persönlichkeit
> Sänger   Silvester   Stiefvater   Vorbild

> bullying   society   role-model   celebration
> celebrity   decision   girl   siblings
> singer   stepfather   fireworks
> New Year's Eve   hospital

 Lesen 2

Refresh your memory! Decide if these opinions are positive (**P**) or negative (**N**).

1 Ich glaube, dass der Weihnachtsmarkt immer schön ist.
2 Dieses Fest interessiert mich nicht.
3 Ich finde die Stimmung zu laut.
4 Die Musiker haben mir gefallen.
5 Das hat so viel Spaß gemacht.
6 Ich finde, dass es zu viele Menschen auf dem Markt gibt.

 Hören 3

Refresh your memory! Listen (1–5) and match each person with the correct description (a–e).

a Gets on well with siblings. Has long hair.
b Has long hair and wears glasses. Gets on well with brothers and is sporty.
c Has a good relationship with family. Has short hair.
d Has grey eyes and is polite. Gets on well with sister.
e Gets on well with brother. Has brown eyes and is honest.

 Hören 4

Party time! Emily is talking about three celebrations. Write **P** if she is talking about a celebration in the **past**, **N** if it is something happening **now** and **F** if it is something she is planning for the **future**.

1 Sister's party
2 Emily's birthday
3 Boyfriend's birthday

> Listen out for different tenses. There will also be clues in the time phrases that are used, such as *letztes Jahr, nächsten Monat*.

 Lesen 5

Translate these sentences into English.

1 Ich feiere gern meinen Geburtstag zu Hause, weil das Spaß macht.
2 Ich kann sowohl meine Freunde als auch meine Geschwister einladen.
3 Wir singen und tanzen und manchmal kochen wir etwas Leckeres.
4 Letztes Jahr habe ich ein Musikfest besucht, das am Strand war.
5 Nächsten Sommer organisieren wir eine Schulabschlussfeier.

6 Role models. Read Yusuf's post on an internet forum.

> Mein Onkel ist mein Vorbild, aber er ist überhaupt nicht berühmt. Vor fünf Jahren hat er meine Tante geheiratet. Sie ist die Schwester von meinem Vater. Jetzt haben meine Tante und mein Onkel drei Kinder. Meine Tante ist in ihrem Beruf als Anwältin sehr erfolgreich und manchmal muss sie ins Ausland fahren.
>
> Also bleibt mein Onkel zu Hause und passt auf die Kinder auf – eine schwere Arbeit, finde ich! Er ist aber nett, hilfsbereit und nie ungeduldig. Er malt und sieht mit den Kindern fern. Er kocht auch oft **Sauerbraten** und die Kinder finden das lecker. Meiner Meinung nach ist er für junge Männer das perfekte Vorbild.

die Anwältin lawyer (f)

Complete the sentences. Write the correct letter, **A**, **B** or **C**.

1 Yusuf's uncle is …
  A famous.   **B** successful.   **C** married.

2 Yusuf's uncle and aunt have …
  A three children.   **B** two children.   **C** four children.

3 Yusuf's aunt …
  A works from home.   **B** lives abroad.   **C** has a good career.

4 Yusuf says his uncle is …
  A nice, but finds his work hard.   **B** patient and kind.   **C** helpful, but not very patient.

5 Read the last paragraph again. What would you do with **Sauerbraten**? Write the correct letter, **A**, **B** or **C**.
  A eat it   **B** watch it   **C** paint it

7 Complete the 90-word writing task.

> An Austrian friend has asked you about your family and friends. Write a reply.
>
> Write approximately **90** words in **German**.
>
> You must write something about each bullet point.
>
> Describe:
> - your best friend
> - where you went with friends last week
> - what activity you will do with your friends next weekend.

Try to extend and add variety to your writing:
- Give opinions in different ways:
  ich liebe/mag …
  … gefällt mir
  ich … gern / lieber / am liebsten
  meiner Meinung nach …
  ich glaube, dass …
- Use synonyms to show you are familiar with a wide range of vocabulary.
- Use adjectives and qualifiers to describe people.
- Vary the conjunctions you use and check your word order: *denn, weil, dass, sondern*.

8 Read the text aloud and prepare responses to the follow-up questions.

> Ich bin ziemlich groß für mein Alter und habe blaue Augen und schwarze Haare.
> Ich verstehe mich gut mit meinen Brüdern.
> Ich habe auch eine wirklich tolle Beziehung zu meinen Eltern, die seit vierzehn Jahren verheiratet sind.
> Dieses Wochenende gehen wir zu einem typischen Fest.
> Meine Schwestern wollen nach den Prüfungen den Karneval besuchen.

Think carefully about how to pronounce these sounds:
v, w, z
u, ü, y

Follow-up questions:
Beschreib dich!
Wie kommst du mit deiner Familie aus?
Was macht ein guter Freund oder eine gute Freundin?
Wie findest du Feste?

Kapitel 4 Wiederholung

 1 Refresh your memory! Copy and complete the sentences.

1 ▭ habe ich Kopfschmerzen.
2 Du musst ▭ ins Fitness-Studio gehen.
3 ▭ habe ich mir beim Skifahren das Bein gebrochen.
4 Er treibt ▭ Sport.
5 Sie trinkt ▭ Kaffee mit Milch.
6 Mein Plan war, ▭ laufen zu gehen.
7 Sie verbringt ▭ Zeit auf ihrem Handy.
8 Ich möchte ▭ spazieren gehen.

- since yesterday
- twice a week
- three years ago
- regularly
- mostly
- more frequently
- less
- more often

 2 Refresh your memory! Listen. Copy and complete the grid. (1–6)

	Where does it hurt?	What were they doing?
1		

 Remember that **beim** + <u>verbal noun</u> means 'while doing something': Das habe ich **beim** <u>Tennisspielen</u> gemacht.

 3 Refresh your memory! Match up the sentence halves.

1 Ich habe beschlossen,
2 Er ist unglücklich, wenn er
3 Wenn ich mehr Zeit hätte,
4 Es hilft sehr, über Probleme
5 Man soll auch nicht
6 Ich würde sagen, dass

a würde ich ins Kino gehen.
b vergessen, genug zu schlafen.
c sprechen zu können.
d mein Leben zu ändern.
e ich ziemlich gesund esse.
f keine Energie hat.

 4 Priorities in life. Arda, Lena, Noah and Emma are talking about what is important to them in life. Complete these sentences. Write the correct letter, **A**, **B** or **C**.

1 Arda thinks the most important thing is …
  A meeting people.   **B** relationships.   **C** helping other people.

2 Lena is helped by …
  A her friends.   **B** her future plans.   **C** role models.

3 Noah finds it important to …
  A have role models.   **B** live a healthy lifestyle.   **C** do well at school.

4 Emma's actions make her feel …
  A well.   **B** tired.   **C** emotional.

Lesen 5 *Lifestyle changes.* Read Lara's diary entry.

a Complete these sentences. Write the correct letter, **A**, **B** or **C**.

1 Lara is quite … with her life at the moment.
 A content   B unhappy   C disappointed

2 Lara would like to …
 A change a few things.
 B keep everything the same.
 C change lots of things.

3 Yesterday, Lara went to bed …
 A early.   B later than planned.   C at 10 p.m.

b Answer the following questions **in English**. You do not need to write in full sentences.
 1 What is Lara's second aim?
 2 What will Lara do with regard to her friends?

> Remember that you do not need to understand every word of a text to be able to answer the questions. You might not have come across *lieb* (kind, dear) before, but you don't need to know it to respond to the question about friends. Focus on the language you do know!

---

31. Dezember

Im Moment bin ich mit meinem Leben ganz zufrieden, aber ich möchte einige Sachen ändern. Zuerst möchte ich ein bisschen mehr Energie haben, damit ich mich besser konzentrieren kann. Ich habe beschlossen, früher ins Bett zu gehen – um 22 Uhr. Leider habe ich das gestern nicht geschafft und deswegen bin ich heute Morgen immer noch sehr müde.

Mein zweites Ziel ist es, mehr Zeit mit meiner Familie zu verbringen. Meine Karriere und meine Freizeitaktivitäten sind mir wichtig, aber meine Familie ist mir noch wichtiger.

Meine Freunde sind mir auch sehr lieb. Es ist nicht immer möglich, mit ihnen auszugehen, aber ich werde versuchen, sie häufiger anzurufen.

Lara

Sprechen 6 Complete the photo task.

> You will be asked to talk about the content of these photos. You must say at least one thing about each photo.
>
> After you have spoken about the content of the photos, you will be asked questions related to any of the topics within the theme of **People and lifestyle**.
>
> Your responses should be as **full and detailed** as possible.

> For the photo description, you can say how many people are in each photo and describe what they look like (their age, gender, clothing) as well as what they are doing; describe the location and mention the weather. Give an opinion about whether you think the young people are living a healthy or unhealthy lifestyle.

Schreiben 7 Translate these sentences into German.
1 We play football twice a week.
2 In my opinion it is important to eat breakfast.
3 He is trying to drink more water every day, in order to be healthier.
4 Last week I spent too much time in front of the computer.
5 I have decided to go to bed earlier in the future.

> Think carefully about how these sounds are pronounced when you write down what you hear:
> s, ski, schw   o, ö
> a, ä   u, ü
> au, äu   -ig

Hören 8 *Dictation.* You will hear <u>five</u> short sentences. Write down exactly what you hear in German.

Kapitel 5 Wiederholung

Refresh your memory! Sort the prepositions into the correct categories.

- accusative only
- dative only
- either accusative or dative

um	über	mit	aus	an	auf
für	gegenüber	ohne	zwischen	nach	
	zu	durch	seit	unter	

Refresh your memory! Write the plurals of these nouns.

1 Haus
2 Stadt
3 Freund
4 Geschäft
5 Auto
6 Baum
7 Theater
8 Museum

Refresh your memory! Is each sentence below in the accusative (A) or the dative (D)?

1 Ich gehe ins Kino.
2 Das liegt im Stadtzentrum.
3 Sie ist im Park.
4 Das steht vor der Kirche.
5 Stellen Sie das vor die Tür, bitte!
6 Sie warten vor dem Kino.

Berlin. You read this online article about Can, who lives in Berlin.

Can ist in Berlin geboren, aber seine Eltern kommen aus der Türkei. Er verbringt die Ferien in der Türkei, aber Deutschland ist sein Lieblingsland und er fühlt sich dort wohl, weil alle seine Freunde hier sind. Seine Schule liegt seiner Wohnung gegenüber und die Umgebung ist sauber und schön, obwohl es auch laut sein kann. Früher gab es ein Sportzentrum und ein Kino in der Gegend, aber nun ist alles geschlossen. Jetzt gibt es hier nichts mehr und er muss nun immer in die Stadt gehen, wo es viel zu tun gibt.

Sein Wohnort gefällt ihm gut, aber er ist nicht perfekt. Es gibt Busse und die Straßenbahn, aber sie sind teuer und am Abend nicht sicher. Seine ideale Stadt würde bessere Geschäfte anbieten und der Wohnort wäre grüner mit vielen Bäumen und Pflanzen, weil er sagt, dass ihm frische Luft das Wichtigste ist.

Complete the sentences below. Write the correct letter, **A**, **B** or **C**, for each question.

1 Can feels at home …
  A with his friends.
  B in Turkey.
  C in Germany.

2 Can's school is …
  A clean.
  B opposite his home.
  C noisy.

3 In Can's local area, there is …
  A nothing to do.
  B quite a lot to do.
  C a lot to do.

Answer the following questions in English.

4 What facility would Can's ideal town provide?
5 What is the most important thing for Can?

Where I live. Charlotte, Felix and Layla are talking about where they live. Listen to the recording and answer the questions in English.

1. Why does Charlotte say the castle is famous?
2. Why does Felix shop online?
3. Where is the large supermarket which Layla uses?

> Each extract will include more information than you need to answer the question, so listen to the end of each extract to make sure you take into account everything that is said.

Complete the 150-word writing task.

> Write about where you live for an online magazine.
>
> You **must** include the following points:
> - the pros and cons of shopping in your town
> - which activities you will do in town at the weekend.
>
> Write approximately **150** words in **German**.

> Before you start writing, spend a few minutes planning. Think about the structures, tenses and vocabulary you want to use. Stick to vocabulary and structures you know, to avoid making mistakes.
>
> When you have finished writing your response, check for accuracy by looking for specific types of errors. For example, first check all your verbs, then look at word order, prepositions and cases.

Translate these sentences into English.

1. Meine Großeltern wohnen in einer kleinen Stadt im Süden von Österreich.
2. Unsere Wohnung liegt am Stadtrand.
3. Es gibt viele Geschäfte, aber wir haben kein Kino.
4. Ich fahre mit dem Fahrrad zur Schule, aber gestern bin ich mit dem Auto gefahren.
5. Morgen werde ich zum Strand gehen, weil ich meine Freunde gern treffe.

- Use your knowledge of individual words to work out the meaning of compound nouns.
- Think about the cases used after prepositions, to ensure you end up with the correct translation.

Read the text aloud and prepare responses to the follow-up questions.

> Ich wohne in der Nähe von einem Wald am Stadtrand.
>
> Unsere Umgebung ist wirklich sauber mit vielen schönen, alten Gebäuden.
>
> Man sagt, dass frische Luft sehr gesund ist.
>
> Vor fünf Jahren hat man ein neues Stadion in der Gegend gebaut.
>
> Hier gibt es viel Verkehr und wir fahren am schnellsten mit der Straßenbahn ins Stadtzentrum.
>
> *Follow-up questions:*
> - Was machst du in deiner Gegend?
> - Welche Gebäude gibt es in deiner Stadt oder in deinem Dorf?
> - Wie findest du Einkaufen?
> - Möchtest du in der Zukunft lieber in der Stadt oder auf dem Land wohnen? Warum?

Think carefully about how to pronounce these sounds:
s, ss and ß
sp, st and sch
w

Kapitel 6 Wiederholung

Refresh your memory! Write down the correct form of the demonstrative adjective *dies-* to complete each sentence.

dieser   dieses   diesem

1 ___ Ausflug ist super!
2 Ich finde ___ Wetter toll.
3 Fährst du mit ___ Zug?
4 Sie bleiben in ___ Ferienort.
5 Heute besuchen wir ___ Museum.
6 Sie hat an ___ Küste gewohnt.

Refresh your memory! Listen and write down the object and the problem each person mentions. (1–6)

room | Wi-Fi | does not work | dirty
bed | money | broken | uncomfortable
sunglasses | laptop | forgot | lost

Refresh your memory! Write down the correct past participle from the box to complete each sentence so that it makes sense.

1 Sie ist im Meer ___.
2 Sie haben die Museen ___.
3 Ich habe meine Tasche nicht ___.
4 Er ist nach Amerika ___.
5 Es hat den ganzen Tag ___.
6 Ach, nein! Ich habe mein Geld ___.

geflogen   verloren   geschwommen
geregnet   besucht   gefunden

My Swiss holidays. You read Yusuf's blog about his holidays in Switzerland. Answer the following questions in English.

> Dieses Jahr im Frühling habe ich mit meiner Familie in der Schweiz Urlaub gemacht. Wir sind von Berlin geflogen und dann mit der Bahn zum Hotel gefahren. Es hat viel geregnet, aber trotz des schlechten Wetters hat uns der Urlaub viel Spaß gemacht. Wir waren sehr aktiv und haben viele Ausflüge auf dem Land gemacht und Schlösser entdeckt.
>
> Leider hat meine Schwester ihre Tasche verloren, meine Mutter hat ihr Handy im Hotel gelassen und ich habe meine **Brieftasche** im Zug vergessen! Nach der langen Reise wollte ich ein Getränk kaufen, aber das konnte ich nicht. Wegen des Essens und der Landschaft kann ich trotzdem dieses Hotel empfehlen.

1 Name **two** activities Yusuf did with his family while in Switzerland.
2 Name **two** problems members of Yusuf's family had during their trip.
3 Read the last paragraph again. What would you keep in a **Brieftasche**?
   A money   B documents   C clothes

> Look at the questions before you start reading the text so that you know which details you need to identify. Make sure you include the correct number of details in your answers.

220 zweihundertzwanzig

5 ***Holidays.*** Some German teenagers are talking about their recent holidays. What opinions do they have? Listen to the recording and write **P** for a **positive** opinion, **N** for a **negative** opinion and **P+N** for a **positive and negative** opinion.

1 Paula
2 Linus
3 Anna
4 Achim

For this type of task, listen out for words and phrases such as *aber, jedoch, leider* or *auf der anderen Seite*, which can indicate a change of opinion. You might hear a word which sounds negative, such as *nicht* or *kein*, but remember this could also be saying that something **isn't** bad, which would make it a positive.

6 Complete the role-play task.

You are talking to your Austrian friend on the phone about a journey you are making to visit him/her.
1 Say what transport you are using and give an opinion about the journey.
2 Say who you are travelling with. (Give **two** details.)
3 Say **one** thing that you are eating on the journey and why. (Give **one** detail and **one** reason.)
4 Say what time you are arriving.
5 **?** Ask a question about how your friend likes to travel.

Use your planning time to recap on the vocabulary you know related to the topic and work out what you can say for each part of the task. For the question (point 5), think about including the word *gern* with the verb.

7 Translate the following sentences into German.

1 We are spending a week in a hotel near a lake.
2 The landscape is beautiful, but it rains every day.
3 Despite the weather, we go for walks in the mountains.
4 It is fun, although I lost my bag.
5 Most of all I like travelling through Austria.

8 ***Dictation.*** You will hear <u>five</u> short sentences. Write down exactly what you hear in German.

Think carefully about how these sounds are pronounced when you write down what you hear:
long *a*, short *a* and *ä*
long *e* and short *e*
long *o*, short *o* and *ö*
w and *v*
s, *ss*, and *ß*

zweihunderteinundzwanzig

Kapitel 7 Wiederholung

 1 *Refresh your memory!* Match up the words to form correct compound nouns. What do these words mean in English?

Tier Verkehrs wasser schutz
Trink Natur problem verschmutzung
Luft Umwelt arten mittel

 2 *Refresh your memory!* Listen and write down the missing modal verb in the first gap. Use an infinitive from the box to fill the second gap.

finden   kämpfen   vermeiden
reduzieren   schützen   beenden

1 Man ___ Menschenrechte ___.
2 Man ___ den Welthunger ___.
3 Man ___ für eine bessere Zukunft ___.
4 Man ___ Lösungen zu Umweltproblemen ___.
5 Man ___ Konflikt ___.
6 Man ___ den Verkehr in Städten ___.

 3 *Refresh your memory!* Prepositions taking the genitive case. Write the correct preposition to fill each gap. Then translate the phrases into English.

1 (*instead of*) ___ der Luftverschmutzung
2 (*despite*) ___ der Flüchtlingskrise
3 (*because of*) ___ des Wetters
4 (*during*) ___ des Tages

 4 *Important issues.* You hear a podcast discussing the findings of a survey on what is important to young people.

1 What priorities are mentioned? Complete the table in **English**.

last year	now	the future
career		

2 Freya and Konrad give their own views. Which **two** concerns does each person mention? Write the **two** correct letters for each person.

A	refugees	D	divorce
B	hunger	E	unemployment
C	war	F	climate change

 5 Read the sentences aloud and prepare responses to the follow-up questions.

Meiner Meinung nach ist Hunger das größte Problem für unsere Generation.

Viele Tiere und Bäume sterben wegen des Klimawandels.

Meine Freunde sind mir das Wichtigste, weil ich mit ihnen über alles sprechen kann.

Um die Luftverschmutzung zu reduzieren, sollte man neue Energien entwickeln.

Follow-up questions:
- Was machst du, um der Umwelt zu helfen?
- Wie findest du Elektroautos?
- Was ist das Wichtigste in deinem Leben?
- Wovor hast du Angst?

Think carefully about how to pronounce these sounds, letters and words:
-tion
-er
r
Remember where the stress falls in a compound noun.

The environment. You read this article about three environmental activists. Read the statements and write **A** if only statement **A** is true, **B** if only statement **B** is true, and **A+B** if both statements **A** and **B** are correct.

Viele junge Leute wollen die Welt retten, weil die Zukunft der Welt ihnen zu wichtig ist.

Emily schwimmt jeden Tag im Meer, und hat die Unterwasserwelt immer gern entdeckt. Sie kämpft gegen Wasserverschmutzung, weil sie findet, dass diese Verschmutzung das größte Problem der Umwelt ist. Sie isst weder Fisch noch Fleisch, weil sie glaubt, dass Tiere nicht für Menschen leiden sollen.

Lukas kämpft, um seine Umwelt zu verbessern. Er denkt, dass das größte Problem das Sterben von Pflanzen ist, deswegen ist er Mitglied einer Organisation geworden. Die Mitglieder kämpfen für Naturschutz und es ist ihnen am wichtigsten, die Zerstörung der Wälder zu stoppen, um Luftverschmutzung zu reduzieren.

Paula findet, dass die Menschen nicht umweltbewusst sind. Sie macht eine Aktion, um die Menschen zu informieren, wie sie die Natur schützen können. Sie macht sich Sorgen, dass viele nicht genug Verantwortung für die Umwelt tragen. Paula versucht, den Menschen zu helfen, um den Klimawandel zu vermeiden.

1. **A** Emily has recently taken up swimming in open water.
   B Emily thinks that no other environmental problem is as serious as water pollution.
2. **A** Emily is a vegetarian.
   B Emily doesn't like to see people suffering.
3. **A** Lukas has joined together with other people to help protect nature.
   B Lukas thinks it is possible to reduce air pollution.
4. **A** Paula aims to raise awareness of climate change issues.
   B Paula thinks that many people are concerned about the environment.

Complete the 150-word writing task.

You are writing about the environment for an online magazine.

Write approximately **150** words in **German**.

You must write something about both bullet points.

Describe:
- what makes a good living environment
- what you did last week to help the environment.

Plan your answer before you start writing. Think about the structures and vocabulary you want to use for each bullet point and remember to vary your vocabulary to avoid repetition. Aim to use complex structures (modal verbs, prepositions, conjunctions, word order, adverbs) and complex verb forms (perfect, imperfect, conditional, imperfect subjunctive). Once you have finished writing, remember to check your work for any mistakes.

Translate the following sentences into English.

1. Meiner Meinung nach ist Familie das Wichtigste in meinem Leben.
2. Ich will in meinem Beruf nicht unter Druck leiden.
3. Wegen der Verschmutzung habe ich an einer Klimawandelaktion teilgenommen.
4. Man sollte das Auto weniger benutzen, um die Natur zu schützen.
5. Mein Bruder wird in Zukunft aufhören, Fleisch zu essen.

Kapitel 8 Wiederholung

 Refresh your memory! Subordinating conjunctions. Rewrite each pair of sentences in one sentence, using the conjunction in brackets. Start sentences 4–6 with the subordinate clause.

1. Ich weiß noch nicht. (was) Ich werde später studieren.
2. Sie will reisen. (bevor) Sie geht auf die Uni.
3. Er ist sich nicht sicher. (ob) Er soll ein Zwischenjahr machen.
4. (sobald) Wir sind alt genug. Wir möchten eine Ausbildung machen.
5. (als) Ich war jung. Ich wollte Lehrerin werden.
6. (während) Sie studierte an der Uni. Sie hat in einem Geschäft gearbeitet.

 Refresh your memory! Write the correct reflexive pronoun to complete each sentence.

1. Er sorgt ___ um seine Noten.
2. Wir treffen ___ nächste Woche.
3. Kannst du ___ das gut vorstellen?
4. Ich kann ___ nicht gut konzentrieren.
5. Fühlst du ___ wohl?
6. Interessiert ihr ___ für diesen Beruf?

| mich | euch | dich |
| dir | sich | uns |

 Refresh your memory! Find the <u>six</u> sentences that require the addition of the word *zu*. Write down the number (1–8).

1. Ich möchte Arbeit ___ finden.
2. Ich plane, Geld ___ verdienen.
3. Ich habe vor, Lehrer ___ werden.
4. Ich versuche, mich ___ verbessern.
5. Es ist schwierig, eine Stelle ___ bekommen.
6. Ich will ein Zwischenjahr ___ machen.
7. Ich habe Lust, ein Haus ___ kaufen.
8. Ich habe mich entschieden, kochen ___ lernen.

 You hear a podcast describing a website called *Mein Taschengeldjob*. What does it say? Listen to the recording and write **A**, **B** or **C** for each question.

1. What do we learn about Marie and the website?

A	Marie was unable to find a job last month.
B	Marie went on the internet to look for work.
C	Marie's organisation aims to help young people.

2. What else do we find out about the work of the organisation?

A	You need to have work experience before applying for vacancies.
B	The organisation matches up companies and job seekers.
C	Young people have to pay to use the service.

> The listening exam will contain different types of questions, such as multiple-choice questions, identifying opinions and open questions. You will have to use different skills to answer the various types successfully.
> In a multiple-choice question like this one, check the exact wording of the statements, as there will be something similar, but not identical, in the incorrect answers. You may also need to listen out for negatives.
> The recording for this type of question is often split into two or three parts and there might be a change of speaker or topic.

My future plans. You read Joel's blog post about the future. Answer the following questions in English.

Letzten Sommer habe ich der Umwelt in unserer Gegend geholfen, aber dieses Jahr habe ich mich entschieden, nach meinen Prüfungen einen Job zu suchen. Meine Schwester möchte auch ihre Zeit benutzen, um etwas Sinnvolles zu tun. Deshalb plant sie, Tieren zu helfen, aber ich möchte lieber Geld verdienen, um in der Zukunft reisen zu können.

Ich weiß nicht genau, was ich machen werde, wenn ich die Schule verlasse. Mein Bruder hat vor, eine Ausbildung zu machen, weil er etwas Praktisches machen will. Für mich wäre das keine Möglichkeit, da ich weiterstudieren möchte. Ich weiß nicht, ob ich direkt auf die Uni gehen werde oder ein Zwischenjahr machen sollte, um mich besser kennenzulernen.

Leider bin ich mir auch unsicher, was ich später werden möchte. Ich kann gut organisieren und andere überzeugen. Außerdem habe ich viel Verständnis, deshalb sollte ich vielleicht Chef einer Organisation werden. Ich möchte auf jeden Fall heiraten. Ob mein Partner will oder nicht, weiß ich nicht, aber ich denke schon, dass ich später auch vielleicht Kinder haben möchte.

1. Why does Joel's sister want to help animals this summer?
2. Why does Joel want to earn money?
3. Why would Joel like to take a gap year?
4. Name **one** quality Joel has when dealing with people.
5. What is the **one** thing that Joel is sure about?

Complete the photo card task and prepare responses to the follow-up questions.

You will be asked to talk about the content of these photos. You must say at least one thing about each photo.

After you have spoken about the content of the photos, you will be asked questions related to any of the topics within the theme of **People and lifestyle**.

Your responses should be as **full and detailed** as possible.

Follow-up questions:
- Möchtest du lieber in einem Café oder in einem Geschäft arbeiten? Warum?
- Was für einen Samstagsjob hast du schon gemacht?
- Was willst du nach den Prüfungen machen?
- Was sind deine Pläne für die Zukunft?

Translate these sentences into German.

1. I can concentrate well and I am honest.
2. I have not yet decided what I would like to study.
3. Last year I worked to earn money.
4. My dream career would be to become a teacher.
5. As soon as I leave school, I will travel abroad.

Think carefully about how these sounds are pronounced, when writing down what you hear.
qu
j
ä, ö, ü

Dictation. You will hear <u>five</u> short sentences. Write down exactly what you hear in German.

Conversation questions

You can use these questions to help you prepare for two different sections of the speaking test:
- the questions which follow on from the **reading aloud task**.
- the questions that you will be asked during the **photo card task**.

In the **reading aloud task** there are four follow-up questions. All four questions are in the present tense and are focused on the same topic as the reading aloud task.

In the **photo card task**, there is an unprepared conversation relating to the theme of the photos in which you have the opportunity to show the examiner that you know a range of structures and tenses in German.

Kapitel 1 (pages 6–29)

Theme 1: People and lifestyle
1. Welches Fach magst du nicht und warum?
2. Was ist dein Lieblingsfach? Warum?
3. Beschreib einen typischen Schultag.
4. Was machst du in der Pause/Mittagspause?
5. Was hast du gestern im Unterricht gemacht?
6. Wie findest du Schuluniformen? (Was würdest du gern/lieber in der Schule tragen?)
7. Wie findest du die Schulregeln in deiner Schule?
8. Erzähl mir von einer Schulveranstaltung im letzten Jahr.
9. Was ist deine Meinung zu Hausaufgaben?
10. Wie findest du Lernen in einer Gruppe / mit Computern?

Kapitel 2 (pages 30–53)

Theme 2: Popular culture
1. Was ist deine Lieblingsmusik? (Wer ist dein Lieblingssänger / deine Lieblingssängerin?)
2. Was machst du gern in deiner Freizeit?
3. Was hast du letztes Wochenende gemacht?
4. Was wirst du nächstes Wochenende machen?
5. Was würdest du machen, wenn du mehr Freizeit hättest?
6. Was hast du neulich im Kino / online gesehen? (Wie war es?)
7. Was sind die Vor- und Nachteile des Lebens als Star?

Theme 3: Communication and the world around us
8. Was machst du online?
9. Was sind die Vor- und Nachteile von Technologie, deiner Meinung nach?
10. Wie hast du gestern soziale Medien benutzt?

Kapitel 3 (pages 56–79)

Theme 1: People and lifestyle
1. Beschreib deine Familie!
2. Wie bist du? (Wie siehst du aus? Wie ist dein Charakter?)
3. Wie sieht dein (Bruder) / deine (Schwester) aus?
4. Beschreib einen guten Freund / eine gute Freundin!
5. Hast du eine gute Beziehung zu deinem (Stiefvater) / deiner (Tante) / deinen (Großeltern)? Warum (nicht)?
6. Wer ist dir wichtig? Warum?

Theme 2: Popular culture
7. Hast du ein Lieblingsfest? (Welches Fest würdest du gern besuchen?)
8. Hast du schon ein deutsches Fest erlebt? (Wie war es?)
9. Wie hast du deinen letzten Geburtstag gefeiert?
10. Was möchtest du machen, um das Ende des Schuljahres zu feiern?

Kapitel 4 (pages 80–103)

Theme 1: People and lifestyle
1. Was ist dein Lieblingssport? (Wie oft machst du das?)
2. Welchen Sport machst du nicht so gern?
3. Welchen Sport würdest du gern probieren?
4. Was möchtest du in deinem Leben ändern, um deine Gesundheit zu verbessern?
5. Was machst du, wenn du schlechte Laune hast?
6. Was hast du neulich für deine Gesundheit gemacht?
7. Deiner Meinung nach, was sollte man machen, um gesund zu sein? Warum?
8. Glaubst du, dass es einfach ist, gesund zu sein?
9. Was ist deine Meinung zum Teamsport?
10. Welche Vorteile oder Nachteile gibt es beim Sport?

Speaking test revision

How to prepare:
- Read through the questions to check you understand them. Focus on the question words (like *Was …? Wo …? Wie … ?* etc).
- Check the verbs and time phrases to understand which time frame the question is about.
- Then practise answering the questions using full sentences.
- Think about how you could extend your answers using more complex structures, particularly for answering questions during the **photo card task** conversation.

Ways to extend your answers:
- Join together ideas with connectives: *und, aber, auch …*
- Add in opinions and justify them: *ich mag … (nicht) / ich … (nicht) gern, weil …*
- Use opposing arguments: *Auf der einen Seite … auf der anderen Seite … jedoch …*
- Add in examples of recent activities in the past tense.
- Add in examples of different tenses.

Kapitel 5 (pages 104–127)

Theme 3: Communication and the world around us
1. Beschreib deine Gegend! (Wohnst du gern in deiner Stadt / deinem Dorf?)
2. Was sind die Vor- und Nachteile von deinem Wohnort?
3. Wie war deine Stadt / dein Dorf früher?
4. Wie fährst du am liebsten zur Schule? Warum?
5. Kaufst du lieber online oder in einem Einkaufszentrum ein? Warum?
6. Wie wäre dein idealer Wohnort? (Wie wäre dein Traumhaus?)
7. Beschreib mir dein Haus / deine Wohnung!
8. Was hast du gemacht, als du zum letzten Mal in die Stadt gegangen bist?
9. Meinst du, dass deine Gegend gut für junge Leute / Touristen ist?
10. Was würdest du an deinem Wohnort ändern?

Kapitel 6 (pages 132–155)

Theme 3: Communication and the world around us
1. Was machst du gern in den Ferien?
2. Was sind die Vor- und Nachteile von einem Urlaub am Strand / in den Bergen?
3. Wie findest du Freizeitparks / historische Gebäude?
4. Würdest du lieber in einem Hotel oder in einem Ferienhaus wohnen?
5. Was denkst du über Urlaube im Ausland?
6. Was hast du in den letzten Ferien gemacht?
7. Beschreib mir einen Ausflug, den du gemacht hast oder den du gern machen würdest!
8. Erzähl mir von einem Problem, das du im Urlaub gehabt hast.
9. Wie wäre dein Traumurlaub?
10. Was wirst du in den nächsten Ferien machen?

Kapitel 7 (pages 156–179)

Theme 1: People and lifestyle
1. Wer ist dein Vorbild?
2. Was ist dir wichtig im Leben?
3. Worum machst du dir Sorgen?
4. Worauf hoffst du?

Theme 3: Communication and the world around us
5. Was ist das größte Umweltproblem, deiner Meinung nach?
6. Bist du umweltfreundlich? (Was machst du?)
7. Was hast du neulich gemacht, um die Umwelt zu schützen?
8. Was sollten wir machen, um unsere Welt zu verbessern?
9. Bist du für oder gegen grüne Energien?
10. Sollte man Veganer*in sein?

Kapitel 8 (pages 180–203)

Theme 1: People and lifestyle
1. Was wirst du nach deinen Prüfungen machen?
2. Hast du schon eine Arbeit gemacht?
3. Was für einen Job würdest du (nicht) gern machen?
4. Wo möchtest du später arbeiten? Warum?
5. Was wäre dein Traumberuf?
6. Was sind die Vor- und Nachteile von deinem Traumberuf?
7. Was sind deine Eigenschaften und Fähigkeiten?
8. Wie wichtig ist dir ein gutes Gehalt?
9. Möchtest du in der Zukunft heiraten?
10. Wie sieht die Zukunft aus, deiner Meinung nach?

German phonics

Here is a list of all the sounds that you need to understand and produce.
The **SSCs** (sound-symbol correspondences) will be assessed in the **reading aloud** and **dictation** tasks.

The **reading aloud task** will be the second task in your speaking test. You will have **15** minutes' preparation time for the whole speaking test. The task will contain **five** sentences (50 words minimum) from a specific theme.

The **dictation task** will form part of your listening paper. You will have to transcribe **30** words (in **five** sentences). Some of the words will not be on the vocabulary lists. Practising the sounds on these pages will help with both the **reading aloud** and **dictation** tasks.

Sounds	Key words and other examples	Pages with a focus on this sound	Further examples to practise
long a / ah / aa	Tag / Jahr / Haar	pages 33, 133	Jeden Tag wasche ich mir die Haare.
short a	kalt / alle / zusammen	pages 33, 87, 133, 184	Am Anfang hatte ich Angst.
long e / eh / ee	lesen / nehmen / leer	pages 8, 134	Ich nehme Tee am Meer.
short e	wenn / denn / denken	pages 8, 134	Meine Eltern sprechen Englisch.
ei / ai	Polizei / Mai / frei	page 31	Ich weiß, wir drei sind meistens frei im Mai.
z	Zeit / Zimmer / zu	page 66	Der Zahnarzt zieht zehn Zähne.
w	schwer / Welt / wieder	pages 15, 66, 112, 142	Werden wir wirklich im Winter wandern?
ie	lieben / spielen / Energie	page 31	Sieben Mitglieder singen viele schwierige Lieder.
long o / oh	Person / ohne / Sohn	pages 37, 87, 133	Das Kino, wo ich wohne, ist so groß.
short o	Kopf / soll / obwohl	pages 37, 133, 184	Die Sonne im Oktober ist oft nicht im Osten.
long i / ih	wir / ihr / ihn	page 31	Interessiert ihr euch für Musik?
short i	bitte / wissen / Himmel	page 31	Das ist nicht im Inhalt.
hard ch	machen / mochte / Buch	page 136	Ihre Tochter sucht auch ein Buch.
soft ch	Mädchen / möchte / euch	pages 8, 136	Vielleicht sprechen die Mädchen über Bücher?
long u / uh	Buch / Zug / Uhr	pages 7, 59, 87	Er hat einen Stuhl, eine Uhr und einen Kuchen.
short u	Grund / und / Hunger	page 59	Die Umwelt in seiner Umgebung ist schmutzig.
long ü / long y / üh	Tür / früh	pages 7, 8, 59, 87, 184	Die grünen Türen und Stühle sind überall berühmt.
short ü / short y	Stück / fünf / Typ	pages 7, 59	Ich bin glücklich, dass es fünf typische Brücken gibt.
long ä / äh	spät / Mädchen / wählen	pages 41, 184	Das Mädchen isst regelmäßig europäischen Käse.
short ä	Geschäft / lächeln / kälter	pages 41, 87, 133, 184	Es wäre besser mit mehr Geschäften in den Städten.
long ö / öh	Größe / höher / schön	pages 37, 87, 133	Die Berge sind größer und höher in Österreich.
short ö	zwölf / können / Töchter	pages 37, 184	Zwölf Schlösser öffnen für die Öffentlichkeit.
äu	Geräusch / träumen / Gebäude	page 87	Sie träumt häufig von Gebäuden und Bäumen.

228 zweihundertachtundzwanzig

Speaking test revision

Sounds	Key words and other examples	Pages with a focus on this sound	Further examples to practise
sch	schnell / schreiben / schwimmen	pages 35, 81, 108	Man lernt schnell Schwimmen in britischen Schulen.
sp-	sportlich / Spaß / spannend	pages 8, 35, 108	Sport treiben ist spannend und macht Spaß.
st-	stehen / Stadt / studieren	pages 35, 108	Er stand eine Stunde am Strand und in der Straße.
s- / -s-	singen / sind / leise	pages 85, 108, 143	Diese Sänger singen sofort sieben Lieder am See.
ß / ss / -s	Fuß / dass / blaues	pages 108, 143	Ein schönes großes Schloss liegt am Fluss.
er	er / erst / Erfolg	page 163	Er ist ernst, erfolgreich und hat Energie.
unstressed -er	Zimmer / Vater / Theater	page 163	Sie hat nur eine Schwester, aber vier Brüder.
v	Vater / viel / vergessen	pages 66, 142	Mein Vater ist voller Verständnis und Vertrauen.
au	auch / auf / Haus	page 87	Die Frauen laufen gern im August.
consonantal r	Problem / reden / richtig	page 167	Der Lehrer hat ein riesiges rotes Fahrrad im Raum.
vocalic r	klar / Uhr / Meer	page 167	Nur am Morgen gibt es mehr Verkehr.
eu	Euro / heute / neulich	page 39	Eure neuen Freunde sprechen heute kein Deutsch.
th	Thema / Theater / Mathe	page 8	Er hat Mathe und Theater studiert.
unvoiced -b / -d / -g	halb / Land / Weg	page 143	Im Urlaub hat er sein Geld im Zug verloren.
-ig	wenig / neblig / zwanzig	page 88	Ich bin lustig, ruhig, oft schwierig, aber nie traurig.
j	jemand / ja / jede	page 181	Jedes Jahr im Juni oder Juli hat die Jugend Urlaub.
-tion	Situation / Information / Tradition	page 157	Man braucht Information in dieser Situation.
qu	bequem / Qualität	page 187	Das Wasser von der Quelle schmeckt gut, aber der Weg ist nicht bequem.

1 Listen to and repeat each sound, example word and practice phrase. Make a list of the sounds or words you find most challenging and keep practising them. Then find other words for each sound to test your pronunciation.

Role-play skills

What do I need to know about the role-play?
- It is an imagined conversation with a friend about a topic.
- It is the <u>first</u> part of the speaking test (before the **reading aloud** task).
- The teacher speaks first.
- You will say something for each of the **five** bullet points.
- You should speak in the present tense for all bullet points except one which will be in a different tense.
- You will need to ask **one** question.
- Three of the bullet points will require two details, two pieces of information or an opinion <u>and</u> a reason.

Themes and topics

There are three themes and nine subtopics. Look back at these modules for some role-play or conversation examples. There are also role-play cards on the exam pages at the end of each module, and in the revision module.

Themes and topics	Module
Theme 1 – People and lifestyle	
1 Identity and relationships with others	Modules 3 and 7
2 Healthy living and lifestyle	Module 4
3 Education and work	Modules 1 and 8
Theme 2 – Popular culture	
1 Free-time activities	Modules 2 and 4
2 Customs, festivals and celebrations	Module 3
3 Celebrity culture	Modules 2 and 3
Theme 3 – Communication and the world around us	
1 Travel and tourism, including places of interest	Module 6
2 Media and technology	Module 2
3 The environment and where people live	Modules 5 and 7

> In order to score full marks, you will need to give a verb in your answer. Make sure you answer **both parts** of the bullet point.
> For example, if you are asked to **say what subject you like and why**
> Don't say: Mathe.
> Instead say: Ich <u>mag</u> Mathe, <u>weil</u> der Lehrer gut ist.

> Make sure you state **two** activities or give **two** details when you are asked to do so.
> For example, if you are asked to **say what you like to do at the weekend** and **give two details**
> Don't say: Ich spiele gern Tennis.
> Instead say: Ich spiele gern Tennis <u>und gehe gern ins Kino</u>.

Useful words and phrases

Meiner Meinung nach	In my opinion
Ich finde …, weil	I find … because
Ich spiele	I play
Ich esse	I eat
Ich gehe/fahre	I go
Es gibt	There is/are
Ich habe … gespielt	I played
Ich habe … gegessen	I ate
Ich bin … gegangen/gefahren	I went
Es gab	There was/were
Ich werde … spielen	I will … play
Ich werde … essen	I will … eat
Ich werde … gehen/fahren	I will … go
Es wird … geben	There will be …

Learn these key question words and phrases:

Wann?	When?
Was für …?	What type of …?
Was?	What?
Welcher/Welche/Welches?	Which?
Wer?	Who?
Wie?	How?
Wie lange?	How long?
Wo?	Where?
Kann man …?	Can you …?
Hast du …?	Do you have …?
Gibt es …?	Is/are there …?
Können Sie bitte die Frage wiederholen?	Please can you repeat the question?

Questions

The last bullet point requires you to ask a question. This is a key part of the task and you should practise asking questions for every topic.

Role-play example topics	Example questions
Free-time activities Ask your friend a question about hobbies.	**Hörst du** gern Musik? **Was ist** dein Lieblingssport?
The environment and where people live Ask your friend a question about their local area.	**Gibt es** ein Schwimmbad in deiner Gegend? **Was machst du gern** in deiner Gegend?
Education and work Ask your friend a question about school.	**Wie findest du** deine Schule? **Was denkst du über** die Schulregeln?
Healthy living and lifestyle Ask your friend a question about food.	**Was isst du** zum Frühstück? **Bist du** Vegetarier?
Customs, festivals and celebrations Ask your friend a question about celebrations.	**Wie feierst du** deinen Geburtstag? **Wie findest du** Silvester?
Travel and tourism, including places of interest Ask your friend a question about holidays.	**Was machst du** in den Sommerferien? **Wohin fährst du** auf Urlaub?
Media and technology Ask your friend a question about social media.	**Welche** sozialen Medien benutzt du? **Wie findest du** Instagram?

Example role-play

Look at the example role-play card below and the model conversation on the right.

- You are talking to your German friend.
- Your teacher will play the part of your friend and will speak first.
- You should address your friend as *du*.
- When you see this – **?** – you will have to ask a question.

In order to score full marks, you must include at least one verb in your response to each task.

1. Say **one** place you go in your free time.
2. Say **two** activities you do for your fitness.
3. Say what sport you did last weekend. (Give **two** details.)
4. Say what you think of basketball and why. (Give **one** opinion and **one** reason.)
5. **?** Ask your friend a question about hobbies.

Teacher:	Wohin gehst du in deiner Freizeit?
Student:	Ich gehe gern ins Kino.
Teacher:	Und was machst du für deine Fitness?
Student:	Ich spiele Tennis und ich gehe schwimmen.
Teacher:	Welchen Sport hast du letztes Wochenende gemacht?
Student:	Letztes Wochenende bin ich laufen gegangen. Es war sehr anstrengend.
Teacher:	Und wie findest du Basketball? … Warum?
Student:	Ich finde Basketball nicht so toll, weil es langweilig ist.
Teacher:	Verstehe.
Student:	Was sind deine Hobbys?
Teacher:	Ich lese gern.

Practice role-play

Look at the role-play card and prepare your answers to the numbered points.

- You are talking to your Austrian friend.
- Your teacher will play the part of your friend and will speak first.
- You should address your friend as *du*.
- When you see this – **?** – you will have to ask a question.

In order to score full marks, you must include at least one verb in your response to each task.

1. Say what kind of films you like and why. (Give **one** opinion and **one** reason.)
2. Describe a recent visit to the cinema. (Give **two** details.)
3. Say who your favourite actor is and why. (Give **one** opinion and **one** reason.)
4. Give **one** negative aspect of being famous.
5. **?** Ask your friend a question about films.

Remember to use the plural noun here. (point 1)

You will need to use the past tense here. (point 2)

This can be a short answer as you only need one detail. (point 4)

Look at the 'useful words and phrases' box on page 230 to help you to give and justify your opinion.

Remember to invert the subject and verb if asking a yes/no question and add a question word at the start if you are seeking specific information.

Photo card task

The **photo card task** is the final part of your speaking test and is made up of **two** parts:

The photo card contains two photos relating to one of the three themes:
- **Theme 1 – People and lifestyle**
- **Theme 2 – Popular culture**
- **Theme 3 – Communication and the world around us**

Each theme is made of three topics (see page 230).

1 Response to the two photos
(one to one and a half minutes)
Give a detailed description of both photos on the photo card.

2 Unprepared conversation
(four to five and a half minutes)
Take part in a conversation on one or more topics from the theme specified on the photo card.

Response to the two photos

During your preparation time, **PLAN** how you are going to respond to the content of the two photos. Prepare a detailed description of both photos. This could include, for example, **People/things**, **Location** and **Activities**.

People/things
Who/What can you see?

Location
Where are they?

Activities
What are they doing?

Now check your accuracy carefully.

Check:
- verbs
  - regular / irregular
  - correct verb ending
- adjective agreements
- word order

To gain top marks you must give a full, detailed description of both photos using **accurate language** and **correct pronunciation**.

Auf dem ersten Foto / Auf dem zweiten Foto	gibt es / sieht man / kann man … sehen.	(vier) Personen / Kinder / Erwachsene. einen Jungen / ein Mädchen / ein Paar. ein Auto / einen Bahnhof / eine Straße. viele Geschäfte/Häuser/Bäume.
Es gibt auch / Man sieht auch		
Ich denke, dass es	eine Familie / eine Gruppe von Freunden ist. Schüler und Schülerinnen sind.	
Die Person auf der linken/rechten Seite	ist (groß/klein) und hat (kurze/lange) Haare. trägt Jeans / eine schwarze Hose / ein weißes T-Shirt.	
Das Essen	sieht	lecker
Die Leute/Gebäude	sehen	glücklich/schön/alt/modern

aus.

Die Personen/Leute/Menschen	sind in	einem Park / einem Bahnhof. einer Schule / einer Stadt. einem Geschäft / einem Restaurant / einem Hotel.
		auf Urlaub / am Strand / in den Bergen.
Ich würde sagen, dass	es Sommer/Winter ist. / die Leute glücklich aussehen.	
Das Wetter scheint	schön/schlecht/gut/warm/kalt zu sein.	
Im Hintergrund sieht man	Häuser / Gebäude / viele Menschen / Berge / Wolken / einen Garten.	
Sie / Die Leute/Personen	spielen / essen / kaufen / sitzen / lernen / hören / gehen / fahren / tanzen …	
Die Person in der Mitte / auf der linken/rechten Seite	spielt / isst / kauft / sitzt / lernt / hört / geht / fährt / tanzt …	

To say what people are doing, use the **present tense**. There is no present continuous in German.
*Das Mädchen **spielt** Fußball.*   The girl is playing/plays football.
*Die Schüler **lesen** ein Buch.*   The students are reading/read a book.

Example photo card task (Theme 3: Communication and the world around us)

During your preparation time, look at the two photos. You may make as many notes as you wish and use these notes during the test.

Your teacher will ask you to talk about the content of these photos. The recommended time is approximately **one and a half minutes**. You must say at least **one** thing about each photo.

After you have spoken about the content of the photos, your teacher will ask you questions related to any of the topics within the theme of **Communication and the world around us**.

Sag mir etwas über die Fotos.

Example answer:
*Auf dem ersten Foto sieht man fünf Personen: drei Mädchen und zwei Jungen. Ich denke, dass es eine Gruppe von Freunden ist. Im Hintergrund sieht man ein Gebäude auf der linken Seite. Sie sind in einem Bus und ich glaube, dass sie auf Urlaub sind. Ich würde sagen, dass es Sommer ist, denn die Sonne scheint. Sie tragen alle Sommerkleidung und eine Sonnenbrille. Sie lächeln und sie sehen glücklich aus.
Auf dem zweiten Foto gibt es drei Personen …*

Unprepared conversation

You will then take part in an unprepared conversation on one or more of the three topics from the theme stipulated on the photo card.

 Listen carefully to the questions and take care with how you start each answer. Are you using the correct tense?

 If you make a mistake, just correct yourself. If you want the teacher to repeat a question, ask *Können Sie das bitte wiederholen?*

 Use the example questions on pages 226–227 to practise answers to the questions you might be asked. This is an opportunity to show off your German!

In the Speaking Test, an **'extended response'** is one which contains at least three clauses, each with a **verb**. For example:
*Ich **war** letztes Wochenende im Sportzentrum und ich **bin** dort **geschwommen**. Ich **liebe** Schwimmen, aber ich **schwimme** am liebsten im Meer.*

Examples of complex language include:

- a wide range of tenses (make sure you use the correct auxiliary verb: *ich habe/ich bin*)
- a wide range of conjunctions (*weil, dass, ob, wenn, da, obwohl …*)
- the subjunctive (*hätte, würde, wäre*)
- modal verbs (*ich möchte, ich darf (nicht)*), also in the imperfect: *ich konnte/wollte/musste*)
- comparatives/superlatives (*besser / am besten / lieber / am liebsten*)
- infinitive constructions (*Ich habe vor, nächste Woche … zu …*)

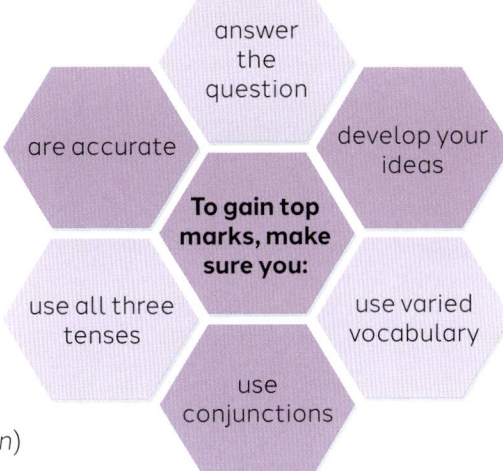

Verb tables

Key:
* = this verb form won't appear in exams, but you may use it in your own work.

Regular verbs

Infinitive	Present tense	Imperfect tense	Perfect tense	Future tense
Regular verbs				
wohnen *to live*	ich wohn**e** du wohn**st** er/sie/es wohn**t** wir wohn**en** ihr wohn**t** Sie/sie wohn**en**	ich wohn**te** du wohn**test** er/sie/es wohn**te** wir wohn**ten** ihr wohn**tet** Sie/sie wohn**ten**	ich habe … **ge**wohn**t**	ich werde … wohnen
arbeiten *to work*	du arbeit**est** er/sie/es arbeit**et** ihr arbeit**et**	ich arbeit**ete**	ich habe … **ge**arbeit**et**	ich werde … arbeiten
Reflexive verbs with accusative				
sich freuen *to be happy,* *make happy,* *please, look* *forward to*	ich freue **mich** du freust **dich** er/sie/es freut **sich** wir freuen **uns** ihr freut **euch** Sie/sie freuen **sich**	ich freute mich	ich habe mich … **ge**freut	ich werde mich freuen
Separable verbs				
einkaufen *to buy,* *shop,* *go shopping*	ich kaufe ein	ich kaufte ein	ich habe … ein**ge**kauft	ich werde … einkaufen

Key irregular verbs

Infinitive	Present tense	Imperfect tense	Perfect tense	Future tense
haben *to have*	ich habe du hast er/sie/es hat wir haben ihr habt Sie/sie haben	ich hatte du hattest er/sie/es hatte wir hatten ihr hattet Sie/sie hatten	ich habe … gehabt	ich werde … haben
sein *to be*	ich bin du bist er/sie/es ist wir sind ihr seid Sie/sie sind	ich war du warst er/sie/es war wir waren ihr wart Sie/sie waren	ich bin … gewesen	ich werde … sein
werden *to become*	ich werde du wirst er/sie/es wird wir werden ihr werdet Sie/sie werden	ich wurde du *wurdest er/sie/es wurde wir *wurden ihr *wurdet Sie/sie *wurden	ich bin … geworden	ich werde … werden
wissen *to know*	ich weiß du weißt er/sie/es weiß wir wissen ihr wisst Sie/sie wissen	ich wusste du wusstest er/sie/es wusste wir *wussten ihr *wusstet Sie/sie *wussten	ich habe … gewusst	ich werde … wissen

Verbs with changes in the *du* and *er/sie/es* stems

Infinitive	Present tense	Imperfect tense	Perfect tense	Future tense
anfangen *to start*	du fängst ... an er/sie/es fängt ... an	ich fing ... an	ich habe ... angefangen	ich werde ... anfangen
brechen *to break*	du brichst er/sie/es bricht	ich *brach	ich habe ... gebrochen	ich werde ... brechen
empfehlen *to recommend*	du empfiehlst er/sie/es empfiehlt	ich *empfahl	ich habe ... empfohlen	ich werde ... empfehlen
essen *to eat*	du isst er/sie/es isst	ich aß/ass	ich habe ... gegessen	ich werde ... essen
fahren *to go, drive*	du fährst er/sie/es fährt	ich fuhr	ich bin ... gefahren	ich werde ... fahren
fallen *to fallen*	du fällst er/sie/es fällt	ich fiel	ich bin ... gefallen	ich werde ... fallen
geben *to give*	du gibst er/sie/es gibt	ich gab	ich habe ... gegeben	ich werde ... geben
gefallen *to please*	du gefällst er/sie/es gefällt	ich *gefiel	ich habe ... gefallen	ich werde ... gefallen
halten *to stop*	du hältst er/sie/es hält	ich *hielt	ich habe ... gehalten	ich werde ... halten
heißen *to be called, mean*	du heißt er/sie/es heißt	ich *hieß	ich habe ... *geheißen	ich werde ... heißen
helfen *to help*	du hilfst er/sie/es hilft	ich half	ich habe ... geholfen	ich werde ... helfen
lassen *to let, allow, have something done*	du lässt er/sie/es lässt	ich ließ/liess	ich habe ... gelassen	ich werde ... lassen
laufen *to run*	ich laufe du *läufst	ich lief	ich bin ... gelaufen	ich werde ... laufen
lesen *to read*	du liest er/sie/es liest	ich *las	ich habe ... gelesen	ich werde ... lesen
nehmen *to take*	du nimmst er/sie/es nimmt	ich *nahm	ich habe ... genommen	ich werde ... nehmen
schlafen *to sleep*	du schläfst er/sie/es schläft	ich schlief	ich habe ... geschlafen	ich werde ... schlafen
sehen *to see, watch*	du siehst er/sie/es sieht	ich sah	ich habe ... gesehen	ich werde ... sehen
sprechen *to speak*	du sprichst er/sie/es spricht	ich sprach	ich habe ... gesprochen	ich werde ... sprechen
sterben *to die*	du *stirbst er/sie/es *stirbt	ich/er/sie/es starb	er/sie/es ist ... gestorben	er/sie/es wird ... sterben
tragen *to carry, wear*	du *trägst er/sie/es trägt	ich *trug	ich habe ... getragen	ich werde ... tragen
treffen *to meet*	du triffst er/sie/es trifft	ich *traf	ich habe ... getroffen	ich werde ... treffen
vergessen *to forget*	du vergisst er/sie/es vergisst	ich *vergaß	ich habe ... vergessen	ich werde ... vergessen
werfen *to throw*	du *wirfst er/sie/es *wirft	ich *warf	ich habe ... *geworfen	ich werde ... werfen

Verb tables

Key:
* = this verb form won't appear in exams, but you may use it in your own work.

Other useful verbs

Infinitive	Present tense	Imperfect tense	Perfect tense	Future tense
akzeptieren *to accept*	ich akzeptiere	ich akzeptierte	ich habe … akzeptiert	ich werde … akzeptieren
anbieten *to offer*	ich biete … an	ich *bot … an	ich habe … angeboten	ich werde … anbieten
ändern *to change*	ich ändere	ich änderte	ich habe … geändert	ich werde … ändern
antworten *to answer*	ich antworte	ich antwortete	ich habe … geantwortet	ich werde … antworten
beginnen *to begin*	ich beginne	ich begann	ich habe … begonnen	ich werde … beginnen
bekommen *to receive, get*	ich bekomme	ich bekam	ich habe … bekommen	ich werde … bekommen
bemerken *to notice*	ich bemerke	ich bemerkte	ich habe … bemerkt	ich werde … bemerken
beobachten *to observe*	ich beobachte	ich beobachtete	ich habe … beobachtet	ich werde … beobachten
besitzen *to own, have*	ich besitze	ich *besaß	ich habe … *besessen	ich werde … besitzen
bestellen *to order, reserve*	ich bestelle	ich bestellte	ich habe … bestellt	ich werde … bestellen
bitten *to request, ask for*	ich bitte	ich *bat	ich habe … *gebeten	ich werde … bitten
bleiben *to stay*	ich bleibe	ich blieb	ich bin … geblieben	ich werde … bleiben
bringen *to bring*	ich bringe	ich brachte	ich habe … gebracht	ich werde … bringen
denken *to think*	ich denke	ich dachte	ich habe … gedacht	ich werde … denken
diskutieren *to discuss*	ich diskutiere	ich diskutierte	Ich habe … diskutiert	ich werde … diskutieren
entscheiden *to decide*	ich entscheide	ich entschied	ich habe … entschieden	ich werde … entscheiden
(sich) entschuldigen *to excuse, apologise*	ich entschuldige	ich entschuldigte	ich habe … entschuldigt	ich werde … entschuldigen
(sich) erinnern *to remind, remember*	ich erinnere	ich erinnerte	ich habe … erinnert	ich werde … erinnern
erkennen *to recognise, admit*	ich erkenne	ich *erkannte	ich habe … erkannt	ich werde … erkennen
erlauben *to allow*	ich erlaube	ich erlaubte	ich habe … erlaubt	ich werde … erlauben

Verb tables

Infinitive	Present tense	Imperfect tense	Perfect tense	Future tense
erleben *to experience*	ich erlebe	ich erlebte	ich habe … erlebt	ich werde … erleben
erreichen *to achieve, reach*	ich erreiche	ich erreichte	ich habe … erreicht	ich werde … erreichen
fehlen *to lack, be missing, be absent*	ich fehle	ich fehlte	ich habe … gefehlt	ich werde … fehlen
finden *to find*	ich finde	ich fand	ich habe … gefunden	ich werde … finden
fliegen *to fly*	ich fliege	ich *flog	ich bin … geflogen	ich werde … fliegen
gehen *to go*	ich gehe	ich ging	ich bin … gegangen	ich werde … gehen
gehören *to belong*	ich gehöre	ich gehörte	ich habe … gehört	ich werde … gehören
genießen *to enjoy*	ich genieße	ich *genoss	ich habe … *genossen	ich werde … genießen
gewinnen *to win*	ich gewinne	ich *gewann	ich habe … gewonnen	ich werde … gewinnen
heiraten *to marry*	ich heirate	ich heiratete	ich habe … geheiratet	ich werde … heiraten
kennen *to know*	ich kenne	ich *kannte	ich habe … gekannt	ich werde … kennen
kommen *to come*	ich komme	ich kam	ich bin … gekommen	ich werde … kommen
kriegen *to get*	ich kriege	ich kriegte	ich habe … gekriegt	ich werde … kriegen
lächeln *to smile*	ich läch(e)le	ich lächelte	ich habe … gelächelt	ich werde … lächeln
lachen *to laugh*	ich lache	ich lachte	ich habe … gelacht	ich werde … lachen
(sich) legen *to lay, put, (lie down)*	ich lege	ich legte	ich habe … gelegt	ich werde … legen
leiden *to suffer*	ich leide	ich *litt	ich habe … gelitten	ich werde … leiden
liegen *to lie, be lying down*	ich liege	ich lag	ich habe … gelegen	ich werde … liegen
lösen *to solve*	ich löse	ich löste	ich habe … gelöst	ich werde … lösen
(sich) nennen *to name, call*	ich nenne	ich *nannte	ich habe … genannt	ich werde … nennen

zweihundertsiebenunddreißig

Verb tables

Infinitive	Present tense	Imperfect tense	Perfect tense	Future tense
rufen *to call*	ich rufe	ich *rief	ich habe … gerufen	ich werde … rufen
schaffen *to create*	ich schaffe	ich *schuf	ich habe … geschaffen	ich werde … schaffen
schaffen *to manage*	ich schaffe	ich schaffte	ich habe … geschafft	ich werde … schaffen
schenken *to give (as a present)*	ich schenke	ich schenkte	ich habe … geschenkt	ich werde … schenken
schreiben *to write*	ich schreibe	ich schrieb	ich habe … geschrieben	ich werde … schreiben
schließen *to close*	ich schließe	ich *schloss	ich habe … geschlossen	ich werde … schließen
schwimmen *to swim*	ich schwimme	ich *schwamm	ich bin … geschwommen	ich werde … schwimmen
singen *to sing*	ich singe	ich *sang	ich habe … gesungen	ich werde … singen
sitzen *to sit*	ich sitze	ich saß	ich habe/bin … gesessen	ich werde … sitzen
stehen *to stand*	ich stehe	ich *stand	ich bin … gestanden	ich werde … stehen
steigen *to climb, rise, increase*	ich steige	ich *stieg	ich bin … gestiegen	ich werde … steigen
treiben *to do (sport), drive, pursue*	ich treibe	ich *trieb	ich habe … *getrieben	ich werde … treiben
trinken *to drink*	ich trinke	ich *trank	ich habe … getrunken	ich werde … trinken
tun *to do, put*	ich tue	ich *tat	ich habe … getan	ich werde … tun
üben *to practise*	ich übe	ich übte	ich habe … geübt	ich werde … üben
verbringen *to spend (time)*	ich verbringe	ich verbrachte	ich habe … verbracht	ich werde … verbringen
verlieren *to lose*	ich verliere	ich verlor	ich habe … verloren	ich werde … verlieren
verstehen *to understand*	ich verstehe	ich *verstand	ich habe … verstanden	ich werde … verstehen
ziehen *to pull, move*	ich ziehe	ich *zog	ich habe … gezogen	ich werde … ziehen
zwingen *to force*	ich zwinge	ich *zwang	ich habe … *gezwungen	ich werde … zwingen

Modal verbs

Infinitive	Present tense	Imperfect tense	Perfect tense	Future tense
dürfen *to be allowed to, may*	ich darf du darfst er/sie/es darf wir dürfen ihr dürft Sie/sie dürfen	ich durfte du durftest er/sie/es durfte wir durften ihr durftet Sie/sie durften	ich habe ... *gedurft	ich werde ... dürfen
können *to be able to, can*	ich kann du kannst er/sie/es kann wir können ihr könnt Sie/sie können	ich konnte du konntest er/sie/es konnte wir konnten ihr konntet Sie/sie konnten	ich habe ... *gekonnt	ich werde ... können
mögen *to like*	ich mag du magst er/sie/es mag wir mögen ihr mögt Sie/sie mögen	ich mochte du mochtest er/sie/es mochte wir mochten ihr mochtet Sie/sie mochten	ich habe ... gemocht	ich werde ... mögen
müssen *to have to, must*	ich muss du musst er/sie/es muss wir müssen ihr müsst Sie/sie müssen	ich musste du musstest er/sie musste wir mussten ihr musstet Sie/sie mussten	ich habe ... *gemusst	ich werde ... müssen
sollen *to ought to, to be supposed to, should*	ich soll du sollst er/sie/es soll wir sollen ihr sollt Sie/sie sollen	ich sollte du solltest er/sie/es sollte wir sollten ihr solltet Sie/sie sollten	ich habe ... *gesollt	ich werde ... sollen
wollen *to want (to)*	ich will du willst er/sie/es will wir wollen ihr wollt Sie/sie wollen	ich wollte du wolltest er/sie/es wollte wir wollten ihr wolltet Sie/sie wollten	ich habe ... *gewollt	ich werde ... wollen

Imperfect subjunctive and conditional

haben	mögen	sein	sollen	werden
ich hätte du hättest er/sie/es hätte wir hätten ihr hättet Sie/sie hätten	ich möchte du möchtest er/sie/es möchte wir möchten ihr möchtet Sie/sie möchten	ich wäre du wär(e)st er/sie/es wäre wir wären ihr wäret Sie/sie wären	ich sollte du solltest er/sie/es sollte wir sollten ihr solltet Sie/sie sollten	ich würde du würdest er/sie/es würde wir würden ihr würdet Sie/sie würden

Go back to pages 43, 88, 113, 171 and 184 to refresh your memory on the imperfect subjunctive and the conditional.

Derivational morphology

Prefixes and suffixes are used to change the meanings of words. In your reading exam, you will come across words which are based on words from the vocabulary list but used with prefixes and suffixes.

The prefixes *Lieblings-* and *Haupt-*

Translate the nouns into English.

1. der Lieblingssport
2. der Lieblingsort
3. das Lieblingszimmer
4. die Lieblingsfarbe
5. die Hauptstraße
6. die Hauptperson
7. die Hauptstadt
8. der Hauptbahnhof

The prefix *Lieblings-* can be added to describe your favourite item, and the prefix *Haupt-* can be added to describe the main item.

The prefix *un-* and the suffix *-los*

Translate the adjectives into English.

1. unmöglich
2. unglücklich
3. unsicher
4. unhöflich
5. hoffnungslos
6. arbeitslos
7. charakterlos
8. sinnlos

The prefix *un-* is added to an adjective to make the opposite negative meaning. The suffix *-los* is added to nouns to create adjectives meaning '-less' or 'without …'.

The suffixes *-keit* and *-heit*

Translate the nouns into English.

1. die Freundlichkeit
2. die Notwendigkeit
3. die Ähnlichkeit
4. die Möglichkeit
5. die Krankheit
6. die Klarheit
7. die Schönheit
8. die Wahrheit

The suffixes *-heit* or *-keit* can be added to adjectives and adverbs to create nouns where the English equivalent usually ends in '-ty' or '-ness'. Remember that nouns with the suffixes *-heit* and *-keit* are always feminine.

The suffixes *-ung* and *-er*

Write out the verbs these nouns have come from.

1. die Öffnung
2. die Bedeutung
3. die Veränderung
4. die Einladung
5. der Arbeiter
6. der Maler
7. der Fahrer
8. der Besucher

The suffix *-ung* can be added to the verb stem to change a verb into a noun with an equivalent meaning. The suffix *-er* can be added to the verb stem to create male people nouns.

Play a game of word tennis by adding a suffix to a noun.

- Das Haus.
- Das Häuschen. Die Katze.
- Das Kätzchen …

The suffixes *-chen* or *-lein* can be added to create nouns where the English equivalent meaning is 'little'. The new noun will often have an umlaut. How would you say 'puppy' or 'booklet' in German?